# INSTRUCTOR

# BIG BOOK of absolutely EVERYTHING

## 1001 Great Ideas To Take You Through The Year

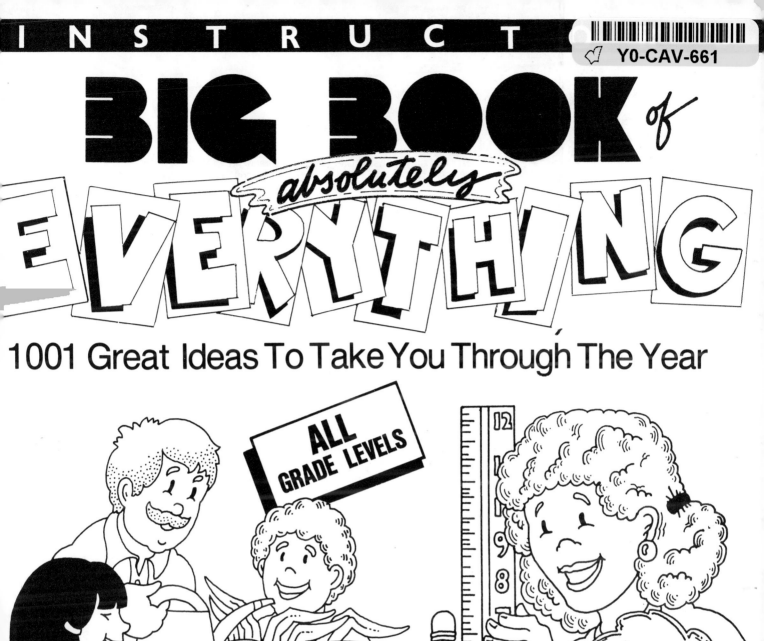

**ALL GRADE LEVELS**

Edited by **Rosemary Alexander**

SCHOLASTIC INC., 2931 East McCarty Street, Jefferson City, MO 65102
Or call (800) 325-6149 between 7:30 a.m. and 5 p.m. Central Time. In Missouri, call (800) 392-2179.

ISBN 0-590-49029-X

12 11 10 9 8 7 6 5 4 3 2 1                                    0 1 2 3 4/9
                                                                     43

Printed in the U.S.A.

Materials in this book previously appeared in INSTRUCTOR Magazine during the years January 1978 through August 1986.

INSTRUCTOR BIG BOOK OF ABSOLUTELY EVERYTHING was compiled and edited by Rosemary Alexander and produced by Judy Cohn, Jane Schall, Anne Rickards, with assistance from Paul Rowley, Louise Aitcheson, Vanessa Byrd and Brenda Johnston. Book design and cover illustration by Design 5, New York City.

# Table of Contents

# Introduction

We're not fooling! This ISTRUCTOR Big Book is packed full of everything you need from classroom management hints to reproducible worksheets. And to help you find just the idea you need in an instant, it's organized by season and subject, with a thumb index on each page and a subject index in the back.

Treat yourself to the best of INSTRUCTOR's teacher-tested activities. **Year 'Round Planning** gives you ideas appropriate for every season of your school year. **The Basics** spans all subjects from reading to career education. You'll find ideas to enhance skills for all grade levels along with enrichment and learning fun.

We've put **Early Learning** in a chapter all to itself so preschool and primary teachers can focus in on specific techniques and skills for this very special age group. And because **Computers** are here to stay, we've included a chapter that will help you and your kids get acquainted with these ''grand machines'' and program them on to greater heights.

**For a Better Classroom** covers much of the business of teaching. Take a look at these ideas to help organize your classroom and make your life easier.

Getting to the heart of teaching, **Relationships** will help you communicate more effectively with kids, parents, and colleagues. This chapter has activities no one can have enough of!

**Bulletin Boards** and **Crafts** will put a little color in your life (and your classroom). These ideas enhance learning while they perk up your room.

Here is a Big Book packed with ideas you can read today and use tomorrow. It will take you through the year again and again with ideas galore and good, solid teaching activities about . . . everything!

# Year 'Round Planning

Welcome to a new year! This chapter of INSTRUCTOR'S BIG BOOK OF ABSOLUTELY EVERYTHING gets you off to a great start with get-acquainted activities for you, your new students, and the whole school. There are fall activities, "spookers" for Halloween time (in all subject areas), even an activity to convince a reluctant Pilgrim that America is the place for him!

December brings ideas with holiday spirit to welcome in the new year. There are calendar activities, a review of New Years' customs around the world, and a celebration of Dr. Martin Luther King. February is packed full of reproducibles. Kids can design a nifty groundhog hole or write an imaginary conversation between Presidents Washington and Lincoln. Finish the year out with a "Summer Security Packet" to send home with kids. All in all, this first chapter will help you work wonders the whole year through.

# First Days/Year 'Round Planning

## FIRST-DAY ICE BREAKERS

The first day of school can be an unsettling time for many children as they face a new classroom full of unfamiliar faces. Here are some activities you can use with pupils to help them break the ice and get to know one another quickly and painlessly.

1. Divide the class into pairs and have each child make a name tag for his or her partner. Let them cut letters from newspapers and magazines and illustrate the tags if they desire. And, to encourage the exchange of addresses and phone numbers, require that this information appear on each tag.

2. Have each child write a descriptive paragraph about a classmate. Begin by asking each student to write his or her name on a strip of paper, then collect the names and put them in a hat for students to draw from. Now, start at the front of the room and ask each child to state his or her name so everyone can identify the person whose name they've drawn from the hat. Students are to describe physical attributes and clothing, limiting their descriptions to positive comments only. When everyone is finished, the kids can take turns reading their descriptions aloud while the rest of the class tries to guess who is being described. That person then reads his or her description and so on until everyone has had a chance.

3. Any first-day activity involving pairs or small groups of students is great for improving the friendship level in your classroom. One such activity your kids are sure to enjoy is pantomime. Have pairs or trios work together to choose an animal, then decide on a pantomime to represent it. The rest of the class must guess which animal is being mimed.

4. Another animal game that's great for the first day, or any day for that matter, is "Barnyard." Write the names of several farm animals on slips of paper, making sure to repeat each animal two or three times. Then have each child draw an animal name and cover his or her eyes with blindfolds. Students are then to get down on their hands and knees and imitate the sounds their animals make. The purpose of the game is for every child to find at least one other student who's imitating the same animal. *-Margaret E. McIntosh*

## LOCKER LOOKERS

On the first day of school each year I take a picture of each child. I use these pictures to put on children's lockers; each month we make some kind of decoration to put on the lockers with a hole in it big enough for the picture to show through. In September it may be balloons; in October, pumpkins; in November, pumpkin pies, and so on. This helps me locate each child's locker, and students are proud of having their pictures where everyone can see. In May we put the pictures in Mother's Day cards for children to take home. *-Sue Williford*

## GETTING TO KNOW YOU

Learn more about your youngsters through songs, games, and finger plays. Start the first day by singing, to a familiar tune like "Skip to My Lou," "If you have an older brother, will you please stand up? If you have an older brother, will you please sit down?" Continue your song with other questions. (Do you take piano lessons? Do you go to the library?) On the second day of class begin another get-acquainted game by saying, "I have a friend. His name is Johnny. Johnny and I will exchange chairs." Each time you play the game, choose a different action. (Patty and I will shake hands. Judy and I will hop on one foot. Josh and I will blink our eyes.) On the third or fourth time, encourage the child whose name has just been called to play the leader and select the next name. Play Mystery Person the next day. Start by saying, "Someone in this class has blue eyes, curly hair, sits near the back of the room," and so on. Pause between clues to give youngsters an opportunity to guess who the mystery person is. Merely pointing doesn't count. The mystery person must be pointed to and his or her name given to be a correct answer. Let children take turns selecting a mystery person and asking the questions. A finger play will help children identify classmates as well as work off excess energy. Say, "There's a person in our class who likes to pretend he is different animals. He likes to fly like a bird" (wave your arms up and down and the children follow suit). "Sometimes he trots in place like a pony" (all trot in place). "Sometimes he creeps around like a tiny mouse" (creep). "Let's all point to . . . Johnny." *-Jane K. Priewe*

## HOW-DE-DO

At the beginning of the school year, I noticed that quite a few children in my second grade didn't know each other's names. To get them more quickly acquainted, I invented "How-de-do." I cut narrow strips of paper and write each child's name on one of the strips. Every morning one child would draw a slip, read the name on it, and then try to identify that person. If he or she couldn't do this, the person whose name was drawn stood up and said, "How-de-do, I'm Alex Smith." By the end of the month most names were known, and some children also had overcome their beginning-of-the-year shyness.           -Margaret Chianis

## A SECRET WELCOME

Welcome your students to school by having them use their math skills to break a secret code. Tell children that each letter of the alphabet represents a number; A equals 1, B equals 2, and so on, with Z equaling 26. Give them math problems to work with answers that correspond to the letters that make up "Welcome to fourth (or the grade you teach) grade." For example W is the twenty-third letter, so the first problem could be 11 + 12. Adapt problems to fit the level of your students.

Write each problem on the chalkboard and draw vertical lines to separate the words. Tell students to solve each problem and print the letter of the alphabet that matches the answer underneath. Who can be the first to crack the secret code?

-Patricia Davis

## GETTING ACQUAINTED

Here's a good way to help new classmates get to know each other quickly. Have each child print his or her name vertically on a sheet of paper. Put names all together in a box and let the students draw one each. They must talk with and observe the person whose name they've picked and write short remarks about them, such as hair color, favorite food, hobbies, and so on. Each remark must begin with a letter in the child's name. At the end of the day, have the students share their comments so everyone will feel better acquainted.           -Mina Berger Lewis

## SOMETHING FOR THE NEW YEAR

To bring in the new school year, ask your students to look for an object they think will be new to most class members. This "new" object can be something old, or even antique, something made by the student him- or herself, or merely something that is most likely to be unfamiliar to others. Explain to the students that they are to bring the object into class and be prepared to explain in a few clear sentences what it is, what it's used for, where they found it, and so on. They may also demonstrate its use if desired. The rest of the class may ask questions when the presentation is finished. This activity provides a good opportunity for oral expression and is also informative for the audience. You'll be pleasantly surprised by the unusual objects your students come up with.

-Sandra J. Frey

## THANKS FOR THE MEMORIES

As soon as school starts in September, be a collector. Save a copy of an interesting story the class writes, a copy of an important test, a letter written to the class, or a few notes jotted down about a fun time you and the class had together. Save these items in a box. Then during the last week or so of school, select several children to come to the front of the room, draw from the box, and tell about the slip they have drawn. It's a good review of the highlights and events of the past year, and you and the class will enjoy the reminiscences.           -Margaret Chianis

## POLITE PUPPETS

Peter Please and Thelma Thank-you are giant puppets who can teach good manners to your students. To make your own Peter or Thelma, cut out a head and neck from a double thickness of knit material. Sew front and back together, leaving an opening at the neck through which to stuff the head with old stockings or cotton. Close the neck opening. Sew yarn hair to the head and felt features to the face. Make Peter's body from a child's shirt and pants and Thelma's from a child's long-sleeved dress. Stitch around the clothing so that it lays flat. After attaching each head to the desired clothing, lightly stuff old mittens for puppet hands and sew to the shirt or dress sleeves. Cut out legs and feet for Thelma and feet for Peter from knit material, and sew and stuff as you did puppet heads. Attach to the appropriate clothing. Sew heavy string or yarn to the puppet heads and a piece of elastic to each puppet sleeve. Help pupils tie the string around their necks and slip the elastic over their hands so they can wear the puppets. Ask pupils to demonstrate how the puppets would respond in different social situations.

-Ellen Javernick

## GET-ACQUAINTED GRAPHING

Here's an effective socializing activity that utilizes graph paper. Have each child choose a category such as favorite foods, best-loved books, or most embarrassing moments. He or she writes the name of several foods, for example, in boxes in the top row. He or she then asks each class member his or her choice from the list, writing the child's name in the proper column. This game is noisy but helps pupils get to know each other better, and at the same time teaches children a little about making graphs. -Mary A. Lombardo

| NAME | EYE COLOR | HAIR COLOR | FAVORITE ANIMAL | FAVORITE SEASON | NUMBER OF BROTHERS AND SISTERS |
|------|-----------|------------|-----------------|-----------------|-------------------------------|
| WILLIAM | | | | | |
| JODI | | | | | |
| ANNAMARIE | | | | | |
| NORMAN | | | | | |
| DIANE | | | | | |
| GEORGE | | | | | |
| ANGEL | | | | | |

## GET ACQUAINTED

Help children renew old friendships and establish new ones. Use the reproducible at right with students' names listed down one side of the page and information to find out about across the top (hobbies, favorite sports, names of pets). Ask your students for additional suggestions. Divide your class into small groups and have them fill in the charts together. Later, take time to share responses and use the information to make graphs, compose story problems, build categorizing skills, and help children feel more comfortable in your room. Don't forget to add a column for yourself!

*-Margo Kavanaugh*

## GET-ACQUAINTED GAME

Play this get-acquainted game the first day of school. Holding a ball of yarn, tell the class your name and something about your teaching experience, family, hobbies, and favorite food. Then toss the yarn to someone who doesn't seem too shy. That person states his or her name and tells the class about himself or herself. When this child is finished, he or she holds on to the yarn and throws the ball to

someone else. The yarn is passed from person to person, crisscrossing the room, creating a giant spider web.

When the ball has gone to everyone, the last person throws it back to the person who threw it to him or her. If the last person is, say, Mary, Mary introduces the person who threw to her and recites what she has learned about that person: "I'm throwing the yarn back to Bobby Smith, who said he likes pizza and loves to play baseball." Bobby then does the same to whoever threw him the ball and so on until the ball returns to you and the spider's web is gone.

Prepare the children for the game by telling them that later they will be introducing the child who throws them the yarn. Be prepared to prompt children so that no one is embarrassed by forgetting or being forgotten. If everyone sits in a circle, your yarn will get less tangled. You'll see that the ball of yarn can increase your students' composure and lessen their self-consciousness about speaking before a group.

*-Kathy Conlan Phillips*

## DOORWAY TO SUCCESS

Use your classroom door to welcome kids each month in a special way. If you're a "door-closer" then decorate the outside of your door; "door-openers" can decorate the inside so passersby can also reap the benefits. Here are some theme ideas: "We're real winners!" with a horseshoe for everyone; "My class is berry good" with everyone's name on a berry; "We're a bunch of good eggs" with individually designed eggs; and "Kids at work!" with individual signs. Children will have their own theme ideas and enjoy making a decoration with their name on it to add to the door. You might want to try "We're unique and we love it!" and have each student think of a personal symbol.

*-Leslie Snyder*

## GETTING TO KNOW YOU

Ease students out of summer vacation gently, and begin the school year on a friendly note. Ask students to describe in detail what they would do on "The Perfect Day." Would they go bicycle riding, mountain climbing, or beachcombing? See three movies in a row or read six "Encyclopedia Brown" books? Eat hamburgers and french fries, or nothing but ice cream all day long? Have students read their papers out loud. Not only will they get to know something about one another, you will gain insight into the character of your students, too.

*-Julia Smith*

## BALLOON BOOST

Want to give your kids' spirits a lift on the very first day of school and help them learn their classmates' names at the same time? Try giving each child a colored balloon labeled with his or her name to be attached with string to desks, wrists, or lockers. Make sure you have plenty of extras on hand to replace the balloons that don't make it through the day! *-Joan Valente*

## My Class Graph

| Name | | | | | |
|------|--|--|--|--|--|
| | | | | | |
| | | | | | |
| | | | | | |
| | | | | | |
| | | | | | |
| | | | | | |
| | | | | | |
| | | | | | |
| | | | | | |
| | | | | | |
| | | | | | |
| | | | | | |
| | | | | | |
| | | | | | |
| | | | | | |
| | | | | | |
| | | | | | |
| | | | | | |
| | | | | | |
| | | | | | |
| | | | | | |
| | | | | | |
| | | | | | |
| | | | | | |
| | | | | | |
| | | | | | |
| | | | | | |

## PERSONAL TIME LINES

The beginning of school is not only a time of anticipation and excitement, but of getting acquainted with new friends. Help your kids reflect on their own lives while finding out about classmates by making autobiographical time lines during the first week of school.

Give each child a sheet of white butcher paper, approximately four feet long. The kids are to draw a line from left to right across the paper. Then they should divide the line into sections representing each year of their lives, beginning with their individual birth dates. Have them label the sections by year. Now instruct them to decide on one major event for each year of their lives. (Students may have to confer with parents concerning the first two or three years of their lives.) The chosen events should then be printed beside the appropriate years and illustrated with crayons or felt-tipped pens. As time lines are completed, have pupils share their creations with small groups of classmates. Then display the time lines for as long as it takes for the kids to get acquainted or reacquainted. If possible, bring them out again at year's end to give your kids a chance to reappraise the important events in their lives.

*-Beth Diaz*

## I'VE GOT A NAME

Sometime during the first week of school, pass around a blank sheet of duplicating paper and instruct students to print their names on it in any direction they choose. When everyone has signed the sheet, take your entire class to the office and let them watch as you duplicate the master sheet. Give each child a copy and encourage students to learn to spell all the names on the list. And before you leave the office, make sure you introduce your class to the staff!

*-Nancy S. Turner*

## MAKE THAT GOAL!

During the first week of school, discuss class goals for the coming year. Help children understand the concept of goals by giving some simple examples. Talk about the object of a game or the purpose of a fund-raising event. Hand out small slips of paper, and ask children to write down one of their goals for the coming year—one they wouldn't mind sharing. Trace the statements (misspellings and all) in a random pattern on a mimeograph master. Include a goal of your own. Run off copies and use them as handouts for Open House Night. Parents and children will love discovering one another's (and your) goals!

*-Helen Wubbenhorst*

## WHAT I DIDN'T DO THIS SUMMER

Ask children to write or tell things they did *not* do this summer that made them glad or sad. For example: "I didn't have homework to do this summer, and I'm glad!" "I didn't ride in a hot-air balloon this summer, and I'm sad." "I didn't get to meet Buck Rogers this summer, and I'm sad." "I didn't get kissed by a toad this summer, and I'm glad!" For younger students, this could make a lesson in rhyming, while older kids can practice using commas, contractions, and exclamation points.   *-John L. Cook*

## ASK THEM

During the first few weeks of school, most teachers are busy assessing their students' reading levels, math competencies, and writing abilities. Prescriptive and diagnostic tests reveal academic information that's undeniably important. However, there is lots of valuable information that testing and simple observation may not reveal—information that students themselves can provide if given the proper vehicle. One such vehicle is the questionnaire. Kids love to fill them out, and they will give you added insight into your students' opinions, thoughts, and feelings. Devise a questionnaire asking a variety of personal questions about home and school life, opinions on specific academic areas, and so on. Examples of questions might include:

1. What did you like most about school last year?
2. If you had one wish, what would it be?
3. What are you afraid of?
4. What academic subject do you like best?
5. Is there someone you can talk to if you have a problem?

Explain to the class that individual answers will be kept confidential. Give the kids ample time to answer your questions and encourage them to be thoughtful and honest in their responses.

*-Jim Derby*

## SOMETHING ABOUT ME

On one of the first days of school, have children write down one statement that tells something about themselves and not sign their name. This should be something that they would like everyone to know. Put the slips in a box. Whenever there are a few minutes to fill, draw a statement from the box and read it aloud. Let kids guess who wrote it and have the child come forward, tell his or her name, and elaborate on the statement. This gives every child a chance to tell something he or she may not have shared otherwise and is a good way to get to know each other.

*-Rebecca Graves*

## WHAT DO YOU KNOW?

Start this year off by finding out how much your students know about things that concern them. Younger students should know their telephone numbers, the color of their eyes, their middle names, the first names of their parents, the year they were born, and similar details about themselves and their families. Ask them some of these questions. Older students should know much more. Ask them names of senators, governors, and mayors, facts about current events and the daily school schedule, the name of the teacher next door. See if they can answer some "should knows" about their families: "What is your mother or father's middle name? What was your grandmother's last name before she married? What make of car does your family drive? Name an ancestor who immigrated from another country." (As many students don't live in a two-parent family, they should answer only those questions that apply to them.) Your students will probably not be able to answer every "should

know" question the first day of school. Encourage them to do some research. Tell them there will be more quizzes like this in the future.   *-John L. Cook*

## JOSHUA LIKES JOKES

This simple game can make the task of learning 30 new names a lot of fun—it works on the associative principle, which students can use to remember other facts as well. Ask each student to think of something he or she likes that begins with the same letter as his or her first name; Patty could like Popsicles or Mike could like motorcycles. Have children keep one other thing in mind, too, in case someone else mentions their first choice.

The first child gives his or her name and what he or she likes; the second child repeats what the first child said and adds his or her own name and like. Continue in this way, with each child repeating what the other children have said, until someone misses; then you can either give hints or start all over again with the next person in line.

If you have a few minutes left at the end of the day, see if anyone can remember everyone's name and what he or she liked. Have students change seats if you want to make it really difficult. You can also use this game while taking roll, with each child responding with a favorite bird, color, animal, and so on, that begins with the first letter of his or her name.

*-Patricia Davis*

## LEAF CITY

Use some of autumn's bounty to create these projects.

**Leaf City** To turn leaves into Leaf City inhabitants, paste leaves of different shapes on wrapping paper in random order. Use crayons or felt-tip pens to add heads, arms, legs and other details to the leaves. Now add paper scraps, bits of wallpaper, yarn, and fabric to make houses, stores, cars, and background items for your creatures.

**Paste-a-leaf** With crayons or tempera paint, draw tree branches on construction paper. With white glue, paste clusters of real leaves on the branches.

**Print-a-leaf** Trace several leaves on fine-grained sandpaper to form a design. Apply heavy pressure as you crayon in the leaves with autumn colors. Put a sheet of thin white construction paper over the sandpaper to obtain a print. Press with a preheated iron (set at medium.)

**Leaf tiara** For each tiara, cut a tagboard strip one to two inches wide and long enough to fit the wearer's head. Either tape or staple the ends together or fasten a piece of yarn to each end so the tiara can be tied on. Paste on leaves with white glue.

*-Roberta Karstadt*

## VIEW FROM A SCHOOL BUS

Because most of my students come to school on the bus, I ask them to draw on construction paper a view of their house as they see it when they get off the bus. Along a long brown piece of paper that looks like a road, we display each picture in scale distance from school and from the other houses. Sometimes we add mailboxes and a school bus to our mural. If we display our houses in the school hallway, we find children in other grades like to guess who lives in which house.

*-Kathleen Benoit*

## LEAF SHAPES

Collect a variety of fall leaves from different trees or cut out leaf shapes from construction paper. Place all the leaves together in basket. Prepare a set of cards on which you have drawn several basic shapes, allowing three cards for each shape. Shuffle the cards and put them facedown in a pile. Pupils draw a card, then search in the basket for a leaf that resembles or contains that shape. Ask kids to explain why they matched a particular leaf and shape.

*-Kelly Riley*

## MIGRATION MATCH

Cut out five different birds in flight from wildlife magazines. Trace the shape of each bird on black construction paper. Cut four or five such silhouettes and glue each set together on blue construction paper. Pupils match each picture to its flock. *-Kelly Riley*

## A NEW KIND OF RUBBING

Mount pictures of several different kinds of leaves on tagboard. Follow the outline and leaf veins with a thin ribbon of white glue. Let dry overnight. Fasten pastel colors of duplicating paper to the tagboard with paper clips. Gently rub the side of a crayon, or several crayons, over the leaf patterns to simulate the varying shades of fall leaves. *-Aileen M. LeBlanc*

## LEAF IT ALONE

Here are fall projects using many leaves from the area. Have the children gather leaves from trees, shrubs, and house and garden plants. The leaves can be arranged into anything from simple leaf collages to geometric designs to portraits.

Discuss various project ideas with the students before they do their collecting so that they are aware of how size, shape, color, and texture of the leaves may be used in their designs. Glue leaves on cardboard and preserve the projects by spraying them with clear enamel or lacquer.

*-Dennis J. Esposito*

## CALENDAR CAPERS

Instead of using an ordinary wall calendar this year, turn your bulletin board into a giant calendar that will involve a variety of subject areas and skills. Simply cover the board with white paper each month and draw the appropriate number of squares with a black felt-tipped marker. Place symbols representing special days and weeks in the appropriate boxes. For instance, you might use a tree for Arbor Day, a bunny for Easter, fire engines for Fire Prevention Week, and so on. Use these special days as the basis for morning discussions. Also, keep books, newspapers, filmstrips, and other related materials on hand so kids can find out more about each special day.

In addition, you can make symbols for sunny, rainy, cloudy, foggy, or snowy weather and place them on the calendar each day. On the last day of the month, have kids tally the various kinds of weather and place the information on bar graphs. Which type of weather occurred most frequently that month?

-Carole Bergevin

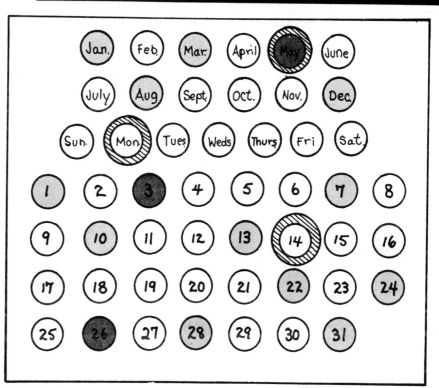

## FOREVER YEARS

This colorful perpetual calendar can be used for years. It's easily seen, and you'll never have to answer, "What's the date?"
Cut a 20-inch square of heavy cardboard or thin plywood. Spray or paint it a wild color. Collect 50 plastic, colored spray-can lids. Using white paint, print abbreviations for a day of the week on seven lids, for each month of the year on 12 lids, numbers 1 through 31 on the rest of them. Arrange the lids on the background. Place the months at the top in two rows, skipping space to separate them from the days of the week; arrange dates in three rows of eight and a bottom row of seven and glue. From heavy cardboard cut three ½-inch rings a little larger than the lids. Paint them white. Slip a ring around the proper month, day, and date. Move circles on day and date each morning.

-Jane K. Priewe

## MARK YOUR CALENDARS

Make up a special events code to use with your class calendar. Laminate cards that symbolize

birthdays (a cake), music days (a musical note), gym days (a basketball), plant-watering days. A calendar committee can have the responsibility for pinning the special event symbols on the calendar for the week or month according to a list you make out for that period. On a particular date, a committee member moves the special event codes for the day from the calendar over to a special events poster and announces the events.

-Judy Meagher

## SUN CALENDAR

Create a sun calendar in your classroom. All you need is a sunny window and Scotch tape. Begin as close to the fall solstice (September 22) as possible. Choose a window with a de- pendable shadow. Every week at the same time, check the shadow and mark the place with a piece of tape. This time-measuring technique will stimulate students' interest in ancient cultures, ceremonies connected with solstices, seasonal changes, and other types of calendars.

-Barbara A. Clark

13

## APPLES

It's the apple season, and here's just the bulletin board for it. Cut out a large red apple and red letters spelling APPLES! for the top of the board, and trim board with a red border. Cut out pairs of apple shapes from white and red paper. On the white shapes write an activity having to do with apples, such as: How many words can you find in the word *apple*?—make a list. Write a story called "The Day I Met My First Worm." Cover each of these white shapes with a matching red shape, staple them together at the top, and attach to the board. Then let children take turns coming to the board, lifting up a red apple, and doing the activity described underneath. -*Patricia Vlk*

## HAPPY APPLE DAY

Celebrate Johnny Appleseed's birthday (September 26) by letting your students work on Johnny Appleseed booklets. Each page in the booklet can cover a different subject area. For a reading page, run off copies of the story of Johnny's life and pass one out to each child. Make a history page dealing with some aspect of Johnny's times, a spelling page that includes pertinent words (*tree, pioneer, animals*), and a math page with addition or

subtraction problems involving apple seeds, animals, and miles traveled in Johnny's life. Have kids write on their creative writing page stories on such topics as "If I were an apple" or "If I could have talked to Johnny Appleseed." Let them make covers for the booklets out of red construction paper. -*Betty Bengston*

## TIED-DRIED APPLES

Tasty dried apples can be a treat this month, and one that will teach kids about a method of food preservation. Allow one apple for every two students. Have kids help you wash, peel, core, and slice apples into hollow rings. Cut lengths of string 36 inches long. Show pupils how to tie the apples onto the strings, spacing slices nine inches apart. Hang the strings from the ceiling where heat will circulate around them. The rings should be ready to eat in about two weeks.

You might want to read about other methods of drying your apples. Discuss which dried fruits kids are used to eating. Try some of the more unusual ones (papaya, pineapple). Together make a dried fruit salad!

-*Willie Ann Helton*

## FROM APPLES TO NUTRITION

Use a celebration of Johnny Appleseed's birthday to kick off some nutrition activities.

**Delicious dips** Sample a variety of delicious dips during snack time. Let pupils help you prepare guacamole, onion, yogurt, or whatever kinds of dip you prefer. Pupils can also help cut up raw vegetables or arrange crackers to serve with the dips.

**Junk the junk food** Get kids on the road to better eating habits with a discussion of *junk food*. Ask pupils to help you make a list of junk foods. Stress that eating such foods in moderation is okay, but that eating too many sweets or snacks is unhealthy. Give pupils magazines and have them cut out pictures of potato chips, cookies, pretzels, and so on, to add to a bulletin board. Tack the foods in and around a paper garbage pail under the heading "Junk the Junk Food."

**Graphing grapes and grapefruit** Set out a sampling of fruits to determine students' taste preferences. Bring in pink and white grapefruit, red and yellow apples, and red, green, and black grapes. Label each fruit and place small dishes in a row on a table. On chart paper mark off a column for each variety of each fruit. Have pupils sample each fruit, then choose which type of each fruit they like best. Mark those preferences in the appropriate columns on the chart. When everyone has tasted the fruits, make a bar graph based on the results.

-*Diane Parette and Marie Jordan-Whitney*

## FIRE PREVENTION WEEK

Here are some activities for Fire Prevention Week to familiarize students with what to do in case of fire.

**1.** Stop, drop, and roll is a technique used to extinguish clothing fires. Spread mats on the floor. Tape balloons to children's clothing, then have them stop, drop, and roll on the floor until all the balloons have burst.

**2.** Using play telephones, call in a fire alarm. Tell kids not to hang up until the operator says to.

**3.** Role-play different scenarios involving reporting fires. For example, how will children report a fire that's happening next door? What if the fire is in their own home? (Get out fast, then call from a neighbor's.)

**4.** Teach children that because smoke rises, they should always lie on the floor if caught in a fire. Explain that a hot door indicates that the fire is right outside it. Have kids practice crawling around the room, touching the classroom door, then reacting based on how you describe the door. (If it's cool, they may open it; if it's hot, they may not.)

*-Kenneth Carlson*

## LEARN NOT TO BURN

A fun and effective activity to help children learn fire safety is to create a smoke obstacle course. A simple obstacle course consists of a smoke detector, cot, telephone end table, floor mats, and simulated smoke. Use a cardboard door and window, or an actual door and window built on braces. To simulate smoke, have four students hold a sheet about three feet from the floor over the pretend bedroom area and gently wave the sheet. Each student completes the obstacle course by identifying the sound of a smoke detector, demonstrating how to roll out of bed, crawling under the smoke, feeling the door to make sure that it isn't hot, and using the door or

the window to exit the "smoke-filled" room. After the child is safe, he or she then goes to the phone, calls the fire department, and gives the proper identification and information about the fire. Have each student take a turn holding a corner of the sheet as well as traversing the course. Directly involving the students in these two tasks allows them to closely observe, as well as participate in, the correct fire detection and protection procedures.     *-Jeanette Mines Ryan*

## A BANNER MONTH

Use the banners that flew from Columbus's flagship, the *Santa Maria,* for October room decorations. The top flag is the Royal Standard of Spain and features emblems of the two Spanish kingdoms, Castile and Leon. Because there were so many castles in the kingdom, Castile was represented by two gold castles on red fields. Leon

means lion in Spanish; that kingdom was represented by two red lions on white fields. Columbus's own swallow-tailed flags carried a green cross on a white field. The cross symbolized Christianity and the green symbolized hope. The gold crown and the letters "F" and "Y" stood for the king and queen of Spain, Ferdinand and Ysabella. It was their financial backing that enabled Columbus to sail. Banners can be made out of discarded white sheets. Use crayons to color in designs. Press the banners on the wrong sides with a warm iron. To deepen shades, recolor and press again. (Be sure to place papers beneath the sheeting when you use the iron.)

Children might also like to design flags they would have used had they been the famous sailor. Hang flags from dowels or a broomstick. After studying Columbus's trip, parade to another classroom to share your knowledge.     *-Jane K. Priewe*

## COLUMBUS DAY PLATES

Let your students combine art and social studies by designing commemorative plates for Columbus Day. After a classroom discussion on Columbus, supply white paper plates, glue, and an assortment of colored markers and construction paper. Have pupils use these materials to illustrate an aspect of Columbus's explorations. The paper-plate designs could include a picture of Columbus's three ships, of the explorer himself, or of his first view of the New World. When the decorating is finished, cover each plate with a square of plastic wrap so the children can use them at lunchtime in the cafeteria. Perhaps your class could work with the school nutritionist to prepare an Italian menu that would parallel the Columbus Day theme.     *-Mary Cobb*

## TOUCHDOWN

It's football season—the perfect time to reinforce basic skills with a game of "Touchdown." Divide your class into four or five even-numbered teams. Now make large construction paper footballs, one for each team. Fold the footballs in half, lengthwise, and print review questions for any subject area inside. Use tape to attach a construction paper flap to the fold-line of each football (see illustration), and print the answers to the questions on this flap. When you're ready to play the game, give each team a football. The first member of each team is to attempt to answer the

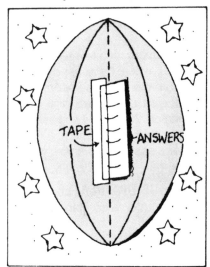

first question listed inside the folded football. Then check his or her answer on the flap. If a player answers correctly, he or she may "pass" the football to the next player, who attempts to answer the second question. If a player answers incorrectly, he or she must "punt" the ball to the next player, who will try to answer the same question. The team member who correctly answers the last question on the list must shout "touchdown!" The first team to score a touchdown wins.

-Ann Fausnight

## BEWITCHING STORIES

No doubt about it—Halloween is a high-interest subject for creative writing assignments! But for a little extra motivation, have your kids make a life-sized witch to urge them all to brew up bewitching stories. Witches can be made from old clothes stuffed with newspaper (a la scarecrow), a heavy tagboard outline covered with black tissue paper, papier-mâché—anything goes! When the witch is completed, prop her up in a chair, and place a "magic pot" in front of her. (This can be made from papier-mâché, or try covering your classroom garbage can with metallic paper.) Finally, place three or four story starters on the wall behind the witch. As kids finish their stories, they should place them in the witch's pot for classmates to read during free time. Here are some possible story starters to use.

**1.** You are riding your bike in the country and you see an abandoned house. You've just walked inside when the door slams shut. It is locked. Night falls, and you hear a chilling sound . . .

**2.** You wake up on Halloween morning to find that you've turned into a jack-o'-lantern! What do your parents and friends say? Tell about your adventures as an orange pumpkin.

**3.** You're walking home from a friend's house one night when you come face to face with a ghost! The ghost invites you on a very exciting trip.     -Jean Antony

## HALLOWEEN STORIES

Let your children be taken in by a ghost this Halloween, and they may write some ghoulishly good stories. First, draw an outline of a ghost—not a Casper type, just an ordinary sheet-over-the-head ghost—and sketch in a face. Then draw lines dividing the ghost's flowing white body into 20 sections. Use the reproducible at the right or create your own.

Next, write a phrase about Halloween night in each of the sections. Some phrases I used were "black bats," "safe and sound," "across the sky," and "creepy feeling."

Run off copies of your story ghost and give a copy to each of your students. Let them construct their own seasonal stories, using as many phrases from the ghost's body as possible. As they use a phrase they can color that section of the ghost.

Use this reproducible for other learning activities: drill on math combinations, vocabulary words, and so on.     -Connie St. John

## A CHAT WITH A BAT

Vampires have the gift of gab; mummies, too, can be downright blabbermouths. Encourage students to choose their favorite monster or character, and make up a list of questions to ask in an interview. They can speak with Bigfoot, The Invisible Man, Godzilla. (They'll need two lists for Dr. Jekyll/Mr. Hyde.)

-Sylvia J. Foust

## POETRY POINTERS

Use Halloween to inspire students to write their own poetry. Introduce your class to the diamite—a seven-line poem written in the shape of a diamond. Provide a concrete form for the children to follow by writing the following parts of speech on your blackboard:

Subject Noun
Adjective   Adjective
Verb   Verb   Verb
Noun   Noun   Noun   Noun
Verb   Verb   Verb
Adjective   Adjective
Synonym
(for subject Noun)

Now explain to the class that the subject is Halloween and all the other parts of speech must relate to it. This exercise will help your students see that poetry can be real and concrete and is an excellent way to sneak in a grammar lesson, too!     -Carol Gold

# The Learning Ghost

### HAUNTED BOOKS

Here's a neat way to motivate your kids to read more books this month. Before the first week in October, make a large construction paper witch sitting on a broomstick with a caption above her head reading "Join me at the graveyard party on October 31." Tack the witch to a wall in

your classroom or in the hallway outside. Then make several construction paper cutouts of items you might encounter while traveling through a haunted house, and place them in progressive order beside the witch. Start with a path leading to the house, followed by a large front door, skeletons, monsters, trapdoors, spiders, and so on. End the display with a graveyard scene. The number of items you place between the witch and the graveyard will depend on the number of books you'd like your kids to read before October 31. Now have each student in your class make a small construction paper ghost with his or her name printed across the front. Place all ghosts on the wall surrounding the witch. As kids read books, they may advance their ghosts to the next item on the wall. The goal is to reach the graveyard by Halloween.

*-Tina Breakall*

### EASY-MAKE PUPPETS

Halloween puppets are fun to make and use, yet provide many benefits to young children. First, the exercise will improve manual dexterity and hand-eye coordination. Second, puppets provide outlets for creative expression. And third, they're great for enhancing oral reading. Let your kids try making some of the puppets described below.

**1. Geometric puppets** Cut different-sized circles, rectangles, squares, triangles, and ovals from colored construction paper. Let children use these precut pieces to make figures. For instance, ovals can be used for heads, rectangles or two triangles with points intersecting for bodies, and small rectangles and half circles for legs, feet, arms, and hands.

**2. Cereal-box puppets** Have each child bring in one empty cereal box. Let kids cover their boxes with plain construction paper, then add features. Show them how to poke holes in the bottoms of their boxes and insert dowels for handles.

**3. Shadow puppets** Any type of puppet can become a strange, eerie creature when you cast its shadow on the wall of a darkened room. Use the light from your overhead projector to cast the shadows. Perfect for puppet plays!

*-Ruth Crisman*

### POETRY BASH

There are coffins in the graveyard
With names on the stones,
But when it's dark and spooky
No one dares go alone!

No reason for students to write poetry alone, either.
Your students can work together to think up nouns, verbs, and adjectives pertaining to Halloween. Next, groups of six can work with topics just developed. Each group can write one stanza about "ghosts and goblins" or "coffins and gravestones," and so on.
The next day, have students return to their groups and edit their stanzas for rhyme and rhythm. Next, they can evaluate all the stanzas as a class, and decide on their order. (If you duplicate the stanzas, students can cut them apart and arrange as they wish.) Students will want to add a title.

*-Nancy Poz and Diane MacFarland*

### SPIDER STEW? *EW!*

Ask students to make up the recipe for arachnid casserole—otherwise known as spider stew. Perhaps they'd like to invite some dinner guests. Do they know how to catch a ghost?
Students will have fun writing "how-to" manuals for all sorts of Halloween happenings. Suggest titles: "How to Comb the Werewolf's Hair," "How to Dance with a Skeleton," and "How to Wrap a Mummy." Students sensitive to the needs of witches may choose to write "How to Ride a Broom." (Not all witches are naturals, you know.)
And for witches who lead modern, liberated lives, students can dream up hi-tech conveniences, such as "Cordless Electric Broom" and "Automatic Bat Catcher." They can diagram their inventions on poster board and prepare a sales pitch—in the event they meet rich witches with wish lists.

*-Sylvia J. Foust*

## A WEB OF LEARNING FUN

Creepy, crawly, and interesting, spiders can be used as a unit with any age level, especially at Halloween time. Display an assortment of spider books with 15 or 20 accompanying questions. What do spiders eat? What happens when their offspring are born? Have children make simple spider bodies out of black construction paper. Explain that each time a question is answered correctly, you will provide a leg. Pipe cleaners or curled construction paper work fine. Questions can be answered in written form or simply whispered in your ear. (While "growing," spiders can hang from desks, chalkboard ledges, or a bulletin board.) Eight answers later, each child has a great Halloween decoration! When everyone has completed a spider, have a celebration with spider cookies. All you need are enough big marshmallows for everyone in the class, a can of crunchy Chinese noodles, a bag of chocolate chips, and some wax paper. Each child carefully sticks eight noodles into the marshmallow for legs, working on the wax paper. Melt the chocolate chips and spoon a little over each spider "skeleton." When the chocolate hardens, your cookies are done!

And for your Halloween party, don't forget the Spider Web Game. All you need is a big ball of yarn and everyone sitting in a circle. Start by holding the end of the yarn, saying your name, and passing on the ball. Weaving around and across, the yarn is passed child to child, each saying his or her own name and all the ones that came before. When someone misses, or there is only one person left, that person has to unweave the web, saying everyone's name in turn.

-Gloria Bernadt
and Patricia A. Livoy

## HALLOWEEN "HAUNTICS"

If you've got a plastic jack-o'-lantern, you can use it to hold Halloween figures on which you've written different activities for pantomime and creative movement. Make several figures of ghosts, tombstones, haunted houses, witches, black cats, owls, and so on. Then print one of the following activities on each figure. Put them all together in the jack-o'-lantern, and let kids take turns drawing figures from it and performing the printed activities.

**1.** Pretend you're a ghost and frighten the class.

**2.** You see a ghost in a haunted forest. React!

**3.** Pretend you're entering a haunted house at midnight. React to the sights and sounds.

**4.** Pretend you're a black cat walking on a fence on Halloween night.

**5.** You're a witch cooking and stirring her brew. Tell what ingredients you're using.

**6.** Pretend you're walking through a graveyard on Halloween night.

**7.** Hoot like an owl in a haunted forest.

-Rebecca Graves

## HULA MASKS

Start with a sturdy headband, and add a string to each side so it ties under the chin. Onto this headband, staple strips of paper that are an inch wide and 16 inches long. Strips should hang down all the way around like a hula skirt.

Students can wear their hula masks plain, or with a mustache pasted on. The strips don't need to hang straight down. By bending, pleating, twisting, curling, and fastening together, kids can create crazy hair and faces. Some strips can be short, some long. They can add eyebrows, earrings, and stars, or even sunglasses.    *-Pecky Kaupelis*

## TWO HALLOWEEN GAMES

These seasonal games will help make learning (and teaching) more fun. The first is an exercise in listening. The second game teaches number order.

### Who Is the Noisy Ghost?

All children but one sit in a circle with their heads bent over. They are the ghosts. The remaining child is the "Ghost Robber" and he or she walks around inside the circle. One of the ghosts in the circle, who has been picked previously, says, "Boo!" The ghost robber tries to guess which one is the ghost who booed. If he or she guesses incorrectly, the person who was the ghost who booed becomes the ghost robber.

If the student guesses correctly, he or she may remain the ghost robber. The game continues until all have a chance to be ghost robber.

### Find the Missing Goblin

Prepare two sets of cards with the numbers 1-10 printed on them. Each card should also have a picture of a Halloween goblin. Place one set of cards along the bulletin board with one or two numbers missing. Let the child find the missing goblins from the stack of extras and put it in correct sequence with those on the bulletin board.    *-Janie Hall*

## OH, SO GAUCHE

Genevieve Ghoul is an interior decorator with terrible taste. Ask students to design a home just as Genevieve would, using a shoe box as the inner sanctum. Color schemes can be *horrific.* Furniture can be *monstrous.* Genevieve, of course, will design as the customers desire—blood-red rugs or electrified lab tables. Students can decide who lives in the room—ghosts, monsters, Frankenstein! The rooms can be frightfully silly—or truly scary. Encourage students to write a story about something that happens in their haunted rooms. They can stack the boxes and make a house.    *-Delores B. Payne*

## GOBLIN CLICKERS

Try this easy art idea for Halloween that will really "click" with your students. The only materials they'll need are covers from baby food jars (or any other jars that size), felt circles approximately 3″ in diameter, felt scraps in various colors, scissors, sewing needles, thread, and white glue. Have kids set each jar cover between two circles of felt. Now instruct them to sew around the edges of the felt with tiny stitches, staying as close to the rim of each jar cover as possible. (You'll probably have to assist younger children with this part of the project.) When the edges are

sewn, show kids how to tie off the thread, then have them trim away any excess felt. Now let kids make facial features for the goblin clickers from scraps of felt, then glue them in place on the top sides of the felt-covered lids. To make a goblin click, kids need only press the center of the lid!

-Mary Cobb

## MOST UNUSUAL JACK-O'-LANTERN

Tired of the same old gap-toothed pumpkin faces? You may be seeing so many of the same designs of faces because you keep giving your students only pumpkins to carve.

I asked my seventh graders to think of all the different vegetables of the autumn harvest and to bring in some out-of-the-ordinary vegetables to carve. They returned with winter squash; gourds of all shapes, colors, and sizes; carrots; and onions. The different forms and sizes seemed to suggest different faces to the students, and we ended up with some very fresh designs. I ran this activity as a most unusual jack-o'-lantern contest. Our winner was a freestanding carrot jack-o'-lantern.      -Bernice Norris

## HAVE A PUMPKIN DAY

Want to try something a little different for your Halloween celebration this year? Why not have a pumpkin day? Begin

displaying hints about the coming attraction a few days in advance. These hints should peak curiosity without giving too much information. Then, on the big day, tack a bright construction-paper pumpkin to your classroom door with the words "Today is Pumpkin Day" written across it. Also, make several pumpkins of various shapes and sizes and place them around your room. In addition, place a real pumpkin on a table in a corner of your classroom. This will be your Pumpkin Day activity center. On small construction paper pumpkins, print activities like the ones that follow, then let kids take turns coming to the center and completing them. You'll probably want to adapt these activities to your students' grade level or make up more of your own.

**1.** Make up different words, using only the letters in *pumpkin* or *jack-o'-lantern*.

**2.** Research pumpkins, using an encyclopedia, and answer these questions: Is a pumpkin a fruit or a vegetable? How are pumpkins grown? When did the tradition of carving jack-o'-lanterns begin?

**3.** Write out instructions for carving a pumpkin.

**4.** List all the jobs involved in the production of a pumpkin pie, from growing the pumpkin to selling the pie.

**5.** Invent a machine for carving pumpkins. Draw a picture of it.

**6.** Write your own version of a fairy tale called "Jack and the Pumpkin Stalk."      -Carole Prince

## JUICY JACK

With a poem and some fresh and dried fruit you can put together a fun and healthy Halloween project. I wrote the poem, and my second graders put together "Juicy Jack." Jack's body is an orange, his arms and legs are toothpicks, and his hands and feet are minimarshmallows. To create a face for our Jack, we used raisins for a mouth, halved

prunes for ears, and halved cherries for a nose. We used peanuts still in their shells for his eyes. We attached all the facial features with toothpicks broken in half. The crowning touch—some called it a stem, some thought it looked like a tuft of hair—was a small spearmint leaf.

The poem about our healthy hero goes as follows:

I'm a jack-o'-lantern
Small and bright.
But I'm sweet and juicy
When you take a bite!
My eyes are made of peanuts,
My nose a cherry sweet,
My mouth is made of raisins,
You will love to eat my feet!
Everything about me
Into your mouth can pop,
Together we'll have lots of fun
As home from school we hop!

-Mary Jo Freebody

## NOW YOU SEE THEM

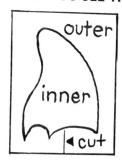

Ghosts can materialize before your students' eyes. Cut a stencil out of oaktag as shown at left, then place it, minus its ghost-shaped inside, on children's pictures. In a central place, have a few students at a time apply paint by dipping a toothbrush in white tempera, and stroking it over a tea strainer or window screen. Less paint makes a "shy," transparent ghost. More paint makes an outgoing, no-holds-barred apparition!

Students can use the inner part of the stencil, too; paint spattered around a ghost cutout makes colorful atmospheric effects.

-Pecky Kaupelis

**SMART COOKIES**

INGREDIENTS:
1 c. Kindness
3 c. Manners
5 T. Responsibility
2 c. Cooperation
3 t. Helpfulness
4½ T. Neatness
¾ c. Enthusiasm

### HAPPY BIRTHDAY, COOKIE MONSTER

The Sesame Street character, Cookie Monster, was born November 10, 1969. Celebrate its birthday with a cookie learning center and a smart cookies bulletin board.

Have the Cookie Monster greet kindergartners from a bulletin board that exclaims, "Crumbling Cookies! Look who's here!" Upon entering the room, each child removes the paper cookie with his or her name on it and drops it into a cookie jar at the learning center. This will enable you to check recognition abilities and attendance. Other tasks at this station include spelling one's name on the magnet board, matching puzzle pieces, and tracing cookie-cutter shapes. On the final day for the center, Cookie Monster offers sugar cookies with names in frosting. Older students will want to be smart cookies by sharing in the making of a bulletin board. Draw a jolly chef and, under the heading Smart Cookies, list the ingredients:

1 cup kindness
3 cups manners
5 T. responsibility
2 cups cooperation
3 t. helpfulness
4½ T. neatness
¾ cup enthusiasm

Directions should say: Combine all above ingredients. Mix well for 196 days in Room _____. Smart cookies will be done by June 198_.

Makes _____ cookies. After you have discussed the recipe with the class, let each child make his or her own large cookie from colored construction paper. Use crayons or markers to put happy faces on the cookies, and arrange them around the recipe.

*-Kathleen Cullen Weisenborn and Anne M. Owens*

### PACKING LIKE PILGRIMS

Did you know that each family on the Mayflower was allowed only one trunk for all personal possessions? This interesting fact can be the start of a Thanksgiving activity your students will really enjoy. Begin by drawing a large packing trunk on a master and give a copy to each child. In the blank area

surrounding the trunk, have them draw the objects they think their family should take along if it were embarking on a journey like the one the Pilgrims made. You'll be surprised and amused by the results, and will gain some meaningful information about your students' values and concerns as well.

*-Brenda H. McGee*

### FEED THE BIRDS

With a bird feeder outside your classroom window, pupils can observe the winter activities of birds. A cylindrical cardboard can with a plastic lid makes a great bird feeder. Attach a larger plastic top through the base of the container with a screw and nut so the feeder has a base for the birds to sit on. To let food gently spill out, cut a small hole or two near the bottom of the can. Attach a wire and hook through the top of the can so the feeder can hang from a tree. Children can paint or decorate their bird feeder, fill it with bird food, and hang it outside your classroom window. Try keeping a class book of bird activities and illustrations.

*-Phyllis Scarcell Marcus*

### AUTUMN ACTIVITIES

Include fall themes in skill-building activities this month.

**Caps 'n acorns** Cut 26 acorns and 26 matching caps from construction paper. Print a lowercase letter on each acorn and an uppercase letter on each cap. A group of children spread the caps facedown. The acorns are dealt out so that each player receives the same number. Players draw caps from the pile; if a cap matches an acorn in his or her hand, the player puts it down on the table; if it doesn't, it goes back in the pile. Play continues until all the acorns are capped.

**Scurrying squirrels** Cut five squirrels from oak tag. Cover five small cans with brown paper to resemble tree trunks. Gather a large quantity of real acorns, or

cut out paper ones. On each of 20 to 30 cards write a numeral from 1 to 10, a set of objects that would represent one of those numerals, or a number word from one to ten. To use, five players each take a squirrel and a tree. Each child takes turns drawing a card, counting out the number of acorns indicated, and placing them in the can. When the cards have all been drawn, count to see which squirrel gathered the most nuts.
*-Kelly Riley*

## PLUCK A FEATHER

When your bulletin board turkey looks tired, replace its feathers with feather shapes containing math story problems. Here are a few to write on different feathers.
**1.** Mr. and Mrs. Stuffin' are planning their Thanksgiving meal. The turkey will cost $9.99, bread is $1.99, sweet potatoes are $.98. How much have they spent so far? Check newspaper ads for other prices and finish out their Thanksgiving menu and costs.
**2.** The holiday dessert is always pumpkin pie. If 87 people are going to eat pie, and each pie only has three (large) slices, how many pies do they have to make?
**3.** Mr. and Mrs. Stuffin' kissed their last guest good-bye at 11:35 P.M. If the party started at 2 P.M., how long did the party last? Place the answers to problems on the back of each feather so children can check their work. Provide extra feathers so children can make up their own Thanksgiving story problems.
*-Pat Goldys*

## TURKEY PLUCKIN' CONTEST

Work with your school's media specialist in this contest that will reinforce your students' library skills while providing information about Thanksgiving. The

specialist will have to supervise the activity, so meet with her in advance to schedule half-hour periods in the center for six students at a time. Then make six construction paper turkeys with detachable feathers for easy plucking. On each feather, print one question about Thanksgiving that the students must answer using reference material. Make sure that each turkey has a different set of questions and that each question is followed by a clue to the appropriate reference book. Then give each child an answer sheet numbered from one to six. After a signal is given by the media specialist to start the contest, students are to pluck their first feather and locate the answer to the question that appears on it. When they've found the answer, they must write it down on the answer sheet and move on to the next feather. The first student to find all six answers wins and is entitled to a certificate of excellence.
*-Betty White*

## BUCKLE UP

Here's a great way to reinforce math skills while everyone's in the Thanksgiving spirit. On 3" x 5"

cards, draw pictures of Pilgrims' faces. Then make one hat for each face—but leave off the buckles. In the upper right-hand

corner of each card, print a math problem. Then write one answer on each of the buckles, which you can make from brown construction paper. Now attach small pieces of magnetic tape to the backs of the buckles. Kids take turns matching the buckles to their appropriate hats to complete the Pilgrim pictures.
*-Ruth E. Berry*

## FIND THE TURKEY

Here's a simple game you can use to spark creative writing projects at Thanksgivingtime. Choose five different colors of construction paper, then cut several small turkeys from each color. Now think of five Thanksgiving words your kids might use in creative stories and print one letter of each word on a different turkey. Make sure all the letters for each word are printed on turkeys of the same color. Now mix up all the turkeys and hide them in different places around your classroom. Have kids find the turkeys, then form groups according to color. Group members should attempt to unscramble the Thanksgiving words and tack them to your bulletin board. When all five words have been identified, have kids use them in original Thanksgiving stories.
*-Dee Zachrich*

## SELLING AMERICA

What made America attractive to the Pilgrims? Ask your students to list as many answers as possible. Next, have them design brochures convincing enough to ''sell'' the new real estate to the most doubtful Pilgrim. Take turns letting children present their brochures with a special sales pitch.
*-Sylvia J. Foust*

### BOOKS TO GOBBLE ABOUT

Here's a reading motivation idea you can begin now and continue right up through Thanksgiving. Use brown construction paper to make a large turkey head and body and tack it on your bulletin board along with the caption, "Books to gobble about." Then cut several construction-paper tail feathers of different colors and leave them on a small table beside the bulletin board. After a child has read an entire library book and given a written or oral report on it, he or she may go to the table and select a feather. Then let the child print his or her name across the feather along with the title of the book read and attach it to the turkey's body.

*-Carolyn Putnam*

### TURKEY TAIL SUPREME

Save all odds and ends of braid, lace, rickrack, and ribbon for your youngsters to cut up and glue on crayoned turkeys for colorfully different tails. *-Jo Fredell Higgins*

### BUDDIES, BATTER, AND BUTTER

You've probably heard of cross-age grouping and cross-age tutoring, but have you ever heard of cross-age cooking? At Thanksgiving, when everyone's thoughts turn to food, this can be an effective way to improve relations across grade levels and boost self-images, too. Primary children, who are often isolated from the school mainstream, will enjoy interacting with older students, and the older kids will gain a sense of importance as they contribute their reading and computational skills to the cooking project. Of course, it won't be possible for the children to whip up a three-course meal in school, but the simple recipe for 12 cranberry muffins below will give them just as much satisfaction. Depending on the number of kids involved, you'll probably have to double or triple the basic recipe.

> 2 cups sifted, all-purpose
>   flour
> 1 cup sugar
> 1½ tsp. baking powder
> 1 tsp. salt
> ½ tsp. baking soda
> ¼ cup butter or margarine
> 1 egg, beaten
> 1 tsp. grated orange peel
> ¾ cup orange juice
> 1½ cup raisins
> 1½ cup chopped
>   cranberries.

Sift all dry ingredients into a large bowl. Cut in butter until mixture is crumbly. Add egg, orange juice, and orange peel. Stir until mixture is moist. Fold in raisins and cranberries. Spoon mixture into muffin tins and bake at 350 degrees for approximately 20 minutes. Remove from tins and cool on wire rack.

Pair the older kids with younger ones and assign the pairs different tasks, such as measuring, stirring, and sifting. These tasks will probably have to be shared, so supervise the activity closely to make sure every child gets a chance to help. After the batter has been evenly distributed in the baking pans, let the children proceed to the cafeteria to watch their muffins get placed in the oven.

When the muffins have cooled enough to eat, hold a cranberry muffin party for the two groups in the cafeteria. You might want to plan ahead to have the children make paper placemats and table decorations for the party during art classes. Encourage the kids to maintain their newly formed relationships with their cooking partners long after the muffins are gone. *-J.E. Rockwell*

### FABULOUS FLOCK

Spice up your art class at Thanksgiving with these *turific* ideas. The body of our first gobbler is a supersized paper wad. Have each student crumple and pack newspaper into a football-sized ball. Smooth colored tissue paper over the wad, overlapping the ends on one side. Now cut a 12-inch-wide semicircle for the tail, and glue the overlapped side of the wad to it. Add a paper head and feet, then fringe the tail and paint on feathers.

A fabric sample cut from a discarded upholstery book provides kids with another turkey--one with a textured body! Onto the center of a small rectangle or square of fabric, place a turkey's round face. Attach cutout feathers and feet to the back edges of the fabric to give a 3-D effect. Give students an exercise in coordinating colors by insisting that the fabric or paper used for their turkeys' feathers, heads, and feet complement the colors of the body.

Kids can draw a turkey totem with markers on a long, narrow sheet of paper. Give pupils pictures of real totems for ideas, encouraging them to draw their turkeys turned in different directions, as the figures on real totems are. Cut out the finished totems and mount on paper.

Also, create a tom turkey who's decided to wear the disguise of a Pilgrim, perhaps to avoid coming to Thanksgiving dinner *as* dinner! For a humorous approach to the annual feast day, have pupils draw turkeys in human attire. What celebrities might their birds "dress" as?

*-James Perrin, Jr. and Joan Lunich Schenk*

## GOBBLE UP THE GOOD WORK!

Have kids make a large turkey out of brown butcher paper and attach colored construction paper feathers. Children can make their own cornucopias, with the opening as large as an 8 1/2" X 11" piece of paper. Now display the bounty of their work.

*-Barbara Jacober*

## STUFFED TURKEYS

Stuff strips of newspaper into a brown paper lunch-bag. Leave enough room at the top to close the open end with a rubber band or yarn. Paste colored construction paper feathers to this end for the turkey's tail. Using construction paper, draw and cut out the neck and head of a turkey—include a beak and wattles—and tape or paste this to the bottom of the bag. These are made very quickly and easily, so your class can have a whole flock of turkeys this Thanksgiving.

*-Cheryl Bogrow*

## THANKSGIVING DINNER

Have your kids search through history and reference books to find out what foods were served at the first Thanksgiving. Then instruct them to check newspapers for food ads and find out what each item costs today. Make a chart with the information discovered, illustrated with pictures from magazines of the different foods—how would the Pilgrims fare today?

*-Nancy Camarigg*

## WE GIVE THANKS

Here's a great way to get your entire school involved in a Thanksgiving project and have kids thinking about the real meaning of Thanksgiving at the same time. Give each child a

feather made from red, orange, or yellow construction paper. On this feather each child should write his or her name and one thing he or she is thankful for. Then place these feathers on a giant Thanksgiving turkey made from brown construction paper. Display the giant turkey in the school hall for all to read and enjoy! *-Wendy J. Vogt*

## TOM TURKEY READS

Tom Turkey is used in my Reading Center to stimulate fun and interest in sharing books in creative ways other than the traditional book report. He and his feathers are made of lightweight cardboard, laminated for durability. Each feather is numbered and describes an activity to do after reading a book. The student picks a number and I record his or her choice. Together, we determine the length of time the child will need to complete the activity. On that

date, the pupil shares the project with the rest of the class. Tail feathers are attached with brass fasteners so children can move them as they read the choices. Some of these are: Make a cartoon strip about the book you just read. Write a new ending for your book. Write a short play about your book. Design a crossword puzzle using words from your book. *-Jan Kennedy*

## LADDER OF THANKS

Here's an interesting project for Thanksgiving called a "Ladder of Thanks," made from empty fabric bolts. (These are easily obtained as hundreds are discarded at any fabric store and salespeople will usually be glad to save them for you.) Punch holes in the ends of the bolts so they can be tied together for hanging with yarn or string. When six or seven have been tied together, glue or draw letters down one side to spell "Thanksgiving." (Colorful lettering is most effective.) Have the children think of things that they are thankful for that begin with the letters in the word "Thanksgiving." Then let them draw small pictures of these things on squares and paste them on the appropriate section until it is filled. Make two holes at the top of the ladder to hold supporting yarn for hanging.         -Ruth Byers

## THANK GOODNESS FOR THANKSGIVING

Incorporate these activities into your classroom observance of Thanksgiving. They can extend your study to a variety of topics.
*Social studies*
**1.** Read *If You Sailed On the Mayflower* by Ann McGovern (Scholastic, 1975) and other books that will help children imagine the hardships of the Pilgrims' journey across the ocean, the trials of the first winter, and the joys of the first bountiful harvest.
**2.** Ask children to close their eyes and think of one thing they might smell on Thanksgiving Day. Ask them to think of one thing they might taste on Thanksgiving, a sound they might hear, something they might touch, a person they might see. Encourage children to share these sensory thoughts. Transcribe onto charts.
**3.** Talk about the kinds of manners children should use on Thanksgiving. Make a list of dos and don'ts at the dinner table. Talk about ways children might help: polish silverware, set napkins in place, entertain the younger children.
*Science*
**4.** What fish and meats were on the menu at the first Thanksgiving feast? Make a list that includes wild turkey, goose, duck, deer, lobsters, clams, and oysters. Ask children to name the animals on this list that we eat today. Do children think people will always eat these foods on Thanksgiving? What could prevent them from doing so?
**5.** The Pilgrims came to America in a sailing ship. Use this fact as a springboard for a lesson on the wind. Explain to pupils that wind is one form of energy. The wind is powerful enough to carry a ship like the Mayflower across the ocean. It can turn machinery to pump water or to run windmills. It can be strong enough to blow over trees or take the roof off a building. on a windy day, go outside and look for signs of the wind (hair blowing, leaves scattering).
**6.** Compare the seeds of fruits that are frequently eaten at Thanksgiving, such as cranberries, apples, grapes, pumpkins, grapefruit. Display the seeds and ask children to compare them, looking at size, shape, and texture. Ask pupils if you can tell the size of a fruit by the size of its seed.
*Language development*
**7.** Place the word *Thanksgiving* on a flannel board. Point out the *th* letter combination and make its sound. Now place a turkey without a tail on the board and hold up a bunch of flannel feathers. If pupils can think of a word that begins with the *th* sound, they may place a tail feather on the turkey.
**8.** Make Thanksgiving dinner for the birds. Have each child spread one side of day-old bread with peanut butter and sprinkle with birdseed. Cut a hole in the bread, and string ribbon through it. Hang on trees outside.
**9.** Make "I'm thankful for you" cards for each child to send to a special someone. Pass out paper, crayons, glue, and odds and ends of materials, and let pupils make cards of their own design.
                    -Marilyn Bennet

## FRIENDSHIP SOUP

Preparing a meal together can help little ones understand the spirit of friendship that made the first Thanksgiving significant. Ask each child to bring to school one of the following vegetables; a turnip, a celery stalk, a tomato, a green pepper, a few peas, an onion, a zucchini, some spinach leaves, a cauliflower section, a handful of green beans, several mushrooms. Have kids wash and dice the vegetables, then place them in a pot. Add 6 cups water and 2 cups tomato juice. Bring soup to a boil, then simmer for 30 minutes. Add ½ cup margarine and 2 bouillon cubes, then simmer 30 minutes.
                    -Carol Gobrecht Andreen

## THE SPIRIT OF CHRISTMAS

My class adopted a "grandmother," an 87-year-old whose family is no longer living. She lives in a nursing home, and my students make things for her regularly.

Last year she came to our Christmas party. For a gift, we stitched two throw pillows for her. Each child made a design on burlap, and I stitched the pieces together and stuffed them.

Since she was born and raised in our home state of Kansas, we had her return to our classroom for Kansas Day. She contributed a wealth of information on Kansas history.

Having a class grandmother has given my students someone to care about. She feels wanted and loved, and the children are happy for making her happy.

-Diane Kaufman

## SEASONAL STORIES

To get kids started writing stories during this holiday season, try setting up a flexible story board, made from a piece of 32" × 16" cardboard. Draw a large Santa and some stockings (one stocking for every story idea) on a green background. Cut out the words "Merry Christmas!" from red paper and glue across the middle. Have kids choose one of the story topics (sticking out of the stockings) and change it into a *merry* Christmas story. Try these for starters:

**1.** The year the elves went on strike and refused to make Christmas presents.
**2.** The year the toys were stolen on December 24.
**3.** Santa started out from the North Pole, but lost his map.
**4.** Santa came down with a bad fever on Christmas Eve.

-Phil A. Long

## CHRISTMASTIME RHYME

Get out those old Christmas cards you've saved from last year, and use them for a word game your kids will really enjoy. It's based on the traditional card game Old Maid, but with a slightly different twist. Cut the front of each Christmas card to approximately 3" x 5". Then print 20 pairs of rhyming Christmas words (toy-joy; sleigh-hay; candle-handle) on small slips of white construction paper and paste one word across the front of each card. For the last card, choose one with a large picture of Santa's face to take the place of the old maid.

-Carolyn Wilhelm

## NEW LOOK FOR AN OLD POEM

You can rewrap the poem "A Visit from St. Nick," by Clement Clark Moore, in a different kind of package this year by turning it into an unusual grammar lesson. The poem is a real favorite with kids and happens to be a good source of instruction as well. Below are a few ideas for teaching grammar through this well-known poem.

**Nouns** Have the children work in small groups to make lists of all the different nouns found in the poem. Then instruct them to place these words in categories of people, places, and things.

**Verbs** Ask your kids to list all the different words the author used to express movement, such as *sprang* and *flew*. Also have them list all the replacements for the word *said* that are found in the poem, such as *shouted* and *exclaimed*. Now let the children incorporate these words into Christmas stories of their own.

**Adjectives** Adjectives, like nouns, can be listed by small groups of children and separated into categories like, "Which one?" "What kind?" and "How many?"

**Similes** You'll find this poem to be a good source of similes, especially in the description of St. Nick. Start with these examples to introduce the use of similes, then have your kids look elsewhere in the poem for others. In addition to these grammar exercises, you might want your kids to do a little research on Clement Clark Moore to find out who he really was, when and where he lived, and what else he wrote.

-Marilynn R. Hall

## HOW MANY DAYS?

How often have you heard the question, "How many days are there until Christmas?" Here's an idea that can help you answer this all-important question in a meaningful and instructional way. Make 25 construction-paper cutouts of objects relating to Christmas, such as evergreen trees, wreaths, bells, or miniature Santas. On December 1st tack these to your bulletin board; then remove one every morning until the big day arrives. This helpful idea, which also reinforces counting skills, can be adapted to any holiday.  *-Peggy Booth*

### A TIME TO SHOW YOU CARE

Holiday times can be times of frenzy — trying to get all the decorations and projects made at school and getting families at home ready for the season. Often gifts for each student are left to the last-minute crunch of, "What should I get?" Try purchasing or making a card for each student and setting aside an hour or two to write short messages praising each student's assets and expressing the pleasure gained from knowing that child. Often these comments will be the most important gift you could give to a child and will create an extra special start for the new year.

*-Kathleen Thompson*

DEAR SUSAN,
YOU ARE A VERY
GOOD STUDENT AND A
PLEASURE TO TEACH!
YOUR TEACHER

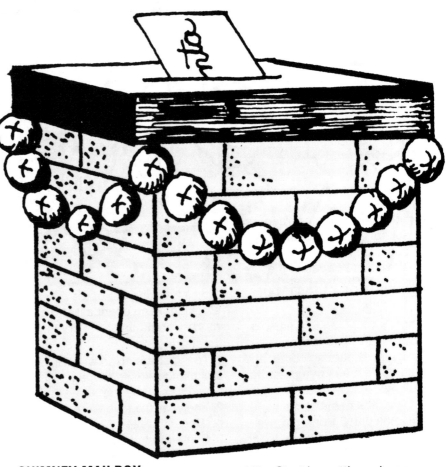

### CHIMNEY MAILBOX

My fourth-grade class placed a chimney mailbox near the primary wing with a sign reading, "Send a letter to Santa." Each morning, a member of my class picked up the letters and brought them to our room to be "cancelled." Then each letter was answered by one of my 26 Santas. They always stressed the holiday spirit and avoided promising special gifts. The letters were stamped with holiday stickers. Our delivery person would leave the letters outside the appropriate classroom and announce the delivery by shaking sleigh bells.

*-Arthur J. Bamel*

### COUNTDOWN TO CHRISTMAS

Here's a bulletin board display that will give your class a vehicle for counting down the days until Christmas. It's also a good way for kids to practice research

skills. Start by cutting a large construction paper Christmas tree, then make construction paper ornaments and attach them to the branches. Number each ornament according to the number of students in your class. Now have your kids research holiday customs from around the globe and either illustrate their findings or print them in brief paragraphs. They might also want to print holiday recipes from other countries. Each contribution should be printed or drawn on pieces of paper that are small enough to fit under the ornaments on your tree. Put each one under a different ball. Starting December 1, allow the kids to lift one ornament each day and share what they find underneath with the rest of the class.  *-Sue Kreibich*

## CHRISTMAS COOKBOOKS

Looking for a low-cost, useful Christmas gift for mothers or grandmothers? Make Christmas cookbooks! Before the holidays begin, divide students into recipe committees for different categories such as main dishes, vegetables, soups and salads, cookies and candy, and cakes and pies. Committee members then bring in one or more recipes for their sections of the cookbook. Appoint proofreaders to check for errors in each group; then duplicate recipes and help students collate pages of the cookbook. Make front and back covers from felt or construction paper and decorate with glitter, sequins, or beads. Tie each cookbook together with yarn, cord, or metallic braid.  *-Beth Diaz*

## "HE'S ONLY A PAPER MAN"

For ornaments that will be treasured for several Christmases, make paper gingerbread men from grocery bags. Trace around a gingerbread-man cookie cutter and cut from a doubled piece of brown bag. On the top man, paste two black-button eyes, a red-felt nose, and a smiling ribbon mouth. Then paste front to back around the edges, leaving one side unpasted. Stuff a bit of crushed tissue paper into tummy and head. Add a pinch of ginger or cinnamon to make him smell like the real thing! Finish pasting edges together. Tie a ribbon around your little man's neck. String a thread through the top of his head and hang.  *-Jane Priewe*

## SILHOUETTES

It's not too early to start thinking about inexpensive presents you can make for your students to take home to their parents at Christmastime. A child's silhouette is one of the most meaningful gifts you can give—and surprisingly simple to make, too. All the materials you'll need to make silhouettes of every student in your class are 12" × 18" sheets of black and white construction paper, the light from a filmstrip or overhead projector, and your classroom door. Simply tape a sheet of black construction paper to the door and position the child so his or her head is in the center. Flash the projector light onto the child's head so it casts a shadow on the paper behind it.

You may have to move the projector to adjust the size of the shadow. Tip the child's head up slightly for a good chin line and hold that position with your finger. Then carefully outline the shadow with your free hand. Finally, cut around the outline you've drawn and paste this silhouette on a sheet of white construction paper. Label with the child's name in black construction-paper letters. If you start early, and make two or three silhouettes each week, you can finish them all before the hectic Christmas season even begins. You'll be surprised at how eagerly your kids will await their turn for a "sitting." *-Peggy Dewire*

### HOLIDAY WISHES

A child at any grade level can create a gift of sharing. This activity can be called "Wishes." Explain to your class that in the three weeks before vacation, they will be writing three paragraphs—one a week to allow time for revision and recopying. Introduced one at a time, the topics will be: My Wish for the World; My Wish for My Parents (or someone special in that child's life); and My Wish for Me.

The idea of making wishes is appealing to all children. Stress only one wish per paragraph so children can work on elaborating why they are making the wish. Encourage the class to help if a child is having trouble thinking of enough reasons. Sharing can be a heartwarming and growing experience as children discuss concerns for the world. When writing the second paragraph, students may want to talk about who is important to them and why. When children rewrite the final copy, they can decide on special stationery or how to decorate borders. The paragraphs can be framed with construction paper or mounted for a wall-hanging and wrapped as a set. This is a gift that parents will value.      *-Darlene Papa*

### A GIFT OF FEELINGS

Coupon books are old favorites for children to make and to give parents. Because this is the season of warm wishes, your students might enjoy giving "feeling" coupons rather than those that guarantee a bed be made or the garbage be taken out.

Hold a class discussion about things that go on at home that require understanding and patience. Looking at these situations, suggest coupons that children can make to give an emotional boost to the people they live with. (They may use the ones the class comes up with, or

special ones, depending on family situations.) Try the following for starters: a coupon that guarantees at least 10 minutes of quiet when it looks like things are getting frazzled; a coupon that provides a loving hug when mom or dad is blue; a coupon that gives 10 minutes of uninterrupted listening to a problem mom or dad has; a coupon to turn off the TV at the first request; a coupon that stands for going to bed without being reminded; one that says all homework will be done before Sunday night; or one that says peace will be made with a brother or sister.

As you provide these and other suggestions, children will not only think of their own ideas but also will begin to grasp what it means to be a parent. This becomes a gift not only of actions but of growing understanding.
*-Sylvia Remer*

### PICTURE THIS

Choose a holiday scene from cards or magazines. Paste toothpicks around it to make a frame. (An easy shape to use is a square with two more toothpicks pasted on top to form a peak.) Let the paste dry thoroughly. Carefully trim the picture away from the outside of the frame. Add two or four more rows on the peak to make it look like a roof overhang. Hang with yarn.
*-Jane K. Priewe*

### SANTA'S NEW SUIT

For a new art idea, I display a drawing of Santa dressed only in his winter underwear. Pupils welcome the chance to design the old fellow a brand-new, modern-styled suit, hat, coat, and boots.
*-Brenda McGee*

### CHRISTMAS BASKETS

Old Christmas cards can become beautiful baskets to hold candy, cookies, and nuts during the holiday season. To make them, you'll need a stapler, hole punch, glue, scissors, cardboard, and narrow ribbon. For the bottom of

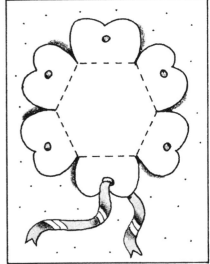

the basket, draw a hexagon on cardboard, each of its six edges 3" long, and cut it out. Then, for a pattern for the sides, draw a heart and cut it off at the point so that the bottom is about 3" across. Trace this pattern onto two attractive cards, cut out and glue the two heart-cards together. This will be one side. Bend and crease this side 3/8" from the bottom, fit onto one edge of the hexagon, and staple them together. Finally, punch a hole on each side of the heart about 1" from the top. Repeat this procedure until there are six colorful sides; then thread a piece of ribbon through each pair of adjoining holes and tie into a bow to hold sides together.
*-Irene Lindberg Munday*

## LET'S LIGHT THE MENORAH

The eight days of Hanukkah are a festive time for Jewish families. Songs, blessings, games, food, and the sharing of gifts are all a part of this happy holiday. Teach this poem to children before the holiday begins.

### Let's Light the Menorah

Let's light the menorah
For the festival of lights,
One candle every evening
For eight great joyous nights.
Latkes, games, and sharing,
Happiness and cheer.
Let's light the menorah
For Hanukkah is here.

### Make a menorah

You'll need: a block of Styrofoam 12 inches by 4 inches by 2 inches, scissors, blue crepe paper, aluminum foil, transparent tape, nine blue or white birthday candle holders, and nine blue or white birthday candles. Cover the sides of the Styrofoam block with crepe paper and the top with a double layer of foil. Insert the nine candle holders in the block, spacing them evenly. The centermost holder for the *shamash*, or ninth candle, should be a little higher than the others. Place the nine candles in the holders so children can see the effect. If you are going to light the candles, only place as many candles in the holder as the day you are celebrating, plus the shamash.

### Hanukkah mobile

Cut several dreidls, candles, lions, and Jewish stars from white construction paper. Color with blue crayons. Dab on glue and sprinkle with gold glitter. Punch a small hole about 1/4 inch from the top of each and thread a piece of blue ribbon through the hole. Tie securely. Use different lengths of ribbon and hang from a coat hanger.                —*Carol Quinn*

## HOLIDAY GLOW

Fold a 9-inch by 12-inch piece of colored construction paper in half lengthwise. Draw a squiggly candle shape and cut out. Unfold

and glue the candle to a 12-inch by 18-inch sheet of black construction paper. Add a flame cut from yellow or orange paper. Drip glue along and around the candle as well as emanating from the flame. Immediately sprinkle with gold or silver glitter.

—*Joy Lindner*

## HANUKKAH COASTERS

Involve your kids in the Hanukkah celebration this year by having them make decorative coasters to bring to the family dinner table. Start by giving the children several cardboard discs each— one for every member of the family—and instruct them to cover these discs with light-colored construction paper. Now let the kids decorate their coasters with a few of the symbols of Hanukkah, such as the dreidl, menorah, or Jewish star. Symbols may be drawn or painted on the discs or cut from construction paper and glued in place. When the decorating is completed, laminate the discs for extra durability. Families will love this creative addition to the holiday table.    —*Gary Riccardi*

## TWO DREIDL GAMES

**Spin the dreidl** Probably the most popular Hanukkah game is "Dreidl." It was first played in the little villages of Judea, where Jews would gather in the courtyards to make plans to overthrow the harsh rule of the Syrian Greeks. When Greek soldiers passed by, the Jews would pull out a dreidl and pretend to be playing this harmless game. The dreidl itself is a four-sided top that tapers to a point at the bottom. Each side of the top has a Hebrew letter on it. The letters are נ—*Nun,* ג—*Gimmel,* ה—*Hay, and* ש—*Shin,* the first letters in the Hebrew sentence *Nes gadol haya shom.* This means "a great miracle happened there," referring to the miracle that took place after the Jews won their freedom from the Syrian Greeks. To play dreidl in your classroom, give each child a pile of peanuts. Each player should put one peanut into a central pot. The first player spins a dreidl. (Commercially produced dreidls are available in most areas.) If *nun* comes up, the player adds nothing to the pot and takes nothing out. If *gimmel* faces up, he or she must give one peanut to the pot. If *hay* lands on top, the child takes half the pot; and if *shin* comes up, the player takes all. After each turn, every player must add a peanut to the pot, and play continues.

**Dreidl in the middle** Have classmates form a circle. Choose one child to stand in the middle of the circle and slowly turn or spin as a dreidl would, while you play a recording of a Hanukkah song. Stop the music unexpectedly. The child in the middle must stop immediately and point to the child in the group he or she is facing. The child must pantomime a part of the Hanukkah story. The first child to guess the scene correctly becomes the next dreidl-in-the-middle.       —*Milton Polsky*

### JANUARY-JUNE PREDICTIONS

Begin the New Year by recording your students' predictions for the remainder of the school year. Then seal up their predictions and hide them away to open and read in June.

Consider with students what kinds of predictions to make. Some should relate to the students themselves (how many students will be in the class in June, whether any student in the class will break a bone, how many snow days students will have off). Some will be concerned with classroom activities (how many library books will the class have read). Others may relate to outside-classroom events (which team will win the Super Bowl, what TV program will be most popular). Make this a group activity with majority vote determining what to list. Write the location of the predictions on the calendar on the date in June on which they are to be opened.

*-Sandra J. Frey*

### HOLIDAY THANKS

Over the Christmas vacation, I cut out a large snowman for each student in my class, writing a personal message on each. On the snowmen of those students who may have brought me a holiday remembrance, I include my thanks.

I leave these snowmen on the students' desks the day after vacation. Since everyone receives a note from the teacher, there are no hurt feelings.

*-Phyllis Scarcell Marcus*

### A BRIGHTER JANUARY

January is such a long, long month. Add some sparkle to it with these language arts activities.

**A diary** is an excellent way to have the students write on a continuing basis. Supply each with a notebook or pupils can make their own by stapling pages together. Schedule a definite "writing time"—the first 10 minutes of the day or the last 10. The students can comment on the weather, describe the day's activities, fantasize, or just write. Stress complete sentences, good choice of words, one or two paragraphs. Diary time should be time for reflection, and after a few days the students, hopefully, will look forward to it.

Have the class **research** people born in January. The list is fascinating. Each selects a subject, does research, writes a report, and makes an attractive cover. Display these reports on a bulletin board with the caption, "They Had January Birthdays." Here's a starter list of people:

> Paul Revere
> Betsy Ross
> Jacob Grimm
> Louis Braille
> George Washington Carver
> Carl Sandburg
> John Hancock
> Albert Schweitzer
> Benedict Arnold
> Martin Luther King, Jr.
> A.A. Milne
> Benjamin Franklin
> Daniel Webster
> Lewis Carroll
> Franz Schubert

Have the students **write** a seasonal story. Have titles available but suggest students use their own if they wish. Stories can vary in length but they should be edited and recopied. At the end of the month, compile all of them into individual anthologies. Have each student find a different poem about snow and **read** it to

the class. Just think of the fun as they browse through anthologies—they'll stop to read countless other poems. Each should practice reading the poem privately, so he can read with expression.

*-Helen Mills*

### PUT A LITTLE COLOR IN YOUR JANUARY

January can turn out to the most colorful month of all if you try some of these color-related writing activities. Print each activity on a different duplicating master and provide a border for coloring.

**1. Color similes** At the top of the page give an example: "As red as the valentine I gave my mother on Valentine's Day." Then let kids fill in their own similes using other colors. The last entry on the page could be "as colorful as . . ."

**2. Rainbow poems** "Blue reminds me of sky on a sunshiny day." "Green reminds me of . . ."

**3. Color questions and answers** "Rose, where did you get that red? I got it from your cheeks that day you built a snow fort." "Clover, where did you get that green? I got it from . . ."

**4. Color acrostics** "*Red* cardinals come to my bird feeder when it snows. *Every* winter there seem to be more of them. *Did* you know that the cardinal is Virginia's state bird?"

**5. Color comedies** "Color me red. I painted the barn during a high wind." Children will have fun illustrating their color comedies. You might want to gather some of the finished products with their colorful borders into booklets for readers in the library to enjoy.

*-Addie Martin*

### NEW YEAR CALENDAR ACTIVITIES

Welcome the new year into your classroom with these activities that revolve around the calendar. Tack a new calendar to your bulletin board so everyone can refer to it. Then have students:

1. Make 12-page booklets with illustrations for each month of the year.
2. Do research and write a short report on the way the different months got their names.
3. Make their own calendars for the coming year, circling holidays and red-letter days.
4. List the months in alphabetical order and write one adjective beside each that describes it.
5. Do research and write a short report on how our calendar started.
6. Write a short riddle for each month, to be shared with classmates in a group guessing game.
7. Write a paragraph about each month, describing what it's like in terms of weather, special days, and so on, and compile them into a booklet called, *The Months.*
8. Choose a new name for each month and explain all choices.
9. Write a list of predictions for the coming decade. What changes in technology do they foresee? Will clothing styles change much in the next ten years?
10. Write a story using one of the following titles:
The Months Go On Strike
My Favorite Month
The Year We Had No April
January Is Too Long
A Decade Begins.        *-Helen Mills*

## SAVE THAT CALENDAR
Here are 10 activities for squeezing a little overtime out of last year's calendar. Your kids can:
1. Cut the calendar apart and arrange the months sequentially.
2. Find the important holidays in each month.
3. Make a list of the months that have 30 days, 31 days, and 28.
4. Paste the months on four large charts, grouping them by season. Then illustrate the charts to show the weather and holiday motifs for each season.

5. Cut the numbers apart and arrange them in sequence.
6. Circle all odd numbers in red and all even numbers in blue.
7. Cut out the numbers and use them to make flash cards or other number games.
8. Use one color and circle numbers you would use if you were counting by twos. On the same sheet, circle (with another color) all the numbers counting by threes. Using other colors do the same for counting by fives, tens.
9. Put the numbers in a box to use in making classroom decisions. For example, the team captain who picks the lowest (or highest) number takes his team up to bat first.
10. Cut between the number rows, horizontally. Tape the strips together to use as a number line for computation.        *-Connie Zane*

## SALUTE DR. KING
Honor Dr. Martin Luther King, Jr., with a choral reading of his famous speech, "I Have a Dream." (Check your library for biographies that include the entire speech, or find it in *Representative American Speeches, 1963-64,* H.W. Wilson Company.) Have your class arrange the speech so that some sections are read by one person, some sections by a group, and others by the whole class. Help children make up hand and body movements to accompany the reading. Here, for example, is one sample paragraph:

"I have a dream that one day every valley shall be exalted, every hill and mountain shall be made low (*cast holds hands and lowers itself slowly*), and the rough places will be made plain and crooked places will be made straight." (*Class makes jagged angles with hands and arms, then slowly straightens limbs, making a soft, peaceful sound.*)
Students may wish to add props or music.        *-Milton Polsky*

## INDIAN DATING
Indian names for the months of the year were beautifully descriptive: January, Snow Moon; February, Hunger Moon (wolf's ribs showing); March, Crow Moon; April, Green Grass Moon; May, Planting Moon (the planting stick); June, Wild Rose Moon; July, Thunder Moon; August, Green Corn Moon; September, Harvest Moon; October, Fall Leaf Moon; November, Hunting Moon; and December, Long Night Moon. These were "written" with pictures. Have children date papers this way. The symbol for day is ✦ so January 5 would be: |||||✦ (⟨⟨        *-Jacqueline Koury*

## RING IN THE NEW

The following mini-unit will help students gain a better understanding and appreciation of other cultures as they celebrate the new year.

**The First first** The custom of celebrating the New Year on January 1 started in Rome in 153 B.C. The Romans had previously designated March 25, the vernal equinox, as their New Year's Day. However, citizens began to observe the New Year on January 1, the day after newly elected officials assumed their positions. In 45 B.C., the Roman emperor, Julius Caesar, established a new calendar. Caesar chose the name January for the first month of the year in honor of Janus, the Roman god of gates and doors. The Romans prayed to Janus at the beginning and end of all important events. He was depicted as having two faces looking in opposite directions. In his left hand he held a scepter (the symbol of power) and in his right hand he held a key with which he could lock the door to the past year and open the door to the new. Ask students to design a poster to represent January.

For his successful calendar reform, the Senate rewarded Caesar with a month of his own, "July." Have students find out how other months received their names.

Next ask students to research the differences between Caesar's calendar (the Julian) and the calendar we currently use (the Gregorian). While the Julian calendar was an improvement over the preceding calendar, it was still out of sync with nature. So, in 1582 Pope Gregory XIII instituted leap year to regularly correct the calendar's flaw.

**Uproar unlimited** All over the world the New Year is greeted with great noisemaking. Cannons blast, sirens sound, and bells ring. Have students speculate as to why noisemaking is such a universal custom. What does New Year noise symbolize in various countries? Most commonly, the great din is meant to drive away evil spirits and sins so as to start the new year with a clean slate. In China it is said that the forces of light (Yang) banish the dark forces (Yin) as cymbals crash and firecrackers explode. If you are brave, let students drive away the evil spirits that may be lurking in your classroom.

**Sing out** In Liberia, people follow the custom of singing the old year out and the new year in. Ask students to write their own songs to sing out the old year and welcome in the new.

**Good-luck tokens** In Austria, the New Year is commemorated with the minting of good-luck tokens called *Gluecksmuenze*. On one side of the token such lucky symbols as a chimney sweep, four-leaf clover, pig, mushroom, or baby are engraved. New Year's wishes are engraved on the reverse side. Have students design their own good-luck tokens. The designs can be transferred to gold paper, cut out, and exchanged among friends.

**Festive foods** In many countries pork is an important New Year's food. Because the pig roots for food in a forward manner (as opposed to some animals that scratch backwards), it is considered to be a good-luck symbol, representing progress. Austrians enjoy pig-shaped New Year candies called *Glueckschweinchen*, or "lucky little pigs."

In Liberia, baked chicken (rooster, not hen) is eaten on New Year's Day. Because the rooster awakens people with its early morning crow, it symbolizes the awakening of a new year. Can students think of any other foods that are thought to bring good luck?

In Iran, it is the custom to include seven foods beginning with the letter *s* in the New Year's dinner. The belief is that this will bring happiness in the coming year. Can students think of seven "s" foods? Have them write a nutritionally balanced menu consisting of seven foods beginning with the same letter.

**Starting with a clean slate** All over the world, New Year's is a time for making changes, for starting with a clean slate. In China and Japan, all debts must be settled before midnight on New Year's Eve in order to start the new year fresh. In China, people put lighted candles in a debtor's yard if he or she has not settled accounts. Germans believe their behavior on New Year's Day will affect their luck for the rest of the year. In Vietnam, it is forbidden to argue on the first. In the United States, no New Year would be complete without making resolutions. Discuss realistic resolutions with your students. Then have children write one or two goals they will try to achieve by the end of January.

**Looking into the future** Lead-pouring is a popular New Year's custom in Germany and Austria. Young people there drop a little melted lead into a bowl of cold water, watching as the lead cools and hardens into unusual shapes. The youngsters then try to tell their fortunes for the coming year by the things they see represented in the shapes of the cooled lead. A boat or plane shape might represent a trip. Your students can experiment with "lead-pouring" using melted wax. Give each student a plastic cup half-filled with cold water.

Light a long candle and drip a little wax into each child's glass. Students can then try to foretell future events from the shapes that form. Have them write a short story about their future, using their wax shapes for inspiration.

*-Kelly Riley*

## IT'S HAT DAY!

It's official—Hat Day comes on the third Friday in January. It's time you joined in the fun!

Tell your students they may come to class on this day wearing the headgear of their choice. (You might prepare children for Hat Day by wearing an outlandish—or at least unusual—hat to school the week before. After you've piqued their curiosity, explain to students that next Friday will be Hat Day.) When children arrive on the big day, they will naturally be interested in classmates' hats, so first of all invite each child to come to the front of the class, model his or her hat, and tell about why he or she likes it. Then line up all the hats on a table and try some of these "hat lessons."

**Hat stories** Before Hat Day, select some of the many stories and poems about hats and stock them on your classroom shelves. Read a few favorites like *Caps for Sale* by Esphyr Slobodkina; *The Cat in the Hat* and *The 500 Hats of Bartholomew Cubbins* by Dr. Seuss; "The Quangle Wangle's Hat" by Edward Lear; and "Mr. Smeds and Mr. Spats" from *A Light in the Attic* by Shel Silverstein. Later in the day, children can write their own stories and poems about magical hats, edible hats, hats that grow on trees, or other hat adventures.

**Hat words** Hat Day provides an excellent opportunity to teach new vocabulary words. Write some of the following on the chalkboard. Discuss briefly, then have each child choose one and find out its precise meaning: beanie, bearskin, beret, bonnet, bowler, busby, calpac, cap, coronet, crown, deerstalker, derby, fedora, fez, glengarry, hard hat, headdress, helmet, miter, morion, mortarboard, nightcap, opera hat, Panama hat, shako, skimmer, skullcap, sombrero, sou'wester, Stetson, tam-o'-shanter, ten-gallon hat, tiara, top hat, tricorn, turban, watch cap, yarmulke.

Discuss some of these expressions with students: "pass the hat," "I'll eat my hat," "hats off to . . .," "mad as a hatter," "at the drop of a hat," "he's talking through his hat," "it's old hat to me," "put on your thinking cap," "he tossed his hat into the ring." Can children think of other expressions? How about making up some of their own?

Ask students to find out the meaning of the term *millinery* (the design, production, and sale of women's hats). Where does the name come from? (Milan, Italy)

**Hats now and then** Try to find several examples of hats that indicate the wearer's occupation, such as those worn by coal miners, cowboys, fire fighters, matadors, clowns, football players, military personnel, or construction workers. Choose one child to come to the front of the room and try on these different hats, while the others guess the occupation. Discuss why that hat style might have developed. You might also invite a guest who belongs to one of these professions to speak to the class about his or her career. Now look into some hats of yesteryear. In the 1400s, European women wore tall, cone-shaped hats called *hennins* (also called *steeple headdresses*—princesses are often wearing them in fairy-tale pictures). In the late 1700s, the Gainesborough hat, with its wide brim and showy feathers and ribbons, was popular. Students may like to find pictures of other hats worn in different historical periods, such as the medieval headdress and cap, Persian turban, beret, cavalier hat (like those worn by the Three Musketeers), top hat, and bonnet. What historical hats are still worn today? (beret, turban)

**Investigating hats** Gather up all the cardboard, egg cartons, scraps of cloth, cans, colored paper, and yarn you can, and let children make their own hats. Challenge them to make a hat that can fly or one that two people can wear at the same time.

**Hat stats** Have students measure their head sizes in centimeters and then graph the information on a classroom chart. (This will help them create hats that really fit!) Make another chart with a graph showing hat color preferences in the class.

If you have access to a computer, here are two simple hat designs children can draw, using the Turtle graphics capabilities of Logo.

| Hat A | Hat B |
|---|---|
| FORWARD 100 | RIGHT 30 |
| RIGHT 90 | FORWARD 100 |
| FORWARD 50 | RIGHT 120 |
| RIGHT 90 | FORWARD 100 |
| FORWARD 100 | RIGHT 120 |
| LEFT 90 | FORWARD 125 |
| FORWARD 25 | BACK 150 |
| BACK 100 | HIDETURTLE |
| HIDETURTLE | |

Now ask children to program their own hat designs.

**Hat art** Let children find and cut out pictures of different kinds of hats in magazines and paste them on pieces of construction paper to make lively hat collages.

*-Peter Rawitsch*

## HOME SWEET BURROW

Fantasy can be a wonderful addition to your art program. My youngsters exercised their creative imaginations by drawing their ideas of Mr. Groundhog's underground home. This is a February activity with a decided difference! A classroom discussion can encourage imaginative "house plans."

*-Marilyn Carden*

## GROUNDHOG PUPPET SHOW

Let kids celebrate Groundhog Day this year with their own groundhog puppets and stages. To make the stages, have each child trim off the top half of a brown paper lunch bag. In the middle of the bottom of the bag, cut out a rectangle 2 inches long and ½ inch wide. (The bottom of the bag will be the top of the groundhog's "stage.") Next, cut out from brown tagboard a groundhog in profile, standing up on its hind legs. Draw in eyes, nose, and whiskers on each side of its head. Then glue the groundhog to an ice-cream stick. The next step is to run off copies of the poem that goes with the props. The poem, titled "Little Groundhog," goes like this:

Little groundhog down below
Underneath the wintry snow.
Come on out and tell us true,
Is spring coming?
Is winter through?

Paste a copy of the poem on one side of the paper-bag stages. Now you are ready for the performance. Each child holds his or her paper-bag stage in one hand, and the groundhog in the other. Children keep their puppets covered in the bag as they all recite the first two lines of

the poem. On the third line, "Come on out and tell us true," they bring their puppets up through the holes in the bottom of the bags. One final touch is to paint the bag with white paint so it appears that the groundhog is poking up through a snowbank to see if the sun is shining.

*-Amy Marotta*

## GROUNDHOG DAY REPRODUCIBLE

Use the reproducible at the right for these activities.

**1.** Celebrate Groundhog Day, February 2. See if you can see your shadow. (Official "groundhog time" is 7 A.M.) Record your weather prediction for this spring.

**2.** Pretend you are applying for Punxsutawney Phil's job (the official groundhog) and use this sheet to write your application. (List special qualities and background.)

**3.** Create story problems about Groundhog Day. Each person can write three, trade papers, and then work someone else's problems.

**4.** List observations that prove that spring is (or is not) on its way (smells, sights, sounds).

**5.** Groundhogs are animals that hibernate. Can you think of other animals that hibernate?

**6.** Write the history of Groundhog Day. Where and when did it start? Has the groundhog ever been wrong?

**7.** Write and illustrate a story about the groundhog who slept until February 3.

**8.** Describe Groundhog Day from the groundhog's point of view.

**9.** Determine how the daily weather report is scientifically predicted. *-Rebecca W. Graves*

## THE GOUNDHOG'S SHADOW

Trace two groundhog outlines 7″ × 3″, one on black and the other on brown construction paper. Cut out both and paste the black groundhog onto a piece of white construction paper. Then fold a small strip of oaktag accordion style and glue one end to the black groundhog and the other to the brown groundhog. Press together; when dry, you'll have your own 3-D forecaster for Groundhog Day! *-Peggy Dewire*

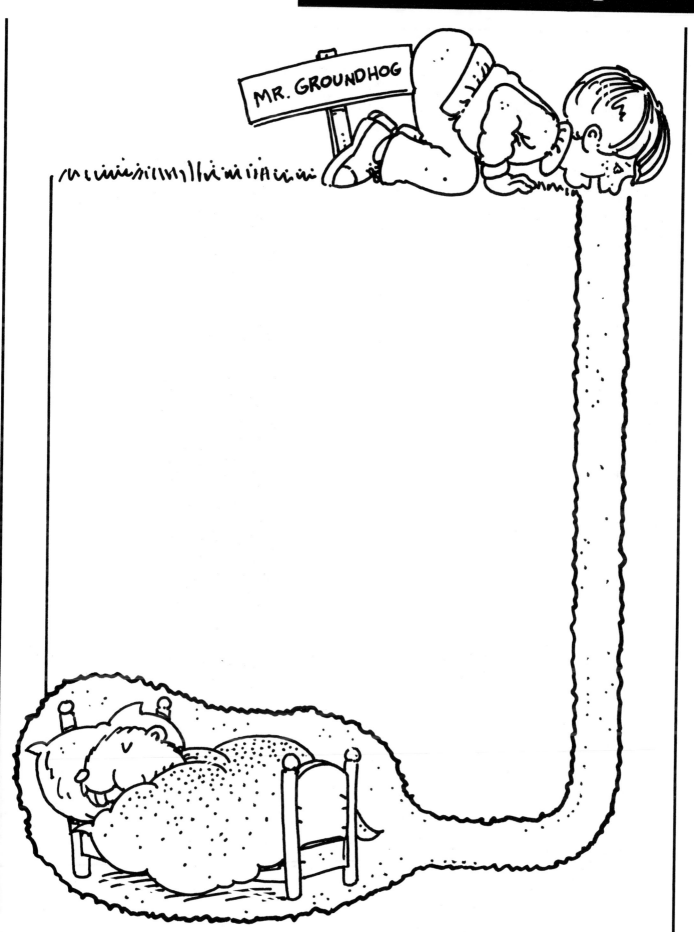

MR. GROUNDHOG

## CHINESE NEW YEAR

Celebrate Chinese New Year's Day by making a dragon that your kids can wear. The dragon is made of a dozen large, green plastic trash bags. You begin by cutting each bag open and laying it out on the floor so you have one flat piece of plastic. Then you sew or staple the bags together so you are left with one long sheet of plastic. Tape thin strips of yellow tissue paper along both edges of the plastic. These edges will be the bottom of the dragon. Next, cut a long strip of yellow construction paper, fold it vertically in half, and tape or staple this "spine" along the middle of the bags. Drape the plastic over five or six children so the spine runs along the top. (The plastic will be completely open at the children's waists, so there is

no safety problem.) Cut holes for the lead child's head and arms. Fashion a dragon's head from a cardboard box covered with scraps of the green plastic. Add Stryofoam eyes and paper horns, nostrils, and tongue. Bunch together and tie or staple the extra plastic behind the last child in the dragon. This will form the dragon's tail. If you want a smoke-puffing dragon, roll powder into a paper tube and close the tube with cotton balls. One puff from the lead child and you have a magic dragon. Let your dragon pay a surprise visit to a neighboring classroom!

-Betty Dietloff

## CREATE YOUR OWN FORTUNE!

Your class can celebrate the Chinese New Year by making this famous Chinese treat. Compose short fortunes and write them on 2-inch by ½-inch strips. Next, have on hand the following ingredients: 1 egg white; 3 Tbsp. sugar; pinch of salt; 2 Tbsp. melted butter; ¼ cup flour; 1 drop vanilla extract; ¼ tsp. instant tea mix; 1½ tsp. water.

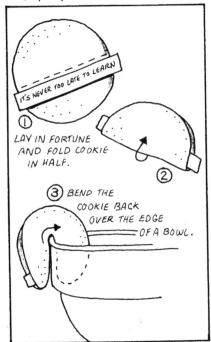

① LAY IN FORTUNE AND FOLD COOKIE IN HALF.

② IT'S NEVER TOO LATE TO LEARN

③ BEND THE COOKIE BACK OVER THE EDGE OF A BOWL.

Beat the egg white, sugar, and salt with a fork, and stir in melted butter, flour, vanilla, tea, and water. Chill the batter for 30 minutes. Grease a cookie sheet; preheat the oven to 350 degrees. For each cookie, drop a teaspoon of batter on the sheet to make a thin 3-inch circle. If you don't have help, bake only two at a time. You will have about 10 seconds to fold the cookies after they're baked before they cool. This recipe, from *Glamour* Magazine, makes one dozen. Bake cookies three to five minutes or until the edges are golden brown. Remove the cookies with a spatula and put on a nonstick surface. Place a fortune across the middle of each cookie. Fold the cookie forming a half-circle, keeping edges even. Work quickly to fold all the cookies while they are warm and soft. Bend folded edge of cookie over the rim of a bowl, pushing down gently. Hold for a moment; then repeat with a second cookie. *Note:* Cool, wipe clean, dry, and grease baking sheets before baking a second batch. Have at least two cookie sheets—one cooling (you can run cool tap water on it) and one in the oven. Cookie batter doesn't cooperate on a hot cookie sheet. Enjoy!

## GEORGE WASHINGTON QUIZ

On February 22, when George Washington is the star of the day, challenge your class with this quiz:

That so many places can say "George Washington slept here" is not really surprising, for George was the most widely traveled American official of his time.

Using the clues below, name the locales where the Father of our Country made snooze news.

**1.** George slept in a cradle in this Virginia county—his birthplace.

**2.** George left the country with his ailing brother in 1751 to sleep in this West Indies island.

**3.** In this Massachusetts town, George slept under the first flag of the United States.

**4.** George slept soundly in this estate, located on the banks of the Potomac.

**5.** Our first president was ready for a nap after driving the British out of this seaport city.

**6.** At Christmas time, a weary George slept in this New Jersey town after defeating Hessian troops.

**7.** In the terrible frozen quarters of this Pennsylvania site, George had trouble catching a little shut-eye.

**8.** George enjoyed a well-earned snooze in this Virginia town after receiving the surrender of Cornwallis.

**9.** President Washington slumbered comfortably in this city after his inauguration in 1789.

**10.** George caught forty winks in this city when serving as a delegate to the first Continental Congress.

**ANSWERS; 1.** Westmoreland County, Virginia **2.** Barbados **3.** Cambridge, Massachusetts **4.** Mount Vernon **5.** Boston, Massachusetts **6.** Trenton, New Jersey **7.** Valley Forge **8.** Yorktown, Virginia **9.** New York City **10.** Philadelphia, Pennsylvania. *-Erma Reynolds*

## LINCOLN'S BIRTHDAY ACTIVITIES

Abraham Lincoln was the sixteenth president of the United States. His birthday this month offers a great opportunity for your kids to research, write, and gain insight into the life of a man who helped make this country great. Following are some activities your students might like to try.

**1.** Make a list of all the things you can think of that were named after Lincoln.

**2.** Read the Gettysburg Address and select your favorite sentence. Neatly print it on an index card and use it as a bookmark. You might want to make several bookmarks and give one to each member of your family.

**3.** Pretend that you are Willie or Tad, Lincoln's young sons, and that you're living in the White House. Write a story describing a typical day for you.

**4.** Use reference books to trace Lincoln's early career. What were some of his occupations before he became president? How did these occupations help him in the presidency?

**5.** The Lincoln-Douglass debates were important events in history. Research these debates to find out what topics were discussed. Now hold a debate in your classroom on the topic, "Who was the greatest president? Abe Lincoln or George Washington?"
*-Helen Mills*

## PRESIDENTIAL REPRODUCIBLES

Use the reproducibles on the next two pages for these activities.

**1.** Write an imaginary conversation between Lincoln and Washington. What would these presidents like to ask each other? President Reagan? What would kids like to ask them?

**2.** Make an invitation to an imaginary presidential dinner party. Be sure to include the guest list (at least 10 people, living or dead).

**3.** Write a personal definition of freedom. (A good bulletin board: Ask other people in your school to also share theirs.)

**4.** Write questions for "Presidential Pursuit ." Research these presidents and create some stumpers.

**5.** Do math problems on the presidential reproducibles. Arithmetic was Washington's favorite subject. Kids can do theirs in his honor!

**6.** Draw at least five different American flags throughout history, or design a new one.

**7.** Write a recipe for cherry pie! Find out if George Washington really cut down a cherry tree. Maybe your class could bake pies together.

**8.** List other famous people born in February, when they were born, and why they are famous.
*-Florence Zimmerman*

## OTHER FEBRUARY ACTIVITIES

**1.** Write a singing telegram in honor of the first singing telegram delivered in February 1933.

**2.** Design your own comic strip in honor of the first comic strip published in February 1896.

**3.** February is American Heart Month. List all the ways that you can be good to your heart.

**4.** In honor of Thomas Edison's birthday, see how many of his 1,097 inventions you can list.
*-Florence Zimmerman*

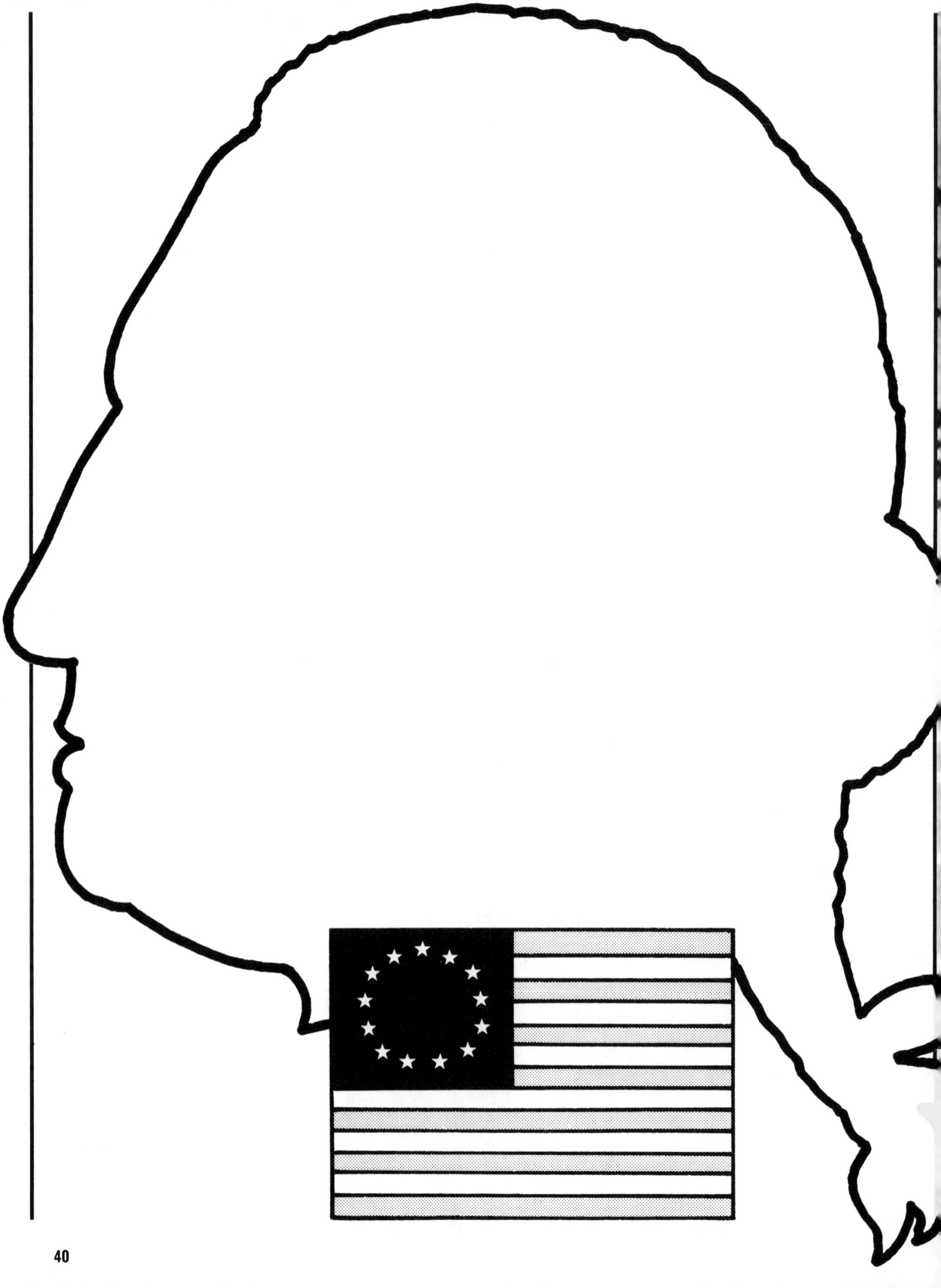

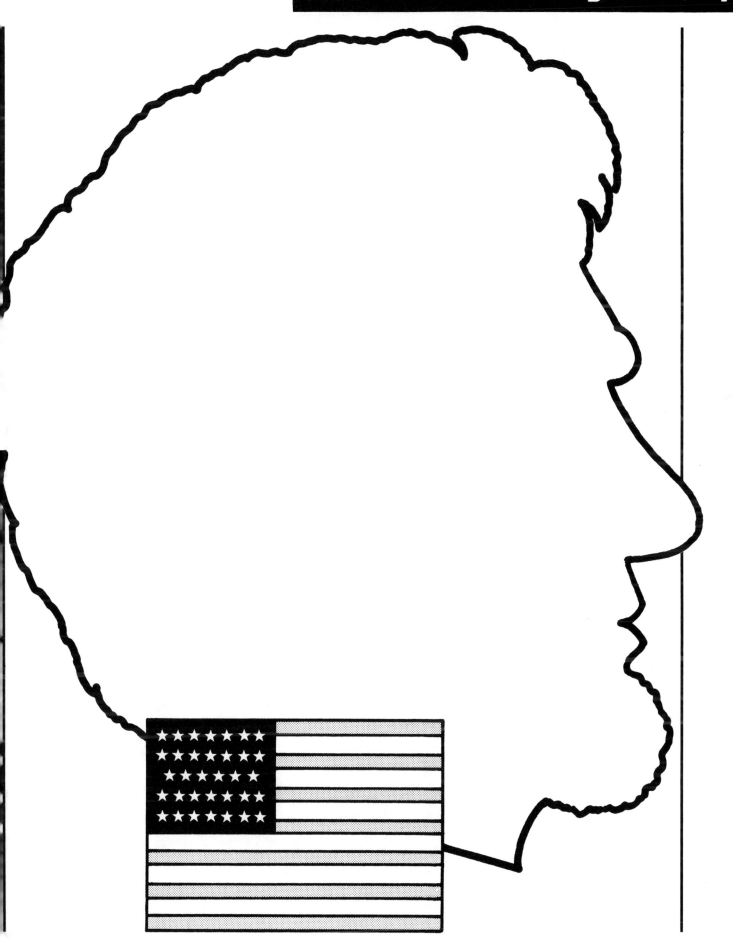

## SUSAN B. ANTHONY DAY

February 15 is Susan B. Anthony's birthday. One of the first women to vote in the United States, she fought for women's rights until her death in 1906. Celebrate her birthday this year by using these consciousness-raising activities (geared to the intermediate grades).

**1.** Ms. Anthony was brought to trial in 1872 for voting illegally. She was fined, but refused to pay on the grounds that the law denying women the vote was wrong. Read selections from the proceedings of this famous trial with your class. Then discuss equal rights and sexism in our society. Can students think of examples of sexism today? Do students think women are being treated equally? Why or why not?

**2.** Read the class a story in which the father has a nurturing role. Discuss family roles. How many fathers cook, do the dishes, or help with the housework? How many mothers fix broken appliances, change the oil in the car, or play catch with the kids? Have students write a story in which there is no sex discrimination or role assignment according to sex. Advise them to be careful not just to put men in traditional women's roles, or vice versa.

**3.** Ask students to take a stand on an important issue such as "The ERA should be ratified," "Women should be drafted," or "Girls should have sports facilities equal to those for boys." Assure students that their opinions will be respected if they are based upon fact rather than prejudice. Some students may want to try supporting an opinion different from their own.

At the end of the day, your students should be more aware of old attitudes, societal stereotypes, and historical facts, as well as new possibilities for the future. —*Sarah M. Butzin*

## BLACK AMERICANS WHO MADE A DIFFERENCE

Famous black Americans, both past and present, are listed in column one. Column two lists each person's claim to fame. Ask your students, "How many can you match correctly?" Then have them find out more about those they are not familiar with.

1. Thurgood Marshall
2. George Washington Carver
3. Booker T. Washington
4. Ella Fitzgerald
5. Willie Stargell
6. W. C. Handy
7. Alex Haley
8. Althea Gibson
9. Oscar Robertson
10. Duke Ellington
11. Jesse Owens
12. Lou Gossett
13. Langston Hughes
14. Frances Ellen Watkins
15. Martin Luther King
16. Harriet Tubman
17. Lorraine Hansberry
18. Daniel Hale Williams
19. Guion Bluford
20. Matthew Henson

A. Basketball player
B. Jazz musician
C. Actor
D. Explorer
E. Plant scientist
F. Author
G. Educator
H. First black astronaut
I. Author of *Roots*
J. Civil rights leader
K. Track star
L. Supreme Court justice
M. Heart surgeon
N. Poet
O. Singer
P. Playwright
Q. Liberator-abolitionist
R. Baseball player
S. "Father of the Blues"
T. Tennis player

*Answers:* 1:L, 2:E, 3:G, 4:0, 5:R, 6:S, 7:I, 8:T, 9:A, 10:B, 11:K, 12:C, 13:N, 14:F, 15:J, 16:Q, 17:P, 18:M, 19:H, 20:D —*O.J. Robertson*

## THE LEARNING TRAIN

This learning train activity will require the cooperation of at least seven other teachers in your school. To prepare for this activity, each teacher should choose a historical event to focus on and work with the students to decorate their classroom in a manner to commemorate that event. Then two students should be selected from each class to research the topic and act as speakers on the day of the big journey.

On the morning of the "trip," all eight classes should meet at the "station" (gymnasium or cafeteria) and form eight long "trains." Each student should be given a paper "ticket," and one teacher should act as the "conductor" for each group. Ask an older student, another teacher, or your principal to be the "town crier." Give that person a bell to ring to start the trains moving. Each train is to go to a different room, hear a short lecture by the designated speakers on the event they're representing, and participate in some commemorative activity, such as signing a mock copy of the Declaration of Independence, or walking through ice water at Valley Forge. When the town crier rings his bell again, each train must move to a different room. The children get their tickets punched at every stop.

—*Madeline Plosila and Cheryl McLaughlin*

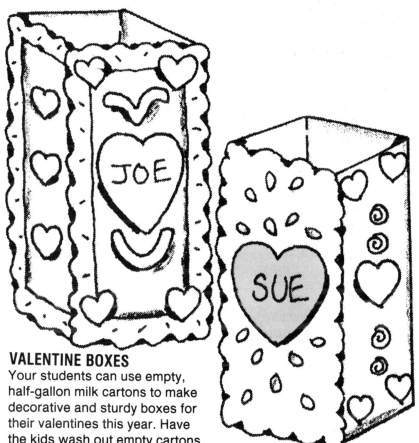

## VALENTINE BOXES

Your students can use empty, half-gallon milk cartons to make decorative and sturdy boxes for their valentines this year. Have the kids wash out empty cartons at home and bring them to school at least one week before the holiday. Using scissors, show them how to *carefully* cut the folded tops off their cartons. Then have them cover the cartons with white or red construction paper. Make sure they cut the paper to the size of the milk cartons *before* pasting. When the glue is almost dry, show the kids how to use their hands to smooth any bubbles in the paper. Now their boxes are ready to be decorated. Let the children choose from such materials as lace doilies, yarn, pipe cleaners, crepe paper, contrasting colored construction paper, and so on to design their own decorations. As a finishing touch, the kids can cut out large red or white construction-paper hearts as name tags and glue them to the front of the cartons.

When the valentine boxes are completed, place them on a large table in a corner of your classroom. Line them up in rows across the table, leaving spaces between each row, and making sure that all the boxes are facing in the same direction. Place strips of masking tape in the spaces between the rows to represent streets. Label them Heart Lane, Valentine Road, Cupid Avenue, Love Route, and so on.
Post each child's name and his or her valentine box address on your bulletin board for classmates to refer to when sending valentines.
-Barbara Lasche

## Rx FOR YOUR VALENTINE

A miniature planter makes a thoughtful gift for any special someone. The basic ingredient is a 3″ tall plastic medicine container. Remove cap from container and apply glue to the top outside of cap and the center of a paper doily. Place the cap, glue side down, on the doily, holding for several minutes until it is set. This forms the base. Next, affix the name of your friend to the bottle, using foil letters. Glue the bottle into the planter base.
Now for the gardening! You'll need pebbles (for drainage), potting soil, and a plant cutting (with at least two nodes, or bumps on the stem where leaves grow). Place a few pebbles in the bottom of the planter and fill the rest with potting soil to within a half inch of the top. Water lightly. Then place the plant cutting into the soil and add a few more drops of water. Your living token of friendship is now ready for giving! Remember to tell your friend not to overwater the plant or it will rot.
-Rosalind Schilder

## HEART TO HEART

This year, celebrate Valentine's Day in your class with a real "heart-to-heart" project that will do wonders for your students' self-esteem. Have each child make one large, construction-paper heart. The students may decorate the hearts in any way they choose, but must be sure to leave enough space in the center for five short sentences or phrases. Now divide your class into pairs. Each member of a pair is to write five positive sentences or phrases about his or her partner in the center of the heart. Then have the kids cut their hearts into five or six puzzle pieces, place them in envelopes, and give them to their partners, so every student has a "broken heart." The kids may then "mend" their hearts to read the flattering messages. You might want to have the children glue their hearts to white construction paper and place them all on a heart-to-heart bulletin board.
-Charlene Czerniak

## VALENTINE VILLAGE

Here's a friendly bulletin board community your kids can use to mail their valentines. Have each child fold the bottom edge of a 12″ x 18″ piece of colored construction paper one-third of the way up to make a pocket, and staple sides together. These pockets will be used for the students' houses. Instruct them to cut from other paper a slanted roof, paper doors, windows, and shingles, then glue all cutouts onto their houses. Finally, have children print their names and addresses on doors. Arrange the houses on your bulletin board around the words VALENTINE VILLAGE (low enough for children to reach), and they're ready for mail delivery!                —Linda Bilyeu

## HAVE A HEART!

Do you have a heavy heart when you try to dream up creative activities for Valentine's Day? This lesson will leave no intermediate-age students brokenhearted! A week before Valentine's Day ask your students to begin collecting expressions with the word "heart" in them. Encourage children to interview friends, parents, and especially grandparents for old sayings. Have a contest to see who can bring in the most expressions. As students bring in their findings, post them on a bulletin board. Have each student choose two favorite expressions to illustrate and label.

Some sayings you might want to *learn by heart* are: heartless, sweetheart, wear your heart on your sleeve, take heart, and eat one's heart out. Your students will really enjoy it, *cross my heart*!
                —Margaret Miles

## ALL DAY VALENTINES

When Valentine's Day rolls around and class excitement reaches a feverish pitch, try "dressing up" your usual curriculum with these Valentine-related activities:

**1.** Have the kids write and illustrate their own Valentine's Day stories, using one of these suggested titles:
> "My Mysterious Valentine"
> "The Case of the Broken Heart"
> "The Valentine Dog"
> "Valentine's Day in the Twenty-second Century"
> "Mr. Valentine and Me"

**2.** Create a special kind of spelling list by having each child write a word on the chalkboard that reminds him or her of Valentine's Day. The kids can study the list together and get together in pairs for oral quizzes. You might want to have the class alphabetize the list, divide the words into syllables, or use them in sentences.

**3.** Let kids make strings of four hearts each (paper-doll style) out of red construction paper. They then choose verbs from the spelling list or vocabulary lesson and write a different form of the verb on each heart, such as "begin," "began," "begun," "beginning."

**4.** When it's time for social studies, let children imagine that they are founders of "Valentown." They must draw up a constitution, write town laws, and decide on a system of government. You may want the kids to draw maps of their towns or representative flags.
                —Sally Stempinski

## HEARTY PENGUIN

A playful penguin puppet is easy to make. To a small white paper bag, attach a black construction paper head and limbs with glue. The eyes are gummed paper reinforcers. Add a gummed foil heart and he's ready to strut! Now read this Valentine Rhyme:

> I met a penguin yesterday,
> So jolly, fat, and fine.
> I pinned a red heart on his chest,
> And named him Valentine!

(Of course, *your* penguin might be a girl.)                —Sally Barrett

## HEARTLAND CITY

This valentine activity makes February prime time for a map studies unit. Draw the basic outlines of a small town on a large piece of white butcher paper. Label the streets Cupid Drive, Valentine Avenue, and other valentine-related names. Discuss where the business, housing, school, and recreation districts should be. Then divide students into committees, one for each district, and have them create construction-paper buildings, people, and pets for their area of the town—using heart shapes as often as possible. The map can be used later for other activities dealing with directions, estimating and comparing distances, spelling, capitalization, and even creative writing.                —Patti D. Nielsen

## MY FAVORITE THINGS

This Valentine's Day, have your students discuss the things they love most—playing in the snow, rabbits, hot dogs, and so on. Then have each child paint a picture of one of his or her cherished objects or favorite activities on a large, red construction-paper heart. Staple the hearts to a long piece of red yarn and hang it across your room for a terrific "heart" gallery!
                —Mary Parent

## CLOTHESPIN WIND CHIMES

Children will be delighted to hear the wind ringing through these cheerful, tuneful wind chimes! First give each child five wooden clothespins and have him or her decorate the tops of each with marking pens. (Kids may want to draw clothes and faces for ''people chimes.'') Then let each child find a stick about a foot long and as big around as his or her finger. Use string or yarn to tie all the decorated clothespins to the stick, making sure each piece of string is long enough for the clothespins to swing freely in the wind. Seal the finished chimes by dipping them in varnish and letting them hang outdoors to dry.

*-Mary Bunton*

## SOUNDS OF SPRING

Sharpen listening skills and enjoy the new season. Have children take turns using small cassette players to tape record different sounds of spring. Remind each student to keep a written record of the sounds. As each child plays his or her tape to the class, have the rest of the students listen carefully and write down their ideas of what the sounds are. Encourage children to find spring stumpers.

*-Clifford Gordon*

## SPROUT A GARDEN

Growing sprouts from seeds is a good way to introduce kids to plant growth and to the habit of nutritious snacking. The following procedure for sprouting seeds is foolproof. First, rinse a half cup of seeds or beans in cold water. Mung beans, soybeans, alfalfa seeds, and radish seeds are all good for sprouting and for snacking. Next, punch holes in the lid of a quart jar. Fill the jar halfway with water and soak the beans or seeds overnight. The next morning, shake the water out of the jar and place the jar

with the seeds in it on its side. Put the jar in a warm, shady spot. Rinse the seeds, which will start to sprout soon after they've soaked, three times a day for three days, shaking out the water each time. After the final rinse on the third day, place the jar in direct sunlight. This will turn the sprouts green. After three days the sprouts will be about three inches long and delicious.

*-Dorothy Needham*

## MINIATURE GREENHOUSE

Don't throw away old plastic ''bubble'' umbrellas—they make great classroom greenhouses for starting seedlings and cuttings. Simply open the umbrella, then unscrew the handle. Push the center pole into a small box of soil, then group other boxes of seedlings around it. Place the greenhouse on the floor in a sunny part of your classroom. The plastic will trap moisture, providing perfect conditions for seedlings to sprout. You'll have healthy classroom plants in no time at all! *-Rose Glick*

## CLASSROOM GARDENING

As spring approaches, you can make your children aware of the rebirth of nature by planting an indoor garden. Use it as an interesting science project or

early preparation for Arbor Day. You'll need one 2-liter plastic soft drink bottle for each child in your class, soil, an assortment of planting seeds, ice cream sticks, scissors, and colored markers. Pull off the black bottom from each bottle. Now cut off the tops, slashing them an inch or so below the neck. Give each child a black bottom filled with soil. Have children plant their chosen seeds in it.

Now give the kids one ice-cream stick each and have them draw colored lines on it to aid in measuring the plant's growth. They are to place their sticks in the soil and cover the containers with the remaining portion of the bottle. When seedlings begin to appear, take off this bottle part.

*-Jita J. Jablons*

## TWIGGY

Probably the most notable change from winter to spring is the change from bare branches to leafy ones. This takes place with incredible speed. Have each of your students take a piece of yarn or string and mark a bud on some living tree or bush by tying the string around the stem closest to that bud. Students should then observe the bud and record their observations in their notebooks over a two-week period. Have them predict what they think will happen to the buds, when it will happen and what their buds will turn out to be. They may also want to cut a branch (about 10 centimeters long with one or more buds) to bring to the classroom and place in water. Is it the water or the temperature that signals a bud to begin developing? Interesting theories can be developed and experiments devised to test them. *-Terry Dixon*

## SHENANIGANS FOR ST. PAT

Do you celebrate March 17 in your classroom? Ireland, rainbows, and the color green can provide a day full of St. Patrick's Day learnings. Here are some subject-related ideas.

**Language Arts** Make up a St. Patrick's Day vocabulary list: blarney stone, shillelagh, emerald, troll, jig, gnome, shenanigan, chartreuse, leprechaun, shamrock, harp, and British Isles. By using a dictionary, students can answer questions about the words. Would you buy a blarney stone to put into a wedding ring? Is a shillelagh to be held or played? What color stone is an emerald? Where does a troll live? What does a gnome guard? Is a shenanigan a small hat worn in Ireland on St. Patrick's Day? Is chartreuse a color or a dance? Does a leprechaun look like a little boy or an old man? Write your favorite Irish poem in your very best handwriting for your students to copy. Be sure to write on a lined master for duplication. Why not use a green master available at your local office supply? Two poem possibilities are Aileen Fisher's "St. Patrick's Day" and "Wearing of the Green." Students can illustrate one.

**Mathematics** Make a vertical bar graph of the color green with collected data: the number of students wearing green, using green pencils, using green erasers, liking green as their favorite color, and having a green room in their house. Compare with other colors.

**Social Studies** Concentrate on map skills. Pass out atlases. Have students draw a map of the British Isles without tracing. Label the countries: Republic of Ireland, Northern Ireland, England, Scotland, and Wales. Locate each country's capital city with its name and a star. Locate and label the oceans and seas around the British Isles. What countries make up the United Kingdom of Great Britain and Northern Ireland? How many Irelands are there? Why? Draw France and the United States on your map. Label.

**Science** Try making rainbows. What makes a rainbow? To produce the spectrum, position a prism over a clean glass pie plate full of water on the light from an overhead projector. Name colors. Do colors appear in some order? Collect objects which produce the spectrum: jewelry, water-filled bowls, and cut-glass objects. Place them in sun or near very strong light. Examine them in various positions. Study the spectrums produced.

End the day with a hunt for the Little People's pot of gold, found at the end of the rainbow. Use foil-wrapped coins of chocolate candy tied in a gold mesh bag. Serve green-frosted cookies or cupcakes and lime drink.

*-Christine Trudel*

## SAINTS PRESERVE US, IT'S A SHENACHIE!

Saint Patrick's Day is a wonderful time to learn a little history and something about a different culture.

Last year my sixth-grade class decided to celebrate St. Patrick's Day in a special way. We set about trying to find a genuine Irish storyteller (or shenachie) by placing the following ad in our local newpaper: "Looking for a shenachie to tell stories to sixth graders. Call . . . ."

After an interest story in the same newspaper (prompted by our ad), responses started rolling in. We followed all leads and found a couple who were taking part in a teacher-exchange program. They were glad to come, tell stories, and share their experiences with us.

In preparation for the visit by our shenachies, we planned a green luncheon. Every student signed up to bring something green for a potluck lunch. Some of the things they brought were green deviled eggs, green onion dip and celery, guacamole and broccoli, pickles, cucumbers, tossed salad, green potato salad, fruit salad, green cookies, green cakes, green ice cream (pistachio and mint) and, to finish off, green gum!

Our combined luncheon and visit by the shenachies was a huge success! We all learned a lot about Ireland's history and traditions. We also found out that a meal fixed all in one color may be nutritional, but really lacks eye appeal!

*-Ruth Allen*

## LEPRECHAUN SEASON

Why not brighten up St. Patrick's Day and your ethnic history program with a little class participation? Begin with a presentation on St. Patrick's Day and the leprechaun's relation to Irish folk culture. Encourage students to research and share additional information. Then spark imaginations and creativity by challenging them to create a foolproof leprechaun trap. You might want to have them work in small groups for this activity and finish by drawing a large diagram of their traps to share with the rest of the class.

*-Michael and Lorraine Upton*

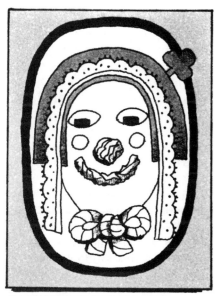

## A TOUCH OF IRISH LACE

Irish ancestors or not, try using bargain lace to trim "family" portraits. Twist colored tissue paper into noses and a mouth. Add a bit o' bulky yarn for hair and a bow. 'Tis 3-D art you've created! And a happy sight it is!

*-Pat Lang*

## OFF TO THE PEAT BOG

Here's an idea for a St. Patrick's Day game your kids will really enjoy. It stars Leopold Leprechaun who leaves his home in an old oak tree to make his yearly visit to the peat bog— where his pot of gold is hidden! Make your game board on a large sheet of poster board starting with the old oak tree and ending with the pot of gold. Divide the board into equal-sized sections and print the names of Irish towns and cities in several of the spaces. Use the suggestions below to fill in the rest of the board. Students move around the board by rolling a die and advancing the designated number of spaces. If they land on spaces with instructions printed on them, they must move backward or forward the specified number of spaces. The first player to reach the pot of gold is the winner.

1. You stop to pick shamrocks. Lose one turn.
2. You take a boat ride—advance to Galway Bay.
3. You trip over a shamrock and advance two spaces.
4. Return to the potato patch for a bag of potatoes.
5. Wait for the bus to Blarney Castle. Lose one turn.
6. Return to Galway Bay for a fresh seafood dinner.
7. You stop to kiss the Blarney Stone. Lose one turn.
8. You're hungry for Irish stew. Advance to Dublin.
9. Return to Limerick—you missed seeing the Norman Castle.
10. You stop to cool your feet in the Shannon River. Lose one turn.

*-Jane K. Priewe*

## LEPRECHAUN VISITORS

Looking for a way to perk up the atmosphere in your classroom while waiting for St. Patrick's Day? Sometime around the first of March, spend a few minutes after school "messing up" your classroom and leave some tiny green footprints on the windowsill. When the children arrive the next day, explain that leprechauns must have visited during the night. Repeat this process for two or three days. On the third day, have the class work together to compose a letter to the leprechauns, asking them to refrain from disrupting the classroom and requesting that they offer information about themselves. Leave the letter on your chalkboard. Before school the next day, leave a note from the leprechauns below the class's letter.

> We live in mushrooms.
> Our beds are made of green grass.
> We eat berries and drink morning dew.

Then, when it's time for an art lesson, ask the kids to draw their impressions of what the leprechauns look like and tack them to your bulletin board. Then have each child write his or her own letter to the visitors, asking questions about them and explaining how important it is to be a good worker and neat housekeeper.
When St. Patrick's Day rolls around add unflavored gelatin to lime Jello and have it set in a long shallow pan. Cut it into squares and sprinkle with green cookie sugar. Put one on each child's desk on top of a green paper shamrock. Clean up the room and bring in some fresh flowers or a shamrock plant. Leave one final letter on your chalkboard from the leprechauns.

> Dear Boys and Girls,
> Thank you all for the letters teaching us to be good workers. Tonight at midnight we will go back to our own land. Happy St. Patrick's Day!

*-Millie Lindell*

### EASTER EGG LEARNING

The large plastic eggs that panty-hose come in or the smaller ones that are sold in stores at Eastertime can be put to good use in your classroom. If you don't have enough eggs of your own to use, ask your students' parents to donate any extras they won't be needing at home.

**Egg-citing language arts** Print vocabulary words your kids have been studying on small slips of paper, one word per slip. Place four or five words inside each egg, then put all the eggs together in one basket. Have students choose eggs from the basket and put the words found inside in alphabetical order, write their definitions, or use them in complete sentences. You can also try printing words with one letter left out and instruct your kids to supply the missing letter. Or place several words inside each egg that together will form a complete sentence when unscrambled and taped side by side in the proper order.

**Math activities by the dozen** If you have 12 small plastic eggs and one empty egg carton, you can put together a mini-math center. Try printing math problems on small slips of paper, one problem per slip, and place one inside each egg. Then put all the eggs together inside the carton and close the lid. Have kids take turns opening the eggs one by one and solving the problems inside, timing themselves as they do so. The student who solves all 12 problems in the shortest amount of time is the winner.

**Classy egg organization** Try filling a large plastic egg with slips of paper on which you've printed the names of all the students in your class. Pick a name from the egg whenever you have a special job to be done by just one student. Or use them to call children up for show and tell, reading groups, or the lunch line.

To make all your egg-tivities a little more enticing, you might want to have your students help you decorate the eggs before you begin to use them. Supply the kids with tempera paints, colored construction paper, cotton balls, and so on. *-Carolyn Wilhelm*

### SPELLING WITH THE EASTER BUNNY

Present new spelling words with a visit from the Easter bunny. Begin by drawing a simple design, 10 inches high, of a bunny on construction paper. Cut this out and use it as a pattern to cut out enough bunnies for each student to have one. Glue or staple the bottom of a basket to the front of each bunny, leaving the top of the basket open. Then cut out copies of the week's spelling words and place a set in each of the baskets. On the back of each rabbit either draw lines for the students to write on or

paste on a sheet of writing paper. Present each student with one of the spelling bunnies, and have the students write sentences using each of the spelling words, on the bunnies' backs. *-Lorraine Lee*

### EGG SHUFFLE RELAY

Reinforce word-building and spelling skills with this Easter game. First, make Easter baskets out of margarine tubs, using tagboard strips for handles, then cut out construction paper eggs and write one letter of a spelling word on each egg. Place several eggs in each basket so that the letters on those eggs form a word. Number the baskets. Then have children sit in one or two circles, and distribute the baskets, one for each child, in numerical order. When you say "go," each child is to form one or more words from the eggs in his or her basket and record them on an answer sheet. When you say "stop," children are to pass baskets to the right and begin the process again. Continue until all students have had a turn with each basket, then check the answer sheets together.

*-Lorraine Lee*

### "DOWN THE BUNNY TRAIL"

You'll hatch a batch of eager readers with this activity that integrates reading with a colored-egg hunt. Before school, hide a basket of eggs or other goodies in a good place. Then set up a trail of clue-giving paper bunnies which leads to the hidden treats. Put a child's name on the front of each bunny and the clue he will read on the back such as "Look under the sink." When the student finds bunny #1 under the sink he will read the name of the child on that bunny who will then read his clue and find the next bunny, and so on, until each child has had a turn and the final clue locates the basket.

You can write each clue to coincide with the reading level of the child whose name appears on the front. Simple clues, such as "Look in the closet," can be mastered by less competent readers, while the abler student can be challenged with more complex hints like: "You will find a bunny hidden in the encyclopedia. Look under 'rabbits'." Students enjoy having their own bunny with their name and individual clue.  -Connie Zane

## BUNNY IN THE GARDEN

After a study of the four basic food groups, my first graders and I planned a healthy snack for the Easter season. The snack was a rabbit (each child got his or her own) from foods of the four basic groups.

We started by placing a bed of lettuce on a butter plate to represent a garden. This was our vegetable. A scoop of cottage

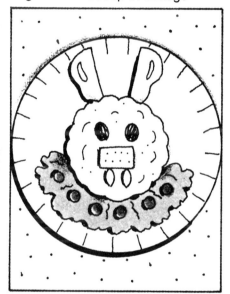

cheese represented the rabbit's head and provided protein from the milk group. Additional protein came from two blanched almonds that formed the rabbit's teeth. Fruits included raisin eyes and pear-slice ears. A square whole wheat cracker was the nose and provided healthy grains found in the bread and cereal group.
  -Carolyn Wilhelm

## A NATURAL EASTER BASKET

Science and art join forces in this Easter activity. Have each child bring in a berry basket to line with aluminum foil and fill with potting soil in class. Pass out grass seed

and show how to plant the seeds—approximately ½ to 1 inch deep. Have children water soil and place all the baskets in a sunny spot. Then have them record on an experience chart the day when the grass sprouts, amounts of water needed weekly, and so forth. When the grass has grown approximately two inches high, have students make colorful handles from heavy oak tag and staple them to the sides of berry baskets. Now, for the extra fun! Have children dye Easter eggs to place in their baskets. Then have them draw the figure of a bunny to cut out and clothe with crayons, felt-tip pens, and construction paper. After bunnies are in their baskets, surround them with nutritious goodies like a small box of raisins, whole peanuts, and a wrapped slice of banana bread, (which, if you have the facilities, can be made in the classroom).  -Lynn Barwell

## RABBIT REVIEW

Draw a large rabbit on poster board and place plastic grass all around. Tack large plastic eggs in the grass and around the rabbit. Fill each one with construction paper flowers or eggs (10 or 15). One of the flowers or eggs should have directions explaining what to do with the math problems or skill questions on the rest of the set. You may want to review skills in vocabulary, contractions, abbreviations, homonyms, antonyms, alphabetical order, and so on. This spring bulletin board can be a cheery way to help children use their spare time to review and retain what's been learned in your room this year.
  -Linda M. Brown

## NATURAL DYE EASTER EGGS

Long before there were chemical dyes people used different natural substances to dye material. At Eastertime I use some of these natural dyes to color eggs with my students. You need a hot

plate, water, some pots, a cheesecloth for straining, some vinegar, and the dye substances. Substances that make good natural dyes are beets, blueberries, orange peels, onion skins, nut shells, tea leaves, coffee, and various green vegetables and herbs. Place the dye substance (experiment to see how much is needed to actually dye an egg) in a pot of water and bring the water to a boil. Then let the dye substance steep for a few minutes. Just before you put the eggs in the water, pour the water through the cheesecloth, straining out the dye material. Place a few teaspoons of vinegar in the pot of colored water. This helps hold the dye on the eggshells. To get different shades of color, leave the eggs in the water for different lengths of time.  -Patricia Wilmott

## HERE COMES PETER COTTONTAIL

This Easter season, bring the popular song "Here Comes Peter Cottontail" to life for your students with this creative art and music project. Divide the song into approximately equal parts and assign one part to every child in your class. Have the kids illustrate their parts on large sheets of white construction paper, and neatly print the words on 12" x 18" strips of yellow or pink paper. Staple the strips below the illustrations. Now have the kids present their art work to fellow students by visiting other classrooms. Bring along a record player and recording of the song. Your students should stand in a line at the front of each room and step forward with their illustrations as their part of the song is played. Your children will really enjoy this activity, which can be adapted to any seasonal song.
  -Ellen D. Townsend

## MAY DAY WRITING CENTER

Establish a May Day writing center in your classroom to give primary students a chance to write creative stories and make May Day cards for friends and relatives. Gather several long paper streamers of different colors and tape them to one point in your ceiling. Twist the streamers, staple artificial flowers to them, and tape the ends to the outside of a table (preferably a round one). This will achieve a ''May Pole'' effect that's sure to capture your kids' attention. Add a dictionary, writing paper, colored construction paper, a seed catalog for flower pictures, crayons, and colored pencils. Then have your students try some of these activities:

1. Tape individual words to the table such as *May, wish, you, happy, my, for, flowers, day*, and so on. The kids then use these words and others when writing the inscriptions on their May Day cards.
2. Have the students write short stories about things that might happen on May Day.
3. Tape several unfinished sentences to the table, the kids to fill in the blanks. You should provide a list of appropriate words for them to choose from. Some sentence possibilities include:
In May, I feel as _____ as a _____.
In May, I can play _____.
May is so nice because _____.
4. Make several large construction-paper flowers and write four or five different May words on each one. Students then make their own construction-paper flowers and print the same groups of words in alphabetical order on each one.

*-Carolyn M. Wilhelm*

## FLOWER BASKETS

The delightful custom of making and hanging May baskets is probably kept alive by the

nation's elementary teachers! Baskets can be prepared from very simple materials. If real flowers are not available, tissue paper, egg cartons, yarn, scraps of fabric, and chenille wire can be used to make blooms.

Young children like to make simple cornucopias from rolled paper cones. Cut the edge of cone into petallike points and staple on a paper handle.

One variation on the traditional basket might be a braided-yarn plant holder containing a plastic margarine or whipped-topping bowl with prerooted cuttings of hardy plants. Children should start cuttings two to three weeks ahead.

Very little children can crayon designs on a plastic foam cup, then insert a colored pipe-cleaner handle. They could also staple together a shallow box cut from a rectangle of decorated construction paper with corners slit and overlapped and a narrow strip of contrasting paper used as a handle. A mini-May basket is quickly made from half a walnut shell with a pipe-cleaner handle. Older children enjoy the more challenging woven-paper basket. First they fold two long rectangles of paper in half and round off unfolded corners with scissors. Across the folded edge of one, they cut equal-width strips as long as paper is wide. Across the folded edge of the other they cut equal width strips about ¼ inch longer than the paper's width. With split ends of papers at right angles to one another, strips are interwoven by overlapping and inserting alternate strips inside one another. As rows are done, they are slid down to make space for the next woven row.

*-Elizabeth Tschida*

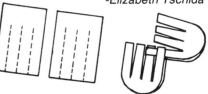

## MAY BASKETS

Foster good community feelings by taking these May baskets, filled with goodies, to a nearby hospital or nursing home. To make the baskets, cut out two identical circles from wallpaper samples or construction paper. Glue back sides together. Place the circle over a can that's about half as big around as the circle, then turn down and flute sides of circle. Attach a handle made from a pipe cleaner.    -Rebecca Graves

## MOTHER'S DAY BOOKS

Your students can make their mothers front-page news for Mother's Day with this project. Start by making a small book by folding two pieces of white paper into quarters. Slit the folded tops to make a 16-page book. Each child puts a picture of mom on the cover of the book. It can be a photograph, drawing, painting—whatever the child wishes. The rest of the book is for artwork, stories, and messages dedicated to students' mothers. A piece of colored string tied around the middle of the book holds the pages together.    -David Bloom

## "A STITCH IN TIME" CARD

Make a card for Mother that she can use and enjoy all year. Fold a piece of construction paper of the color and size desired for the card. On the inside, glue a heart- or flower-shaped piece of fabric and push a threaded needle into the fabric. On the facing page, write this poem:

Mother, on this special day,
There is something I want to say:
I love the way you cook and sew
More than you will ever know.
I love everything you do,
And most of all, I love you!

The children can use their creativity in choosing the fabric and design for the holder, and in decorating it.''    -Juliann D. Hickerson

## A BRIGHT GREETING

A 3-D sun is easy to create and makes a wonderful theme for a Mother's Day card. Cut out four identical circles and paste them together. Press this "paste-filled pancake" over a jar bottom to dry into a flowerlike form. Cut fluted edges into points. Paint in sunshine colors. Glue sun to cardboard and add the appropriate sentiments. One suggestion is: "You are the sunshine of my life."

*-Joan Mary Macey*

## BOOK OF THE DAY

When you turn the word MOM upside down, it spells WOW. Children use this idea to design booklet covers. Fill-in-the-blank pages are duplicated for the inside of the books. They read: My Mother loves me when _____. My Mother looks prettiest when _____. If I could give my Mother something special from me, it would be _____. My favorite thing about my Mother is _____. The funniest thing I can remember about my Mother is _____. I want to say "Thank you, Mother" for _____.
Children can add a picture they draw of their mother and/or poem and other pages that each mother loves to receive.    *-Sharon Rankin*

## ROOM MOTHERS

For Mother's Day my first graders like to make special gifts to let our room mothers know how much we appreciate everything they do for us. After we make a paper frame, we place the following poem inside:

**To Our Room Mothers**
You've been so very good to us.
You've been kind in every way.
You've made us treats and helped
On all our special days.
Today we'd like to thank you
For all you've done this year,
And to tell you that you're special
And so very, very dear.
Today we'd like to tell you
In our very own way—
We've decided that today is
"Happy Room Mothers Day"!

After each student signs his or her name on the frame, the frame is dated and then laminated. Then each child draws a picture showing something special the mothers have done for the class. We bind these to make a meaningful book and use our frame as the cover.    *-Lynne Hepker*

## A GIFT OF LOVE

This job is one of the nicest gifts students can give parents. Have them bring in jars large enough for an adult's hand to fit in. Cover the jars with ripped pieces of masking tape, 1" long, in alternating rows like brick patterns. Then rub shoe polish on and off until dry, and shellac the jar when polish has thoroughly dried. You'll probably want to give it two coats. Poems written by your kids on construction paper can be attached to the jar. Have kids fill the inside of the jar with paper strips, folded in half, on which they've printed various jobs. Students decide on these jobs themselves, after a class discussion on the true gift of love—the giving of oneself. There should also be some blank slips kids can fill in later, for individual needs; about 60 slips altogether, enough for one job a week for a year. For a final touch, tie a ribbon around the jar.

These jars make attractive gifts to keep on a kitchen counter or mantle, and kids will love giving them. *-Melissa Donavan*

## LET'S NOT FORGET FATHERS

Though our school is over before Father's Day, I try to have my students make something for dad before they go on summer vacation. All fathers seem to be proud to receive their own handwritten Certificate of Merit Awards, sealed and signed by loving youngsters. My students follow and/or adapt this form:

*FATHER'S MERIT CERTIFICATE*
*This is to certify that* _____
*has fulfilled the role of father.*
*He is also an expert at* _____,
*especially when* _____.
*When dad gets a bit upset, all you have to do is* _____.
*If you need* _____, *there's dad.*
*If you need* _____, *there's dad.*
*If you need* _____, *there's dad.*
*If you need* _____, *there's dad.*
*This certificate is hereby awarded this* _____*(date).*

_____
(signature)
Ever-Present Witness

A circular "seal" is cut with a pinking shears and affixed appropriately. Each certificate is mounted in a paper "frame."
*-Bernice Cohan*

## THEY DO IT ALL FOR HER

On Mother's Day what mother can resist an A paper or papers that her youngster has saved and enclosed in an attractive folder, decorated and lettered, "Happy Mother's Day"? Children work hard to earn an A, and this little motivator seems to help counteract the distractions of spring weather.
*-Shirley Shratter*

## POCKETS FULL OF MESSAGES FOR MOTHER'S/FATHER'S DAY

Looking for a way to turn a commercial day into a thoughtful week? A book with pockets full of messages will make moms and dads happy for a whole week before Mother's or Father's Day. The book should have eight pages, with each of the inside pages containing a pocket for the parent to open—one a day—during the week before the holiday.

To make the book, use two 12″ × 18″ sheets of construction paper, one white and one a color. Fold each sheet in quarters, making the white piece the front cover, the back cover, and pages two and seven. The colored sheet will be pages three, four, five, and six. On the inside pages, tape or glue in paper pockets.

Students can illustrate the cover with three sayings about what they like the most about their mom or dad.

For the first pocket of the book, the children write on an index card two extra chores they will do that day for their parent. Kids should think of chores they normally don't perform.

Use another card for page three's pocket. On this card, the children write, "Tonight I am going to read something special to you. Please let me know when we can spend a few quiet moments together." Encourage the children to look for a poem in an anthology or to pick a favorite passage from a book. For page four: "I am all yours for a half hour tonight. For that time I will do anything for you, or with you, that you choose."

On the next card, have children write about a memory they have of their parent. Encourage them to describe the remembrance thoroughly so that the parent will feel its significance.

For the last pocket of the book, children either can draw a picture or make a badge or bookmark. The badge or bookmark could read: Number One Mom/Dad or The World's Greatest Mom/Dad. On the inside back cover of the book have each child write a thank-you letter to the parent, pointing out specific things he or she appreciates—leading the Brownie troop, taking them camping, driving them to activities. *-Tom Bernagozzi*

## ONE LAST GAME

During the last week of school keep a stack of index cards on the corner of your desk. Tell children to write a question on each card anytime they think of one that pertains to something they've studied during the year. Answers must be included and children can use textbooks to refresh their memories.

The last day of school divide the class into two groups. Ask the questions yourself or choose a panel of three or four students. Ask the first person on one side the first question for two points. If he or she can't answer, it goes to the rest of the team for one point. If no one from the first team has the correct response, the question is given to the second team. Anyone on that team can answer for one point. Questions alternate back and forth.

*-Irene K. Palko*

## REVIEWS FOR A HAPPY ENDING

Who feels like reviewing the term's lessons when the sun is shining, birds are singing, and warm breezes are wafting through the open window? Your students might if you try a few of these games to put spring into your reviews.

**Hole-in-one** Golf anyone? Make a list of 18 review questions. Divide the class into teams of about five. Ask a question of the first player on Team One. If he or she answers correctly, that's a hole-in-one for one point. If the player misses, the second player on that team tries for two points. Set a four-stroke limit—if after four tries a team hasn't gotten the answer, move to the next team with a *new* question. The team with the lowest score after 18 "holes" wins.

**Tick tock, cuckoo clock** Call out a topic (such as animal babies) and pairs of related words (cat—kitten, goat—kid). If the words go together, pupils shout "tick tock."

If the words do not correspond (for example, dog—calf), children say "cuckoo clock."

**Sound & Silence** Determine a category. Then call out a list of words and ask students to clap when you call a word from that category. When a word doesn't belong, students remain silent. Here's a sample round of "mammals": "horse" (clap), "mouse" (clap), "Kermit the frog" (silence).

**Stack up** Collect enough pennies, chips, or blocks to build two or more stacks high enough to collapse. Divide the class into two or three teams and ask a question of the first person on each team. Whoever answers correctly first starts the team stack. Players carefully add to their team's stack until it collapses. The game ends when each team's stack has fallen. Each team then counts the objects in its heap. The team with the most objects wins.

**Use your bean** On each square of a large outdated calendar, write a question or math problem. Students toss a beanbag and answer the question on which it lands.

*-Dee Leone*

## HELP FROM SMALL HANDS

My pupils are helping me be a better teacher every year. During the last full week of school, I lead a class discussion of ways we dealt with new subject matter during the year. Then I invite students to list ways I might have made the studies more interesting to them. Students are encouraged to discuss their ideas with their parents before submitting them. Unsigned lists are placed in a large envelope near the back of the room.

I find that as my pupils look for novel methods of dealing with concepts they are really reviewing the year's work. Parents are also reminded of the wide scope of learning which has taken place during the year. I then take home

the envelope and use the leisure of my summer months to examine the suggestions. Often, I use their ideas to informally plan ways to present basic subject matter for the next school year.

*-Mary Ann Wilson*

## SUMMER SURVEY

"What are you going to do this summer?" This end-of-the-year math activity will involve your class with the whole school and community. With your students, make up a survey of 5 to 10 questions about the up-and-coming summer season: Are you going anywhere? Do you have a part-time job? What would you do if you could do anything? Decide who you want to survey. Allow about a week for data gathering. Graph the results for a great math bulletin board. *-C.R. Fivver*

## HOW DO YOU FEEL ABOUT NEXT YEAR?

*Terrifying scare*
*to get lost in the halls there*
*at the junior high*

Use haikus for an end-of-the-year bulletin board. Have children fold an 8 ½- by 11-inch sheet of manila paper lengthwise and draw a self-portrait on it. Use a large, light-colored sheet of construction paper to make a shirt or blouse to attach. Discuss the general rules of haiku poetry (17 syllables: five on the first line, then seven, then five). On their item of clothing have children write a haiku about how they feel about being in the next grade. *-Pam Dailey*

## ANOTHER LOOK AT PARTIES

Your end-of-the-year party can be a peaceful, pleasant one with these helpful hints. Begin about two weeks early with discussion about foods, guests, manners, and even the art of table conversation. Plan the menu during a discussion of nutrition. Have students nominate their favorite food by drawing its picture or by writing its name in one of the five groups you offer: fruits, vegetables, meats or meat substitutes, desserts, drinks. The food in each category receiving the most votes is put on the party menu. Send the menu home so parents and children can decide what they would like to contribute. Have children suggest people in the school and community they would like to have attend. You may want to remember the people who have helped make this year a special one. Decide how many guests are appropriate and discuss as a class each child's reason for choosing a particular person. After a vote has been taken, ask children to come up with good questions and table conversation that would be interesting to guests. Hand-decorate invitations and ask guests to respond in writing. Name tags, place mats, centerpieces, and napkin holders are other items students can make. They should plan the number of utensils, chairs, cups, and plates needed, too. Have lunch together as a class before the party so that you can discuss manners and table conversation without the hum of the cafeteria. Decide what kind of music guests might like, games that everyone could play, and how to make everyone feel comfortable. You won't be the only one who thoroughly enjoys the party.

-Nanci Hamilton-Hoffman

### GOING, GOING, GONE

Begin preparing your kids now for an end-of-school class auction to "sell off" old and unneeded class posters, games, crayons, plants, and so on. They can start earning play money now to be used later on in the auction. Five- or ten-cent "payments" can be given to the children for various reasons, such as perfect spelling tests, neat desks, and consistently good behavior. To make the game even more exciting, declare some days "double money" days in which the kids may earn twice as much play money. Continue this for a month or so and hold the big auction just before the end of school.            -David Pickering

### SAY THANKS TO SCHOOL VOLUNTEERS

My students and I have a unique way to say thanks to all the volunteers and aides who help us in the classroom. We invite them to a box-lunch social at the end of the school year. I start two weeks before the lunch by getting a supply of cake boxes from a local bakery. Each child decorates one of the boxes at school. I send a note home to parents, asking them to prepare a special box lunch for one of our volunteers. The lunches are packed in the decorated boxes. Then the students write a short profile of each helper. They include memories of the school year in these. I run off copies of the profiles and staple them together to make "thank you" booklets. A week before the lunch, I send invitations to the volunteers. I then pair each child with an adult so the students know who they are bringing lunch for. If there are more children than adults, I include school secretaries, custodians, nurses, and other support staff. The children present the booklets before lunch and then eat with their "own" volunteer.            -Margaret Johnson

### HAND-ME-DOWNS

As each school year ends, I have my class plan a small legacy for the pupils that will follow them in my room the next year. One way the youngsters have found to "welcome" the next class is to leave a supply of cutout letters to use on bulletin boards. During the last days of school, students cut the letters from construction paper. (Each child can draw and cut four or five of the same letters.) Then I seal the alphabets in an envelope so they won't fade. I use some of the letters on my "Welcome" board in September, and my new students use the rest to create original boards.            -Robert Conklin

### CLASS SCRAPBOOK

A scrapbook of your students' creative work is a nice way to remember your class at its best. Collect the top essays, stories, poems, art, and letters by your students. (Each child should have at least one piece in the collection.) Ask each contributor to write a short autobiography. Then have an artistic student draw a cover, or work out a cover design as a class. Bind this together with string or yarn and you have your scrapbook. My classes make one copy at the end of every year, and I keep these in my classroom. Students are honored to be represented in the book, and they love to return to my class to see and read their best work of that year.

-Jean Antony

### A CHANCE TO SAY SO LONG!

After a whole year together, it's nice to set aside a block of time just to say good-bye. One way is to have children make "mailboxes" (folders will do) and tape them to their desks the last week of school. Hold a class discussion about how hard it is sometimes to say good-bye. Ask children to write a wish for each classmate on small pieces of paper, and sometime during the last week of school drop one in each mailbox. Stress that children don't have to sign their names and that the wishes should be positive. A class discussion about what children hope their summer will bring might help students think of specific wishes they would like to pass on.

-Nancee Boynton

## SUPER SUMMER SIZZLERS

Here are some fascinating activities to keep your students writing during the summer.

**1. Keep a diary:** A summer diary can provide children with memories long after vacation has passed. Encourage kids to use their diaries for accounts of family trips or to record ideas, feelings, and impressions.

**2. Write reviews:** Bring in TV magazines, newspapers, and publications containing reviews of TV shows, plays, and concerts. Have the students read and discuss these reviews, then try writing some of their own. Encourage them to continue doing this over the summer when they see a production that particularly interests them.

**3. Write a brochure:** Have kids select well-known or little-known vacation attractions. They are to write advertising brochures, including information on opening and closing dates, prices, and things to see and do. They might want to write two or three similar brochures about places they visit during the summer.

**4. Plan a vacation:** Have students plan a mock vacation including detailed information on things like transportation, itinerary, length of time, and financial needs.

**5. Write letters:** Encourage children to write to you over the summer. Also, provide a list of class members' addresses so the kids can write to each other, too!

*-Julie S. Polak*

## SUMMER LEARNING WITH PARENTS

Are you worried that your primary students will forget over the long summer vacation some of the skills they've acquired this year? Try sending home a list of activities parents can use to reinforce those skills at home.

**1.** When guests come to dinner, have your child set the table. Have him or her count the number of knives, forks, and spoons needed. When finished, have your child count every item on the table, including plates, napkins glasses, and so on.

**2.** When riding in the car or walking on the street, point out common words to your child such as *gas, stop, caution, exit, entrance*, and so on. He or she will soon learn to associate these words with the objects, places, and directions they refer to.

**3.** When shopping in the grocery store, read aloud the label found on every item you place in your cart, and make sure you show it to your child as you do so.

**4.** Place several common objects found in your house on the floor or on a table. Have your child tell you which is largest, smallest, thinnest, widest, and so on.

**5.** Let your child count the number of items you put in your washer or dryer on wash day.

**6.** Have your child count every light bulb in the house.

**7.** Read a short story aloud to your child. Have him or her tell you what happened.

**8.** When buying new shoes, jeans, toys, and so on, show your child the price tag and have him or her count out the correct amount of money to give to the clerk.

**9.** Let your child use a ruler or yardstick to measure several items in your home, such as the television set, the dining room table, your living room carpet.

**10.** Point out the different shapes of objects found in your home, such as circles, squares, rectangles, and so on. Let your child practice drawing and cutting similar shapes from construction paper.

**11.** Have your child count all the books found on a bookshelf or in a bookcase.

*-Florence Rives*

## SUMMER SECURITY PACKET

Are you increasingly concerned that students' minds will wither on the TV-vine over the summer vacation? Why not send kids home with a Summer Security Packet, full of suggestions for independent projects, plus a sheaf of leftover worksheets. It will protect kids from boredom and parents from the threat of ''*Now* what can I do?''

I have found it useful to include in the packet a letter to parents, offering ideas for helping children with the activities suggested. The letter may also thank parents for their support in your teaching endeavors. I like to let parents know that their enthusiasm is the most valuable resource their child will draw upon this summer, and assure them that time spent messing with old magazines, pens, crayons, and glue is worthwhile.

Both parents and children will appreciate suggestions for places to visit during the summer. Put together a list of local zoos, museums, walking tours and historic sites, along with such information as phone numbers, people to contact, charges, and schedules of hours. To compile this section you may wish to enlist the help of a parent who can call these places during the day to verify information. You might also add a list of follow-up activities. Include in your packet the reproducible on page 56 for pupils to keep and refer to during the summer. *-Nancy Fielder*

## BEST-SELLERS

During the last month before school is out, ask children to list at least three books they've read that they really like. The list should contain the author's name and a short description of the book. A little time in the library to search and remember will be valuable. Compile all the descriptions into a master list, add a few recommendations from your librarian, and kids will have a great reading selection for summer. *-Peggy Zimmerman*

## When There's Nothing to Do This Summer

*When you are alone:*
1. Draw a large picture of yourself wearing a bathing suit. Label 12 parts of your body (eye, nose, and so on).
2. Ask someone to give you a crazy beginning for a story. Add to the idea to create your own story. Tell it to a pal.
3. Tell a story using only pictures—no words. You can draw the pictures yourself, or cut them out of magazines.
4. Collect things from nature (pinecones, twigs, acorns, and so on). Use them to make a mobile.
5. Count things: Number of houses on the street, cars driving by in 15 minutes, windows in your house, cups in the cupboard, birds that land on a particular spot, and so on. Make a booklet to hold your numbers.

*With a friend:*
1. Plan a scavenger hunt. Together, make a list of 10 things to find outdoors. The first one to bring all 10 back is the winner.
2. Take turns making up a story. Tape record it and add sound effects.
3. Cut a sentence from a magazine. Cut it into separate words and scramble them. Can your friend put the sentence back together again?

# Basics

Basically speaking, this chapter has it covered. There are ideas that will enhance skills in reading and vocabulary, language arts, spelling, handwriting, creative writing, science, social studies, physical education, music, and more.

Set aside some skimming time. You might even want to come up with a special code — mark a star for ''do this soon''; a circle for ''wait until spring''; an asterisk for activities kids can adapt into a game; and ''s'' for a reliable fill-in activity for substitutes. Enjoy these tried and true, teacher-tested ideas.

## CEREAL BOXES AND READING

Everyone likes to read cereal boxes at the breakfast table, and kids are no exception. So take advantage of this and create a mock breakfast table in your classroom, using empty cereal boxes as motivational devices to introduce or reinforce word attack and comprehension skills. Set up a small table in a corner of your room (don't forget the tablecloth!) and place several *empty* cereal boxes on top of it. Now have the kids work in pairs or small groups on the following activities:

**1.** Make a list of all the words found on the boxes featuring a particular vowel combination, such as ea. Determine whether the words' pronunciations follow the general rule for that combination.

**2.** Make a list of 10 or 15 interesting words found on the cereal boxes. Think of synonyms, homonyms, and antonyms for these words.

**3.** Make a chart comparing three different types of cereal. Include such things as price, main ingredients, size of box, and percentage of daily nutritional allowance provided by a single serving. Then discuss which cereal is the most nutritious and economical.

This idea can be adapted to any age group to cover a wide range of word attack and comprehension skills.

*-Evelyn H. Blake*

## DESIGN A SIGN

"Second Graders Are Super!" "When in Doubt, We'll Find It Out!" Invite your class to design signs. They provide a good incentive for reading and are a great way to develop vocabulary. My second grade chose 50 messages to write and illustrate on construction paper. When finished, they taped a ruler to the back for a handle, marched down the halls, and visited many classrooms. By the time the parade was over, every second grader could read all the signs.

*-Suzy Weaver Kline*

## BOOKS NONREADERS CAN READ

Very young children need early experiences with books to prepare them for reading. Here are some examples of "books" you can make for your preschool and kindergarten children that they can actually "read" themselves.

**1.** *The Cereal Book.* Make this one by gluing front panels from cereal boxes to heavy paper or cardboard and putting them together in book fashion. This works well with cracker box panels and labels from cans, too!

**2.** *The Hand Book.* Each child and each adult contributes the outline of his hand (or foot), labeled with his name to this book.

**3.** *The Local Stores Book.* Get out your camera and make a tour of the neighborhood. Photograph a variety of stores the children are familiar with, making sure to get a clear shot of the name of the store, and compile these into a book. For a permanent collection, laminate your books!   *-Ginna Hoff*

## CARTOON TIME

You can give your reading program a boost by having your students make cartoon booklets. Cut out cartoons (preferably showing one character speaking) from newspapers and magazines. Cut the captions off and paste on plain paper. Have kids write their own captions and gather cartoons together to make booklets with decorated construction paper covers for other classes to enjoy. You might want to have children try drawing their own cartoons, after first discussing what makes a good cartoon.   *-Edna Knudsen*

## CRAZY READERS

When students are alienated from reading, any available material may seem threatening or too abstract. Try these "Crazy Readers" to entice your students back into the reading fold. The books must be short, made in any shape and out of any kind of firm paper, and bound with yarn. They should also be well illustrated, either with drawings or photos clipped from the media. You might want to try this Crazy Reader, entitled *What Can You Count On?*, for starters. On the inside pages, print the following statements: "You can count on your fingers," "You can count on a chalkboard," "You can count on a calculator," "You can count on the president!" "You can count on Tony Dorsett," and on the last page, "You can count on ME!" Illustrate each of these statements appropriately. Then tape a small pouch to the rear cover, title it "Words to Know," and insert little sheets of paper with one word on each— chalkboard, fingers, calculator, and so on. You can make a whole series of these books and your students will love them—and learn from them too! *-Marie Clauss*

## CLIMB THE BEANSTALK

Word recognition skills will reach new heights when your students play this game. First, you need a "beanstalk." This can be any available tall plant or shrub. Mine is a rubber plant tree which stands about 2 ½ feet tall. Each day I tape words to its broad leaves.

Children climb the beanstalk by reading the word on each leaf. (Sometimes I also ask them to define the word or use it in a sentence.) They keep climbing until they reach the top of the plant or miss a word.

When they reach the top, they pick up the "golden egg" which the "giant" has placed there for them. The egg is a slip of paper which serves as a ticket. Three tickets buy admission to the special activities center housing crossword puzzles, word search games, and other such activities. On special occasions, reaching the top of the beanstalk merits an immediate award such as a new pencil, a puzzle page, or a small box of raisins.              *-Helen Orth*

## VOCABULARY POSTERS

Here's a way of presenting new vocabulary words that really makes an impression. Assign one word to each student. Then have the child design a poster for it, including the word (printed in large letters), its phonetic spelling, its definition, and a sentence containing it. Also, ask the kids to make drawings or cut out magazine pictures that illustrate the word's meaning. Now, to increase your entire class's word power, hang the posters on your bulletin board for the children to study until they're ready to go on to another batch.

*-Jane L. Hillard*

## AUTO MECHANICS

Capitalize on student interest in cars with this neat vocabulary activity. Have your class list as many names of different automobiles as they can think of. Print this list on your chalkboard and don't erase it for a few days so kids can add more names as they think of them. Now instruct each child to choose one name from the list and look up its meaning in the dictionary and write a brief paragraph discussing why a car might be given that name. For instance, students will find that *corvette* is defined in the dictionary as a small sailing ship or vessel. If they've ever ridden in a Corvette, they'll easily see why the name applies! As a follow-up activity, have kids design cars of their own and give them appropriate names.   *-Jean Antony*

## DOT TO DOT

This self-checking vocabulary game will come in handy when your students have a few minutes to spare. Print vocabulary words on an index card, one per card. On a separate set of index cards, print the definitions for each word. Color-code the matching pairs by making small dots with

felt-tipped pens on the backs of the cards. Shuffle each set of cards separately, and have each student draw a card from the word set and attempt to match the printed word with its definition. Kids may check their answers by flipping the cards over to see if the dots are the same color. If a student makes a mistake, he or she should find the matching dot, then flip the card over to learn the correct definition.              *-Sandra F. Frey*

## CLASSROOM PASSWORD

This word-association game makes learning new vocabulary words fun. First, introduce the new words for the week and give a definition for each word. Then ask students to think of five one-word clues they could give a classmate to help him or her guess each of the words. I usually have one child give a clue and let the rest of the students raise their hands to give an answer. If a student guesses the word from the first clue, he or she receives 10 points. If two clues must be given, the guesser receives 8 points, and so forth. If the class cannot guess the word after five clues, I give them the word.

A very simple example of this game would be to use the word "corn." The clues might be "vegetable," "yellow," "cob," "kernel," and "butter." The first clue word should be a general term.

This game can also be played with teams of two players each. When playing with teams, one child in each team gets a chance to give clues while the other player tries to guess the word. When one team fails to guess the word, the other team gets a chance. Alternate between the two teams, again making five clues the limit, until someone guesses the new word.

*-Connie Kubilus*

## WORD OF THE WEEK

Here's a fun and effective way to increase students' vocabularies. Each week, choose a new word to be included in the spelling list, and designate it "word of the week." During the week, center various activities on that word. For example: Have kids look the word up in the dictionary, write a paragraph using it, see if they can find it in a newspaper, use it in a sentence and illustrate it, and so on. After several weeks, have each child select any word and write it on a slip of paper. Put the slips into a "word box" and choose from this box for future words of the week.

*-Mina Berger Lewis*

## WHAT'S MY WORD?

Here is a game I call Ad-lib that introduces new vocabulary words and usually gives everyone a good laugh. The teacher pronounces a new word, spells it, and writes in on the chalkboard. Next, a student is chosen to be the "expert" on that word. He or she comes to the front of the room and, standing with his or her back to the board, answers the class's questions about the new word. Some of the favorite questions are: Is it an animal? What color is it? Is it alive? While the "expert" is doing his or her best to answer the questions, the teacher writes on the board the word's definition and a sentence using the word. I usually allow two or three more questions at this point, and then ask the "expert" to turn around and read the meaning of the word he or she has been pretending to know so much about.

This game, which is especially effective in the content areas, is an enjoyable change from traditional methods of teaching new words. *-Marilyn Drennan*

## SPACE ALPHABET

One of my reading groups enjoyed reading and studying about space flights and moon landings but they found the vocabulary words difficult to learn and understand. That is when we launched our space alphabet book project. Each reader stapled construction paper together to form a booklet, one page for each letter of the alphabet. Then space vocabulary words were printed on the correct letter page. Each word was carefully illustrated. Example: 'L' is for launch, lift-off, lox, lunar; 'M' is for moon, moor, Martian. When the booklets were completed, the authors shared them with the rest of the class. The completed books helped the whole class visualize and better understand space vocabulary.

*-Mary Cobb*

## SUPER SENTENCES

Tired of teaching vocabulary by telling children to "write each word in a good sentence"? Try Super Sentences; they're guaranteed to challenge your students.

Choose two unrelated words and ask the children to use both in the same sentence. For instance, the words "rock" and "fly" can be combined in these ways: "The fly is on the rock." "Don't rock in that chair, or you'll kill the fly." "An airplane can fly, but a rock can't." You will be amazed how creatively even primary school children can combine two unrelated words in a sentence. Gradually work your way up to groups of three or four words for Super-duper Sentences.

*-Anne M. Pacheco*

## SAND CARDS

Do some students have difficulty with the same reading words all the time? If so, here's an idea that can help them learn those troublesome words once and for all. Work with small groups of two or three children and print each word you'd like to reinforce on a large-sized index card. Have the kids repeat the word, then let each of them trace over it with two fingers. Now go over the word with a thin line of glue. Have kids sprinkle sand over the wet glue and wait about 30 seconds. Shake off the excess sand. Your kids will be delighted to see the word appear in three-dimensional form, and you can be sure they'll remember it from then on.

*-Eileen Hodrinsky*

## GIVING WORDS HOSPITAL CARE

Sketch a hospital bed on the chalkboard. Each time a child misuses or mispronounces a word when he or she is reading it, he or she must put the word to bed in the Word Hospital until he

or she has cured it. After the head doctor (the teacher) has heard the word pronounced and used properly 3 or 4 times, the child may remove the word from the bed to make room for another patient. *-Shirley Shratter*

## WACKY WORD WALL

You can put that extra wall space in your classroom to work as an effective vocabulary-builder with this unique idea. Cover blank wall space with a large sheet of poster board or butcher paper and keep a supply of wide felt-tipped pens nearby. Each week, select a different topic or category such as occupations, forms of transporation, holidays, unusual animals, and so on, and label the wall accordingly. Children are to use dictionaries and thesauruses to come up with words pertaining to the labeled category and print them in large letters on the labeled wall. Encourage the kids to choose unusual and unfamiliar words and make sure they check spellings before printing anything. By the end of the week, you'll have quite a collection of new vocabulary words.

*-Pamela Klawitter*

## WHO'S WHO?

Here's a way to get students to learn some unusual but useful vocabulary words. Divide a duplicating master into nine large rectangular sections. At the bottom of each section, type titles or names given to people who have a certain occupation or hobby. Examples are: podiatrist, manicurist, philatelist, haberdasher, mortician, instructor, numismatist, legerdemainist, sleuth, and milliner. Give each student a copy of the sheet and a dictionary to find pronunciations and meanings for the words. Students should draw in the box an object that would be associated with a person of that particular name or title. Students then pronounce and discuss each of the words, explaining their drawings if necessary. Then display the papers to help students further remember who's who among these ordinary people with the fancy names.       *-Sandra Frey*

## A PICTURE'S WORTH

A new word appears on the chalkboard. The class is baffled — what does it mean? This, you explain, is the Word-of-the-Week. Tell your students that once a week they will be given a new word to look up in the dictionary, and write in their notebooks, along with the word's definition(s), correct pronunciation, and a sentence using it correctly. Then ask students to use their imaginations to produce an illustration of the meaning of the word. The meaning should be so clearly presented that it does not need any verbal explanation. Hang them on a bulletin board as a zippy reminder of the meaning of the word, all week long!

*-Frank C. Schilling*

## MIX AND MATCH

Find or duplicate two identical pictures of vocabulary words to be studied. Mount on construction-paper cards and cover with clear plastic food wrap for longevity in handling. Place cards facedown on table. Children draw two cards at a time. Each child states what he he or she has drawn. If he or she has a match, he or she keeps the cards. If not, they are returned to the table facedown. Person holding most pairs at end of the game wins.       *-Mitchell E. Wallick*

## FICTIONARY

Ever heard of a lycanthrope? Your students will have after playing this game. Begin each day's language arts program by writing an unusual-sounding word on the board. Have kids try and guess its meaning, then define it. For the next few weeks, assign a student to bring in a word each day. Once everyone has learned the definitions, they can use these new words to write stories or to stump parents.       *-Margaret Miles*

## WORD DETECTIVES

The pupils in my class had an interesting adventure in word detection. Armed with a tablet and pencil, they became detectives and wrote down all the words they could find in the halls on doors, signs, and bulletin boards. They did this one at a time when

their regular assignments were completed. The words were counted and then written on cards where they were used for various activities. Children alphabetized the words and classified them to indicate people, places, and signs. They illustrated some words, looked up meanings in the dictionary, counted syllables, and found short vowels. The class also made riddles. (What teacher's name is the name of a bird?) The unit was concluded by playing Concentration with the word cards and writing stories about the adventure. Each child got a certificate as a good word detective.      -Vivian P. Leidy

## IN-THE-FUTURE DICTIONARY

In this language arts activity, my students create their own new vocabulary words of the future. Each word must have a vowel or a vowel sound in each syllable. The children must write the word, divide it into syllables, and mark the vowels and the accent. Next, they must tell what part of speech the word is, define the word, and draw a picture to illustrate the word. We then alphabetize our new words and put them together to make our futuristic dictionary. Here's one example of a student's imaginative word: pexilen, pex-i-len, noun, A bug that has ten legs and three eyes. It has a red stripe down its back, like a racing stripe. The pexilen crawls on tomato plants and eats their leaves.      -Nancy Camarigg

## SLANG DICTIONARIES

Help your kids explore the different meanings of words with this activity that centers on slang. Start with a class discussion on the meaning of slang; then have kids list their favorite slang words. Now ask them to define each word and compile them all in a classroom slang dictionary. Make sure they list the words alphabetically and note parts of speech. When the kids' dictionary is complete, have them look up the words in a conventional dictionary. How do the definitions differ? Are any slang definitions listed? As a follow-up activity, have kids ask their parents for slang words that were popular when they were young. Your students will be surprised to find that many of these words *are* listed in the dictionary with their slang definitions. This can lead to a class discussion on how slang words often become acceptable over time.      -Donald P. Kauchak

## ABBREVIATION BINGO

Try an interdisciplinary approach to social studies and English with this game that's played like Bingo. Begin by giving each student a scrambled list of the 50 states to alphabetize. Have them look up the states in a dictionary to find their correct English abbreviations, and they're ready to play. Give each child a card with 25 squares and columns headed by the letters, U S N O A (United States Names or Abbreviations). Each square should contain a correct English abbreviation, and each card should have a different combination. Designate one student to be the caller and have him choose a state to name aloud for the class. The players are to cover the correct abbreviation for that state with a marker if it appears on their card. The first one to cover five abbreviations in a row must call out his winning states by their full names, not by the abbreviations he sees on his card. The game can be varied by printing state names on the cards and having the caller spell their abbreviations.      -Helen Robinson

## TO TELL THE DEFINITION

Here's a vocabulary word game based on the old television show, "To Tell the Truth." Start by choosing three student volunteers. Meet with these students outside the classroom to assign a vocabulary word. Then instruct two of the volunteers to make up incorrect definitions for this word. These false definitions should sound as reasonable as possible. Before going back into the classroom, make sure the third volunteer knows and can recite the correct definition. Back in the classroom, print the chosen vocabulary word in large letters on your chalkboard, then instruct the panel of three to recite their definitions. Now ask the rest of the class to vote on their choice for the correct definition. After the correct definition has been identified, choose another panel and start the game again.
      -John Marshall Carter

## WRITING SCRAPBOOK

Here's an idea for a year-long language arts project that makes use of the weekly periodicals you may subscribe to in your classroom. At the end of each week, take a classroom poll to determine which two articles your students enjoyed the most. Then have one child cut out the articles, date them, and paste them on sheets of light-colored construction paper, approximately 18″ × 24″. After a few weeks, you should have several scrapbook pages from which to plan lessons on particular writing skills.

For instance, you might ask your students to locate as many contractions as possible on designated pages. Then, have them write the contractions in the spaces beside each article along with their regular forms.

Or, you can use the weekly articles to help your kids learn to analyze writing skills. Paragraphing, topic and transitional sentences, capitalization, abbreviations, the solid opening that grabs the reader—all these things will be found in the articles your kids have collected. Point them out to your class and have them try similar constructions of their own. Also your scrapbook can be the start of a continuing art project if you require illustrations to accompany each article. Choose two different students every week to draw the illustrations.

Finally, the scrapbook pages can inspire creative writing projects if used as models for news reporting, interviews, short stories, and so on. You might want your children to start their own class newspaper, using the skills they've acquired from analyzing the collected articles. Invite the entire school to contribute news items.  *-David Appleby*

## BALANCED LANGUAGE DIET

Are your pupils getting a "balanced diet" of successful practice activities?

**Word family chip and dip** Cut oaktag in potato chip shapes and on each print a consonant, consonant digraph, or consonant blend. On several empty dip containers print such basic word patterns as *in, et, ake, ain.* Pupils place chips in appropriate containers and make a list of the words that can be formed. Some chips can go in several containers.

**Parts of speech fruit salad** Cut paper in fruit shapes. Include one for each part of speech, perhaps apples for nouns, bananas for verbs, oranges for adjectives, and so on. On each fruit write one appropriate word and put all in a plastic bowl. A pupil empties the bowl, arranges words into syntactically correct sentences, and copies the five most interesting ones created.

**Homonym steak** Cut shapes from oaktag and on each write a sentence containing a homonym but deleting that homonym and replacing it with a blank. Under the sentence list two or three homonyms as choices. Cover each steak card with clear plastic so pupils can write responses with grease pencil.

**Compound seafood** On fish cutouts, print words that can be combined in a variety of ways to create several compound words. Keep the fish in a fish bowl. Students empty the bowl and combine fish to make compound words, remembering that some fish may be used many times. They list each compound word they form and then write sentences containing their words.

**Creative vegetables** Each pupil draws a vegetable shape and gives it a personality by adding a face and choosing an appropriate name. On the back, he or she writes a paragraph about the newly created personality.

**Irregular verb pie** Cut wedge-shaped pieces to represent bottom crust, filling, and top crust of a piece of pie. On each wedge, write one of the forms of an irregular verb such as *go, went, gone;* or *lie, lay, lain.* Pupils sort the wedges and put the three together for each verb.

*-Lester L. Laminack and Patricia J. Anderson*

## LADDER LETTERS

To reinforce letter recognition, make a ladder with five rungs from construction paper and mount it on the bulletin board. Place a different letter on each rung. Then write each of the five letters on index cards and place them on the floor in a straight line. Each child tries to "climb" the ladder by naming each letter as he or she walks from one end of the letter cards to the other. When the child reaches the last one, write his or her name at the top of the bulletin board ladder. In February, you might write each of the five letters on hearts and staple them to ladder rungs. When children have learned the letters, their names can be placed on a large heart at the top, under the words "Learned by Heart." Try other seasonal symbols for other months.    *-Carol Jackson*

## SAVE THOSE LETTERS!

When you change bulletin board displays, don't discard all those colored paper letters that took so long to cut out and assemble. Instead, toss them all into a large box or envelope and save them for these "rainy day" activities:

**1.** For young children, use them for a letter-recognition fishing game. Attach a paper clip to each of the letters. Now find a short stick or pole and tie a string around it with a small magnet attached to the end. Now call out individual letters and have your students "go fish" for them.

**2.** Have children separate the vowels from the consonants.
**3.** Give each child a group of letters and see how many words he or she can make from it.
**4.** For phonics review, have the children voice the sound that each letter makes.
**5.** Use the letters to label items around the room.
**6.** Practice discrimination skills by having the children sort letters according to color, size, or style.

*-Marilyn Karns*

## FIND THAT LETTER

For some quick challenge practice with the alphabet, ask students to find out the letter which is missing from this sentence:
The quick brown fox jumped over the lazy dog. (s)
Can they make up some sentences of their own which use all (or almost all) of the letters? This provides some good handwriting practice, too.

*-Isobel Livingstone*

## ALPHABET SOUP SLURP

We all know that refined people never slurp their soup. But every once in a while it's fun to disobey the rules of etiquette. That's why this game is such a success. For the game you need an empty coffee can or other container. Cover it and label it "Soup Kettle." In the kettle place slips of paper on which you have printed different letters of the alphabet. Include several copies of each letter.
To play the game, a child is selected to be the chef and pass the soup kettle from classmate to classmate. As the kettle passes, each child takes a letter and tells what it is. If the child names the letter correctly, he or she keeps it. Letters not named correctly are returned to the kettle. At the end of the game, letter holders

pretend to eat their soup by giving a giant slurp.
Make the game more challenging by requiring children to name the letter they draw and then to give a word that begins with that letter.

*-Helen Orth*

## HANG AN ORNAMENT

As kids hang ornaments on this bulletin board tree, they'll be learning long and short vowel sounds at the same time! On a blue, white, or red background, place a black construction paper tree stump. Cut out a yellow Christmas tree and a smaller green tree the same shape, with five branches on each side of the trees. Place the large yellow tree on the board, and position the smaller green tree in the center so that a yellow margin shows around it. Use a light pencil mark to divide the tree in half vertically. On each branch write a long or short vowel with black felt pen—long vowels on one side of the

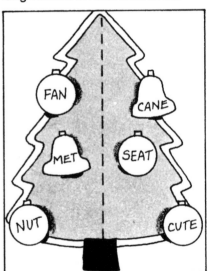

tree and short vowels on the other side. Make sure you place the short vowels on the branches opposite the corresponding long vowels.
Cut out ornaments in shapes like balls and bells, and print words with long and short vowels on each one. Then have kids hang the balls on the appropriate branches.    *-Marilyn Burch*

## MS. E'S BIRTHDAY PARTY

When your kids have learned their vowels, celebrate with a long vowel birthday party. Make huge paper people. Mr. A, Ms. E, Mr. I, Dr. O, and Ms. U are taped so that they appear to sit in chairs. Children cut out or draw five things using each long vowel. Finally, the paper people are placed in front of the room along with a box for each. Children give each person an appropriate present, naming the picture aloud as they slide it into the box.

-Amy Hicks

## GET THE MESSAGE

For practice in alphabetizing, pass out copies of this short puzzler. Print the words at the left in alphabetical order on the lines at the right. Now copy the circled letters in the blanks at the bottom to receive a secret message.

| | |
|---|---|
| violin | _ _ Ⓞ |
| fox | _ _ _ Ⓞ |
| wedge | _ _ Ⓞ |
| cub | _ Ⓞ _ |
| foxy | _ Ⓞ _ _ |
| dew | _ Ⓞ _ |
| cube | _ Ⓞ _ _ |
| under | Ⓞ _ _ _ |
| early | _ _ Ⓞ _ _ |
| fee | _ _ Ⓞ _ |
| erase | _ _ _ Ⓞ _ |

_ _ _ _ _ _ _ _ _ _ _ _
Correct answer: Beware of Dog.

-Isobel L. Livingstone

## VOWEL VOID

Here's a simple idea that's a great time filler. Tell your kids to imagine that vowels have been removed from the English language. Then choose a category, such as animals. Print the name of an animal on your chalkboard, making sure to omit the vowels. For example, "tiger" would be spelled "tgr." The kids are to guess the word, then spell it correctly out loud. The first child to guess may think up the next word. Remember to change categories frequently. -Jean Antony

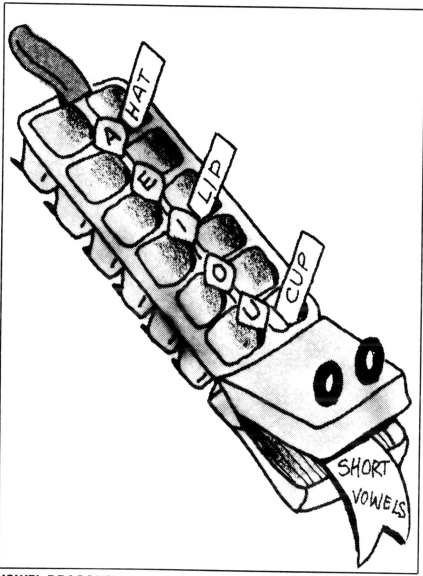

## VOWEL DRAGONS

Two little dragons can be your best allies in helping your students learn long and short vowel sounds. All you need are two egg cartons and construction paper.

Cut off the lid and front flap of one egg carton. Fold the lid in half and tape it to one end of the bottom of the carton to form the dragon's head. Staple the flap to the other end to form its tail. Make eyes from construction paper and attach them so they stick straight up from the top of the head. Cut out a rather long red forked tongue and glue it to the inside of the mouth. Now do the same thing with the other egg carton, but give this one a short tongue. Your two dragons are now complete.

Glue vowels down the center of the partition dividing the egg sections, leaving one spot blank. Write "long vowels" on the tongue of the dragon with the long tongue, and "short vowels" on the shorter dragon tongue. Then let children put words printed on construction paper in the section that's labeled with the correct vowel sound. You can also provide an answer sheet to make this activity self-checking.

-Jean Staffeld

## THE LONG AND SHORT OF IT

A is for Amy. A is for Adam. This activity for grades 1-2 helps children learn the short and long vowel sounds and their notations. Choose those children whose names have the vowel sound you want to teach on a particular day. Their classmates trace the outline of their bodies onto a sheet of brown wrapping paper.

Ask the children to cut out their form and write their names clearly on the front of the form, using a colored pen to mark the long and short vowel sounds. Meanwhile, the rest of the class is cutting out words and pictures of things that have the vowel sound of the day. Finally, have pupils paste their words and pictures onto the forms, which are then hung up around the room. Since every child has at least one vowel sound in his or her name, every child enjoys the spotlight at some time, and will have a life-sized work of art to take home!

-Ellen Sussman

## CATCHING VOWEL SOUNDS

When baseball season approaches, this bulletin board project is a great way to teach vowel sounds. Have kids cut out baseball mitts from brown or white construction paper. With crayons, color in the stitch marks and outlines of each finger. To make the baseballs, cut out circles from white paper, or use the reproducible on page 67. Write a vowel sound on each ball (long *a*, short *e*, and so on). Pass out baseballs to children and instruct each one to write on his or her baseball a word containing the particular vowel sound described on it. Then have kids draw pictures illustrating their words. Glue the baseballs to the mitts, and attach mitts to the bulletin board. Title your display "Catching Vowel Sounds."

-Eileen A. Etna

## CONSONANT CARDS

Most children need drill and practice to cement their understanding of consonant sounds and the formation of syllables. Using posterboard,

make five large cards, one for each vowel. Print the vowels on the right-hand side of the cards. Use scissors or a putty knife to make two slits on the left-hand sides of the cards so that strips of cardboard with consonants printed on them can be pulled through. As the consonant strips are pulled through the slits, students will view different syllables, which they should vocalize individually or in groups. With this handy little aid, you'll be able to test your class's grasp of consonant sounds and syllables quickly and easily.

-Marsha Gilbert-Willhite

## SHORT VOWEL BANNER

This banner, which should be hung low enough for children to touch, is economical and easy to make from cloth remnants that are readily available for low prices at most fabric stores. If you sew, or know someone else who sews, you can probably accumulate enough scraps for this project on your own. Here's how to make your own short vowel banner:
**1.** Start with a large piece of heavy cloth, approximately 15″ × 45″ in size. Burlap or lightweight canvas works well for this. Using a broad, felt-tipped pen, draw horizontal lines across the fabric, forming five 9″ sections.
**2.** Make patterns for the five vowels on paper first, then transfer each pattern to a 6″ × 9″ piece of felt. Each letter should be a different color and stand at least five inches tall. Cut around the patterns and glue one letter to each of the five sections in their proper order.
**3.** Now use the cloth remnants to make figures that correspond to each vowel. For instance, an apple for the letter "a."
**4.** After you've cut the five objects, glue wads of cotton to the back of each. Then put glue around their edges and paste them to the cloth background. The cotton will puff out of the centers and give the objects dimension.
**5.** When the five objects are securely attached, use colored yarn, fake fur, pipe cleaners, buttons, or any other materials to add detail to your figures. Use your imagination and encourage the children to offer suggestions, too.

-Jane E. Doyle

## PICK A POCKET

This activity will give your students valuable practice in learning initial consonants. Cut three or more paper plates in half. Staple each half to a large piece of cardboard so that it forms a pocket, and write a consonant on each one. Tape a large envelope to the back of the cardboard. Cut out pictures of objects from magazines, paste them on index cards, and place them inside the envelope. (The names of these objects should all begin with one of the consonants printed on the pockets.) Then let students take turns drawing a card from the envelope, telling what the picture is and which letter it starts with, and placing it in the correct pocket.

-Linda C. Abendroth

# Catch The Sound

Use this reproducible with the idea on page 66, or create your own word drill with these symbols.

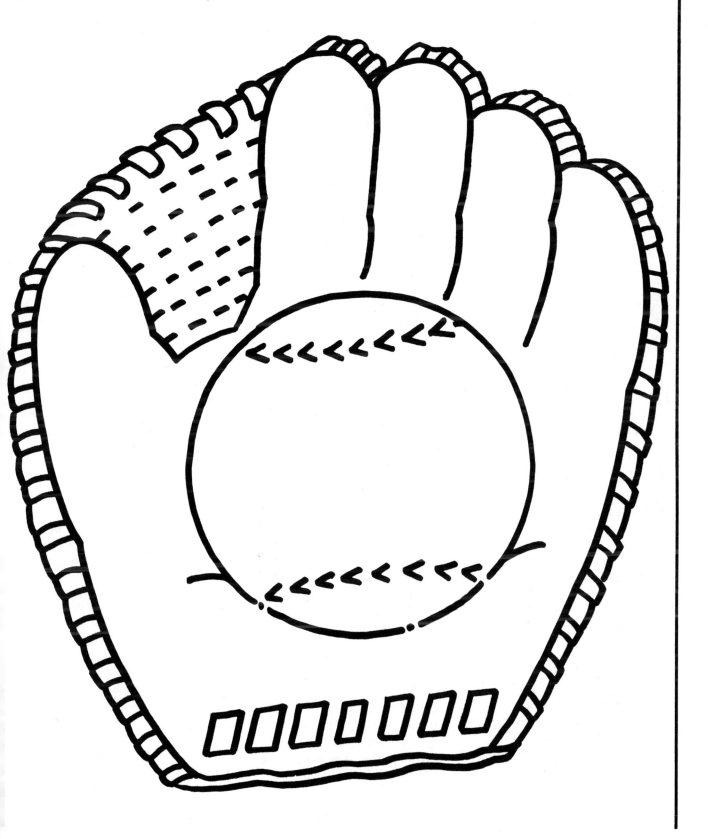

### THE SENTENCE GAME

Here's a simple game that can give students practice identifying complete sentences—no matter how brief they are! To set up the game, draw a series of 22 overlapping circles, approximately 1½" in diameter each. Inside each circle, print either a verb or a pronoun. You should alternate verbs and pronouns as much as possible, but occasionally have a verb following a verb, or a pronoun following a pronoun. When you've

labeled all the circles, mark the first one *start* and the last one *finish*. Instruct kids to use small buttons for markers and have them roll a die to determine which player will start the game. He or she is to then roll the die again and advance that number of circles. Students are to place their markers in the spots where the circles intersect. Then they must read the words printed on the two intersecting circles and tell whether they form a complete sentence. If a player does not answer correctly, he or she must skip the next turn. The first player to reach the finish circle wins!

*-Richard Latta*

### UNSCRAMBLING EGGS

This reading activity requires about a dozen plastic Easter eggs that are hollow and can be opened and closed back up, and tagboard of different colors. Begin by printing a sentence on one of the pieces of tagboard. Then cut up the sentence so each word is on a separate piece and place the cut-up sentence into one of the plastic eggs. Fill all of the eggs with sentences and then place the eggs in a basket. Each child in a reading group then takes an egg and "cracks" it open to get to the sentence pieces. Then the children must arrange the pieces to make a logical sentence.   *-Judy Meagher*

### WORDS FOR SALE

Hold a classroom market with an unusual commodity: words. This word fair will give your students fun practice in using words in imaginative sentences. Each child is assigned a different letter. He or she thinks of about 40 words that begin with that letter, writing each one on a separate file card. Then give each child $20 in play money and open the fair. The students buy words from one another: the buying and selling continue until the children have bought all the words they want or can afford. All words cost a dollar, and the sales are restricted to one word beginning with each letter per child. The buyer's aim is to use as many of his or her purchases in sentences as possible. The sentences must be grammatically correct, but can be wildly imaginative. The child who uses the most words wins that round. Then you can begin the fair again.   *-Hilary Davis*

### PUNCTUATION—DON'T LET IT DRIVE YOU CRAZY

Before we start an oral reading lesson, I tell my class to think of this reading lesson as driving school. As they read they will encounter certain signals that make reading "safe." A period is a red light. A comma is a flashing yellow light. Exclamation points are potholes. Question marks are signs for curves, and quotation marks represent roadside advertising signs.

As each student reads, I keep a list of violations of the driving-reading rules. I then issue tickets for running red lights (not pausing at a period) and tell students when they have been involved in an accident (hitting a pothole by not showing any change in expression for an exclamation point). Our classroom driving school helps children note punctuation in their reading, and it reinforces their knowledge of important traffic signals.

*-Michael Mihalov*

### PUNCTUATION BASEBALL

Baseball inside the classroom? It's Punctuation Baseball and no windows get broken. First pick the bases — pencil sharpener, reading table, radiator. Home plate is in front of the chalkboard. Now a student from one team gets "up." Will the batter move to first base? Pitch a sentence and see. If you throw "I live on High Street," the player had better choose a period to end the sentence. If he or she points to a question mark or an exclamation point (you'll have put all three sentence closers on the board), that student is out, and the next on the team gets a chance. Three outs and the other team's up. Every time a player crosses home plate, it's a run scored.

If you're a ham at all, you'll love pantomiming your "wind-up," and the kids will act out their batting stances, too.   *-Suzy Weaver Kline*

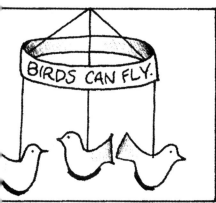

## MOBILE SENTENCES

Here's an interesting and decorative way to help your students write proper sentences and develop punctuation and capitalization skills. Use it as a class assignment or leisure-time activity. Give each child a 3″ by 18″ strip of paper with three or four pieces of yarn cut to desired lengths. Now have each child write one proper sentence on a theme of his or her choice (suggestions are birds, kites, bicycles, and so on) and print the sentence on the paper strip. Be sure to check each sentence for structure, capitalization, and punctuation first. Then have the kids staple their strips at the ends to form a circle. After forming the circle, they are to cut three or four figures representing their sentence subjects from colored construction paper and attach them to the circle with yarn. Hang the mobiles from your classroom ceiling and use them as examples of proper sentence construction.

-Anne S. Cernak

## FAMOUS QUOTATIONS

Many students have trouble deciding how and when to use quotation marks. It's a skill that takes a lot of practice; but unfortunately, that practice can be boring. To make it a little more meaningful for your students, try this idea. Give each student a 4″ square of oaktag, on which he or she can draw a television screen. Inside these screens, have kids paste pictures of their favorite television characters, clipped from the *TV Guide* or your local newspaper. Make sure each child leaves enough blank space below his or her screen to print a brief sentence. These sentences should be quotes from the television characters pictured on the screens. For instance, the sentence below a picture of Mork might read, ''Nanu, nanu,'' said Mork. This activity will make learning quotation marks fun for students, as it draws from their realm of experience.

-Lois Gasparro

## CAPITALIZE ON NAMES

When making up sentences for punctuation exercises, try using your students' names! You'll be surprised at how much their interest increases when they're the subjects. Write a list of honest, but not uncomplimentary, statements about each child in your class, such as ''David Brown hurt his hand in P.E.'' Be sure to leave out the punctuation, then give a copy of the list to every kid in your class. When students have handed in the corrected statements, let them make up their own unpunctuated statements. Have each child choose a partner and make up a sentence about him or her. Now instruct the pairs to exchange papers and insert the correct punctuation, then return papers to original writers to be checked.

-Rebecca Graves

## STUDENT STORYTELLING

Teach punctuation and help children of different ages get to know each other at the same time.
Send an older student to write down the dictated story of a younger one. While the younger child learns to tell a story and to read manuscript writing, the older student learns punctuation, capitalization, and spelling. Setting up an arrangement with a cooperating teacher is necessary, as is preparing the students for this experience.
For a preliminary lesson in punctuation, type 15 paragraphs from books or juvenile magazines, leaving out all punctuation. Read the paragraphs aloud as children follow along and punctuate. Later, point out places where a comma instead of a period should go. Provide sufficient opportunity for practice.
Prepare behavior guidelines on how to visit another classroom before sending your storytakers. Tell the children to introduce themselves to the younger ones and to encourage them to tell a story about a trip, a scary experience, or a make-believe character. The older child should let the younger one see him or her write down the story as dictated, skipping lines to leave room for later changes.
The first visit should take about 30 minutes. After the older student returns to regular class, he or she should check spelling and correctness before turning in the paper. After the paper is approved and before the second visit, the student should copy the story in careful handwriting into a booklet and illustrate it for the younger one. Teach how to write titles and bylines at this time.
The older student then takes the story back to the younger one's classroom. He or she reads the story to the child, then listens as the younger one reads it back. Post booklets on the bulletin board.

-James Charnock

### WORDPLAY

This game reinforces word-recall, spelling, and syllabication skills. Choose a group of children to go to the chalkboard. Dictate a word and spell it so that each child writes it correctly on the board. Set an egg timer for three minutes. When you give the signal "Go!" each child is to write a word beginning with the last letter of the word you dictated. He or she then writes a word beginning with the last letter of *that* word, and continues listing words in this way until the three minutes are up. Scoring one point for every word, the student with the highest score wins. For older students, you might want to score one point per syllable, to encourage longer words.    -Sister Leontine Mulvenna

### EGG WORDS

These rotating eggs will be a great help to you in teaching kids how to divide and pronounce words ending in *le*. Collect several of the white plastic eggs that stockings come in. On one half of each egg, write an ending

such as *-ple* with a colored felt-tipped pen. On the other half, write word beginnings such as *peo-, sta-, pur-,* or *stee-.* Then have children take turns rotating the egg, pronouncing each word that is formed, and discussing its meaning. Try *-tle* and *-dle* words, too.    -Sally C. Laub

### PARTS OF SPEECH SCAVENGER HUNT

Students can learn the parts of speech, and at the same time, take a walk on a nice spring day by going on this scavenger hunt. Divide the class into three groups. Each group should be accompanied by an aide, a volunteer parent, or you. Arm each team with pencils, pads of paper, dictionaries, a thesaurus, and a list of items to search for on the walk.

The list should contain items such as these: list seven nouns you see on Virginia Street; name five proper nouns on Fell Avenue; list six adjectives to describe the church on Franklin Street; list five adverbs to describe the activity around Brokaw Hospital. Instruct each group to start in a different direction and walk for about three or four blocks. The object of the hunt is not to be the first to get back as in an ordinary scavenger hunt; it is to come up with words no other group can think of that day. Award one point for each word that is the correct part of speech and is unique to one group's list.    -Jane Legner

### STOP THAT VERB!

Looking for a quick and easy activity that will help you reinforce verb recognition in your students? Try writing STOP in white chalk on pieces of octagon-shaped red construction paper, one for every student in your class. Spray the signs with hair spray to prevent smudging; or laminate, if possible, and attach them to Popsicle sticks. Give each child his or her own STOP sign and have the class arrange chairs in a circle around you. Choose one of the kids' favorite stories and read it aloud, instructing the children to raise their STOP signs whenever

a verb is read. Your students will practice recognizing verbs, and have an opportunity to hear their favorite stories, too!    -Debbi Paup

### TRAFFIC JAM

Want to give your kids some practice in word endings? This activity will put them on the road to proper usage! Start with a manila file folder, then use a black, felt-tipped pen to draw a three-lane "highway," as in the accompanying illustration. In each lane, print a different word ending, such as **ed, ing,** or **es.** Now make a tagboard pocket and label it **car storage.** Staple it on the front of the file folder; then cut several small construction paper cars. On each car, print a different

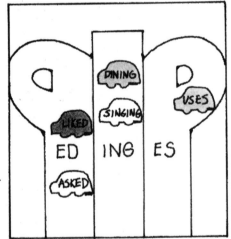

word, using one of the three endings. Place all the cars inside the pocket. Also, on the front of the folder, print the following directions: **Help clear up this traffic jam! Place all the cars in their proper lanes on the highway. Use the word endings printed on each lane to help you. When all the cars are on the road, copy the words and tell which lane each one belongs in.**
   -Gertrude Parker

### SENTENCE SANDWICH

My class enjoyed and quickly grasped the concept of sentence structure with my sentence sandwich "a la teacher."
I took one slice of bread and a slice of beef to demonstrate the

making of the simplest kind of sandwich. I labeled the bread "noun, subject" and the beef "verb, predicate."

Next, I dipped a knife into a jar of mayonnaise labeled "adjective," remarking, as I spread it on the bread, "Just as we add mayonnaise to bread, we add adjectives to a noun."

Then I reached for the salt, labeled "adverb" and continued, "We can add salt to the beef, and we can add adverbs to the verb." As I took a second slice of bread, I said, "A sandwich is a bit more interesting with more bread following the beef. A sentence may also have another noun. This noun is called a "direct object." I laid the bread on the beef slice before I reached for the lettuce, remarking, "Sometimes lettuce goes between the beef and the bread. Sometimes, too, an indirect object goes before the direct object."

After the demonstration, we made a "sandwich" bulletin board and wrote sentences in the demonstrated patterns.

-Wilma Goodman

## QUESTION CARD GAME

Here's a fun game to help your students differentiate between the meanings of the words who, where, why, how, and when. On plain white index cards, print the five words, ten times each. Then, make squares along the perimeter of a plain white piece of poster board. In scrambled order around the board, print words in each square that could answer the questions who? where? why? how? and when? Mix up the index cards and place them facedown in the center of the board. The players take turns drawing a single question card from the pile and moving to the nearest answer on the board. The student who makes it around the board first is the winner.          -Arlene McDowell

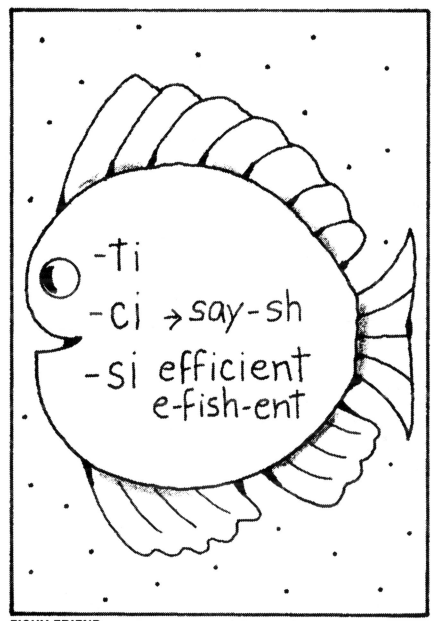

## FISHY FRIEND

A "fish friend" chart helps children improve word attack skills when it is used with a phonetic reading program, or even more when children do not receive formal instruction in phonics.

Although this chart might seem to appeal to only younger students, I have used it for years with sixth graders. It illustrates a simple phonetic rule: -ti, -ci, and -si, when followed by a vowel, say sh. You can copy this chart easily in a few minutes and then place it in a prominent place in the room.

When children read aloud and come across an unfamiliar word containing any of the above digraphs, they will be able to glance at their fish friend and continue to read pro-fish-iently.

-Dorothy Westwood

## PARTS OF SPEECH SCRAMBLE

Here's an action game that will give kids exercise while they review parts of speech. Play it in the gym or where you have plenty of room. First make two identical copies of a list of the parts of speech. Cut into individual pieces of paper. Divide the class into two teams. Give one group of slips to Team A and the other to Team B Have teams face each other and place a ball or other object at an equidistant point between them. Call out a word such as "pretty." Players who have the slip marked *adjective* run to grab the ball and carry it back to their team's position. The successful player earns a point for his or her team. If the player is tagged or if he or she has the wrong part of speech, the opposing team gets the point. If a word called is more than one part of speech ("fish", for example), both *noun* and *verb* run to grab the ball. To add to the excitement, call two or even three words. Or call "grammar," and everybody scrambles. When time has elapsed, the team with the most points wins.      *-Aviva Frenkel*

### ARE YOU ABLE?
Each of the following sentences is a definition for a word which contains the shorter word *able*. Are you capable of finding the answers?

1. Part of a house.
2. Piece of furniture
3. Heavy wire
4. Story with a moral
5. Farm building
6. Valuable fur
7. Pleasant

Answers: **1.** Gable, **2.** Table, **3.** Cable, **4.** Fable, **5.** Stable, **6.** Sable, **7.** Likable
*-O.J. Robertson*

### BIRD PLACES
This activity will help your students master prepositions. Draw a picture of a tree on poster board or tagboard. On index cards, paste or draw pictures of birds, and write one prepositional phrase *(above the tree, in the tree,* and so on) on each bird. Give each child a card and let him or her place it on the tree as it directs.      *-Marina C. Krause*

### SENTENCE RUMMY
This activity, based on the popular card game *Gin Rummy,* is a good way to help your kids learn noun and verb agreement and to practice writing sentences containing complete subjects and predicates. Start by having each child write five descriptive sentences using as many single adverbs, adjectives, and prepositional phrases as possible. Then the kids are to divide their sentences into complete subjects and complete predicates and write the two sentence parts on separate pieces of poster board that have been cut to playing card size. Now divide the class into small groups and let them play the game. One child in each group should be the dealer. This student shuffles the subject and predicate cards together and gives six cards to each player. Remaining cards should be placed facedown in the center of the group. Players first try to match the cards in their hands to make complete sentences, with nouns and verbs in agreement. If a player cannot match any of these cards, he or she may draw another card from the pile. Any time a new card is drawn, another must be discarded from the player's hand and placed faceup beside the other pile. The next player may choose from the previous player's discard or from the original pile. The first player to make three complete sentences from his or her hand is the winner and must shout "Sentence Rummy!"
*-Marshall Levy*

### EERIE ADJECTIVES
When the Halloween spirit begins to haunt your classroom, use it to reinforce your students'

understanding of the comparative and superlative forms of adjectives. Begin with a brainstorming session in which your kids list all the adjectives they can think of that are related to Halloween. When the list is complete, let the children take turns going to the board and writing the comparative and superlative forms of each adjective. As a culminating activity, have each child choose one adjective trio to use as inspiration for a Halloween drawing. Instruct the kids to divide their drawing paper into three sections — one for each form of the chosen adjective. For instance, to illustrate forms of the word "frightening" a child might draw a picture of a haunted house in the first section, then the same house with a black cat on the front lawn, and finally the haunted house, a black cat, and a ghost peeking out of the chimney!
*-Margaret Levine*

### SOME LIKE IT HOT
Here is a challenge for your students in creating compound words and idioms. They must complete the words or phrases that begin or end with the word "hot" by filling in the blanks with words that fit the definition given. The words in parentheses are the answers your students must come up with.
1. Hot (bed) A place to sleep
2. Hot (head) The top of your body
3. Hot (dog) Domesticated relative of wolf
4. Hot (shot) Fired a weapon
5. Hot (house) Where people live
6. Hot (plate) Dish
7. (Red) hot The color of blood
8. (Piping) hot The sound of bagpipes
9. (White) hot The opposite of black      *-Dave Bloom*

## PICK A POCKET

Make this self-help file folder to teach children antonyms, homonyms, and synonyms. First, cut out six pocket-shaped pieces of construction paper. Draw on scallops and topstitching. Label two with the word "Antonyms," two "Homonyms" and two "Synonyms."

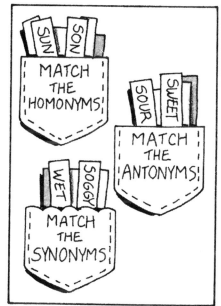

Using different colors of paper, write antonyms, homonyms, and synonyms on separate strips of paper and insert in appropriate inside pockets. Prepare an answer key that shows how words are matched and place it in an envelope or long handmade pocket. Paste this in the inside front cover.

Children now can match words by clipping them together and transferring them to the front-cover pockets. After they're finished, they can check their answers against the answer key.

*-Gertrude Parker*

## FIND THE DUCKLINGS

Children will enjoy putting words together to make compounds when they use this manipulative bulletin board. Start with a plain orange background, then use black letters to label the board "Find the mother's ducklings." Cut out four large ducks and eight ducklings from yellow construction paper; then add eyes and beaks with a black, felt-tipped pen. Now print the first half of a compound word on each of the large ducks (*book,* for example). Think of two other words (such as *mark* and *case*) that might complete the compound, and print them on two ducklings, one word on each. Attach two pieces of colored yarn to each large duck, and stick a thumbtack on the end of each piece. Now have kids make compound words by joining the mother ducks with their ducklings. Great way to reinforce compounding skills! *-Marilyn Burch*

## COMPOUND MATCH-UP

Make a list of compound words. Choose half as many words as there are students in your class. Next cut 2-inch by 6-inch strips of paper out of two colors of construction paper. Print the first part of the word on one color and the second part of the word on another color.

Before school begins or before children come in from recess,

place one strip on each child's desk. The object of the activity is for students to walk around the room trying to find the person who has the other part of their compound word. When two people are successfully paired, their goal is to write 10 more compound words that could be used in a future game. Pairs can take turns setting up future games. Kids can set up games for other classes. *-John D. Roberts*

## SHADES OF MEANING

To help students become aware of the subtle differences in meaning among synonyms, I make a bulletin board labeled "Shades of meaning." To make this bulletin board, cover the board with three vertical strips of paper in three different shades of the same color. Ask students to illustrate three synonyms on three separate sheets of paper. Examples are: little, tiny, microscopic; hat, cap, bonnet. Post the groups of synonyms across the board, one word and picture to each shade of colored paper. *-Isobel Livingstone*

## Match The Ducks

Use this reproducible with the idea on page 73, or create your own word drill with these symbols.

## IF YOU CAN BEAR IT

This cuddly bear is a good display for teaching idioms. Draw this simple outline of a bear on a large sheet of construction paper for a bulletin board display or on a duplicating master for a handout. On and around the figure write phrases with the word "bear" in them: bear in mind, bear out, bear down, bear up, bear market, bear hug, and so on. Leave enough space under each one of the phrases or idioms for you or the children to write in the definition on the lines you've drawn.

*-Deanna Andreano*

## WHAT'S A PALINDROME?

Read it from right to left, and it will be the same as when you read it from left to right. That's a palindrome. "Huh?" you might ask. You catch on quickly. You just made a palindrome. Other single-word palindromes are *pep, eye, pop, wow.* Introduce this phenomenon to your students and challenge them to find palindromes on their own. Writing phrases and sentences that work as palindromes is much more difficult, but it can be done. "Was it a bar or a bat I saw?" "No, it is open on one position." "Too hot to hoot." A popular dictionary prints this example: "Able was I ere I saw Elba." A few commercial names are palindromes. There is a city in California called Yreka. A merchant there calls his shop Yreka Bakery.

You can do the same with numbers. These are easier and a good place to start with your students. Example: 25952.

*-Alan Farrant*

## DRAMATIZE AND DISCUSS

The English language is filled with idioms. Hold a class discussion in which you explain the concept of an idiom; then ask kids to list as many as they can think of. Would students in foreign countries have difficulty deciding what these idioms really mean? After you've discussed this for a few minutes, ask kids to pantomime their interpretations of some of the idioms they've listed. Some particularly good ones to try are *tickled to death, bury the hatchet, keep on your toes,* and *spill the beans.* Classmates must guess which idioms are being pantomimed. This exercise will yield hilarious results!

*-Dave Bloom*

Bear up

Bear in mind

Bear hug

### PERSONALIZED SPELLING LISTS

If you need an alternative to traditional once-a-week spelling lists, try this! Ask children to make a list of difficult words or words that they always have trouble with. Choose one of the lists, print or type the words, and photocopy that child's class picture on the top. Give everyone in class a copy of the list. Children look forward to spelling each week to see whose list has been chosen.                    -Cynthia Bellezzo

### ABC ORDER

When my students have trouble spelling a word, they go to their spelling file boxes before they go to the dictionary. They make their spelling files from shoeboxes or recipe files and note cards. When the children are writing stories and want to use a word that they cannot spell but is not yet in their files, they look the word up in the dictionary or ask me how to spell it. They then write the word on one of the note cards and file it alphabetically. Writing the word on the card and filing it in the correct place is often enough to teach the child the correct spelling. And if the student is still unsure of the spelling, he or she can look it up in the file next time.
                    -Betty Slipetz

### WORD SCRAMBLE

Greet your students each day with scrambled words. Have lists of scrambled words on their desks when they come in. Use spelling words at first, then move on to vocabulary words for English, science, and social studies. As students become more accustomed to this activity, they will not only be able to unscramble more words at one time, but also they'll handle increasingly difficult ones. It won't be long before your students come up with their own suggestions for the next day's scramble.                    -Jacqueline Armin

### TYPE TO SPELL

I have found that a great way to reinforce spelling words each week is to have a typewriter available in the room. Each child takes a turn spelling out each word on the machine whenever he or she gets a chance. This manual activity is exactly what some children need to help them remember the position of letters within words. If your high school has a typing course available to the students, as most do, you might ask your superintendent if you could have one of the old typewriters. You may also be able to pick up one cheaply at a garage sale.     -Thomas Bernagozzi

### SPELLING DICTIONARIES

Children who do not have large spelling vocabularies and are not proficient with a dictionary will really benefit from making and using their own spelling dictionaries. In class, children put together a 26-blank-page booklet, using regular paper and construction paper for the cover. Then they print the alphabet, a letter to a page. (If time allows, the letters may be cut from magazine ads.) When they think of a word they do not know how to spell, they ask their teacher for the correct spelling and copy it in their spelling dictionaries. They keep the dictionaries in their desks and refer to them as they need to throughout the year. Some children take them home to use during vacation. This encourages correct spelling and acquaints children with beginning skills associated with using a regular dictionary.     -Rachell King

### SPELLING SPEEDSTERS

Looking for a gimmick to encourage good spelling? Try speed racing. In this activity, students get cardboard sports cars to move along their own roads on this horizontal bulletin board. When the drivers learn all 20 spelling words on a list, they move their cars to the first flag. The caption reads "No speed limit for good spellers." A toy car is the reward when a student passes all spelling units. Choose different word lists: directional words, emergency words, sports words, equipment words. Give a pretest first, then give each child a take-home sheet of words missed.     -Susan Shiffrin

### SPELL-N-ROLL

This activity will give your class's spelling review a boost of excitement. Divide the class into two teams. These teams take their place in single-file lines at the front of the room. Each line has a die and a desk on which to roll it. You are in between the lines with the week's spelling words and a stopwatch (the classroom clock will do if you don't have one). Teams are given one minute each to spell as many words correctly as they can. Give first player on one team a word. If player spells the word correctly, he or she rolls the die and that number is recorded by a student at the chalkboard. The next speller steps up to the desk and is given another word to spell; if spelled correctly, he or she rolls the die again and the point total is recorded on the board. If the word is misspelled, give the same word to the next student in line, and so on until someone spells the word correctly. Do this until one minute is up, then give the other team a turn. After each team has had 3 one-minute rounds, the points are added up to determine the winning team.
                    - Stephen J. Pesek

## THE SPELLING LADDER

For this game, print each child's name on a 10″ × 4″ card and randomly place cards on a 24″ × 36″ vertical, slotted chart at the front of the room. The student whose name appears at the top of the ''ladder'' is the champion. Begin with the child whose name is at the bottom: he or she has the option of challenging either the champion or any student whose name falls in a slot above his or hers. If the champion is challenged, have these two students stand side by side as you give the first spelling word to the challenger. After he or she has spelled it aloud, without indicating whether it was spelled correctly the first time, have the champion spell the same word. If both students are correct, give them another word. If the challenger misses the word, he or she must sit down and may not challenge the champion again that day, but may challenge other students with higher positions to work his or her way up the ladder. If the challenger spells the word correctly, move his or her card to the top of the ladder and move the champion's card down one slot, as well as all the other cards. Begin the game again with the next student whose name appears at the bottom of the ladder.     -Carol A. Gibb

## THIS GAME SPELLS CHALLENGE

Here's a spelling game that everyone will enjoy. See if you can figure out how the game is played from this example:

My neighbor, Miss Sally Matter, likes her name and some other things, but there are many things she dislikes. Why does she like one thing and dislike another?

—Miss Sally likes guppies, but doesn't like fish.

—She likes aardvarks, but is frightened of snakes.

—Miss Sally likes pebbles, but won't touch a rock.

—She loves pretty dresses, but don't call them a frock.

You've probably seen that Miss Sally is fond of words with double letters in them. The last two examples show how you can make this a rhyming game as well. The variations of this game are endless. You might change the name to Pollyanna and feature words with two or more double letters (likes a **teepee,** not a **tent,** or likes **Tennessee,** not **Virginia**). How about Jean Early who favors a specific combination of vowels (**dream,** not **sleep,** or **break,** not **cheek**).

This game makes a fun assignment if you write a different letter or letter combination on slips of paper and let each child draw a slip to make certain combinations. The game will challenge students in writing, spelling, and creating rhyme.

-Jane Priewe

## BASEBALL SPELLING

To play this game, divide the class into two teams, and have each team choose a catcher and three batters. Position the players not up to bat at appropriate places around the room.

You ''pitch'' a word to the first person up to bat. If the batter spells the word correctly, he or she advances to first base. If he or she misspells it, the catcher must spell it correctly before it is considered a strike (three strikes are an out). The batter may go to first base when: he or she spells the word correctly, the catcher misspells the word, too, or the catcher doesn't notice the batter misspelled the word.

When the next batter is up and has correctly spelled a word, the runner on first base must spell another word correctly to go to second. After the first runner either advances to second or is out, the batter who spelled the word right goes to first.

After the batter has spelled a word correctly, give the next word to the most advanced runner. For example, if bases are loaded, give the runner on third base a word, and he or she either goes home for a run or is out. Then the second base runner gets a word, and so on. After three outs the other team is up to bat. Play for as many innings as you like—the team with the most runs at the end wins.     -Nancy Brandmeyer

## ROW RACES

Unlike spelling bees, which give the good spellers plenty of practice while the poorer ones doodle at their desks, this activity involves the entire class for the duration of the game. Start by having your students position their desks in rows; then assign each row a number and a section of your chalkboard. The kids should also have sheets of scrap paper at their desks. Now dictate a word from your weekly spelling list and have the first student in each row print the word on the section of chalkboard assigned to his or her row. The students at their desks should print the same word on scrap paper so they get a chance to practice it too. Now check the words printed on the board. The students who've spelled the words correctly may put one stroke mark in their section of the chalkboard. Have them erase the words they've printed; then repeat the process with a different word and the next student in each row. After you've dictated all the words, add up the points, and applaud the winning row of the week. You might want to record the weekly winners and give an award to the row with the most points at the end of the semester.     -Sister Mary Glavich

### SPELL TO WIN

Buy or make an assortment of cardboard letters in upper and lowercase. Each set should be a different color. (I use red, blue, green, and orange.)
Divide your class into four groups and give one set of letters to each.

Designate four children to serve as judges for each group. Give each judge a flag that matches his or her team's letters.
Now, choose a spelling word. From their set of letters, team members select those that spell the word. Then members must stand in the correct order, holding the letters. The first group that spells the word correctly gets one point.
Judges must watch their groups carefully and as soon as a word is correct, the judge raises his or her flag to alert the teacher.

*-Joan Lincoln*

### SPELLING SCRAMBLE

Use index cards to create a spelling game at which even the weakest spellers in your class can feel successful. First, print each consonant of the alphabet two times, and each vowel three times (one letter per card). This set of 57 cards is good for one team. Make as many sets as appropriate for your class.
To play: Each team sits on the floor in a circle. Team members spread their cards faceup, so everyone can see. Call out a word and watch carefully. Which team finishes spelling the word first? Which finishes second? Have teams raise their hands as they complete a word, and assign them a number that corresponds to the order in which they finish. When everyone has attempted to spell the word, check each team's choice of letters. Has the fastest team spelled correctly? They get a point. If not, the second-place team has a chance to get the point, and so on. Once everyone has figured out how to spell the latest word, students should rescramble the cards and be ready for action! *-Tina M. Riesett*

### SPELL A SNOWMAN

Get your kids excited about spelling with this flannelboard contest. Divide your class into two teams and take turns asking a member from each team to spell a word. Each time a student spells a word correctly, place a part of a snowman's body on the flannelboard for that particular team. The team that completes its snowman first wins. To make snowmen, use cloth circles for the bodies and small pieces of felt for features, buttons, scarves, hats, and earmuffs. If you have lots of spellers, you can add tiny circles for flakes of snow in the sky. Use this idea all year round—just change the figures according to the seasons.

*-Sister Sharon Stone*

### SPELLING BASEBALL

Spelling bees have always been popular in the classroom, but it's unfortunate that poor spellers usually end up sitting out most of the game. Here's a simple way to remedy this problem, and it's perfect for the baseball season, too. Make a list of spelling words you feel your students should have learned during the year and divide them into four groups: first base, second base, third base, and home plate. Arrange the words in columns according to spelling difficulty, with the simplest words under the first base heading and the most difficult under home plate. Duplicate the list, give a copy to every child in your class, and have them all review the words for a day or two. When you're ready to play the game, divide the class into two teams. Then, use poster board to label the corners of your room first, second, third base, and home plate. Make a tagboard "spinner" labeled with the four positions, and have the teams take turns "stepping up to bat" by spinning for a base. If

they correctly spell a word from the corresponding list, they may advance to that position. If a student spells a word incorrectly, it counts as an "out" for his or her team. Better spellers will naturally get more hits, but everyone can stay in the game for all nine innings!

*-Patricia Landreman*

Penmanship
License
This certifies that

_____ has

permission to use a
pen for certain
assignments.

_____
Teacher

## LICENSE TO LEARN

All students seem eager to begin writing with a pen. Put this interest to good use by opening a penmanship license bureau in your classroom. It will help convince young students of the need for neat, legible handwriting. Have a few students serve as clerks at the License Bureau. Clerks can serve on a rotating basis and are responsible for inscribing the licenses with students' names and the date. Each student files an application ("forms" supplied by the teacher) for the license, carefully printing such information as name, address, teacher, and school. Students then demonstrate their readiness for a penmanship license by copying, in cursive, a sample paragraph. Licenses are issued according to neatness and legibility of applications, as well as effort made. And, of course, second attempts are permitted! A "certain specified assignment"

that is fun for children to pen is to have each student decide what he or she is famous for and write a special award. Students will also get a kick out of penning their own reward stickers on blank labels. These can be put in a "sticker pool" to be used on papers that deserve special honor. 

*-Peggy Heller*

## AIRY ANSWERS

Have children write the following short rhyming riddle as a handwriting exercise and illustrate it as an art activity. Can the class think of other good subjects for riddles? Have them write some.

> A bird with no song,
> You go flying along.
> A bird with no wings,
> You make use of my strings.
> A bird with no feather,
> Will you fly forever?

Answer: A kite 　　*-Mary R. Palmer*

## MAKE A MAGIC WRITING SLATE

Put good handwriting skills at your students' fingertips with this reusable device made from a zip-lock freezer-strength plastic bag. Just put finger paint inside the bag, seal it, and reinforce all four edges with masking tape. Kids then use their fingers to "write" on the clean plastic surface, erasing mistakes with a quick flick of the wrist. 　*-Susan Axelrod*

## WRITING GRAPHICALLY

Graph paper is ideal for handwriting practice! For beginning printers, one-inch squares provide a perfect letter boundary. Either half-inch or quarter-inch graph paper is useful for cursive practice. Writing one letter in each box eliminates excessive or uneven slanting and crowding. 　*-Mary A. Lombardo*

## CURSIVE QUOTES

An enjoyable handwriting exercise for my fourth graders began by my cutting sheets of loose-leaf paper into four or five pieces and writing a short quotation (about twelve words long) on each slip. For the exercise, each child took a quotation and copied it, along with the author's name, on his or her own paper. The children wrote the saying over again until time to exchange with the child at the next desk.

We did this exercise several times, and the quotes were available for use during "free time." They were especially helpful and of interest to students with handwriting problems. Several asked to borrow the quotes to copy at home. The entire class looked forward to this change-of-pace handwriting period, and while they were improving their cursive writing, they were being introduced to some worthwhile thoughts of famous people

*-Theresa Grass*

# Listening/Basics

## LISTENING SKILLS

Here are some practical exercises for developing students' ability to concentrate on what they should be listening to and to block out extraneous noise.

First reduce the noise level in the classroom—turn off fans and humming lights, close doors. Then all the students put their heads down, close their eyes, and listen for half a minute to the many sounds still around us. Talk about the background noise that is always there and how it can affect paying attention to a friend, teacher, or parent—anyone who is talking to us and expecting us to listen. After that discussion begin some of the specific listening activities.

—Pair your children up for team listening. One child talks for 25 seconds. The listener must then repeat what he or she has heard. Reverse roles.

—Give oral directions for both written and physical activities. Children become "secret agents" and must listen carefully because instructions will be destroyed immediately.

—Have children keep a log of sounds heard on the way to school, night sounds, city sounds, sounds from a boat, and so on.

—Listen to classical music with your students and help them recognize recurring themes.

—Ask older children to practice critical listening skills by evaluating a speaker on radio, television, or tape.

—Read aloud a poem or story and ask students to recreate plot, character, or setting or to recognize the author's point of view through careful listening. Older students can listen for figures of speech such as alliteration, hyperbole, metaphor, and personification.

Listening is a skill that can be learned and honed.    -Ellen S. Alvin

## TELL AND DON'T SHOW

Here's a variation on the usual game of Show and Tell that will help you develop listening skills, retention of information, and deductive reasoning in your students. On Show and Tell day, have each child deposit his or her object in a large bag or cardboard box. Then choose one student at a time to stand before the class and describe his or her object without showing it! When the child is finished speaking, put *all* the objects on a table in the front of your classroom and have the kids guess which object has just been described. Or, to make the game even more challenging, allow the class to ask questions about the object after it's been described. In this case, the object won't be seen at all until one of the children guesses what it is. The first one to guess correctly is next to describe his or her object. Another possibility is to assign categories for show-and-tell objects. For instance, one week have the kids bring in articles that are red, or things that begin with a certain letter of the alphabet. (Often, you'll find that the child's family gets involved in searching for an appropriate object at home.) Following are some category ideas to get you started.
• Things that fit in your pocket
• Things that are found in your bedroom
• Things that come from foreign countries    -Josephine Lazzaro

## YOU HAVE 60 SECONDS!

"My kids could talk all day if I just let them!" Teachers have been saying this for years. Here is a game that gives children the opportunity not just to talk but to develop their listening skills. Some simple preparations will help the game run smoothly. Before class begins, write 40 speaking topics on separate cards, such as favorite pets, pizza, birthdays, and holidays. Put all of these in a hat. Arrange chairs in a circle, one for each student, one for you, and an extra chair for "The Speaker's Chair." Make sure you have a watch or clock with a second hand.

Join the children in a circle, have them number off, and at the same time have them write down their number on a card. Collect all the cards, put them in a container, pick one, and call it out. The child who has that number moves to the empty "Speaker's Chair" and draws a topic from the hat. The object of the game is to try to speak about the topic for 60 seconds. For shy children, you may want to give an option to pass on their first few tries.

This is not an easy game! Encourage children with helpful hints and suggestions. If someone is stuck, let the class help, too.    -Daniel Levine

## SECRET DIRECTIONS

Want to improve student listening skills? Try playing "secret directions." What's a secret direction? Just one of the many instructions you normally give your students during the course of a typical day—only you decide in advance which direction will be the secret one each day. For instance, one day the secret direction might be, "Put your pencils down." When you decide to give the secret direction for the day, simply issue it in a normal tone of voice, and do not repeat it. Observe which students heard the direction and followed it correctly, then print their names on a sheet of paper. An hour or so later, tell your class what the secret direction was and who followed it. You might want to reward the best listeners at the end of a week. Kids will pay more attention to all your instructions when they know that one of them may be the secret direction of the day!    -Janice Kempe

## SPEAK UP

Try these ideas for helping children become used to speaking before a group.

1. Teach the class humorous short poems, finger plays, and songs as a class activity. Then each day ask two or three different pupils to perform one for the rest of the class. Send home copies so parents will know what their children are learning.

2. Create a make-believe radio and television studio. A long stick with a cardboard circle on top will be a suitable microphone. As children perform, show them how to stand, without fidgeting, before a camera.

3. Let the children record favorite selections on tapes. Keep samples to evaluate how they sounded initially and how they have improved.

4. Keep a library of cassette tapes and read-along stories. Pupils will learn appropriate phrasing, intonation, pacing, and so on as they listen to these professionally done tapes.

5. Arrange a storytelling contest. Prepare youngsters by familiarizing them with appropriate stories to tell. Start them with short selections and build up to longer ones. Use those with dramatic impact.

6. A daily school news program provides opportunities for reading, writing, editing, and speaking. Remind students to speak slowly and clearly. A playback tape can help them develop better speaking techniques.

7. Initiate an interclass read-to-me program. Make sure upper graders are familiar with the stories they are to read and are fluent in them before they read to younger groups.

8. Encourage parents to have "show times" at home for the children to perform poems, songs, and stories learned at school.          -Bobbye S. Goldstein

## SPIN A YARN

Try this activity to reinforce the concepts of storytelling, logical thinking, and sequencing of events. Cut different-colored skeins of yarn into 12- to 15-inch lengths, tie the strands together, and roll them into one big ball. Have the students sit in a large circle and choose one child to begin making up a story. He or she is to unravel the ball of yarn and roll it into a new ball while talking, stopping when he comes to the end of the first color. Then he hands it to the person to his right, who continues the story until the second color runs out. This continues until the last person in the circle receives the ball and adds an ending to the story.          -Dr. Patricia H. Olson

## THE ARRANGEMENT

To provide a meaningful experience in communication skills try this activity. Before class, cut out of firm cardboard two sets of figures: stars, squares, circles, triangles, and parallelograms. (Do not be concerned about whether your students are able to recognize or name them. The important thing is the variation in shapes. To make it a simpler exercise, vary the colors also.)

In class, have two students sit back to back in the middle of the classroom. Place a desk or other flat surface in front of each. Instruct one of the students who is sitting to arrange the figures in any way on the surface, describing each figure and its location aloud. Instruct the other person to listen and try to arrange the figures in the same way. After both children finish, discuss with the class, as well as the partners, ways communication could have been improved. Have two others try it the next time. You might want to try timing the groups. Does the length of time decrease as communication skills are perfected?   -Donald Lankiewicz

## SELL AND LEARN

Many schools and organizations engage their students in selling some items to raise money. This venture into the world of sales may be used as a learning situation. If students are selling candy, make sure they can rattle off the particulars without a mistake: the price, the size (or weight), and the delivery date. Practice filling out any necessary forms together. Discuss an appropriate time to approach people and stress the importance of being polite (even when a potential buyer is not). Use children who are "paper boys" or "paper girls" to serve as resource people and consultants. Role play different situations that students might encounter. Join in and play some of the roles yourself. Begin by choosing an ordinarily polite child and allow yourself to be a rude customer. (The children get a real laugh out of the teacher playing the villain.) Have children act the roles of other typical clients—an undecided person, a talkative customer, a hostile buyer. Use a Hula Hoop as your stage and have the actors stand within it. This sets the mood quickly. Sometimes the shyest kids become the most aggressive salespeople.          -Shirley Shratter

## ACTION STORIES

Divide your class into pairs and explain that as one student makes up a story, the other must pantomime it. Let each pair decide who will begin telling the story and who will act it out. After the children have been spinning their yarns for a while, say "freeze!" and have the partners switch roles. The new storyteller should pick up the plot where the other left off. At the end of the session, have the children write their stories on paper. You might also want the pairs to take turns sharing their stories with classmates.          -Carol Ann Piggins

## IMPROVISED DRAMA

Put your students' creative and dramatic abilities to use as they explore the concept of "point of view" through fairy tales. Begin by giving each child a copy of a simple fairy tale. Then, rewrite the tale from a different point of view and distribute copies. Ask the kids to tell you how the two stories differ, then have them work in groups to create their own versions and act them out for the rest of the class. After this introduction, your kids should be ready for the following activity. Place two unconnected telephones on stands in the front of your room. Explain that skits will revolve around telephone calls made by fairy-tale characters, but that these characters need not behave in familiar ways. Some suggested situations are:

1. The prince in "Cinderella" is calling around his kingdom trying to find out the identity of the mysterious woman at the ball.
2. One of the seven dwarfs is calling a real estate agent, trying to rent a house for Snow White, himself, and the other dwarfs.
3. Little Red Riding Hood gets a call from her grandmother, whom she really doesn't want to visit.
4. Jack's mother calls a gardener when the beanstalk gets out of hand.

Keep the following points in mind:
1. Be prepared to demonstrate a skit yourself. Rehearse something beforehand, so you can offer your kids a clear example.
2. Don't hesitate to offer a suggestion if a performer is having a difficult time improvising.
3. When a skit is over, call attention to the actor's strong points and note moments that worked especially well, then move right on to the next skit.

*-Paul Lamar*

## SWINGING SKETCHES

Dramatic sketches are a good way to encourage creativity and characterization. Divide the class and have each group pick a well-known fairy tale to update to fit our modern life-style. Imagine modern versions of "Goldilocks," "Cinderella," or "The Three Little Pigs."

### Raving Red Riding Hood

*Characters:* Narrator, Mom, Raving Red Riding Hood, Wicked Wolf, Grandmother

**Mom**—Yoo-hoo, Red! Turn off the TV and come in here.

**Red**—Aw, Mom. "The Hulk" is on; it's my favorite program.

**Mom**—Granny just called and she's feelin' a little "under the weather." I've put together some goodies in this basket and I want you to tool on over and take them to her.

**Red**—Wow, this is heavy! Whadya put in here, bricks?

**Mom**—No, dear. I wrapped up an enchilada TV dinner, a couple of Dr. Peppers, and a bottle of Excedrin. Now, get the lead out.

**Red**—Okay, bye, Ma.

**Mom**—Good-bye, dear!

**Narrator**—Red, being the responsible daughter that she is, takes off without delay. She is walking through the park on the way to Grandma's when she hears someone whistle at her and turns.

**Red**—Who was that?

(She hears the whistle again and the wolf appears.)

**Wolf**—Hi ya, Red!

**Red**—Oh, it's you! I should have guessed. Listen, I don't pay any attention to wolf whistles, so bug off.

**Wolf**—Hey, not so fast, Chickie! Where are you off to?

**Red**—I am not a "chickie," and where I'm off to is none of your business!

**Wolf**—Hey! Hey! Hey! Cool it. Will ya look at those goodies. Goin' on a picnic, Chickie?

**Red**—No, I'm not going on a picnic. I'm going to my grandmother's because she is feeling sick and I've got to get movin'.

**Wolf**—Okeydokey. Bye-bye-ee!

**Narrator**—But the wolf has other ideas. Little does Raving Red know, but the wicked wolf goes bananas over enchiladas! He picked up the scent right away and he's determined to get them for himself. So he scampers off, taking a shortcut to Granny's. When he gets there, he mugs Granny, ties her up, and locks her in the closet.

**Narrator**—Shhh! Raving Red is arriving. (Knock, knock, knock!)

**Wolf**—Come in, dear!

**Red**—Hi, Granny! Sorry to hear you're feelin' bad, but I brought you some things that will perk you up right away. I thought . . . Say, Granny, what big eyes you have!

**Wolf**—It's my new matching eye pencil and shadow, dear. You like it?

**Red**—And, Granny, what big ears you have!

**Wolf**—All the better to hear you, honey. Speak up!

**Red**—And Granny, what big teeth you have!

**Wolf**—All the better to eat them enchiladas, baby!

**Narrator**—With that, the wolf reaches for the picnic basket. But, our Raving Red Riding Hood is nobody's fool. She hasn't been taking karate for three years for nothing! With feet firm, she screams, "Saw-gow-ee" and lands a swift karate chop on the back of wolfie's neck. Now, alerted by muffled noises in the closet, she opens the door and rescues Granny, who has developed a crick in her back from sitting in that tiny closet. The two hug each other. Granny settles into her rocker and is given the goodies.

**Granny**—Red, it's so good to see ya, honey! Have a Dr. Pepper and come sit down. I think we can just catch the rest of "The Hulk"!

*-Merri L. Lebo*

## SURE-FIRE STORY STARTERS

Find five tall sacks, each a different color. Then choose a particular category for each sack and label all five accordingly. Categories might be *time, location, people, animals, action.* Print related words on construction paper strips and place them inside each sack. For instance, in a sack labeled *location* you might have words like *candy factory, spaceship, island,* and *forest.* Have students take turns pulling one card from each sack. Then post all five cards on your chalkboard. Have the kids use these words to write sentences and eventually complete stories. This activity will offer you and your students endless possibilities for creative stories, guaranteed to get everyone's imagination rolling!

-Evelyn J. Jensen

## SET THE SCENE

What do students find most difficult about creative writing? Finding something to write about, of course! Even when teachers assign themes or suggest opening sentences, kids sometimes have difficulty relating to the subjects. The results? Dull, unimaginative pieces that benefit no one—least of all the students . . . or you! Here's an idea that can change that. Try establishing a *setting* and let your kids take it from there. Use your bulletin board to display a large, paper apartment house with several windows. In the windows, place pictures of different types of persons found in magazines. Give each one a name. Now have kids choose one to write about. How old is the person? What does he or she do for a living? Does the person live alone? If so, by choice or necessity? What's the most exciting thing that's happened to

this person in the past week? Is he or she friends with anyone else in the apartment building? The answers to questions such as these can form the basis for many creative stories. Change the pictures several times throughout the semester to keep your students' imaginations working!

-Margaret Sharp Levine

## JUST DESSERTS

Here's a *delicious* way to promote descriptive writing in your classroom. Have students write brief paragraphs about their all-time favorite desserts! Each paragraph should describe how the dessert tastes, looks, smells, and feels. When the compositions are finished, they can be illustrated with original drawings or magazine pictures and assembled on your bulletin board.

-Sister Roberta Ann Leskey

## STORY STARTERS IN A NUTSHELL

Are your students bored with the story starters you offer, no matter how catchy they may seem to you? Well, try this different idea based on the fortune cookie of the Orient that will soon have everyone's imagination running high. You'll need a large number of empty peanut shells (let your kids eat the nuts as an extra added attraction). Before taping halves of shells together to make whole peanuts, place secret messages inside. The messages should be typed or printed on small slips of paper and can relate to any subject you desire. Suggested messages are:
**1.** You have just found a $100 bill. What's your next move?
**2.** You decide to plan a party for all of your friends. The sky's the limit. What kind of party will you have?
**3.** You've just been invited to a party on another planet in our solar system. How will you get

there? What will you wear?
**4.** You find that a piece of jewelry you've inherited from a relative is worth $1000. What will you do with it?
**5.** You have been asked to be the main character in a television show. What will your character be like? Write a short script that shows his or her personality. When your first crop goes stale, substitute a fresh basket of "fortune peanuts."

-Ruth Byers

## WRITING THE NEWS

Here is a way to teach creative writing and sharpen students' observation skills. Go through a stack of old newspapers and cut out large news photos of people, animals, construction, or any subject that suggests action. Be sure to cut off all the photos' captions. When you have at least five more photos than the number of students in your class, you are ready to begin. First, explain the reporter's five Ws—who, what, where, when, and why. Ask students to tell why each of these elements is important in telling a story. Then distribute the photos.

You may have students work alone or with partners. The assignment is for students to write a headline and story to go with the photo. Children who cannot come up with much for a particular picture can exchange theirs for one of the extras. Then have students read their stories aloud to the class. *-Doris Cruze*

## CREATING WITH CANCELLED CHECKS

Looking for a novel activity that will get your kids interested in creative writing? Have your students tell stories based on a series of cancelled bank checks—it's a great way to get them thinking about how incidents relate to one another. Using an overhead projector, flash one cancelled check at a time on a screen at the front of the classroom. These checks may be legitimate ones from your own account or made up and printed on construction paper. Have the kids write down the date, amount, endorsee and endorser of each check. Then, when all the information is gathered, let them put the pieces together to form individual stories. You might want to have the kids try this exercise in small groups first.

*-Richard F. Abrahamson*

## ADS FOR LAUGHS

Most children own things they don't particularly like—unlikely gifts they received, uncomfortable clothes, and so on. Here's a creative activity that will have kids laughing at the objects of their dislike. Have each child write an advertisement for his or her least favorite item and illustrate the ad accordingly. For example, ''Available: one itchy shirt. Strong enough for Raiders of the Lost Ark to wear!'' Of course these items won't really be for sale, but your class can have a lot of fun imagining that they are!

*-Sister Roberta Ann Leskey*

## JABBERING GIRAFFES

''If my giraffe could talk, he'd say, 'Have you been to New York?''' This giraffe writing assignment will develop your primary children's imaginations plus their art and math skills. Tell the children that as you read statements about giraffes that have missing words, you want them to imagine a wonderful giraffe. Ask them to fill in the blanks with any answers they like. (Don't tell them what they will do with the answers.)

When they have completed their sentences, have them draw their giraffes exactly as they have answered, incorporating the exact measurements and colors. Try these sentences:

My giraffe's name is _____.
My giraffe is _____ inches tall.
My giraffe has _____-colored spots. *-Deanna Andreano*

## WANTED: GOOD WRITERS

Writing want ads can help children become aware of their use and will provide practice in clear, concise written communication.

After studying newspaper want ads, have pupils write their own for the following situations:
1. You want to find your lost black kitten.
2. You are seeking a job cleaning yards.
3. You have found a lost collie puppy and are looking for the owner.
4. You want to sell your old one-speed bike.
5. You want to buy a used stereo.
6. Your family is going to have a garage sale. *-Genevieve Bylinowski*

## TWO SIDES OF A STORY

''What good luck, the teacher's gone today.''
''What bad luck, the substitute's worse.''
''Good news, bad news'' phrases are very popular with students. So what better way to study humor in everyday situations than to write a series of these ''two sides of a story.''

Introduce the lesson by asking about the situations when everything seemed great until one little thing spoiled the whole setup. Kids will catch on to the format by the time you write three or four examples on the chalkboard.

Suggest each child write 10 ''good luck, bad luck'' stories. The class could then compile and illustrate a book of the best examples. *-Joy Lindner*

## TURN-ONS FOR TURNED-OFF WRITERS

**What are they saying?** Have each child in your class cut out a magazine picture that tells a story. The best pictures are those that involve two or more people in an easily identified situation. Instruct each child to paste his or her picture on a sheet of construction paper, then write a brief story suggested by the picture. Put all the stories together in a booklet to be read by the children during leisure time.

**Synonym golf** Make a list of 18 vocabulary words to represent the 18 holes in a game of golf, and arrange them on a large sheet of poster board. To advance around the course, players must think of one synonym for each word. Score 18 points every time a player cannot think of one. The student with the *lowest* score at the end of 18 "holes" wins.

**Chain story** Use this activity to reinforce your students' sequencing skills. Cut several construction-paper strips, about one inch wide and nine inches long. Have one student start the chain by writing the first line to a story on his or her strip. Then instruct the child to paste the ends together so it forms a loop, with the sentence appearing on the outside. The next student must read the sentence on that loop, think of another to add, and print it on his or her strip. This continues until every student has had a chance to add to the chain.

**Pick-a-pal paragraph** Have each child choose a character from a recently read story that he or she would like to have as a friend. Now give the students one sheet of construction paper each and instruct them to fold the sheets in half lengthwise. On the outside of the folder, each child is to draw his or her character involved in some event or scene from the story. When the drawings are completed, have the kids write brief paragraphs about their characters inside the folders, telling why they chose the characters they did, how these characters are similar to or different from themselves, and why they would like to be friends.

**Extra! Extra!** For this activity, you'll need to give your class a short lesson in journalism. Explain that the first paragraph of a good news story should cover the 5 Ws—who, what, when, where, and why. Now tell the kids that they are to write brief newspaper articles about books they've recently read and enjoyed, making sure to include the 5 Ws. The students should also come up with catchy headlines to call attention to their articles. Put all the articles together on your bulletin board under the heading "Extra! Extra!" and encourage your kids to read them in their spare time. You might want to award a small prize to the student whose article inspired the greatest number of requests for the book it described.　　　*-Betty Johnson*

## FIVE-STAR WRITING PROJECT

If your students are reluctant to express themselves in writing, try this sure-fire approach. Use television programs as subject matter! Ask your students, as a group, to name 10 different television shows they have recently viewed and list them on your chalkboard. Now instruct each child to choose one television show and describe, in writing, the latest episode he or she watched. What happened in the beginning, the middle, and the end of the show? Who were the main characters? What are their personalities like? When everyone is finished, let the kids take turns reading their descriptions aloud to classmates, or have them exchange papers and evaluate each other's work. You'll be surprised at how eager your students will be to write about their favorite television shows! You might also want the children to illustrate their work. When television is used as a writing tool, it gets a five-star rating!　　　*-Frances Herskovitz*

## RETIRE OVERWORKED WORDS

Try the Retire-A-Word/Retire-A-Phrase method of teaching vocabulary to encourage students to give well-worn expressions a well-deserved break. Here's how it works: Step 1—Make a list of the expressions students use most often that do not add clarity or flair to their writing. Step 2—Discuss each word on your list, asking students what each word means—exactly. Will their writing suffer without this word? Are there better words to take its place? Step 3—After discussing each word's meaning and frequency of use, have students vote on whether or not it should be allowed in their writing. The class can decide on a penalty for using rejected words, such as points off or a clean-up task. Students will soon be more careful.　　　*-Arthur G. Sharp*

## THICKENING THE PLOT

To give kids a make-believe story center in which to write their own suspenseful stories, post these signs on the sides of a study carrel.

**1.** Choose descriptive names for your main characters, and title your story.

**2.** Make up a problem for the main character to solve. Example: The hero must rescue his best friend from the elevator of a burning building. The friend, the only witness to a bank robbery, has been trapped by the villain.

**3.** Create a climax. Give the hero or heroine a "darkest moment"— a time when it looks as if he or she could fail. Example: The hero is accused of being the bank robber and is being detained by the police for questioning. Will the hero be able to get away to save the friend? Or will the friend die and the hero be sent to prison?

**4.** Find an answer for the hero's problem.

Encourage your storywriters to use dialogue. Suggest they illustrate and design book covers for their finished stories.

*-Marion G. Walker*

MONSTER WORDS

FANG
BLOOD
GHOUL
SCARE

## MONSTER MADNESS

My Monster Madness Writing Center has really had kid appeal. After you have duplicated the reproducible on the following page, have children write their assignments directly on that page. Assignments can range from simple word listing to more difficult story writing. Try some of this monster madness in your class.

**1.** Write eight huge scary monster words.
**2.** Write 10 words describing how you would feel if you met a monster on a dark, rainy night.
**3.** List 10 things Madeline Monster has in her purse.
**4.** List 15 things you would find in the Monster family's refrigerator.
**5.** For each letter in the word "monster," write a word that describes a monster. Now use all those words in a sentence.
**6.** Write five questions you would like to ask the Monster family.
**7.** Describe the Monster family pet.
**8.** Write and design an invitation to Baby Gog's birthday party.
**9.** Describe Baby Gog's favorite birthday present.
**10.** Describe where the Monsters will go on vacation and what they must take with them.
**11.** Write Madeline Monster's favorite family recipe.
**12.** Write "the Scariest Story Ever Told." *-Janice Bennington*

## CENTER ON WRITING

Try constructing a creative writing center for your students' extra-time activities. Choose a corner of your room and cover the adjoining walls with word cards containing descriptive adjectives. Also set up a long table in this corner to hold a brightly decorated box and a kitchen timer. Fill the box with tiny objects such as a stuffed toy or spool of thread, and cut a hole in it just large enough for a child's hand. When students visit the center, they select an object from the box, set the timer for five minutes, and write four descriptive sentences about the object they picked. This exercise is sure to get their creative juices flowing and broaden their repertoire of descriptive words. *-Lorraine A. Lee*

## DYNAMIC DIALOGUE

When your students write conversation, is their dialogue dull? Lifeless? Uninteresting? Let's face it—it's not easy to write strong dialogue. Even professional writers struggle to make their characters speak like *real* people! If your students have trouble writing conversation, let them try some of these activities. (Stress proper punctuation at all times!) Print them on index cards and place them on a table in a corner of your classroom along with a stack of writing paper, some pencils, a dictionary, and a thesaurus. You might want to label the center "Let's write dynamic dialogue!" Let kids take turns coming to the center and completing the activities. You'll be surprised at the result!

**1.** Scan a short story you have read recently that contains a lot of conversation between characters. Now change one of the character's personalities and rewrite the dialogue accordingly, keeping the events surrounding it in mind. What would you have said at that point in the story if you had been one of the characters?
**2.** Imagine that you are 16 years old and have just passed your driver's examination. Write a short conversation between you and one of your parents, in which you ask to use the family car for an evening. What will you say to convince your parent to let you use the car?
**3.** Find two magazine pictures of persons with interesting expressions on their faces. Paste both pictures on a sheet of paper and write a conversation that might take place between them.
**4.** Surprise! the president of the United States has just chosen your phone number at random! He's going to call you tonight. What will he say to you? What will he ask you to do? Write your conversation.
**5.** Pretend you have invented the breakfast cereal "Whackies." You are calling people at random to ask their opinions of your product. Write down some of the things people say to you over the phone. For instance, "I'd rather eat my shoes than another bowl of Whackies," said Mr. Jones. *-Rena L. Allen*

# The Mad Monster

Reproduce this page to use with the idea on page 86, or create your own writing activity.

# Creative Writing/Basics

## WHAT'S THE BIG IDEA?

Tactile, visual, and auditory—three different learning styles! It isn't always easy to help primary children understand that a paragraph is made up of a main idea with supporting details. Activities that use different learning approaches can build the understanding needed to be a successful writer.

Begin by telling children to close their eyes, then give each a quarter to feel as a mystery object. Elicit guesses about what is being held. After "quarter" is guessed have children open their eyes. Looking at the quarter, ask them to give supporting details about it, such as: its roundness, the eagle, the year, the ridges around the edge. Stress that in a paragraph the main idea would be the quarter and the other facts would be the supporting details. The next activity is to look at photographs. For instance, use a picture of a child swinging in a rubber tire from a tree. Ask for the main idea (the girl in the swing) and the supporting details (the tree, the rubber tire, the smile on her face).

A listening experience comes next. Pair children and whisper the main idea, "clown," in the ear of one member of each pair. The child who has heard the idea then whispers three supporting details to his or her partner, who is to guess the main idea. Responses are recorded on newsprint tacked to the board under headings, "main idea" and "supporting details." From these words and phrases the class can then write a paragraph about a clown. Have children choose individual topics, listing their main idea and supporting details before they write their paragraphs.

*-Bernice Ruth Winston*

## PARAGRAPH SKILLS

Children frequently have difficulty learning the concept of paragraph writing. One way of helping your students overcome this difficulty is through public speaking. Have students deliver extemporaneous speeches on topics chosen either by you or the students themselves. It is usually best to limit the number of speeches to no more than five a day.

After each speech, involve the rest of the class in a little constructive criticism. This gives you the opportunity to develop specific paragraph writing techniques such as eliminating repetition and organizing thoughts. This is also an ideal time to help your students develop the use of multiple meanings for vocabulary and to begin to think in more complex, but related, language units. Finally, as your students begin writing simple paragraphs, they will more fully understand that their paragraphs, like their speeches, are language units built around topic ideas.

*-Michael Lipton and Lorraine Lipton*

## WORDS INTO PARAGRAPHS

Here's a writing activity that will really get your students thinking. Divide the class into groups of four or five, and have them number their papers from 1 to 20. Give each group a word which group members are to write down next to number 1. Now have each student write a word he or she associates with that word next to number 2. Have students do the same with the next word, and so on, until they have written 20 words. Then instruct all members of a group to share their 20th words with each other. Group members are to use those last words in a paragraph dealing with one main topic. Let kids read the results to the rest of the class— what variety from a single word!

*-Sandra J. Frey*

## WRITER'S EXCHANGE

If you're looking for a way to spark your students' interest in creative writing, try setting up a writer's exchange between your school and another one in your district. Talk to your principal first about the possibility of establishing such a program. He or she can put you in touch with teachers from other area schools who might be interested in participating. Once you've found a school to work with, ask for a list of names and grade levels of the children who'll be writing for the exchange and match them up with similar students in your school. Children will enjoy reading other students' stories and poems and will be inspired to write more of their own, too. You might want to inquire about a postage-free mailing system in your school district or ask for parent volunteers to swap the stories and poems every week or so. Encourage the children to write to their partners each week, and plan a time when the writers can meet face-to-face.

*-Mary Lou Cooper*

## STORY RECORDING SESSIONS

Here's a good activity that will encourage your students to write better holiday stories they can share with younger children. Make sure students understand that their compositions must be related to the holiday at hand, and have them keep these questions in mind as they write their stories:
**1.** Is the material appropriate for younger classes?
**2.** Is the story interesting and does it relate to the holiday?
**3.** Is there a climax and a satisfactory conclusion?
After the stories are written, have each child read his or hers aloud to the rest of the class. Tape them on a cassette recorder. Circulate the tapes among the

younger grades for children to listen to during art periods, free time, or before writing their own holiday compositions. This activity is exciting and fun for both the authors and the younger children who listen to and genuinely enjoy these stories.

*-Theresa Grass*

## WRITERS ON PARADE

Celebrate your students' writing. First, make time in your daily schedule for each child to have at least 20 minutes of writing time. Keep writing topics on hand to help children who have a hard time getting started. As your kids begin to refine their writing skills and come up with finished products, find ways that they can share their accomplishments. Flags and a parade give everyone a chance to rejoice.

Have children make flags that represent their piece of prized writing and march to a prearranged classroom to share their work.

Rather than ask kids to read their work to the whole class, break children into small groups to share both the meanings of their flags and their writing. Next time exchange roles and have that teacher's class come to you!

*-Carolyn Kirmes*

## RECIPE 'RITING

Recipe writing is a fun way to enhance the study of food groups and develop language skills at the same time. Ask students to write their names in bold capital letters down the side of a piece of paper. Tell them to think up a name for their recipe, using the initials of their first and last names. (For example, C.E's Creamy Eggnog.) Then, using the letters in the names, have students write the directions for making their chosen recipe. Make sure the directions are given in the right order! Finally, ask students to recopy their recipes on lined index cards,

using colored markers. Here's a good example:

> Crack exactly
> How many eggs your
> Recipe
> Includes and
> Simmer in a pan;
>
> Eggs should be beaten
> Lightly; pour a
> Little milk at a time
> Into the mixture and stir
> On medium heat; keep
> Temperature low to avoid
>     lumps.    *-Peggy Richardson*

## GUESS WHO?

It's not always easy to motivate students to write creatively, but you can make the task a little easier with the help of a simple game of "Guess Who?" Have each child print his or her name on a small piece of paper, folding it carefully so the name doesn't show. Put all the folded papers in a box or large jar and let each child draw a name. Stress the importance of not revealing the names they've chosen, then have the students write a short paragraph, giving clues to the person's identity. No negative clues are allowed. When everyone has finished writing, have the kids take turns reading their paragraphs aloud to the class. Assign one child the role of tabulator and have him keep a record of the number of guesses it takes the class to identify the person described in each paragraph. The student whose paragraph requires the greatest number of guesses is the winner. Your kids will love this game, especially when they're the subject of a paragraph. It's a good lesson in decoding information, too!    *-Kate Kunz*

## SCRAMBLED EGGS

Get students "egg-cited" about writing with these simple activities. Just cut out a fried egg shape from white paper, add a yellow yolk, and write one of the

following activities on each.
**1.** Make a list of 10 animals that lay eggs. **2.** Write 8 words describing eggs. **3.** Describe a raw egg. **4.** Write the directions for cooking an egg — any style you like! **5.** Create a bumper sticker that will encourage people to like eggs. **6.** Write a new ending for "Humpty Dumpty." **7.** A 6′ purple egg was found on Mars. Describe what came out of it. **8.** Write a conversation between 2 eggs about to be cooked.

When students are finished writing, you can display their papers by making large eggs and mounting the papers on them. Arrange these on a bulletin board with the title "A Few Good Eggs," or "Eggs-cellent Work!"

*-Janice Bennington*

## CREATIVE WRITING RECIPES

Here's a great idea for writing assignments that will have all your kids' minds cooking in no time! Fill a recipe file box with enough index cards for every child in your class. On each card, print the ingredients for an original story. For example, one recipe might include these ingredients: 2 strawberries, 1 bad boy, 2 tennis shoes, ¾ apple pie, 1 deserted lake, and 2 police officers. Instruct kids to choose recipes from the file box and cook up their own stories, using the listed ingredients. No matter what kids come up with, one thing is certain: every story will have its own flavor! *-Josephine Lazzaro*

## DAILY DIARY

To promote positive self-concepts in your class this year, have students make individual journals on the first day of school by stapling together sheets of notebook paper and attaching construction-paper covers. Each day, set aside a few minutes for the kids to write positive statements in their journals about themselves, their classmates, and their school experiences. Have the children review their writing every few weeks. *-Jane B. Spann*

## GRIMMS, MOVE OVER

Folktales can be used as the basis for so many language arts activities. Here are just a few suggestions for your class.

**Readers Theater:** Have children rewrite their favorite tale in the form of a script and produce it for other classes. **Songfest:** Rewrite the tale in the form of a ballad or popular tune. Set the words to music. **Guilty or not guilty:** Many tales lend themselves to a court-room situation with some children acting as news reporters.

**Changing times:** Rewrite your favorite tale in a modern version.

**Tall Tale News:** Using a copy of a local newspaper as a model, write interview articles, news stories, even a classified ad section that relate to favorite tales. You can even include obituaries. **Picture talk:** On long sheets of paper retell the story in picture form, using dialogue in "balloons."

**Dear Abby:** Have children write advice to one of the characters on how to get out of the trouble the story has gotten him or her into.

**Tell a tale:** During a story hour let each child tell his or her favorite story to the rest of the class or to a small group from another class.

**Continue it:** Ask children to write a sequel to their favorite folktale.
*-Darlene Armstrong*

## FAIRY TALES

Fairy tales can be great launching pads for creative writing when you ask students to rewrite them, keeping the basic characters the same but updating the settings. For example, they might have Cinderella lose her high, leather boot at the disco; Little Red Riding Hood could travel from her high-rise apartment across the city to visit her sick grandmother and decide to take a new subway route; and Goldilocks could taste cheeseburgers and try out water beds at the Three Bears' house. Have students read their stories aloud for classmates to enjoy.
*-Barbara Lassman*

## DESCRIBE, IN YOUR OWN WORDS

Children need to learn to describe an object, animal, person, or place in order to communicate orally as well as in writing. These picture games will help them learn this skill. Find pictures of different animals and mount them on cardboard. Hold each one up, one at a time, and ask kids to describe what is pictured, noting size, color, height, and outstanding body parts (goggly eyes, body pouch, long stiff tail, and so on). Then place all pictures on the chalk rail and choose one child to describe one of the pictures without telling which one it is. Ask another child to point to the one being described.

Give each child an animal picture and have him or her write a description on a 3" × 5" card, without giving its name. Put all

cards in a container and place the pictures on the chalk rail again. Children take turns drawing a card, reading the description, and finding the matching picture.
*-Florence Rives*

## CLASSROOM MYTH-TIQUE

If your class is studying myths, why not let your students make their own creatures and beasts? Start out with a discussion of different mythological creatures and their characteristics. Then let students think of characteristics they would like their own creatures to have, make a rough sketch of such a creature, and then a final drawing with all the details; from this drawing they can construct a three-dimensional papier-mâché model and paint it however they wish. Introduce Greek and Latin root words such as *branchi* (arm), *cauda* (tail) *cent* (hundred), *deca* (ten), *dentia* (teeth), *herbi* (vegetable), *opti* (eye), and *probo* (nose); then let kids use these words to name their creatures: for example, pentapoda biopti unigastro gastropoda (five-footed, two-eyed, one-stomach, belly-footed creature). Then do activities such as the following.

**1.** Summarize a day in the life of your creature.

**2.** Make a map of your creature's environment.

**3.** Write a poem about your creature.

**4.** Describe your creature's special or super powers, in contrast to one of the other creatures.

**5.** Conduct a survey of the creatures, using such criteria as most bizarre, most creative, and so on, and graph your results.

**6.** Write a newspaper article about your creature's first contact with humans.

**7.** Perform a pantomime in which you act the part of your creature.

**8.** Put your creature on trial for disturbing the peace.
*-Rich Carpenter*

## SUPER STATIONERY

Personal letters provide a good means of reinforcing basic writing skills, but it's not always easy to interest students in this area. I've found that children are much more receptive when they've been given the chance to design their own stationery. Have them draw their individual designs on a duplicating master and run off about 20 copies for each student. (Be sure to keep the masters so you can make additional copies when the first batch runs out.) Now have the children fill in their designs with crayons or felt-tipped pens. These colorful creations will motivate students to take pride in their letter-writing!

*-Marilyn C. Nicholson*

## "TIME CAPSULE" LETTERS

After returning to school from maternity leave, I gave my students (nine to ten years old) a letter-writing assignment that turned out to be a great experience. I asked each student to write a letter to my newborn son. I told the students the letters would be put in Ryan's baby book for him to read when he was nine or ten years old.

The students were delighted with this assignment. Some of the contemporary occurrences and facts that they wrote about were the space shuttle flights, Reagan's presidency, major sports statistics, and current prices of items from gasoline to fast food.

Writing letters to my son was such a success that I have expanded the project. Now whenever a student in my class has a new sibling arrive in his or her family, we all write "time capsule" letters to the baby. When my students take these letters home, they can feel as though they have added to all that is special about having a new baby in the house. *-Laura Kinsey*

## NOTE OUR MAILBOX

Cure your class's "Note-Passing Disease" by installing a mailbox in your room. The box may be a bona fide mailbox or any large covered box with a slit in the top. Students should feel free to put their "mail" to friends in the box at any time. Mail is delivered at the end of each day.

Our mailbox also helped stimulate some learning activities. We learned very quickly how to correctly address letters, complete with their return addresses. During one social studies period, we investigated the origination of stamps. In the following art class, we designed our own original stamps. Toward the end of the year, all mail had to be addressed in cursive handwriting. *-Linda Pitts*

## BUSINESS LETTERS THEY'LL LOVE

Does your language arts curriculum demand that young children learn to write business letters? If so, then you know how tedious it can be to teach a skill your students don't yet have a need for. They simply aren't interested, right? Well, here's an idea that can change all that. Divide your class into small groups of three or four children each, then have each group form a fictitious company, with group members acting as its chief executives. Each group is to think of a name for its company and a fictitious address. Next, have the groups design letterheads and matching envelopes for their businesses. Then distribute a list of every imaginary business and address to the entire class. Each child must choose a business executive from the list and write him or her a letter of praise, complaint, or suggestion. In turn, the executive who receives the letter must answer back, using his or her company's letterhead. Check each letter carefully before it's sealed in the envelope for "mailing." *-Annette V. Werle*

### WHAT'S IN A NAME?

A baby name book provided the raw material for one of my most successful special projects. As my first graders learned the literal translation of their names, it was difficult to hold them down! I began the lesson by having the students help me alphabetize their names on large chart paper. After all the names were defined and the class was again manageable, we discussed whether the names seemed to fit the students. We all laughed when we discovered the name Brian meant "strong." Brian had been opening thermos bottles that I couldn't budge all week! To finish the lesson, each child drew a picture illustrating the meaning of his or her name. Jason, "the healer," drew a doctor, while Samantha, "the listener," portrayed a girl with gigantic ears.

-Kathleen Richko

### BIG ON WORDS

Add zip to drill on dictionary skills by using *BIG* words: argyranthemous, commensurate, dichotomy, entrepreneur, languette, paramiographer, serendipity, ticopolonga, xanthocyanopsy, zumbookuk. Give pupils the following directions.

**1.** Using a dictionary, find definitions, then try to use each word in a sentence.

**2.** If you are very brave, write a story using all the words. When finished, read it aloud to your classmates.

**3.** Make a mobile of the words. On a card write one of the words, its definition, a sentence using the word, and draw a picture of it. Cut the card into an interesting shape and hang from a string.

-Teddy Meister

### TERRIFIC TRIVIA IDEA

Most kids are fascinated with trivia. Here's a good way to challenge them to find the answers to unusual questions while strengthening their dictionary skills at the same time. The only materials you'll need are a dictionary, your chalkboard, and a class of inquisitive children. Start by searching the dictionary for unusual definitions, prominent historical figures, abbreviations, and archaic words. Create several questions from these facts, write them on the chalkboard, and let the contest begin! You should underline the most prominent word clue in each question and instruct students to start their dictionary search with the underlined word. Be sure you use questions that can be answered from the dictionary alone. Students must answer each question with a complete sentence. The first one to correctly answer all the questions is the winner. Here are some suggestions for super-trivia questions:

**1.** What are the ingredients of *mayonnaise*?

**2.** How much is *twopence* worth in American money? -Sue Witte

### ALL IN THE FAMILY NAME

The origin of names can supply your kids with some fascinating research. Two sources for materials are: *Burke's General Armory* (Arco) and *Surnames of Scotland* (New York Public Library). Your kids will be fascinated to learn that until about A.D. 1100 most people in Europe had only one name. -Dave Bloom

### NEW WORD FUN

Here's a simple way to increase your students' vocabularies while improving their dictionary skills. Before class every morning, print a different vocabulary word in a designated spot on your chalkboard. As soon as students arrive in the morning, they are to look up the word in the dictionary, then write the word and its definition on a slip of paper. Remind students to print their names on their papers as well. Give students five to ten minutes to complete this activity every morning. At the end of the time period, instruct students to fold their papers in half and place them in a box marked "NEW WORDS." At the end of the day, choose one student to draw one piece of paper from the box and tell whose name appears on it. That student is to read his or her definition aloud to the class and spell the word. If the child has not spelled and defined the word correctly, he or she must draw another piece of paper from the box. Return all corrected papers to your students the following day and begin the process again.

-Eileen Marousek

## ENCYCLOPEDIA BLUES

It is often difficult for children to do more than just copy from the encyclopedia when assigned reports on famous people. Here is a way to avoid that.

Have pupils select names of people from a list that you have made. Children then spend time in the library researching interesting facts about their persons: their early life, education, family, friends, life work, and contribution to society. These facts are then to be written in the form of a letter, with a significant date and place for the return address. The letter has to be addressed to a family member or friend mentioned in the person's biography. The body of the letter should contain biographical material as if that person were telling it.

Letters can be exchanged and read in small groups, as well as posted for all to read as the "day's mail."        -Mary M. Burman

## ENCYCLOPEDIASTICS

An easy way to build proficiency in using the encyclopedia is a classroom exercise I call encyclopediastics. To prepare, I comb several volumes to find interesting facts which I then put into question form on index cards. When we play the game, I give each child a volume and five questions to which he or she can find the answers in that volume. For example, the questions for Volume A might include: On what date was the first class graduated from the U.S. Air Force Academy? What are the eight maneuvers used in aerobatics?

-Patricia A. Wilmott

## ENCYCLOPEDIA SEARCH

Use the following poem in your class to introduce and then reinforce reference skills. Make one copy for every child in your class and list the various reference books they may use to find the answers to the riddles at the end of each stanza in the poem. You might want to make this activity into a contest by giving a small prize to the first student to answer every question.

The basset is a type of hound
With a funny-looking torso.
What country did it come
    from?
It wasn't Mexico!

Dr. Seuss has written books
That children love to read.
Can you find his real name
And do it with some speed?

Guided missiles are
    researched
In Huntsville, Alabama.
Find the nickname of that city
And don't ask your grandma!

The Dead Sea Scrolls were
    found in caves
By a shepherd boy one day.
Find the year he found them
    there;
Do it without delay.

The walrus is a kind of seal
That grows to enormous size.
Find how much a grown one
    weighs;
You'll be a bit surprised!

The Pacific is the largest
Ocean in the world.
Pacific has a special meaning;
Can you define that word?

-Marsha Blake

## SEARCH AND ENJOY

Are your students reluctant to dig into reference materials to obtain required information? Do they know where to hunt? Here's an exciting way to introduce reference books and motivate your class to use them. First, be sure to have several sources available in the classroom such as an encyclopedia, a dictionary, a telephone book, a cookbook, an almanac, an atlas, a TV guide, the Readers' Guide to Periodical Literature and so on. After looking at and discussing the use of each reference aid with your class, pass out small index cards with two different problems on each. Have each student read his problems to the class and suggest the source book from which they might obtain a solution. Your kids will love playing detective in this new approach to reference materials.

-Margaret Sullivan

## CAN YOU ANSWER THESE?

Finding the answers to these questions will give students practice in using several different reference books—the atlas, dictionary, encyclopedia, even the Guinness Book of World Records.
1. What is the largest land animal?
2. What is the largest sea animal?
3. Name two microscopic animals.

4. Pandas are found in the country of _____.
5. Where can you find flying squirrels?
6. The ostrich is a bird. Does it fly?
7. What's the difference between an alligator and a crocodile?
8. Can we eat a sea cucumber?
9. What is coral?
10. How does a marmoset move?
11. Who was Moby Dick?
12. What does an ornithologist do?
13. How do homoiothermic animals differ from poikilothermic animals?
14. How do arachnids get their food?
15. What are pintos and mavericks, other than car models?    -Teddy Meister

## A BUG MISTAKE

After reading this poem with your students, ask them to hypothesize about where the name "ladybug" came from. Students can then do research to find out the facts. Students may also enjoy writing their own poems about such interesting insects as the walking stick, daddy longlegs, or the katydid.

### PUZZLED
*Those little bugs called ladybugs*
*May all just look the same.*
*But if some of them are gentlemen,*
*Is that a proper name?*
       -Anita E. Posey

## YOU NAME IT

Have your students play an exciting and challenging identification game that leads them straight to the reference books. Display pictures or realia, one at a time. Each item has a problem-answer sheet attached on which the children work. A typical problem might be "identify the animal that lived in this shell. Give both its common and scientific names." An answer must not be simply a guess; announce a time limit. Some research must lead to the students' decisions. All students' answers are visible, as they each use one piece of paper. Any number may answer in the same way. (This, however, sometimes reveals that independent thinkers are sometimes right!) At the end of the allotted time (usually about two days), answers are checked. If anyone has found the correct answer the class is still in the game, and you challenge them with another more difficult problem!    -Sandra Frey

## PLANT SOME IDEAS

Using old seed catalogs and library reference books, have students find pictures and descriptions of various plants, information on planting times, and planting directions. Encourage students to gather information to plan a class indoor garden or to compile a "Nature Walk Handbook" for the coming spring. Students will be pleased that, after preparing the handbook, they will be able to identify the different kinds of plants on their walks or visits to community gardens.    -Nicholas P. Criscuolo

## NO MORE COPYCATS!

When you assign research projects, do too many of your students merely copy information, word for word, from the encyclopedia? Here's an activity that will help them break that habit. Have each child browse through any volume of the encyclopedia and choose a particularly interesting or informative paragraph. Then instruct the kids to rewrite their paragraphs as if they were short news stories, complete with catchy headlines. If you assign this exercise frequently, you'll soon have no more copycats.
       -Dorothy Zjawin

## ANIMAL DETECTIVES

Use some of the world's unusual animals to motivate research skills. Aardvark, anteater, armadillo, bison, colugo, echidna, ferret, gazelle, hyena, iguana, lemur, manatee, mandrill, pangolin, sloth, tapir, and wombat are all real and come from different parts of the world. Have students act as detectives and hunt down clues to find out what they are and where they come from. Suggest that each student choose one of these intriguing animals and write a storybook about it that a child might enjoy. Have kids read their books aloud or donate them to a younger class.    -Teddy Meister

I'M NO LADY!

## COUNT THE BIRDIES

Here's how to make a counting game for primary students. With black marker, outline and then cut out ten birdhouses from heavy construction paper. Draw and cut out ten birds to perch on the birdhouses. At the top of the first birdhouse put one dot, put two dots on the second house, and so on. On each bird, place a different numeral (from 1 to 10).

Put the game in an envelope with instructions to students to match the birds with the houses during their free time. Have them tape the birds on the house for you to check later. *-Gertrude Parker*

## HUNGRY PAC-MAN

The pie-slice mouth of Pac-Man makes him an excellent greater-than and less-than symbol to use in mathematics equations. In the video game, Pac-Man earns points as he gobbles his enemies. When using him in a mathematical equation, tell children always to place him so that his open mouth faces the larger number. Write out some "greater than, less than" equations and then ask your students to place the Pac-Man symbol correctly. Award them points when they do.

*-Judy Muskauski*

## IRRESISTIBLE MATH

Each Monday, my kindergarten students receive a plastic bag filled with small objects. They estimate the number of objects during the week. Then on Friday we count the contents. We've used pennies, seeds, paper clips, and various other things, but nothing had the success of chocolate chips.

I divided the chips in bags and Monday through Thursday we wrote down several estimates of the number in each bag. On Friday morning several students counted the contents of each one by putting them in groups of tens in small paper cups. (There were more than 700 chocolate chips altogether!)

With the help of parent volunteers, we baked cookies and while the cookies were cooling, each child estimated the number of chips that would be in his or her cookie. These estimates were recorded on a large sheet of paper.

While eating the cookie, each child carefully counted the actual number of chocolate chips in it. Then students reproduced their findings with crayon on a construction paper cookie. Each child glued his or her cookie onto a large graph marked in columns: 0-5 chips, 6-10 chips, 11-15 chips, and 16 or more.

I could then follow up using the graph with questions: Which column had the most? Which had the least? This was a useful and fun math week! *-Ann E. Hestand*

## IT'S IN THE BOOK

If you have students in your class who need practice in sequencing numbers from 100 to 200 (or higher), let them use a textbook for drill. They may simply page through the book on their own or

you may structure the activity by asking questions such as: "Which number is 2 more than 110? 5 more than 131? 10 more than 149?" *-Isobel Livingstone*

## BIRD BROS., INC.

Primary students often get confused when using greater-than and less-than symbols. Here's a surefire way to solve the problem. Draw the two Bird Brothers (see illustration) on a large piece of poster board. Make

their beaks from pipe cleaners to illustrate the inequality signs. The first bird's name is More Than because he is always hungry for more food; his beak is always open. The second bird's name is Less Than because he always wants less to eat; his beak is always closed. Children can run their fingers over the beaks, reinforcing each symbol's direction as they repeat the symbol's name.

*-Gay Lynn Elmendorf*

## COLORED NUMBER FACTS

Here is a way to use color to teach and reinforce arithmetic skills. You'll need 8-by-10-inch cards and many colored pens or markers for this project. First, write a number in the middle of each card in black. This number should be almost as big as the card. Then write, to the side of the large number, two numbers whose sum is the large number. For instance, if the large number is 8, the two small numbers could be 5 and 3, 6 and 2, and so on. Make these numbers smaller and of different colors.

Take one of the cards and place it somewhere in the room where all students can see it. Tell students that they will learn four number facts from each card. The first two facts show that adding one of the small numbers to the other gives you the large number. The second two facts show that subtracting one of the small, colored numbers from the large number will give you the other small number.

Ask students to make a copy of the large card on their own papers. Work on each card until all four facts are mastered. This technique helps children form visual pictures of number facts.

*-Inez Barry*

## THE DRILL DOLDRUMS

Whether in addition, subtraction, multiplication, or division, the drilling of facts is often boring and tedious. Spark those needed drills with something as easy as standing up and sitting down. Write the set of facts to be learned on the board. It's best to work with six facts at a time. As you and your class drill out loud have the students stand up at the end of the first fact and sit down for the next one. For example: 3 X 1 = 3 (stand up!); 3 X 2 = 6 (sit down!); 3 X 3 = 9 (stand up!), and so on. After you've practiced the set of six and students seem to feel comfortable, try mixing facts up or going faster and faster. Always review the learned facts before starting on new ones. Try changing movements; for example, touch noses and tummies. Have children take turns leading.      *-Jan S. Bright*

## MATH TRAINING

Here's a bulletin board display your kids can help construct that results in a "locomotivator" for studying math facts! Give each child a sheet of construction paper to make one car for a classroom train. You should make the engine that heads the train. Instruct the kids to use paper scraps to make details like windows, wheels, and so on. Now have each child print one math fact on his or her car. When the cars are complete, tack them to your bulletin board following the engine. Now you can begin your math lessons with a drill of facts printed on the train. Choose one child to be the engineer for the day. That student should wear an engineer's cap and scarf and use a ruler to point to different cars on the train. He or she can then call on individual classmates to answer the problems printed on them.      *-Carolyn Wilhelm*

## TIC-TAC-TOE MATH

Here's an idea for a math drill your kids will love, and it takes *no* preparation. Have each child draw a tic-tac-toe board. Call out a simple math problem and have children write down the answer in any square they wish. Repeat this procedure eight times, keeping track of what you've called out, until the nine squares are filled. Now call out different problems that can be answered by these same nine numbers. Children must find the answer for each problem and draw an X through it. For example, if one of the first nine facts was 4 + 2, you might call out 2 + 4, 6 X 1, 14 − 8, or 12 ÷ 2 the second time around, depending on the level of your students. The first player to get 3 Xs in a row and call out "Tic-tac-toe!" is the winner!      *-Betty Dale*

## ALL ABOARD THE MATH TRAIN

For practice in addition and subtraction skills, have your students line up to form a "train" around your classroom. Begin by dictating a problem to the first child in line. That child must answer correctly, then think of another problem whose first number is the same as the answer he or she has just given. The second child answers that problem, then thinks of another for the next person in line, and so on around the room. You can keep score by giving the students tickets and then punching holes in them every time they answer correctly. When a child gives an incorrect answer, he or she gets no punch and must move to the end of the line to become the "caboose." In this way, no one sits down and everyone participates for the entire "trip."

*-Cheryl McLaughlin*

## BLOOMING MATH FACTS

Everyone knows that memorizing math facts can be *boring*. But you can eliminate some of the tedium with this colorful idea that will motivate your kids to learn their facts quickly. On a long sheet of butcher paper approximately equal to the width of your bulletin board, draw a row of giant flowers—one for every student in your class. Each flower should have nine petals and a circle center. Number the petals on

each flower from one to nine, and print an individual student's name in each circle center. Now tack the row of flowers to your bulletin board. As a child masters a set of facts, he or she may color in the corresponding petal on his or her flower. By the time your students have all learned their facts, you'll have a blooming flower garden!

*-Betty Dale*

## COUNTATHONS

Discovering a counting pattern and sequence and continuing it correctly is not as easy as it might be for many youngsters. The consecutive counting of large numbers, counting backwards, skip counting by various patterns, bridging decades and hundreds are not automatic skills. Use some countathon activities for drill in these areas. For a "Count to 300" activity, for example, create a chart by that name with many lines on which to write numbers. Every day, as each child enters the room, he or she "counts" by writing the next number on the chart. The winner is the one who writes the 300. Other variations might be: counting to 300 by 2s, counting back to zero by ones from 300, counting by 10s to 1,000, counting to 500 using even numbers only.

*-Joan Yares Schussheim*

## ADDIE ALLIGATOR

Addition and counting will be extra fun with this Addie Alligator head with detachable parts. First, from green felt make the head. For its wide-open mouth, cut sharp teeth from white felt to attach later. Then, prepare white circular eye pieces and a nose. Place a felt numeral on Addie's nose and have children place that many teeth in Addie's mouth. Or put addition combinations in Addie's eyes; children put the answer on Addie's nose and illustrate with the teeth how they

reached the answer. For example, if the problem is 4 + 2 (on eyes), they place a 6 on the nose and make four teeth the uppers and two the lowers. It will all add up to fun.     *-Lois E. Putnam*

## SHOE-BOX MATH

Here's an instructional aid you can create from shoe boxes to reinforce addition and subtraction facts. Start by printing several addition and subtraction problems, without answers, on index cards, one problem per card. Next, collect a set of 11 shoe boxes to serve as answer

boxes. Cut slits in the boxes large enough for flash cards to slip through easily, then print a different numeral, 0 through 10, on the outside of each box. You might want to arrange the answer boxes to form a freight train or a house, as in the illustration. Students are to draw from the set of flash cards, solve each problem, then place each in the appropriate answer box. For instance, if a child draws the card 6 + 1, he or she should place it in the box labeled 7. On the lid of each shoe box, list the facts that should appear in that specific box, so students can check themselves after they've placed all the cards in their appropriate boxes. Your kids will enjoy this creative variation on addition and subtraction drill.     *-Lisa Barnett*

## CALENDAR MATH

Use calendar pages (any month, any year) as ready-made math worksheets. You can provide drill in addition by having students add each successive numeral in order or in subtraction by having them begin with the largest calendar number and subtracting the smallest, as in $30-1=29-2=27$. Repeat this process until you get a negative number.

For multiplication practice, have students multiply sets of odd and even days of the month. To teach fractions, have them use calendar numerals to create fractions equivalent to $\frac{1}{2}$, $\frac{1}{3}$, $\frac{1}{4}$, $\frac{1}{5}$.

*-Robert L. Friedli*

## LIKE PEAS IN A POD

Pea-pickin' time is math skills time in my class. I cut out many shapes of pea pods and write an addition or subtraction problem on one side. A child chooses a pod and works the problem written on the pod. To solve the problem he or she turns the pod over, where the correct number of peas is drawn in. Then by counting the peas in the pod, he or she can check this total against his or her answer.

*-Lori Stein*

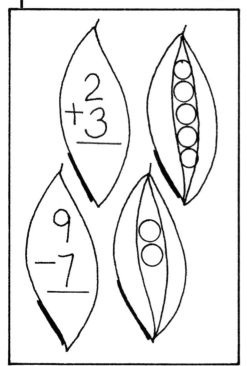

## BIRD FEEDER MATHEMATICS

Looking for a way to enliven your math curriculum on bleak, wintry days? Try a classroom bird feeder that encompasses a host of math skills.

If you choose to *buy* a feeder, have kids use catalogs to compare prices and find the best buy. If you decide to make one, let your students assist you in reading the instructions, purchasing the materials, measuring the wood to proper dimensions, and so on. And when it's time to buy seeds for the feeder, kids can compute cost per ounce to find the most inexpensive.

When the feeder is well stocked, place it outside where it can be seen from a window in your classroom. Then try some of these math activities:

**1.** Have students observe and count the different types of birds that visit the feeder each day during a specified time period. Record findings on a classroom chart.

**2.** Measure the amount of seed eaten by birds each day. Based on that information, can your students determine the average amount consumed by each bird?

**3.** Have kids refer to the cost and weight of a bag of birdseed. Then have them determine approximately how much it costs to feed one bird every day for a week.

Birds will also benefit from these lively activities! *-Paul C. Spector*

## MELT-AWAY MATH

Whose snowman will melt first? Personal snowmen helped my third graders master addition/subtraction number facts. Duplicate a snowman for each pupil. Section and number body into as many parts as you wish. Create as many work sheets as you have sections, each testing one group of addition or subtraction facts. As a pupil completes the first one correctly in the allotted time, he or she can cut off section one of his or her snowman and then move on to the second sheet. Whenever there is an error, the pupil retakes sheet.

The object is to see who can "melt" his snowman first by cutting off all the sections.

*-Linda Pakl*

## HOLLY-DAY MATH

This easy-to-make holiday dominoes game will help kids learn math facts as they enjoy the festive season!

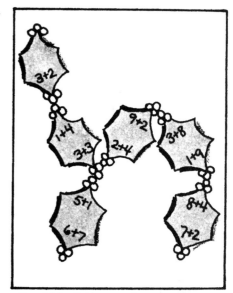

Cut 3″ holly leaves from green tagboard. Add a few hole-punch berries to the ends of each leaf. Then use a marking pen to write equations or solutions on both ends of each leaf. To play, leaves should be divided equally between two players. Children then take turns placing leaves end to end, matching only those ends with equal sums. There may be more than two leaves at any one intersection. The object of the game is to use up all your leaves first. A berry good math activity!

*-Carolyn M. Wilhelm*

## FUNNY FACE SUBTRACTION GAME

After your students have mastered basic subtraction facts, try this game for reinforcement.

You'll need a set of 52 index cards for up to six players. On half the cards, print basic subtraction problems. On the other half, print their answers. Then add an extra card on which you've drawn a funny face. This game is to be played like "Old Maid," with the entire pack of cards dealt to the players. Players should look for matches in their hands and place them faceup in front of them. A match, of course, is a subtraction problem and its correct answer. As players reveal their matches, the rest of the students must check to be sure they're correct. An incorrect match must be returned to the player's hand. After all players have sorted their matches and placed them on the desk or table, the dealer must pick a remaining card from the player on his or her left. Then that player picks from the next student's hand, and so on, until all cards are correctly matched. The player left with the extra card is declared the "funny face."

*-Ruth Ann Johnson*

## FACT FEUD

To play this math game, divide your class into two or three "feuding families." Have everyone line up at the chalkboard. Announce the math operation(s) the game will focus on and call out a number for round one. Each "family member" must then write a fact for that number using the operation(s) for the game. For example, if the game operations were addition and subtraction, and the number was 7, the students might write such combinations as $3 + 4$, $5 + 2$, $9 - 2$, $11 - 4$, and so on. One point is awarded to the family who finishes first. One point is also given for each correct fact. Bonus points are awarded if the whole team gets all its facts correct. No points are given for

facts that do not fit the given number. (To encourage unusual combinations, award points to family members only when someone in their family has not already given that combination.)

*-Cheryl Bartone*

## DOUBLE-DUTY DIGITS

Give young kids a chance to color and count at the same time with reproducibles you can make yourself. Start by sketching the first 10 digits (0-9) onto reproducible masters. Inside these oversized numerals, have a resident artist (Andy Warhol or yourself) draw little persons. When kids see the series, what will they discover? Inside zero, of course, there won't be a child in sight. But the "1" will have one child drawn inside, all the way up to the "9", which has nine tots in all. Kids, with the help of some crayons and coloring time, will get a concrete reminder of what numerals represent. In fact, kids may enjoy drawing the little persons themselves. If you'd like, just reproduce the 10 digits, and leave the artwork up to them.

*-Judy Lynn Tate*

## THE PRICE IS RIGHT

For a different approach to subtraction lessons, try this idea patterned after the popular game show, "The Price Is Right." Place ten empty food boxes with prices still on them in different areas of your classroom. Attach to each box an additional "price tag" that contains a subtraction problem such as: $\$5.37 - \$1.33 = ?$ Students go to each station and complete the problems on the

price tags. If the answer matches the price stamped on the box, the price is right. If the answer is different, the price is wrong and the student must determine the difference between the two numbers and write it on a sheet of paper. After students have visited all ten stations, have them switch papers with the person to their left and check the answers against an answer sheet. If an acceptable percentage of the class has answered all the problems correctly, they are entitled to a special "bonus prize." Inside a large cardboard box, put slips of paper entitling kids to a special privilege such as a short field trip, or a special story-telling session. You'll be surprised at how quickly their subtraction skills improve with this extra shot of motivation.

*-Carolyn Wilhelm*

## PRICING POWER

This classroom version of a TV game show will make practicing subtraction fun for your students. Give each child a pen, pencil, and paper. The object is to bid as closely as possible to the price of a certain piece of merchandise. For the items and prices, use a mail order catalog, sale circulars, or small objects.

First read the description of an item and have students decide on their bids and record them in ink on their papers. Then announce the actual price. Students should use pencil to record this price, then subtract to find the difference between their bid and the actual price. The student closest to the actual price (with the lowest number) is the winner and is eligible for the bonus round. Make sure students know whether they have over- or underbid and how this affects which number is subtracted from the other.

After three to seven rounds, the winners come to the board for the bonus round. A package of items or a special item like a vacation is described. Each player writes his or her bid on the board, then subtracts from the actual price as before to see whether he or she is a big winner. —*Sharon Brinker*

## CARD SHARK MATH

To make math drill fun, all that is needed is a deck of ordinary playing cards with the Jacks, Queens, and Kings removed. Keep the aces to represent one. Shuffle cards and deal them, two at a time, to each of two players. At a given signal, players turn over their cards at the same time. The first one to call out the correct sum of his or her two cards is the winner and gets to keep the cards. The big winner is the one with the most cards at the end of game. To increase difficulty, deal more cards to each one and require the sum. To practice subtraction, instruct students to call out the difference between their highest and lowest cards. Multiplication may also be practiced. This drill will quickly cause the students to learn that knowing a sum automatically enables them to give the answers much faster than they could by counting. —*Sandy Houston*

## THE PROBLEM WITH MATH

Have you found that the word problems presented in most math textbooks are unrelated to your students' interests and experiences? Here's an idea that can change all that. Start by discussing the elements of a good word problem, citing plenty of examples from textbooks. Then divide your class into small groups and instruct each group to come up with four or five word problems of its own. Kids may use newspapers, magazines, reference books, and so on to obtain information for their problems. When each group is finished, pass around a duplicating master and have group members print their problems on it, to be copied and distributed to the class. Repeat this process several times during the year to keep your problem bank filled. —*Sondra Brainin*

## MATH MARATHON

I use this math drill activity to put my fourth graders "through their paces" in computation. Start by making a set of about twenty footprints from construction paper. On one side of each footprint, write a computation problem. You can make it an addition, multiplication, division, or subtraction problem. On the back of the footprint, write the answer to the problem. Next, place the footprints around the room on the floor, close enough together so that a student can step from one to another easily. Each child then takes a turn walking the math marathon trail. To move a step closer to the finish line, he or she must answer the problem on the footprint correctly. If a child misses a problem, the next student in line begins the game and continues until a mistake is make. When a child misses a problem, he or she must sit down and write that problem in a notebook. —*Bruce Lund*

## TAKE ME OUT TO THE BALL GAME!

Possibilities for math problems abound on the back of baseball cards. Addition problems can involve totaling doubles, triples, and home runs for specific players. Have children use subtraction skills to figure out how many more doubles a player hit than triples. Multiplication problems can involve figuring out how many runs a player would hit if he doubled or tripled his total. And don't forget division; ask children to figure out official times at bat per game for players of their choice.

There are countless ideas, including making graphs and figuring percentages. Intermediate-age children can ask each other to figure out batting averages and check their partners' answers with the cards. A player's age can be calculated from his birthdate. Even height and weight statistics can be used to practice metric conversion. —*William Hubbell*

## MATH PROBLEM PHOTOS

My class photographs its math problems! This method not only adds fun to math but also teaches many survival skills.

In small groups the students make up a word problem and decide which steps are needed to solve it. After they arrive at a solution, they illustrate the problem by posing for and taking a photograph.

One such photograph showed two students with price tags attached to their clothes; the word problems that accompanied it were: How much do the two hats cost together? How much more do the overalls cost than the shirt? Whose outfit costs more? We display the photos and the word problems for other students to work. —*Bernie Lucas*

## MATH VOCABULARY ACTIVITIES

If your kids are having trouble with word problems, maybe their real problem is vocabulary. After all, how can kids solve word problems if they don't understand the words? The following activities can help you reinforce your students' general vocabularies and improve their understanding of basic mathematical terms.

1. **Math-term pantomime** Print several mathematical terms your kids have studied on tagboard rectangles, one term on each. Then attach string to the

rectangles so your students can wear them around their necks. Have kids take turns choosing terms and acting out their meanings for the rest of the class.

**2. Around the circle** Have your class form a large circle in the center of your room. Go around the circle, asking each student to name and define a different mathematical term. If a student can't think of one or can't define it correctly, he or she must leave the circle. Terms may not be repeated, so students will have to listen closely.

**3. Teamwork** Have kids work in pairs to solve word problems from texts or workbooks. If one team member doesn't understand a word used in a problem, the other team member must look it up in the dictionary, read the definition silently, and explain it in his or her own words.

*-Sondra Kutzman and Rick Krustchinsky*

## THIRTY-MINUTE MILLIONAIRE

Next time you go to the supermarket, don't throw out the cash register receipt. Save it for class, and ask students to save theirs, too. Gather 35 or 40. Cut off the totals from each receipt. Students will play this game without the benefit of knowing how much each list of items adds up to. Save these totals and make an answer key with them by labeling both pieces of a receipt with the same number.

Announce to students that they should each choose a receipt and add it up. If they get the answer correct, they "win" the dollar amount of that particular receipt. If they add incorrectly, they can choose to try again or pick another tape. Some students will pick several short tapes while others will try adding a longer tape to produce a higher dollar value. Keep track of scores. The "richest" student wins.

*-Judith Brocket*

## TRAVEL

Math facts can be a source of great fun when you put them to use in this simple game. Have a student at the end of a vertical row stand beside the student sitting in front of him or her. Then give them both the same math question. The first one to give the correct answer moves on to stand beside the next student in the row, while the other child must sit down in the seat, whether it is his or her seat or not. Continue in this way through all the rows until one student manages to travel all the way around and back to his or her own seat.

*-Joyce M. Parker*

## COAST-TO-COAST MATH

This activity provides drill in math and helps students visualize the geography of the United States. Begin by drawing an outline of the United States on a large piece of blue construction paper. Draw in the states' boundaries. Label each state and then hang up this blue map in the classroom. Next, draw an identical outline of the country on white construction paper. Again, draw in the states. This time, cut out every state and write math problems on each. Let children choose a state. Then ask them to work all the problems on that state's outline. When they have all the correct answers to the problems, they can glue or tape the state in its proper place on the blue map. If you outline each of the cutout states with a colored magic marker, and ask the children to sign their names to the state they worked on, you will have an unusual class decoration.

*-Doris Cruze*

## HOW BIG IS A DINOSAUR?

If the question is answered with numbers, children will still have a hard time forming an idea of the actual size of a dinosaur. Here's a way you can help bring this concept home to them—by

having them "earn" the length of one of the longest dinosaurs, foot by foot.

Collect some strong tape and as many foot-long strips of sturdy paper as you'll need to make a particular dinosaur's length. Tell students before each activity that if there is at least a certain number of papers (for example, 20) with a certain percentage (80 percent) of correct answers, they can add one strip of paper to the roll which will represent the dinosaur's length. (Determine the number of correct answers and papers for each activity, based on its difficulty.) Keep the roll of paper (to which new strips are taped after each successful activity) rolled up and clipped to keep it in good condition. When the whole length of the dinosaur has been earned, take the children outside or to a long hall. Space them so they can hold the roll as you unroll it. They'll then be able to see and appreciate just how long a dinosaur was.

*-Sandra Frey*

## SNEAKY SNAKE CROSS-OUT

Draw a sneaky-looking snake and a dreadful dragon. (Check coloring books for inspiration or use the reproducibles on the following pages.) On each, write the numerals 1-12. Paste these creatures, complete with numbers down their backs, onto cardboard to make two game boards (for practicing subtraction and addition).

Take two cubes and put the numerals 1-6 on one. Put the numerals 0-6 on the other, leaving off the numeral 1.

Two players will choose a game board and will take turns rolling the two dice. They'll cover up *either* the sum or the difference of the numbers that come up on the roll. If there are already markers on both the sum *and* the difference, the player has to pass. The first player to cover his or her board wins.

*-Judy Lynn Tate*

# Sneaky Snake Game Board

Duplicate this text and mount on cardboard to make individual game boards for math drill. See page 101 for ideas.

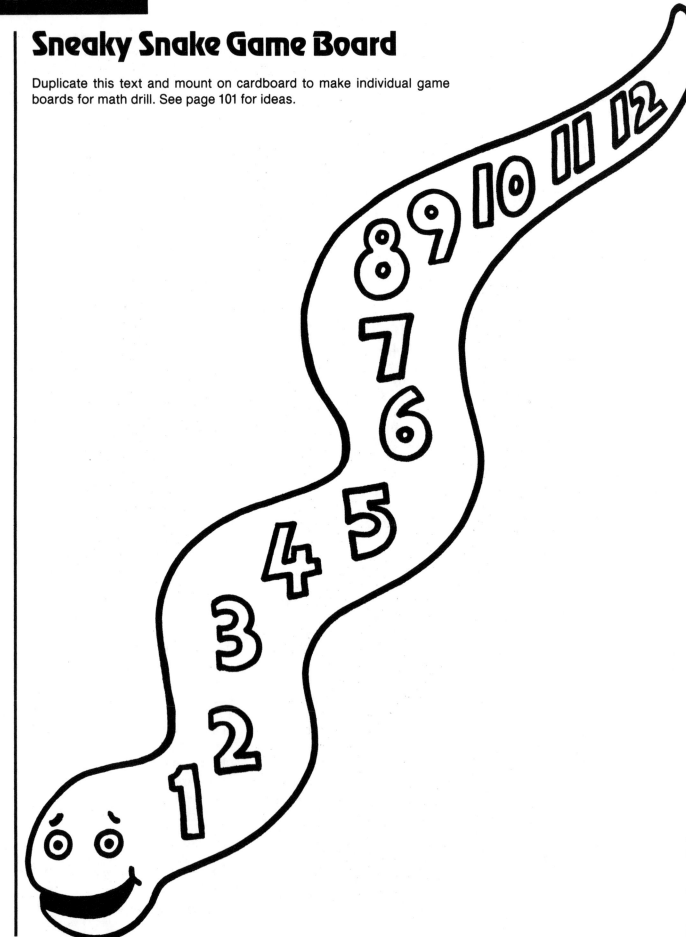

# Dreadful Dragon
# Game Board

Duplicate this page and mount on cardboard to make individual game boards for math drill. See page 101 for ideas.

### AN AFTERNOON OF MATH

Who said mathematics drill has to be dull? When it's organized around an afternoon of unusual games that reinforce skills and concepts, your kids will learn and enjoy themselves at the same time! Following are five games you might want to try with your students. Start by setting up five different stations in your room—one for each of the games described below—and divide the class into five groups. Assign a different color to each group and have the kids make name tags out of appropriately colored construction paper. You should also enlist the help of five parent volunteers to act as group leaders and assure that rotation of the groups from station to station runs smoothly.

**Arithmetic Bingo** At this station, you'll have to provide bingo cards for each child and several small flash cards, each containing a different unanswered equation. The answers to these equations should be printed on the bingo cards. The group leader is to hold up the flash cards as children

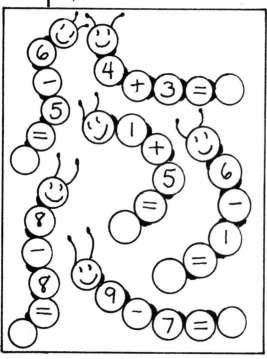

look for the answers on their bingo cards and cover them with red construction-paper discs. The first child to cover a horizontal, vertical, or diagonal row of numbers is the winner.

**Get my taillight right!** You'll need a two-minute egg timer or hourglass for this station; eight brightly colored tagboard cards, approximately 11″ x 14″; 240 green construction-paper discs, and 48 red ones. Use each tagboard card for mounting six "equation worms." These are made by gluing five green discs together. The first disc should represent the worm's head and the next four should each contain different parts of simple, unanswered math equations (see illustration below). Print the answers to these equations on the red discs, which represent the worms' "taillights." The object of the game is for students to match the worms with their appropriate taillights to answer all the equations within two minutes.

**Problems in a nutshell** This station should be set up near a water fountain because all your kids will be eating their share of peanuts! Supply one or two large bags of unshelled peanuts and several sheets of paper that have been divided into six equal squares. The kids are to choose two peanuts from the bag, remove their shells, and arrange the nuts in a row in front of them. Each child is then to decide on an equation based on the number of peanuts found inside the two shells and print it in one of the squares provided. After an equation is written, the children may eat the peanuts and select two more for the next equation. Play continues until all six squares are filled.

**Bean-bag toss** Start with a large sheet of poster board or heavy cardboard and divide it into 16 equal squares. Print one number in each square and place the sheet on the floor. The children are to pitch four bean bags each and write down the numbers they land on. These numbers will be the answers to equations the kids must write themselves. The first child to write four equations correctly is the winner and may start the game again.

**Equations in a bottle** Divide the groups into pairs for this clothespin-throwing activity. Set three or four wide-mouthed bottles or jars on the floor and give each pair several clothespins with equations printed on them in felt-tipped pen. One member of each pair is to stand a designated distance from one of the bottles and attempt to drop as many clothespins as possible inside it. The other student is to remove the clothespins from the jar, read the equations aloud, and check his or her partner's answers. When all the clothespins have been thrown and the equations answered correctly, the partners switch places and play continues.

*-Gretchen Huff*

### MAKING GRAPHS ABOUT REAL LIFE

Making graphs about events in students' lives is an effective way to introduce graph skills. The "birthday graph" is easy to make and use. Make a chart on a large piece of construction paper by drawing in vertical lines to make 12 columns. Label the columns at the bottom of the sheet with the months of the year. Then have each child draw a self-portrait on a small piece of paper. Label each picture with the child's name. Next, ask the children to place their pictures on the chart in the appropriate vertical column. After several chidren have placed

THE FRUITS WE LIKE BEST

MONA

SAM · ANN · NICK

SUE · PETE · SALLY · HANK

APPLE · BANANA · STRAWBERRY · PINEAPPLE

their pictures on the chart, ask them how many birthdays are in each month and what month has the most class birthdays.

This type of vertical line graph can be used to graph other things such as holidays, favorite foods, colors, numbers, the weather, and the different ways students get to school. All you have to do is change the labels for the columns and then use the same pictures of the students to graph with, or make simple cutouts to take the place of written words. For instance, with a weather graph, cut out shapes of the sun, umbrellas, and clouds. Then place the correct pictures in the monthly column so at the end of the month students can count up the number of rainy or sunny days. *-Barbara Bethel*

## GRAPHING WITH M&MS

Graphing is a skill that most students learn slowly and grudgingly, but you'll be surprised at how quickly they can learn when M&Ms are involved in the process. Begin by giving each child his or her own small package of M&Ms. Ask the students to predict how many candies of each color are in their packages, and using an overhead projector and a grease pencil, make a bar graph and a line graph of their predictions. Now divide the class into pairs. Each pair is to make a bar graph showing the color distribution in one package of M&Ms and a line graph for the other. When everyone is finished, discuss how their predictions differed from the actual graphs; then let them eat the M&Ms—this is the part they are sure to enjoy the most. Two things to remember: (1) Be sure to plan the activity for some time after lunch, and (2) Keep sugarless snacks available for those who can't eat candy.

*-Karen McGillivray*

## GRAPH-MATICS

Working math functions on graph paper gets children into the good habit of writing numbers in straight columns, always an aid to accuracy.

Teaching graphing is, of course, another use for this paper. Even very young children can compile, and begin to understand, simple graphs. Tack on your bulletin board two pieces of one-inch graph paper lengthwise to make one double-size sheet. At the bottom of each column to be used, place an upward-pointing arrow to indicate the starting place for the bars and the direction in which they will be built. Number the boxes in the column from the bottom up. At the top of one column you might print, "I like ice cream"; on the other, "I do not like ice cream." (Pictures may be used for nonreaders. Older students can express an opinion on current events.) Each child places his or her name in a box in the appropriate column, following the numerical sequence. The result is a simple bar graph.

Graph paper bingo games utilizing math skills provide both drill and fun. To play, block off an 11 x 11 square, using one-inch paper for young students, half-inch for older ones. In the top left corner box, place the math symbol you will use: $+$, $-$, or x. In the row to the right of the symbol, write in random order the numbers 0 through 9. Do the same in the column below the symbol and you're ready. Let's use multiplication as an example. The leader calls out "36." The player writes 36 in the box where 4 meets 9, 6 meets 6 or 9 meets 4. (He or she can write in just one box, not all three.) The first to complete a row says "Bingo!" In a similar game called "Times Race," an 11 x 11 square is again used, a times symbol put in the top left corner, and the numbers 0 to 9 written in the top row and the left column. (Start by placing them in consecutive order; later, random order can be used.) At the signal, the player fills in the table as fast as he or she can. The elasped time is noted and the next time the student plays, he or she tries to beat that time.

*-Mary A. Lombardo*

## MAKING GEOMETRY SIMPLE

Use these ideas to teach concepts of geometry with common materials and visuals found in your classroom.

**Points and lines**—The concept of a point is difficult to grasp because it must be represented by a dot which has length, width, and thickness. Actually, a dot only represents a position in space. A line represents the motion of a point.

Make a straight line by sticking two pins in cardboard and stretching a string between them. Fold a piece of paper; the crease is a straight line. A horizontal line may be demonstrated by showing that it is parallel to the surface of water in a glass; a telephone pole is a good representation of a vertical line.

**Angles and triangles**—An angle is formed when two lines meet. Children can discover this by opening a pair of scissors or looking at the hands of a clock. The principle that the angle of incidence is the same as the angle of reflection can be demonstrated by rolling balls against a board. This knowledge can be put to use in basketball, tennis, or handball.

The concept of right angle can be taught with a pendulum. The pendulum at rest forms a right angle to the table.

**Circles and ellipses**—The relation of a circle to its diameter can be tested by putting a pencil mark on a tin can and touching the mark against the end of a ruler. Roll the can until it has made one complete turn. Read the circumference on the ruler, measure the diameter and divide the circumference by this number. The result is the constant known as *pi*.

Tilt a glass half full of water. The shape of the water's surface is an ellipse. An ellipse can also be demonstrated by shining the beam of a flashlight against a wall at an angle. To draw a perfect ellipse, put two pins in a piece of cardboard. Lay a loop of thread over the pins, put the point of a pencil in the loop, and draw completely around, keeping the loop tight.

**Parabolas, spirals, and helices**— Parabolas (something bowl-shaped) are familiar as a football sailing through the air, a stream of water shooting from a hose, or the cables hanging on a suspension bridge.

A spiral may be shown by winding string around a nail and pushing the nail into cardboard. Loop one end of the string around a pencil. Place the pencil point on the cardboard and go around and around the nail, unwinding the string.

The helix is a spiral that goes around a center. Make a helix by cutting a narrow paper triangle 3″ on the short side and 10″ on the long side. Starting with the short side, wrap the paper onto a pencil. *-Harold P. Hormel*

## YOUR BEST ANGLE

Teach angle measurement with your overhead projector. Use a black grease pencil and a clear plastic protractor to draw the angle on the overhead. Then project the image on a screen in front of the classroom where everyone can see it. Place the protractor on the angle so the students can see both the angle and the numbers on the protractor. Demonstrate how to read the measurement. Repeat this procedure several times, erasing the angle each time. Complete the lesson by giving pupils a work sheet where they measure a number of given angles. It is most effective to teach acute and right angles first and obtuse and straight angles after the class has mastered the preceding lesson. When a certain degree of competency has been shown, mix the various angles— acute, obtuse, and so on and change their positions on the paper. Put them on a slant, rather than straight up and down.
*-Arlene Page*

## KALEIDOSCOPES ON STRINGS

Here's a creative art idea that will also reinforce your students' knowledge of the basic geometric shapes. Have each child cut a different shape from colored construction paper each day for a week or so. For instance, assign blue squares one day, orange circles the next, and so on. After the kids have made several different-colored shapes, help them string them together on pieces of yarn long enough to extend from the top of your window to the bottom. Hang the "kaleidoscopes" from the ceiling,

and you'll have a colorful window display that can reinforce your next geometry unit. *-Peggy Dewire*

## LET'S GO SHOPPING

Adding and subtracting dollars and cents is a difficult skill for some children to master. Provide extra practice in a fun form by using empty egg-carton "stores." Place a toy grocery item (purchased in toy section of most stores or ordered from dollhouse supply catalog) in each section of carton. (Cutouts can be substituted, but children love the miniatures.) Write the price of each item in its corresponding position on a paper diagram pasted to inside lid of carton. Children then work in pairs. One selects several items from the carton and writes their prices in a column on paper. He totals them and the partner adds the same items. They both compare answers. If they agree, the shopper uses play paper money to pay for the purchase,

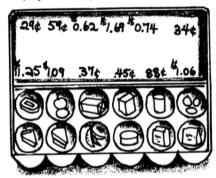

subtracting the price, and figuring out the correct amount of change. The partner also checks this step. Then they change places. This is one math assignment that children will frequently ask to have repeated! *-Jeannine Mann*

## SHAPEY SAYS

Young children sometimes have trouble discriminating between different geometric shapes, but this task is more fun when it's patterned after the popular game, "Simon Says." Have each child cut out a set of large geometric shapes from poster board or oaktag. Then move to an open area and have the children place their shapes on the floor in front of them. Call out directions to the students; those who follow them correctly are allowed to stay in the game. For example, ask them to place their shapes in a specific order, put their left foot on the rectangle, or hold the triangle above their heads.    *-Lorraine Lee*

## CONSUMING MATH

You can make wise consumers out of your students and reinforce their math skills at the same time by turning your classroom into a mini shopping mall. How do you do it? By making several learning centers around your room, each representing a different type of store found in a typical mall. You can make a grocery store stocked with empty food boxes, cans, and cartons; a restaurant complete with menus, tablecloth, and place settings; a travel agency with maps and brochures from resort areas; a pet shop with pamphlets on the care and feeding of domestic animals, and so on. Each station or "shop" should contain several task cards at different levels of difficulty to be completed by each student before he or she moves on to the next area. These task cards should involve word problems and exercises using the computations and other math concepts like fractions, measurement, and percentages. Following are a few examples of task cards you might make for a classroom pet shop. You'll need to provide a list of common pet shop items and their prices for these activities.

**1.** You went to the pet shop to purchase a leash, a bowl, and a rawhide bone for your dog. How much money did you spend?

**2.** You want to buy two packages of colored rocks and some foliage for your fish tank. Your dad gave you five dollars to spend. Will you have enough money? Will you take home any change? If so, how much?

**3.** The pet store is offering 10 percent discounts on all purchases. How much will that fancy bird cage cost you now? How much money will you be saving on the purchase?

For extra motivation, try setting up a "First Classroom Bank of Arithmetic," with you acting as banker. Give the kids daily "allowances" in the form of tokens and let them make purchases at each station. Have the children make personal account sheets of money earned and spent throughout the project. You'll be surprised at how quickly they learn the value of money when they have to balance purchases against their income!

*-Pam Robinson*

## CORRECT CHANGE

Many children and most adults are able to count correct change if an electronic cash register tells them how much to give back. But when the machine is broken or a customer gives a penny or two extra, some children can't figure out the correct change. During the last five or ten minutes of a class, challenge students with "correct change" problems. Give the class a total amount of a purchase and the amount given by the customer. Then ask them to figure out the change to return. For instance: "If I buy a record for $6.27 and give you $10.07, what is my change?" You can make the problems as elaborate as the class can handle. After a few weeks, ask the students to make up their own problems, which you can draw from a box and recite to the class. A few months of this drill and your students will have no difficulty giving or getting the correct change.    *-Carolyn Roberts*

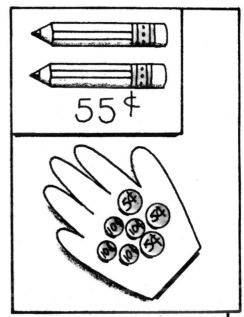

## WHO WILL BUY?

Here's a handy game for practicing math skills. Prepare two sets of cards, with as many cards in each set as there are students in your class. On each card in one set draw a human hand. Glue pictures of various coins to the palm. (Each palm should total a different amount.) For the second set glue a picture of a different item on each card, listing its price underneath. For each price in this set there should be a corresponding amount of coins on one of the hands in set one. Now give everyone two cards, one from each set. First have students count the coins in their hands, then let one student offer his or her item for sale. The person with the correct amount for that item should "buy" it and then offer his or her own item for sale. Continue in this way until all items have been purchased.

*-Lucile M. Knauss*

## MONEY, MONEY, MONEY

Here are some challenge-activities to use in connection with a money unit:

**1.** How many dimes are in a stack ½" high?

**2.** A pile of nickels 2 centimeters high contains how many nickels?

**3.** Stack one each of the different U.S. coins. How many centimeters high is your stack?

**4.** Choose coins to make one dollar.

**5.** Choose 6 coins or bills. Arrange them according to their value: lowest to highest.

**6.** Arrange 50 cents four different ways. Can you think of any other ways to make 50 cents?

**7.** Tell what these slang words mean in money: buck ($1 bill), two bits (a quarter), sawbuck ($10 bill), fin ($5 bill).

**8.** Find out why a coin has ridges on its edge.

**9.** Find out what these phrases mean:
Pennywise and pound foolish.
Pin money.
Don't take any wooden nickels.
A penny saved is a penny earned.
Put your money on the barrelhead.
A pretty penny.           *-Betty White*

## MANY PENNY CANDY

If your pupils are chewing gum or eating candy, do they know how much it costs? Have them find out with the help of simple mathematics. If a candy bar that weighs one ounce costs 15 cents, how much does that candy cost per pound? Multiply 16 (the number of ounces in a pound) times 15 cents. That candy costs $2.40 a pound! That's a lot of money! One candy, very similar to grape-flavored sugar, costs 10 cents for one quarter of an ounce. That is $6.40 a pound! When children figure out how much their candy is costing them, they begin to see apples, oranges, and other fruits as a real nutritional bargain!
*-Richard Latta*

## COUNTING COINS

Here's a fun exercise that helps your students learn to count coins and distinguish between their different monetary values. Fill a small box with play money—quarters, nickels, dimes, pennies,

and a few silver dollars and 50 cent pieces as well. Have the children sit in a circle on the floor and start the game by handing the box to one child. He or she is to empty the box, close it, and pass it on to the next person. The child with the coins in front of him or her has to determine the correct amount of money that was in the box before it gets passed around the circle and is returned to him or her again. If he or she counts correctly, a different amount of coins is put in the box, and the child chooses someone else in the circle to begin the game again.           *-Lorraine Lee*

## INTRODUCING THE MEASUREMENT OF TIME

Two types of ancient clocks, the Egyptian water clock and the European sandglass, provide much more graphic examples of the passing of time than today's clocks do. Give a quick lesson in measuring time by making these ancient models.

To make sand or salt clocks, start with three sheets of construction or writing paper. Roll these into cone-shaped funnels and tape the seams. Make the openings of the funnels different sizes. Then find a two-liter bottle with a mouth large enough to hold the narrow

SALT TIMER
WATER CLOCK

ends of the three funnels. Place the funnels in the opening of the bottle one by one, starting with the funnel with the smallest opening. Fill the funnel full of salt or sand and note the time it takes for the material to empty into the bottle. The funnel with the smallest opening will, of course, be the slowest to empty.

To make the water clock, cut off the top third of a large, plastic soda bottle. When turned upside down, this part forms a funnel. Collect three bottle caps for the end of the funnel, and punch holes of different sizes in each one. Then test and time the cap with the smallest hole by screwing it onto the funnel and placing the funnel cap-end down in the bottom piece of the cut-up bottle. Fill the funnel with water and note the time it takes for the water to empty. Repeat this with the other two bottle caps.
*-Sylvia Weldon*

## COUPON MATH

Don't throw away those coupons that come in the mail. Youngsters love to do math using coupons. Duplicate question sheets similar to this sample and staple one coupon at the top of each sheet. Include such activities as:

**1.** If you use this coupon, how much will you have to pay for the item? Write an equation.

**2.** Draw a picture of the coins you would use to pay for it. Use the fewest coins possible.

**3.** If you pay for it with _____(I fill in the blank with an appropriate collection of coins such as ''a quarter and a dime''), how much change will you receive? Write an equation.

As children learn new math skills, plan problems so they'll need to regroup as they subtract. A supply of toy money may prove helpful in solving some of the problems.           *-Bea Schannen*

## MULTIPLICATION BEE

If a spelling bee can motivate students to learn basic spelling rules, why not use this type of contest with math skills as well? That is what I did with my fifth graders when they started to stumble on their multiplication tables.

Of course, a "bee" of any sort is easy to manage. Just have all your students stand and ask them to sit down when they miss a question. Last one standing is the winner. But I was looking for a way to keep everyone in the game longer, and my solution was to set up an inter-class competition. Once the students saw themselves as a team, they began to help each other and to work as a unit.

The teachers of all classes involved in the competition met to decide on a date for the "bee." We decided the children would need three weeks to prepare. And did we ever underestimate the competitive fire of our students! Within a week no one was sitting down, and we were asking questions from the tables from 0 to 12. We went up to 15 and they stayed right with it; so I started giving them problems with a single multiplier and a two- or three-digit multiplicand!

*-Anne Westbrook*

## MULTIPLICATION HURDLES

Try this neat activity to review multiplication facts. Start by making 10 tagboard "hurdles." Fold 12" sheets of tagboard in half so they stand upright. Then print a different number from 0 through 9 on each one, and place them in random order in a row on your classroom floor. Now print a different number from 2 through 9 on a set of index cards, one number per card, and place them in a small box. When you're ready to play, divide your class into two teams. Have the first player draw a card and read the number on it aloud. He or she must then

multiply that number by the number printed on the first hurdle. If the answer is correct, the player may jump over the hurdle and try the same thing with the next hurdle. If the player jumps over all 10 hurdles holding one card, a point is scored for that team. If a player answers incorrectly, a member of the other team may draw the next card and try to jump the first hurdle for his or her team. Play continues until all the cards have been drawn from the box and answered correctly. The highest-scoring team wins.

*-Sandra S. Click*

## TYPEWRITER MATH

Letting students use a typewriter to illustrate number facts adds to their comprehension of the multiplication process and gives them practice at the same time. Sample examples might look like this:

```
 #   #   #   #   #
 #   #   #   #   #
 #   #   #   #   #
     3 × 5 = 15

     &   &   &
     &   &   &
     &   &   &
     3 × 3 = 9
```

*-Isobel Livingstone*

## MULTIPLICATION TABLES DRAG RACE

Do your students think that learning the times tables is a real drag? Then turn the task into a drag *race* instead! Set up a model racetrack on your bulletin board. The track should have 11 rows—one for every times table between 2 and 12. Then have kids make their own racing cars from construction paper and print their names on them. Tack each car to your bulletin board, beside or below the racetrack. Also tack a sign-up sheet to the board and explain to students that they may sign up for as many races as they choose, but that they shouldn't sign up for races unless they know the times tables for the

corresponding tracks. If a student signs up for race number three, for example, quiz that child on the three times table sometime during the day. If he or she is able to recite the table correctly, place his or her car in the appropriate row on the track. Make sure you keep a record of the times tables each student has learned. The first student to "race" his or her car through every row is the winner!

*-Lorraine Lauri*

## MATH MUSICAL CHAIRS

This game is played for multiplication practice, but it can be used for practice in any other math skill as well. It's played like Musical Chairs. Each child brings one chair to an empty corner of the room, and chairs are put in a circle with one chair in the middle. Children walk outside the circle of chairs, rotating as they would for a game of Musical Chairs. Instead of playing music, though, a student chosen to be the leader holds up flash cards with multiplication facts written on them, reads the problem, and gives the answer. ($3 × 6 = 18$) As long as the answers are correct, students keep walking around the circle; as soon as the leader makes a mistake, children scramble for a chair. The one left without a chair sits in the chair in the middle (the witch's cauldron), to be boiled and bubbled. The leader continues calling out facts as before, children again walk around the chairs, and when a mistake is made everyone, including the child in the cauldron, scrambles for a chair. The child left is now the one to sit in the middle chair.      -Muriel Radebaugh

## ROUND THE WORLD WITH MATH

Students who master their times tables will become world travelers when you use this math motivator. First, cover a large bulletin board with blue paper to represent water. Then draw the continents of the world on the paper. (It may be easier to make a transparency of a world map and then use your overhead projector to trace an outline of the continents.) After labeling the continents divide your board into 10 spaces by stapling nine lengths of black yarn from top to bottom, equal distances apart. Along the top of the board, number each column 1 through 10. At the bottom of each column, fasten an envelope containing its corresponding fact cards. For example, column one would have the ones times facts; column two, the two times facts, column three, the three times facts, and so on. As a child satisfactorily answers the ones number facts, he or she may place a paper rocket or ship anywhere in the ones column. He or she then proceeds in order through the facts and around the world. This continues until everyone has completed a world tour. You may wish to award a prize to the first student who completes the trip, or even prizes to pupils who travel the farthest in one week. It is also a good idea to set a time limit. For example: "Let's all be in Europe by spring vacation."      -Betty Dale

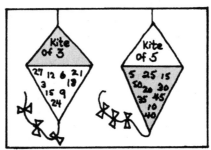

## FLYING HIGH

Emphasize multiplication fact memorization in your classroom with this "flying high" approach. Use kites suspended from your classroom ceiling on strings. Name each "flying object" for one set of multiplication facts, such as "Kite of 5," and have multiples of five printed all over it.

Students will enjoy this variation in classroom decoration and will point to the multiples on the kites and give the corresponding number sentences. Students' names may be written on the different bows that make up the tail of the kite. For example, when Joe learns the five times facts, he may add his name to the Kite of 5. Corresponding work sheets for the kites can be made for either multiplication or division.

If real kites are used, the math class can actually fly them when they are no longer needed, on some windy afternoon.

      -Carolyn M. Wilhelm

## BREAKDOWN MATH

Make the step from doing simple multiplication facts to multiplying multidigit numbers easier by breaking the problems down into nonthreatening sizes.

First cut sheets of 8-by-11 paper into fourths, and give each child three pieces. To multiply a number such as 437 x 8, have students first multiply 7 x 8 on one of the sheets of paper. Have them multiply 30 x 8 on the second sheet, and 400 x 8 on the third sheet. Tell them to fold the sheets so that only the products (56, 240, 3,200) show; line these

products up vertically along the ones' side. Finally, ask students to add the products for the final answer.

After mastering this system, students will often take shortcuts, such as putting all the steps on the same sheet of paper. Eventually, many children will take the final step of solving the problem as it appears on their own.

Use the same method for a problem such as 347 x 35. Students multiply 347 x 5 on one sheet, 347 x 30 on another, line up the products, and add them for the answer.      -Daniel Ellerbrook

## MULTIPLICATION CONCENTRATION GAME

You can introduce your students to unfamiliar multiplication tables with this fun card game that's modeled after the game called Concentration. Begin by cutting 24 small cards from white construction paper (approximately 2″ x 3″). On each one of the first 12 cards, print a multiplication equation (answer included) pertaining to whatever table you'd like to teach. With the remaining 12 cards, make a duplicate set of equations, so that each will have a matching card. When the 24 cards are completed, shuffle them and singly place them facedown in neat rows on a table or desk to begin play. For optimum "concentration" the recommended number of players is two. The first player picks a card and turns it over in place. He must read the equation aloud and attempt in one try to locate the matching card. If successful, he keeps both cards after reading the equation aloud once more. Then he picks another card to begin the process again. If the player is unsuccessful at matching on the first try, he must place the cards facedown again in their proper places after reciting both equations. The second player then takes his turn, and the game continues until all the cards have been matched. The player with the most pairs in his hand at the end of the game wins. After the multiplication equations used in the first game have been mastered, try this variation as a follow-up activity. Divide the cards into two sets as before, but this time, print the equations *without* the answers on the first 12 cards. Print the answers only on the remaining cards. Have kids play this game in the same manner as before, trying to match question cards with answer cards. Students will memorize multiplication equations almost automatically while improving powers of concentration.

*-Joan B. Murphy*

## CALCULATOR GAMES

In addition to figuring number problems, calculators can be used in a variety of enjoyable ways that will give children familiarity with math operations, decimals, fractions, odd and even numbers, and other mathematical elements. When kids have become proficient calculator users, encourage them to make up their own problems and games — meanwhile, here are a few to get you started.

**Find the number** Divide students into teams, then write a large number on the board, such as 1476383. The object of the game is to combine various numbers and operations that will result in this number. Start the teams off by giving them a simple problem like $3 \times 9$ to calculate, then let them devise their own calculations from there. First team to reach 1476383 wins.

**Secret agent** Assign numbers to the letters of the alphabet (a = 1, b = 2, and so on). Then give a series of clues such as $4 + (3 \times 2)$ that kids should calculate. The number in each answer will represent a letter. Give clues so

that the resulting letters will spell out a message. (You might want to make the code more complicated — a = 17, b = 9, and so on.)

**Calculator lottery** Write numbers, fractions, or decimals in separate one-inch squares of cardboard. Place these in a large empty juice can. Have kids take turns picking two numbers from the can and using their calculators to add, multiply, or divide both numbers to get the highest number possible with each turn. Player with the highest score wins.

**Check the invaders** Draw several space figures on the board and assign each one a number. You also might give them names, such as Dork — 80, Menbon — 48, Zickwol — 34. Then designate certain numbers as "ammunition," such as 6, 8, 10, 15, and so on. Students are to use these ammunition numbers to perform subtraction and division operations that will eliminate the invaders by resulting in answers of 0 or 1. For example, suppose 10 and 4 were two ammunition numbers. To fight Dork — 80, a student could divide by 10 to get 8, then subtract 4 and another 4 to get 0. As each student is able to check an invader, he or she can add that invader's number to his or her score; the person with the highest score wins.

**Problem time** Write several figures on the board such as the number of miles from your city to Los Angeles. Then give children a problem to solve, using these numbers; "I am going twice as far as Los Angeles is from here. How many miles do I have to travel?"

*-Dorothy and Sandy Zjawin*

## METRIC RECORDS

Believe it or not, I have found an enjoyable way for children to practice converting weights, temperatures, and other measurements into metric units.

Go to any book of records and find unique records of measurements for your class to convert. For example, the longest recorded fingernail was 24½" or 62.33 centimeters long. The smallest working violin is 2" or 5.08 centimeters long. The lowest temperature ever recorded outdoors was −126.9 degrees Fahrenheit or −52 degrees Celsius. Choose funny or amazing records that will get the students' interest. This will lead the class to computing records in different categories among themselves: longest hair, smallest feet, shortest pencil. They'll have fun converting and keeping these facts, just for the record.

*-Rebecca Friary*

## TEAM FACTORING

You can make even the most routine math operation come alive if you turn it into a team sport— and factoring is no exception. For this lively activity, divide your class into two equal teams; then print the numerals 1 through 40 on the chalkboard. The first team is to choose one of the numerals and attempt to identify all the factors for it that are listed on the chalkboard. Erase each factor as it is identified so it may not be used again in the game. Each team will receive a score equal to the sum of the factors identified. The teams are to take turns choosing numerals and calling out factors until all the numerals have been erased. *-Barbara Bethel*

## NUMBER NEWS

Here's a surefire way to make math one of your students' favorite subjects: publish a math newspaper for your school! The paper can be published once a month, with a class production meeting held once a week. Assign a different student to be in charge of each column; you can include math word searches, activity sheets for lower grades, math comics, optical illusions, and articles such as "Famous Math

People," "Jobs and Math," or "Metric Trivia." Rotate editors each month. Set aside one column for "Math Problems of the Month." For this column, seven students should think up story problems, one for each grade level, K-6, for students in other classes to solve. As the answers come in, have each writer correct the responses to his or her problem. Students who answer the problems correctly can receive a "Math Genius" ribbon or certificate and have their names published in the next issue.                    *-Michael Paskewicz*

## PARTNERS IN MATH

Partners make math proficiency easier. Try this procedure. On Monday, a new concept is introduced by the teacher. Then desks are pushed close and partners work together. Tuesday, children work alone; if they run into trouble, they consult partner. Wednesday, work alone; partner checks work and points out mistakes. Thursday, work alone; teacher corrects; partners determine why examples were wrong. Friday, work alone; teacher corrects and records marks.

Each week a math family is reviewed, for example, 12. Work for that week: addition, subtraction, or problems, include combinations of 12. There are duplicated sheets, records, cards, games.                        *-Rosalie Beck*

## MONSTER MATH

This card game, called Monster Math, is a popular way to drill math combinations. Prepare a deck of 31 cards — 15 of math problems (2 × 8), 15 of the problems' answers (16), and one card to be the monster card. Three to six players can play. Deal out the entire deck. Players sort out any pairs they have, place them on the table, and read them aloud. Play as you would play Old Maid. Each player picks

one card blindly from the player at the left. After a turn, everyone puts down any new pairs. Play continues until a player doesn't have any more cards. The one left holding the monster card is the Monster for that game.

Cards can be made to drill on all sorts of combinations — addition, subtraction, multiplication, division, word problems. To keep the game moving quickly, however, problems should be those that are easily solved mentally.          *-Joan Yares Schussheim*

## NUMERAL PSEUDONYMS

Take a large piece of cardboard, about the size of a pizza box, and divide it into four sections. In each section, draw four horizontal rows of circles, with three circles in each row. In the middle circle of each row, draw one of the operational signs, $+$, $-$, $\times$, and $\div$; leave other circles blank. In middle of cardboard write a number, such as 36. Provide the four players in this game with construction paper markers on which different numbers are printed. Players take turns trying to find other "names" for 36 (6 $\times$ 6, 20 + 16, and so on) by placing their numbered markers in the blank circles in their own section. (Circles may be used more than once; for example, if a student places a 30 and a 6 in the circles on either side of the $+$ circle, on the next turn he or she can then use a 10 and 26 in the same circles.) The player who completes the most combinations for the number shown in the center is the winner.

*-Dorothy Zjawin*

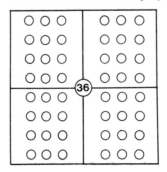

## MC MATH

When pupils begin learning long division, the many steps involved are often confusing. To aid them in remembering, teach them this sentence, "*Does McDonald's Serve Cheeseburgers?*" The main consonant sounds tell the steps to take — Does, divide; McDonald's, multiply; Serve, subtract; Cheese, compare; burgers, bring down. This surefire device has worked for my pupils for several years.     *-Dawn Bonelli*

## ROUNDING TO THE NEAREST STANLEY

Kids in my middle school class always had trouble with rounding numbers. I decided they needed to picture rounding off in personal terms, so I taught them to round off to the nearest Stanley or Melinda. Suddenly rounding off was easy and even a bit of fun! Call five or six people to the front of the room. Hand them each a sheet of paper and a felt marker to write a digit from 0 to 9. Pin the papers to students' backs, and have them stand in a row facing the wall.

Example: Melinda, George, Stanley, Juan, Lisa, and Sue choose 5, 7, 1, 4, 9, and 4 respectively. The class sees the number 571,494. Now, let's round off to the nearest Stanley. Find Stanley. Ask him to look at the person directly to his right, Juan. Is Juan less or more than 5? If Juan was more than 5, he'd be big enough to change Stanley. But he's less than 5, so Stanley will stay as he is. Shattered at his ineffectiveness, Juan becomes a zero! In a chain reaction, Lisa turns into a zero. So does Sue. Melinda and George, in higher positions than Stanley, just stay as they are. As a result, 571,494 rounded to the nearest Stanley becomes 571,000.

How do we round off to the nearest Melinda? We follow the same basic steps. Melinda looks to her right. Is George's number enough to change her? Yes, George is more than 5 and Melinda is changed forever into the next higher number. But, heartlessly, Melinda discards George and he becomes a nothing. So do all the numbers to George's right! The number 571,494 rounded to the nearest Melinda becomes 600,000. (To move on to decimal notation, I place a stool between Juan and Lisa and call it a decimal point.) Your students will giggle and groan as they get rounded and zeroed, but they'll never forget how to do it.  *-Bob Schultz*

## FRACTION BINGO

For this math activity you will need to buy or make bingo cards for your students. In each square on the cards draw a shape that is

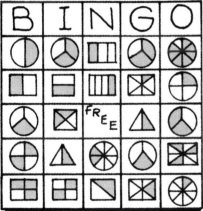

divided into clearly identifiable sections. Then shade in a section of the whole shape. Next, make the call cards for the game. You can use index cards for this. Draw a horizontal line across the middle of each card. Above the line write one of the letters in the word "bingo." Under the line write a fraction that describes the amount of area shaded in one or more of the shapes on the students' cards. To play the game, place the cards facedown, pick one at a time, and call what appears on the card. Students

must then try to locate a shape on their cards that has the same fraction of area shaded and is in the column you called. Continue to follow the regular rules of bingo, calling one letter and fraction at a time and giving students a short amount of time to see if they have a match on their cards.  *-Lorraine Lee*

## FRACTION ACTION

This homework assignment will help students realize the importance of understanding fractions. Ask children to find as many examples of fractions in their homes as they can, and to report on them to the class. They may be surprised to find that their favorite toy was bought for one-third off the original price, or that their favorite team is only one-half game out of first place. They will discover that foods are measured in fractions and that fractions are a part of almost every recipe. Extend this project by collecting some of the recipes that contain fractions. By simply writing out the recipes on construction paper, punching holes in each sheet, and joining them together with yarn, you can create your class cookbook of Marvelous Mathematical Munchies!

*-Rebecca Friary*

## FRACTIONS OVERHEAD

Four overlapping transparencies for the overhead helped in teaching fractions. Transparency one establishes the fact that the set of common fractional numbers falls between the whole numbers 0 and 1 on a number line.

0 ———————————————1

The second transparency has been divided in half and shows the points $^0/_2$, $^1/_2$ and $^2/_2$.

$^0/_2$ ————————$^1/_2$————————$^2/_2$

The third transparency has the distance divided into fourths.

| $^0/_4$ | $^1/_4$ | $^2/_4$ | $^3/_4$ | $^4/_4$ |
|---|---|---|---|---|

The last transparency divides the distance into eighths.

| $^0/_8$ | $^1/_8$ | $^2/_8$ | $^3/_8$ | $^4/_8$ | $^5/_8$ | $^6/_8$ | $^7/_8$ | $^8/_8$ |
|---|---|---|---|---|---|---|---|---|

Use these transparencies to introduce the concept of equivalent fractions—$^1/_2$, $^2/_4$, $^4/_8$.

*-Emile L. Mazze*

## MAKE THE SUN SMILE

Are your students bored with ordinary fraction activities? Then try this neat idea that's sure to bring smiles to all their faces. Start with a plain, manila file folder, and on the inside left-hand page, draw a large sun with a smiling face. On each of the sun's rays, print a fraction that can be reduced. Now attach a short length of yarn to each ray. On the right-hand page of the file folder, place corresponding fractions in their lowest terms and punch a hole beside each simplified fraction. Write these directions across the top of the folder: Make the sun smile by finding the simplest form of each fraction. Students are to lace the yarn from the ray to its corresponding reduced fraction. Answers can be written on the back to make the activity self-checking.  *-Jean Parks, Marquin Barrett, and Harriet Waldrop*

## FRACTION TOSS

The materials needed for this concept-of-fractions game are:
**1.** Pegboard with six evenly spaced pegs. (Board can be made from wood, cardboard boxes, or heavy cardboard.) Pegs are cut from doweling. Fractions should be lettered beside each peg.
**2.** Rings (rubber canning rings may be used or rings cut from cardboard).

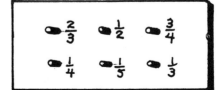

**3.** Set of 10 fraction cards similar to these:

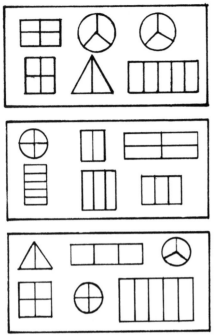

Each player gets five chances to land a ring on any one of the pegs. Once the player lands a ring on a peg, he or she must select the correct equivalent fraction on the top card to score a point. If the player is correct, he or she places that card on the bottom of the pile so there is a new card with fractional drawings for the next player. Answers are on the back of the cards.
Make a variety of boards so you can vary the fractions. This is a good review game for children who finish classwork fast.

*-Lorraine Lee*

## PERCENTAGE PRACTICE
This math activity will come in handy for your students in their daily lives. Find in newspapers five or six sale items that are advertised as being sold at a certain percent off the regular price. Cut off the sale price so students can't see what it is. Then have kids figure each percentage and subtract it from the regular price. Pupils can then figure the sales tax and add it to the new price to get the total for the item.

*-Carolyn Roberts*

## PLAYING WITH PERCENTS
Here's an activity I use with my sixth graders when we study percentages. After learning the procedure for finding percentages and figuring sales tax, I distribute catalogs that I have saved throughout the year. I ask the children to select three things they would like to ''purchase'' from their catalogs. The students fill out order forms and compute sales tax. Then they fill out ''checks'' that I run off on the duplicating machine. This activity provides practice with computing percents, filling out order forms, and writing checks, all activities that require precise figuring and writing.

*-Eleanor Messner*

## ELEMENTARY BANKING
Students can use bottle caps to learn a lot about banking. My pupils used bottle caps for currency and over a period of seven months deposited more than a million of them in the First Elementary Bank of Sherwood-Bates School. Each classroom in the school represented a branch bank, and the learning center was designated the main office. A giant, chicken-wire ''vault'' was constructed in the cafeteria, and thanks to the cooperation of a local bank, savings account passbooks were printed for the kids to record their biweekly deposits.
As deposits grew, the bottle caps became the focus of many math activities involving counting, estimation, word problems, bar graphs, place value, and the four basic operations. Students also computed the interest their deposits earned each month. When the project was concluded and the First Elementary Bank of Sherwood-Bates officially closed its doors, one problem remained: what to do with all those bottle caps? After careful consideration,

the kids decided to give them to a local metal recycling company so the deposits wouldn't be wasted. Students not only learned about banking, but they raised their conservation consciousness as well. All in all, this project was one in a million!

*-Jeane Joyner*

## LODGER LEARNING
Your students will enjoy learning place values when you use this unusual visual approach. Make little ''hotels'' from small cardboard boxes and construction paper, one for each place value through the millions. Give each hotel a name such as Tens' Inn, Hundreds' Hotel, and Millions' Motor Lodge, and equip each with nine rooms. Cut out stick figures in the shape of the numeral one. Select several students to ''register'' at one of the hotels by placing one of the stick figures in a room. Then have the remaining students write down or say aloud the number created by the hotel guests. For instance, if three students registered at the Tens' Inn and two at the Hundreds' Hotel, the number would be 230. Continue until all stick figures have been used.

*-Michael E. Murphy*

## FIND THE PLACE
For a quick test to help you spot those children who have difficulty with place value, duplicate the following chart. Ask students to supply numbers which come before and after the given numbers.

| Number Before | Given | Number After |
|---|---|---|
| | 999 | |
| | 909 | |
| | 800 | |
| | 1,021 | |
| | 750 | |
| | 1,001 | |
| | 4,099 | |
| | 310 | |
| | 9,909 | |

*-Isobel Livingstone*

## SOAP BUBBLE SCIENCE

Here's a way to teach science with soap bubbles. Kindergarten and early primary graders can experience the scientific processes of observing, predicting, inferring, and recording by blowing soap bubbles . . . just for fun. In addition, they'll gain a beginner's understanding of the properties of air and fluids, the shape and nature of a sphere, and even evaporation.

Cover all the desks with newspaper and give each child a paper cup half filled with diluted liquid detergent, a straw, and several pieces of paper on which they can record their discoveries. While preparing the cups, mention that liquid detergent is a fluid that can be poured from one container to another. Show kids how to dip one end of their straws in the liquid, let the liquid drip once, and then blow bubbles through the straw. Have them draw pictures of their bubbles. Ask questions such as: What is inside the bubbles? (Air.) Where did the air come from? (From blowing into the straw.) Why do the bubbles pop? (Because the atmospheric pressure outside the bubble becomes greater than the air pressure inside.) Why do some of them show rainbow colors? (Because light passing through the bubble is refracted and separated into different colors.) Ask students to blow one bubble onto a sheet of paper, circle the wet spot, initial it, and place it on the windowsill for a future lesson in which they can study evaporation.     -Dorothy Needham

## HANDS ON THE SCIENTIFIC METHOD

This bulletin board reminds students of the basic steps of the scientific method.

First, draw on a large sheet of construction paper a large hand with the fingers spread apart.

Then, on the fingers and the thumb print in large letters the five steps involved in solving a problem scientifically. Start with the thumb and print "define the problem." Then write one of the following phrases on each of the succeeding fingers: "Collect information," "form a hypothesis," "test the hypothesis through experimentation," "communicate the results."
     -Calvernetta Williams

## VISIBLE CHANGES

One of the most important ways scientists learn about the workings of the world is to observe changes. You don't need an electron microscope to use this scientific skill. These easy experiments will help your students develop their powers of observation. Each experiment follows the same basic procedure: You begin with observing an object; you do something that will change it; and you note what happens.

Begin by making a chart on the chalkboard. Across the top of the board write "the object," "action," "result." You will present an object to the class and then perform some simple experiment with it. Your students will help you fill in the "result" column after observing the change in the object.

You can use everyday objects such as sugar cubes or salt to create changes. Drop these into water or pour water over them, and the result will obviously be that they dissolve. Or start with a blown-up balloon and then hold it over a radiator or some other source of mild heat. This will make the balloon expand. The possibilities for these experiments are endless. It is not important that you go too deeply into the scientific principles at work with each change. The object of the lesson is to show that objects do change in predictable ways when exposed to certain forces.     -Florence Rives

## SCIENCE ALERT!

A Science Alert is a great way to draw the class's attention to an important event or change taking place in the world of science; students are all the more interested because they are being alerted to this event by two of their own classmates.

Each month I choose two students to be Junior Scientists of the Month and specify one area of science to concentrate on: marine biology, space exploration, endangered species, computer science, and so on. The Junior Scientists use newspapers, magazines, television, and other sources to find a Science Alert in this subject. They then write the alert on a large poster and put it up near the science table. One such poster showed a picture of a butterfly and read: "Monarch butterflies are migrating to Mexico to spend the winter. Watch for them and see how many you can find making their way south to Mexico's Sierra Madre."

The Junior Scientists then plan and conduct weekly science programs related to the alert. All students participate in these sessions; they bring in specimens or information, give demonstrations, or the whole class might discuss the subject of the alert in general. Sometimes the Junior Scientists ask local experts to come talk to the class. The Science Alert can change from week to week or it can remain the same; students may be asked to observe the migration of an insect or bird, keep notes on the position of a constellation or planet in the night sky, or collect caterpillars, fossils, or other specimens. This idea has made my class a roomful of scientifically aware students!
     -Judy Nichols

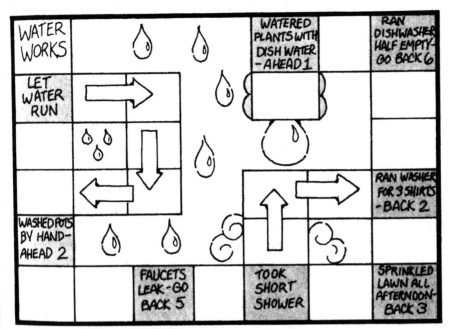

## GOOD TO THE LAST DROP

Here's a great classroom game that will reinforce student awareness of the need for water conservation. Just make a large copy of the game board above, and try it with your class. The rules are simple. Each child cuts out a water drop and writes his or her initials on it. Players start at the waterworks and roll the die to move around the board. The first player to reach the large water drop at the end of the game board wins. If a student lands on a box with directions, he or she must do what it says or follow the detour. If a student lands on a space occupied by another player, he or she must move back one space. A player must roll the exact number required to enter the water drop and win the game. If a player passes two turns in the faucet without rolling the exact number to win, he or she must move back one space each turn after that.　　*-Sandra Markle*

## WATER-CYCLE PUZZLE

Reinforce the basic steps in the water cycle with a little fun and games. Create your own water-cycle puzzle. You'll need poster board, paint or markers, scissors, white glue, cotton, and sand.

Then follow the simple instructions below.

**1.** Draw a large circle on the poster board.

**2.** Divide the outer circle into five dissimilar sections, one for each of the following: clouds, precipitation, runoff, underground water, and surface water.

**3.** Leave the cloud section white. Paint the precipitation section black, the runoff section green, the underground section brown, and the surface section blue. When it is dry, cut the five sections apart, into a jigsaw puzzle.

**4.** To make the puzzle even more fun, spread glue on the white section and paste down white cotton fluff. On the brown section sprinkle sand over a thin coat of glue.

**5.** Print a description of what happens in each part of the cycle on the back of the puzzle pieces. For example, the white section should say, "Water vapor cools (condenses) and clouds form"; on the black precipitation part write, "Water in the form of rain, snow, sleet, or hail falls on the ground"; on the green, "Water runs over the ground, and some goes up the roots of plants"; on the brown, "Other water soaks deep

into the ground and is stored there"; and finally on the blue, "Runoff water collects into streams, rivers, lakes, and oceans. The sun makes this water evaporate and move into the air as water vapor."

**6.** See if your children can fit the pieces of the water-cycle puzzle together, looking only at the colored sides. Then have them try the reverse side.

This puzzle illustrates how water moves through the environment and the importance of each part of the cycle. Discuss with your class what would happen if one part of the cycle was missing. Also consider what could cause a break in the cycle such as overuse of the water supply, changes in weather patterns, too much construction, air pollution affecting the weather, and so on.

*-Sandra Markle*

## HIGHS AND LOWS

One day at the beginning of winter when we had a fresh snowfall, the children were fidgety because of being confined to the building. I issued thermometers, made an assignment, and stood by. The lesson turned into one of my most successful! The assignment was this:

**1.** Lay the thermometer on your desk. Do not touch the bulb with your hand. After two minutes record the room temperature on your paper.

**2.** Hold your palm against bulb two minutes. Record the temperature.

**3.** Breathe on the bulb for two minutes. Record the temperature. Compare your results with a neighbor.

**4.** Take your thermometer outside. Lay on top of snow in open air while you count slowly to 100. Record the temperature.

**5.** Push thermometer down into the snow. Leave it while you count slowly to 60. Record the temperature.

**6.** Hold the thermometer lightly under your arm for two minutes. Record the temperature. You can't imagine the wild excitement as the children watched that mercury fluctuate.

*-Fern Wood*

## SUN SPOTS

Make children aware of solar energy with simple experiments involving temperature differences. First have them feel two spots on one surface (the playground, for instance), one in the sun and one in the shade. Which is warmer? Why?

Second, get one piece of white paper and one of black and place a thermometer under each. Compare temperatures. A third test is to place one thermometer in a closed white box and one in a closed black box. Finally, use two white dishes and two black ones; cover one of each with transparent plastic wrap. Put all four in the sun and record temperature changes every hour. Now ask pupils to answer this question: If you were making solar panels to catch the sun's energy to heat your house, what color would you choose? Why?

*-Rich Latta*

## PULL IN THE CLOUDS

It's not always easy to use a "hands-on" approach when teaching the weather, especially when the subject is cloud formations. Here's an interesting idea that will help you bring clouds a little closer to your students. Cover your entire bulletin board with light blue construction paper to simulate the sky. Now use 1/2″ construction paper strips in a darker color to divide the board into rectangles—one for each student in your class. Have the children cut out their own "suns" from bright yellow construction paper along with a 2″ x 4″ "data tag" to be filled in later.

Every morning, choose one student to go outside and decide what type of cloud formation is present and describe it to the rest of the class. Then give that student some polyester fiber fill (cotton may also be used) to stretch and mold into the cloud formation observed that day. He or she must glue the "clouds" to his or her square and fill in the data card with the date, his or her name, and the type of cloud formation simulated. Also have him or her paste in the sun if it's shining that day and darken the clouds with black chalk, if necessary.

Try to use the same time every day for observation purposes, and continue the activity until every child has had a chance to "pull in the clouds." When the unit is completed, you'll not only have a unique bulletin board, but an effective tool for studying the clouds and a creative chart for analyzing meteorological data as well.

*-David L. Carofano*

## WEATHER WISDOM

There are a lot of methods of predicting the weather that are nothing more than superstitions. But there are many unconventional ways to forecast the weather that are based on facts of nature. Ask your students if they think these signs of a change in weather are reliable or not, and then discuss the natural laws that make them accurate.

**1.** "When the night has a fever, it cries in the morning." This old saying is true because for the temperature to be hot at night, the air must be very humid to hold in the heat from the day's sun. A very humid night leads to rain or a heavy dew in the morning.

**2.** "When spiders forsake their webs one day, look for rain the next." True. Spiders are some of the best indicators of humidity in nature. As humidity rises and rain becomes certain, the spider will leave its web to find better shelter from the rain.

**3.** "Bats fly close to the ground before a rain." True. Bats' ears are sensitive to changes in air pressure, and the low pressure before a rainstorm is painful to their ears. The lower they fly, the less the pain.

**4.** "Flies bite more before a rain." True. Flies are more likely to be found in great numbers in advance of a weather front because the warm air ahead of the front is more comfortable. The more flies there are, the greater the possibility of being bitten!

*-Evelyn Kelly*

## SOLAR REFLECTIONS

Student-built power solar reflectors have helped my third-grade class learn about the importance of energy and the difference they, as individuals, can make in conserving it.

To construct reflectors, glue aluminum foil to large sheets of cardboard. Then nail sheets to a wooden frame. Once reflectors are built, prop them outside large classroom windows at the correct angle to bounce light down from the ceiling. Adjust reflectors at recess time. You will be amazed at how much heat and light can be generated in this crude way. One day when the temperature was −5°F, classroom temperature was 80°F with a window open slightly and the heat turned off! We were also able to turn off six 300-watt lights and save electricity in addition to heating fuel. During summer months, reflectors are stored, but the energy awareness they generate in students continues all year long.

*-Mike Carney*

## WEATHER FORECAST WORD GAME

In each sentence, find a word a weather forecaster might use.

**1.** Did you enjoy your ride in the Thunderbird?

**2.** Do you like spicy food?

**3.** Is the Doc old?

**4.** The cloudberry grows in the northern hemisphere.

**5.** The clearance sale is over.

6. Mt. Rainer is in the Cascade Range.

7. She walked along the pleasant winding path.

8. Haile Selassie was an emperor of Ethiopia.

9. Do you like rice pudding?

10. A dryad was a nymph in Greek mythology.

11. Was he really an old fogy?

12. Brighton is a city in England.

13. August, you know, is the eighth month of the year.

14. Heather is grown in England and Scotland.

15. Was it a mistake?

16. Yes, Mogul may refer to a Mongolian.

17. Sunnyvale is a city in central California.

18. The stormy petrel is a small black and white bird.

19. Warmongers advocate war instead of peace.

20. Do you prefer a milder flavor?

21. Did you ever ride a snowmobile?

22. How many snapshots have you?

23. Have you ever caught a lightning bug?

24. Admiral Dewey defeated the Spanish fleet in Manila Bay.

Key: **1.** thunder; **2.** icy; **3.** cold; **4.** cloud; **5.** clear; **6.** rain; **7.** wind; **8.** hail; **9.** ice; **10.** dry; **11.** fog; **12.** bright; **13.** gust or gusty; **14.** heat; **15.** mist; **16.** smog; **17.** sunny; **18.** stormy; **19.** warm; **20.** mild; **21.** snow; **22.** hot; **23.** lightning; **24.** dew. *-Aleta Slater*

## MAKE A RAINBOW

When you study rainbows, why not make one? Use a prism or an aquarium with square corners. Place either so that bright sunlight streams through it and projects a rainbow on a piece of white paper placed on the floor. Initial the bands of color from the bottom up to form the coined word *vibgyor* (violet, indigo, blue, green, yellow, orange, red). Encourage your children to memorize the new word so they will always have a way of remembering the colors of a rainbow. Then have your students draw big rainbows and write a sentence on each tinted band telling what that particular color reminds them of. For example, ''Violet reminds me of lilacs.'' ''Indigo reminds me of bluejeans.'' ''Blue reminds me of my bedroom.'' *-Dorothy Needham*

## GOOD VIBES

To demonstrate the tremendous energy produced by sound waves, have your students participate in this experiment that shows how sound waves can make air vibrate. Working with a partner, one student raps a tuning fork sharply on a desk while the partner attempts to pass a cotton ball, suspended on a thread, between the tines of the fork. The cotton ball will fly away from the tuning fork quite abruptly because it has run into the fastmoving sound waves. *-Dorothy Needham*

## FADEAWAY

Here's a colorful project you can use as a continuing science lesson. Cut up 12 or more sheets of paper, all of the same dark color. Mount them on a window facing the sun and record the day's date on each. Then take down one sheet per week and put them in a place that doesn't receive direct sunlight, such as a closet. Be sure to mark the date on it as you do so. When all the papers have been removed from the window, arrange them in chronological order, with faded sides showing. Explain to your kids that the longer the paper stayed in the sun, the more it faded—so if you used red paper in the beginning, the last sheet removed from the window will be almost white.

This activity requires minimal preparation and results in a great visual aid for a nifty science lesson on the effects of prolonged exposure to sunlight.

*-James M. Muller, Jr.*

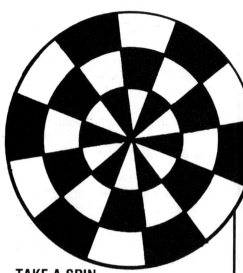

## TAKE A SPIN

Combine science and art for this fascinating project. Materials needed are an electric drill and some index cards. On each card, draw a circle about three inches in diameter and cut it out. Color half of one disc red, the other half blue. Then punch a hole in the middle, put some masking tape over it, and repunch the hole. (The masking tape helps keep the drill from ripping the center hole.) Mount the card on the drill and spin. **(Drill is handled by teacher only.)** Depending on the intensity of the red and blue, you should see a particular shade of purple. Now, color other discs. Blue and yellow will give you a shade of green; red and yellow—orange. Use different percentages of colors. Instead of half red, try one-third red and two-thirds blue, or one-fourth red and three-fourths blue. Can your students detect the difference in the various proportions of colors? Let students experiment with different color combinations and come up with unique colors. Have them record their results.

Finish this exploration with an impressive optical illusion. Copy the black and white design above and spin it. Your students should see color. See how many different designs your students can come up with, and try each on the drill to see what colors are created by the design. *-Richard Latta*

## SANDWICH BAG PRISM

Create a prism from common kitchen supplies to demonstrate that white light is composed of a rainbow of colors! You'll need a small mirror (4″ x 4″) and a clear plastic sandwich bag. Place the mirror in the bag and add water so that a wedge of water is formed between the mirrored surface and a side of the bag. This wedge will act like a prism. Hold the bag so that sunlight will travel through the water and be reflected on a pale surface, such as white paper taped to the wall. The sunlight will be broken up into its component parts, resulting in a vivid color spectrum.

*-Sylvia Williams*

## SHOW 'EM SURFACE TENSION

You can demonstrate the concept of surface tension by sprinkling a little talcum powder in a bowl half-filled with water. Now put a drop of liquid soap in the center of the water's surface. The powder will be pushed to the edges by the break in surface tension!

*-Richard Latta*

## ADAPT AN ANIMAL

The concept of adaptation is an interesting part of the study of animals. Introduce the subject to your class by explaining that an adaptation is anything that helps an animal survive in its environment. Three important ones are body coverings, body parts, and coloration. To identify the adaptations of specific animals, use slides or pictures (though a trip to the zoo is better). Discuss the environments in which the animals live and how their adaptations help them survive. As a culminating activity, prepare large pictures of the desert, forest, prairie, tundra, ocean, pond, and so on. Place these where they can be easily seen and reached. Now have students choose one of the environments and create an animal that can survive there.

Have a child draw his or her animal and cut it out. When it is his or her turn, he or she tacks it to the appropriate picture and describes it. How does each adaptation help the animal survive? What characteristics do not fit the environment? How well could the animal survive in one of the other types of environment? This activity easily leads to a discussion of why animals should not be removed from their natural surroundings, or why destruction of natural environments also leads to destruction of the animals themselves. *-Kelly Riley*

## ANIMAL TRACKS

If you have a wooded area or a large field near your school, you can take your class on a short field trip in search of animal tracks. This activity can be adapted for any age group. Before the outing, look through your library for books on animals and check wildlife manuals and the Girl Scout or Boy Scout Handbook to find information about, and drawings or photographs of, different animal tracks. Take the most portable of these books with you into the field so you can positively identify the tracks as you find them. Display a list of each animal whose tracks you identify, along with students' drawings of the tracks.
The best time to go hunting for tracks is after a light snowfall or any time the ground is soft so the tracks will show up clearly.

*-Pat O'Neill*

## WHAT COLOR IS YOUR TOOTHPICK?

The color of an animal can either protect it or make it easy prey. Here's how you can illustrate this for students. You'll need 200 toothpicks, 40 each of red, blue, white, green, and yellow, and one cup for each student.
Sprinkle the toothpicks at random on a grassy area, and give

children one minute to pick up as many as they can and put them in their cups. When time is called, have each student count the number of each toothpick color he or she picked up. Total the amount of each color picked up and subtract this total from the original number, 40. Compare the totals of the different colors. Repeat the experiment on other surfaces, such as a sidewalk, a rug, or sand. Discuss with kids why some colors were picked clean and why others "survived."

*-Mark Tangarone*

## WINTER DREAMS

A mini unit on animal hibernation is an interesting and informative winter activity. A good book to use is *Winter-Sleeping Wildlife* by Will Barker (Harper & Row, 1958). Assignments can include items like these: Define hibernation. List animals that hibernate. Give their scientific names. Give the name of one animal that hibernates in each of these groups—mammals, amphibians, birds, reptiles, insects, fish, mollusks. Choose a hibernating animal and write a report, draw a picture, chart its behavior, draw a plan of the burrow. How does estivation differ from hibernation? Write to the U.S. Department of the Interior, the U.S. Fish and Wildlife Service, or the National Wildlife Federation for more information. Pantomime an animal going into hibernation and waking up. Write a poem or play about an animal who hibernates. Write a story about hibernators' dreams, or draw a cartoon strip depicting them. Write a song about hibernating to the tune of Brahm's "Lullaby" or your own music. *-Rebecca Graves*

## CLASSROOM BIRD FEEDER

You and your students can make a classroom bird feeder in no time this fall—and all you'll need is a large empty milk carton and a plastic drinking straw. Simply cut

119

out one of the carton's front panels, leaving about a half-inch border all around. Now make a perch by gluing a plastic drinking straw to the bottom edge of the border. Fill the feeder with suet, orange pieces, birdseed, crackers, and so on; then attach a hook or string loop to the top for hanging.  *-Martha J. Beckman*

## OUTDOOR TREASURE TRIP

If your school is in a rural area, here's an idea for a class trip. It takes place on the school grounds, and you can be sure that Mother Nature has done more than her share of preparation. You'll need the cooperation of at least one teacher from every department to direct stations in designated areas of the campus, while classes travel from one to the other participating in the following activities:

**Art station:** Students can sketch, paint, or photograph landscapes, or collect material to create nature collages when back in the classroom. Also, the kids might enjoy collecting litter from the campus and making "litter critters" to display later as reminders not to pollute the grounds.

**Language arts station:** Have your students pause and look at their surroundings while listening, in silence, to the sounds of nature. Then have them write brief poems about their observations and feelings. Haiku is an especially useful form for this type of expression.

**Math station:** This is a good time for kids to get some experience in measuring, guessing heights and diameters, and putting metrics to practical use. Use objects and living things in the environment like rocks, acorns, and so on.

**Social studies station:** Have the kids work in groups or alone to design maps of the campus area. Also, let interested students

prepare a questionnaire on opinions, attitudes, and reactions to the campus treasure trip.

**Science station:** Kids can collect plants to be identified later and then displayed in the cafeteria or library. Also, try conducting experiments involving soil samples or the use of prisms. A field trip such as this can provide you with an excellent opportunity to observe student behavior and performance in a group situation. Plan one in your school this spring and put your students in closer touch with their environment.  *-Margaret Chavin*

## TALK A NATURE WALK

When leading children along nature trails, it's not always easy to point out objects of interest so everyone can hear. Here's an idea that can change that. Take the first child up the trail a little ways while the rest wait quietly. Choose a tree, flower, or stream and tell the child two or three facts about it. Then station him or her there to tell the other children as they pass by. Do the same thing with the next child farther up the trail, and continue to station children at random spots along the trail until everyone has had a chance to "teach." After each child has taught the last person in line, he or she becomes the last in line.  *-Priscilla Olmsted*

## TAKE A WALK ON THE WILD SIDE

If your school is in a rural area or close to a public park, why not take your kids on a nature walk this fall? Make a master list of things to look for such as four different kinds of birds, three kinds of insects, a chipmunk, a pine tree, and so on. As children identify these items, instruct them to cross them off the master list. Then, have kids collect colored leaves to make an autumn bulletin board display.  *-Louisa Zamorski*

## SEEDS OF AWARENESS

To help children become familiar with seeds and plants indigenous to their neighborhood, bring a leaf, bud, twig, or seed to class each day for students to identify. Stick some beggar ticks, burdocks, or other seeds with burrs on your coat one morning and talk about how people and animals act as transporters. Bring in milkweed to illustrate an airborne type of seed; ask students to think of other ways seeds travel, such as water. Encourage students to notice seeds (maple seeds or acorns) on their way to school. Examine the contents of frostbitten marigolds or nasturtium blossoms to see how they produce seeds. Take an evergreen cone containing seeds, put it in a plastic container, and watch it open up and release its seeds. Make it a part of every field trip to have students identify as many kinds of seeds and plants as they can. Carry this out as the seasons change.  *-Joan Mary Macey*

## NITTY GRITTY DIRT CENTER

Set up a display area in a corner of your classroom and label it "Nitty Gritty Dirt Center." On a table in the center, place samples of different types of soil in appropriately labeled plastic bags. If possible, include samples of clay (tiny, solid particles), silt (soil particles slightly larger than clay, but smaller than sand), loam (soil with decaying plant and animal matter), sand (fine or coarse grains), and gravel (large, hard particles). Of course, it may not be possible to find all these samples in your area—do the best you can.

You'll also need a bag of dried beans, a long-handled spoon, a magnifying glass, crayons, one plastic-foam cup per student, a small cake pan, scissors, 12 empty quart jars, and white construction paper.

Before you introduce the center and accompanying experiments, give each student a paper bag with his or her name printed across the front. For homework, instruct each child to go home and collect one full bag of soil each, and print where the soil was found on the back of the bag. Each child will use his or her bag of soil for the following experiments. Print the directions for these experiments on index cards and let kids take turns going to the center and completing the activities.

**Experiment #1: What is soil?** Fill one of the quart jars half full with dirt from your bag. Add water to within 5 centimeters of the jar's lip. Stir gently with spoon until dirt and water are well mixed. Let jar sit overnight. Then on white construction paper, draw, color, and label a soil chart like the one illustrated, showing how the dirt separated in the jar. Refer to the soil samples in plastic bags to help you label each level on your settling chart, and make the width of each layer on the chart equal to the width of that layer in your jar. When finished, clean your jar and return it to the center for someone else to use.

Now try this pinch test. Place a small pinch of soil on notebook paper. Rub your finger through soil. At the bottom of paper, list words that describe how soil felt: Was it coarse, gritty, sandy, velvety, powdery, or crumbly? Look at your soil through a magnifying glass and draw a picture of what it looks like.

**Experiment #2: How well will plants grow in your soil?** Put bean seeds into small cake pan; cover with water and let sit overnight. Poke a small hole in bottom of plastic-foam cup. Print your name on outside of cup and fill it with soil from your sample. Then plant three bean seeds just beneath the soil's surface. Sprinkle with water, and put cup in a warm, sunny place. Record the number of days it takes before the first sprout appears. Measure your plant daily for five days, recording its new height every day. Also, make notes about how the plant looks: Is it green, healthy, and full-leafed, or pale, spindly, and droopy, with small leaves?

This Nitty Gritty Dirt Center may not be the cleanest part of your classroom, but it will provide a wealth of projects your students can really dig into!  *-Sandra Markle*

## MEASURING AIR IN SAND

Sand seems solid, but it isn't. How much air is in a given quantity of sand? Challenge your students to find out using water and two measuring cups. Measure out a quantity of sand. Measure out a quantity of water. Pour the water into the sand. The combination will measure less than the two quantities added arithmetically. The difference is the amount of air that was in the sand.  *-Rich Latta*

## DANDY ACTIVITIES

Center some springtime activities on a common springtime sight— the dandelion. After studying a chart of the parts of this plant, take off for the dandelion patch growing near your school.

**1.** Divide the class into groups of four or five. Have each group measure a 100-square-meter area and estimate the number of dandelions in that area by finding the number in one square meter and multiplying by 100.

**2.** Have kids practice mathematical skills in other ways, such as counting the leaves on each plant, the seeds on a mature blossom, and the lobes on each leaf, and measuring each blossom.

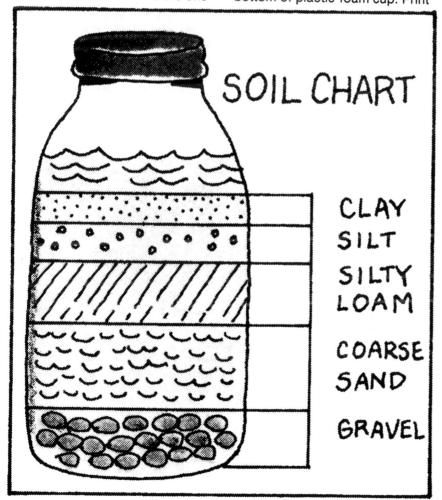

SOIL CHART

CLAY
SILT
SILTY
LOAM
COARSE
SAND
GRAVEL

**3.** If you have a microscope handy, use it to view the stamen and pistil.

**4.** Have students write stories about how the dandelion got its name.  *-E. Harold Harper*

## STATIC ELECTRICITY STUDY

Winter is the ideal time to begin a study of static electricity—the cold, dry air is perfect for experiments on this subject, which you can perform using common materials found at home. Begin by explaining the concept of electrical charges: positive (lack of electrons), negative (abundance of electrons), and neutral (balance of electrons— most material is in this state). Then, to introduce the concept that like charges repel and unlike charges attract, take a plastic lunch bag and rub it vigorously on two pieces of wool yarn. Suspend one of the strands of charged yarn; it will repel the second strand and attract the plastic bag. (If you have another plastic bag, see how it similarly repels the first bag while attracting the yarn.) Testing to find if a material has gained a charge can be easily accomplished by building an electroscope. Get a wide-mouthed, clear jar with a screw-on cap and punch or drill a hole in the cap. Then take two small strips of Christmas tinsel or tin foil from gum wrappers, and attach them to the head of a common nail with a drop of glue. Be sure the foil can move freely. Melt paraffin around the nail to hold it in place and insulate it in the jar cap, point sticking up. Screw cap back on jar. You now can test different objects for static charges. The presence of a charged object (such as the yarn) will cause the leaves of foil to repel each other.

Experiments like this allow students to investigate and discover some of the laws of electricity in a safe and enjoyable manner.  *-R. Richard Larke*

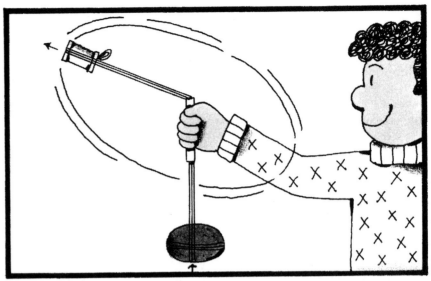

## A POWERFUL FORCE

Everyone has had fun holding a water-filled bucket by its handle and swinging it in a circle. At any angle you swing the bucket, no water spills. Why? Because centrifugal force holds the water in the container.

Here's another activity to demonstrate the power of centrifugal force. You'll need a wooden spool, a 4″ length of plastic straw, a large potato, and 1 yard of knitting yarn (tripled for strength).

Thread one end of the yarn through the center hole in the spool. Thread the other end of the yarn through the straw. The yarn should slip freely up and down through the straw. Tie the free end around the potato: (See illlustration.) Before proceeding further, make sure all knots are tight so that the potato or spool won't come loose.

Now, holding the straw in one hand, lift the potato with your free hand so that the spool hangs five or six inches out of the straw. Swing the spool in a circle parallel to the floor. When you have the spool swinging fast, let go of the potato. The faster the spool whirls, the wider its circle gets and the higher the potato rises. Although the spool weighs less than the potato, the centrifugal force created by the rotating spool easily lifts the large potato. Ask your students if they can think of any practical uses for centrifugal force. Does anyone know of a case where it is used? (One answer is in drying laundry).  *-Jane Priewe*

## STARCH SEARCH

Any broad-leafed plant, such as a geranium, that can spare a leaf will show students how the sun helps green plants manufacture food. Tape a one-inch-wide strip of aluminum foil across the center of the leaf and place the plant on a sunny windowsill. After a few days remove the leaf and briefly soak it in ethyl alcohol to remove the chlorophyll. Rinse and dry it thoroughly and remove the foil. Drop some diluted iodine (about 10 parts water to one part iodine) on various parts of the leaf. Children will observe that the iodine on the uncovered parts turns purplish black, which indicates the presence of starch. Iodine placed on the part that was covered remains reddish brown, showing the absence of starch. Without sunlight, the leaf could not produce food. Have children sketch before and after pictures of leaf, labeling the changes. Put diluted iodine on powdered starch, raw potato, instant potato flakes, white bread, and rice to reinforce this concept.  *-Dorothy Needham*

## 50 STATES CARD GAME

Here's a simple game that will familiarize your students with characteristics of the 50 states. Using a set of 50 3" × 5" index cards, print several clues about a particular state on each card. Have the kids arrange their desks into rows, with each row representing a different team. Now shuffle the set of cards and place them facedown on your desk. When the students are ready, draw the top card and direct the first clue on the list to team number one. If any member of the team can correctly name the state to which that clue applies, place the state card on the first desk in the row. If a team member guesses incorrectly, direct the second clue on the list to team number two. Continue until the state is correctly identified. The row with the most cards at the end of the game is the winning team. You may want to have the kids change seats a few times during the course of the game so no team is a consistent winner. The level of excitement will rise to a high pitch with this activity, and your students will learn something about our country.          -Stephen Pesek

## CITY-STATE MATCH GAME

To help children readily associate the names of large cities with their corresponding states, try this card game. Cut large sheets of tagboard into 52 playing card-sized pieces. On 26 of these, print the names of large cities in the U.S.A. and on the remaining 26 cards, print the names of the states they can be found in. Groups of children play the game by taking turns drawing one card at a time from the deck and discarding every pair of city-state cards they draw. When the deck is gone, the players continue by drawing from one another's hands. The object of the game is

to make as many matches as possible and not be the last person left holding a card. Assign someone to check the discarded pairs and make sure they match correctly. If a player makes an incorrect match, he or she must take the cards back and forfeit two draws before he or she can reenter the game. This idea can also be used for cities and countries around the world.
-Florence Rives

## ADOPT A STATE

Have your students acquire firsthand information about a state of their choice by sending letters to three potential sources: the chamber of commerce of a major city; the state bureau of tourism; and an elementary school classroom of the same grade level in a small town. These three sources can provide information about the state's area, physical features, types of industry, and areas of recreation and entertainment. Children can ask elementary "pen pals" for a copy of the local or school newspaper; what their school is like; what kinds of houses they live in; what the weather is like; and so on.

Let children use school letterhead. You can even take a field trip to the post office to watch your letters being postmarked and sent all over the country.

While waiting for responses, research other sources of information, design individual covers, write brief state histories and prepare a state fact sheet, make a state collage, draw a U.S. map indicating the child's particular state, create an original puzzle or riddle about the state, and illustrate and explain the state symbols. Responses can also help children put together a closeup portrait of a small town in the state and to design an illustrated "tour" of the state. As enthusiasm builds, children

will think of other ideas to expand their state notebooks. Culminate this experience with a "Meet-My-State Day" where all your students can display and share their booklets with each other and the whole school.     -Judy Jenkins

## GEOGRAPHY IN DISGUISE

Children in the middle grades usually don't like to memorize dates, products, or even the correct locations of the fifty states unless they travel a lot themselves. Here's a practical aid that appeals to youngsters and makes learning geography a lot easier and a lot more fun. Turn to the sports pages of your local newspaper or ask your students to list the names of some well-known baseball, basketball, or football teams. Now divide your class into small groups and give each group several different names. They are to work together to find out why the teams acquired their names. For example, the Pittsburgh Steelers got their name because they represent the steel capital of the U.S.A., and the Miami Dolphins are so named because Florida is noted for dolphins, especially at "Sea World." Any type of reference material may be used for this activity.     -Alse Riesenfeld

## TAKE ON THE NEIGHBORHOOD

Distribute laminated copies of neighborhood maps to teams of students. Ask each student to mark the location of his or her home, then figure out which student lives farthest north, which farthst south, which east, which west. Who lives closest to a park, a post office, or a public library? Are there any shortcuts students know about that aren't on the map? Ask kids to mark them in with colored markers.
-Rosalind Schilder

## PHOTO ESSAY EXCHANGE

Set up an international photo-essay exchange to help your students learn about foreign countries this year. Begin by selecting a country that your students are interested in. Write a letter to the appropriate government official asking for the names and addresses of public and private schools in particular towns. If possible, write this letter in the language of the country. When you receive your answer, write to one school at a time and inquire if any teacher with students at a comparable age level to your own would be interested in participating in this exchange. Find out if the children are studying English or if they have someone who can translate for them. Explain that the text accompanying the photos will be kept to a minimum to facilitate translation. Suggest some good beginning themes such as your community, your school, the local government, or leisure activities, and offer to send your photo-essay first. Be sure to set an approximate date for its arrival. Plan the pictures you will take with your class ahead of time so you can decide which ones will be necessary to tell your story. Other pictures may be taken as well, but by planning your shots in advance, you'll be sure to get the essentials.

When the pictures are taken and developed, mount them on heavy oaktag with appropriate captions and explanations below. Protect your finished pages by placing them between corrugated cardboard sheets before wrapping them in heavy paper for mailing.

You'll find that your students not only learn about a foreign country this way, but discover things about their own surroundings that they've never noticed before.

*-Bruce Porell*

## DISCOVER AMERICA, DISCOVER FRIENDS

Bring geography and American history to life for your students with this fascinating activity that can be extended through the whole year. It involves research on various parts of the country and culminates in a collection of items representative of your area to be sent to students in another school. First, divide your class into five groups. Assign each group a different area of the United States to research. These areas should have different cultural styles, life-styles, and regional dialects, if possible. Have each group find out as much as possible about its assigned region—including the name and address of one elementary school in that area. (These can be obtained by dialing telephone information or consulting phone books on file at your local library. If possible, contact a teacher at the school to be sure he or she will cooperate on the project.) Other things to investigate include history of the area, industry, agriculture, famous people born or living there now, school styles and curriculum, dress, recreational activities, and tourist spots.

When the initial research is completed, the groups can begin preparing their packages. Have them collect and place in a large packing box, significant items from your area such as city and county maps, tourist information pamphlets, drawings or photos of your school, lunch menus from the cafeteria, class snapshots, pressed flowers from the school grounds or surrounding neighborhoods, samples of your school or classroom newspaper, facts about your city, and so on. The last article to be placed in the box should be an informal questionnaire for the receiving class to fill out. It should contain questions the kids write themselves, seeking information on town, school, and so on. Also, make sure that each group writes a letter to accompany the package, explaining the program and encouraging the other class to participate with similar packages. When all the articles are assembled, have the groups address their packages carefully. You may be able to mail them from your school at a library postal rate. If not, a class trip to the post office would be an instructional addition to the program.

Your students should find their new friends eager to participate in the program they've started. When return packages are received, have the kids compare the interests and life-styles of the different classes they've contacted, and post their results on a bulletin board in the front of the school. *-Joyce D. Jensen*

## INTERNATIONAL TASTING PARTY

Add a new dimension to learning about other lands with an international tasting party. Your class probably represents a mix of ethnic backgrounds. Send a note home to parents explaining your plans and asking if any would care to participate by providing a "dish" that represents their nationality. Ask all those who respond positively to send in a copy of their recipe a week or so before the party is to take place. These recipes should be compiled into an international cookbook by the students. Reading and writing the recipes will acquaint students with many vocabulary words they're probably unfamiliar with. You might want to write some of these words on the board to be sure everyone understands them. You can also incorporate some map study into the unit by having the children look up the countries where the dishes they'll be eating are usually served.

On the day of the party, set a long table for dining and use a globe as the centerpiece. Be sure to provide nametags for all the parents who participate, the students, and yourself.

Encourage the children to taste a little of everything. Finish the unit by having the kids write thank-you notes to all the parents who contributed food. This activity will not only help your students develop a taste for international cooking, but will reinforce vocabulary, social studies, and writing skills, too!

-Nancy C. Sheridan

## POSTMARK, USA

With the help of the *United States Post Office Zip Code Directory*, search for a personalized city for each child. Jill Brown's could be Brown City, Missouri, while Scott Wise's could be Scottsdale, Georgia. Try to arrange it so that each student in your class has a different state.

Then have kids draft an introductory letter to Postmaster,

United States Post Office, in "their" town. They should request two things of the postmaster: first, to hand-stamp their return envelope with the name of the town or city, and second, to send some information about the town or to pass the letter on to someone in the town who could. While waiting for returns, take advantage of pinpointing locations on the map. When letters come back, each student should read his or hers aloud. Our class's responses were great. Amy received photographs of Amity, Washington. James's letter was read at the town meeting in James Store, Virginia. Tamala received postcards from a resident of Tamal, California, and Kevin, a key ring from Kevin, Montana. Ross received the best response. The town historian in Thompsonville, Michigan, sent a copy of the town's history.

For two stamps, many happy returns should come your way.

-Mark Truszkowski

## CURRENT COUNTRIES

Cut out shapes of various countries currently in the news and hand out a different one to each student. Students must find out what country they have. (You may want to give a clue—a capital city or important river.) After watching for their country in the news for a few days, they must report what they have learned about the country's geography, people, and current events.

-Susan J. Kreibich

## WHERE IN THE WORLD ARE YOU?

This geography activity tests students' knowledge of local, national, or world geography. The activity can be done in pairs or in small groups, and uses maps

taken from daily newspapers. Cut the maps from the newspapers and paste part or all of each map on a separate index card. For the next step, you will need colored adhesive dots. We used different shades of green for countries, states, and other land masses, and blue for bodies of water. Using sections cut from the adhesive circles, cover several localities and bodies of water on the map so a student cannot read the name of the colored area. Leave one or two named places showing so the student can have a reference point. The player's objective is to name each colored area after being prompted by questions from a moderator. For instance, your first card might show a portion of a map showing the state of Massachusetts, its bordering states, and the Atlantic Ocean. All state and ocean names, except for Massachusetts, would be covered by a sticker. To begin, the moderator would ask the student who picked this card what country the map was a part of. Then the student would be asked to identify what each colored dot was pasted over. In this case, the covered areas are the Atlantic Ocean and the states of Vermont, New Hampshire, Connecticut, and Rhode Island. For maps of different countries and continents, the first question can be broader: Where in the world are you?

I make up a sheet with questions for each map and let a student act as moderator. Each player has a record sheet to keep track of his score. Award one point for each correct answer.

-Mary Lickteig

## RECYCLE THAT ENVELOPE!

Save your Christmas card envelopes for this geography project that's perfect for the weeks after Christmas. This project will give students a chance to become better acquainted with zip codes and two-letter state abbreviations. They will also give kids practice in recognizing states by shape and location, finding cities in alphabetical listings, and locating cities by using the letter-number grids on maps.

Have students trace an outline map of the United States, 3′ × 5′ or larger, using an overhead projector, onto light-colored paper. After map is drawn and mounted on the bulletin board, pin state names to each state. When kids are familiar with state shapes and locations, remove names to make room for postmarks.

Atlases, road maps, encyclopedias, zip code directories, and a list of two-letter state abbreviations should be available for students' use. As postmarks are brought to school, they should be cut out, the state identified, the city located on a road map or atlas, and the postmark then pinned in the correct location on the map. Discuss this project with students right after Thanksgiving, so they begin saving postmarks as soon as Christmas cards arrive. Then when kids come back after Christmas, you'll have an abundance of teaching materials to work with!  *-Arline M. Bolz*

## SING FOR SOCIAL STUDIES

Map study can be a source of delight for your kids when you set it to music. How? Start by having kids list popular songs that mention U.S. states or cities in their titles, such as ''I Left My Heart in San Francisco,'' or ''New York, New York.'' Then let kids locate each city or state on a large map of the U.S. When students have exhausted song possibilities, have them try movies or television shows like *Dallas, Hollywood Squares,* or

*Mr. Smith Goes to Washington.* Kids will enjoy this different approach to social studies!  *-Marilyn Siegel*

## DRAW A SNOWMAN IN THE ALPS

Make map study a treat for your kids by having them draw pictures on maps instead of labeling cities, states, and landmarks. For instance, after a geography unit on Europe, design a map quiz, including directions, such as the following:

**1.** Draw a sailboat in the Mediterranean Sea.
**2.** Draw a bunch of grapes in Spain.
**3.** Draw a windmill in the Netherlands.
**4.** Draw a lighthouse at the Strait of Gibraltar.

Accompany your directions with simple sketches so students will have ideas to work with. This is one quiz every kid will enjoy!  *-William A. Rower*

## AIR PHOTOS HELP MAP SKILLS

To help improve map-reading skills, I found a photo of our school taken from the air. It really helped the kids to make a line drawing of the shape and major features of the familiar building. They then used the photo and drawing to draw the school as a map. I had them do the same with air photos of other buildings.  *-Rebecca Graves*

## EARTH BALLOONS

Give your students a creative geography lesson by building globes from balloons. To make these globes you will need large blue balloons, string, different-colored construction paper, glue, and felt pens. The balloons are blue to represent that portion of the earth's surface that's covered with water.

First, blow up the balloon and tie

it closed. (Do this first in order to see how big your earth will be so you can then make your continents to fit the scale of the globe.) Next, glue a piece of string around the middle of the balloon to mark the equator. Small circles of string also can be glued at the top and bottom to represent the North and South poles. The difficult and challenging part of this project is drawing, cutting, and fitting the paper land masses. Encourage your students to use different-colored construction paper for each continent. This will help to create a beautiful and easy-to-use globe. Glue the continents in the correct positions. With a black felt pen, you can then label the continents and the oceans. If you are working with large balloons, you might draw in some specific countries.  *-Gertrude Parker*

## PLAN A TRIP

With maps from a vacation trip, I decided to plan a map study unit for my fifth graders. Using each state map, I chose a major city and a place off the main highways, and asked students to plan a trip from one to the other. For example: WEST VIRGINIA *You live in Huntington and want to take a camping trip to Holly River State Park. What routes will you take, how far is it, and about how long will it take you to get there? If you come within 15 miles of the answer on the card, you are a good trip planner.* Because some maps give mileage to the nearest tenth, I review the concept of adding numbers with decimals. I also remind students how to use the number and letter cross-reference format and the map legend and scale. This useful activity can easily be extended to figure how much time would be needed for food and fuel stops, and how much money to take along.  *-Mary Louise Angone*

## TURN LEFT AT OLIVE STREET

While driving several of my students home from the circus, I noticed that although they could direct me to their houses, they were unaware of the names of streets in their neighborhood. So I made a map of major streets in the area and included special points of interest such as McDonald's, the bank, supermarket, and so on. Then I made up cards with directions on them. These ranged from very simple — "What street is the movie theater on?" — to complex — "Begin at home, pick up shoes at shoe repair shop, stop at the bank, then meet your brother at the supermarket." I put the cards in piles according to difficulty and let students pick from the different sets according to their ability. Each student could then "run an errand" using the map and a pointer, and saying the names of streets and the directions taken along the route. If the student followed directions correctly, he or she could then make up an errand for someone else to try.        *-Janet A. Buchholz*

## MAP OF US

Who among your students wouldn't be thrilled to have a river, lake, or city named in his or her honor? You can give them this experience by creating a class map of US (not U.S.) in which rivers, bays, mountain ranges, cities, and towns are named after your students. A map with a Bonnie Bay, Cunningham Creek, Brownsburg, and Port Patti is a good way for everyone to get to know one another's names in these first days of school and will help provide you with map-reading lessons as well. Draw your "eighth continent" on the chalkboard or on a handout sheet. Then have students help you locate and label cities, towns, rivers, railways, mountains, oceans, bays, and lakes. Now use your map of US to introduce basic

map-reading skills. For example, you could present a lesson on symbols ("How do we know Tommytown is the capital?") or directions ("Is Lake Lonnieandluke located north, south, east, or west of the Rock Rogers Mountains?").
*-John L. Cook*

## WHAT'S IN A NAME?

This game reinforces map locating skills and draws on each student's imagination and vocabulary. Provide your students with a list of phrases that describe the names of cities. An example is "a hot weather town—Summerville, Georgia." Students first try to figure out the clue to the city's name and then they locate it on the map. Here are a few to get you started. In Pennsylvania find a town in the center of things (Middletown) and a town named after the ocean east of the United States (Atlantic). Using the North Carolina state map, find a place that is winter white and steep (Snow Hill) and a town named after a pig that sways back and forth (Rockingham). On the New York state map there is a city named after an island that is 90 miles south of Florida (Cuba) and a place whose namesake is a flower that has thorns on its bushes (Rose).        *-Vara Hitchcock and Sharon Crawley*

## MINUTE MAPS

Need an interest-boosting time filler or a challenging extension activity? Have pupils make simple maps or blueprints to solve the following problems.
**1.** You've just been chosen to design an amusement park. Make a map showing the location of ticket booths, rides, restrooms, and concession stands.
**2.** Plan a castle fit for a king. He insists it have a moat, kitchen, dungeon, garden, chapel, living quarters, stables, kennels, and gatehouses.

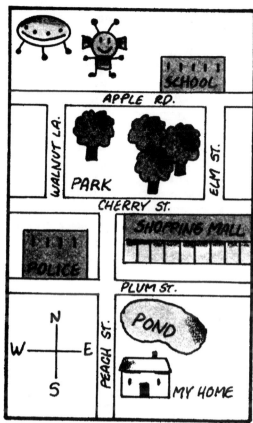

**3.** Here's a whale of a problem. It's time for Horatio Whale's yearly migration, but he has lost his bearings. Research the matter and see if you can chart a path for him. (You can let pupils decide where Horatio is now or you can pinpoint his location so all are working on the same migratory route.)
**4.** Just suppose a UFO landed and a space creature needed to get from school to your house. Draw a map so this extraterrestrial being can find the way.        *-Sylvia Foust*

## SILLY-CITY MAP STUDY

Try this game idea that focuses on cities and towns in the U.S. with unusual or amusing names. Let your students work with a large map of the United States or assign a different state to each child. You'll have to find maps with major cities clearly marked. Specify that the children are to find 10 cities each with unusual names and list them on a sheet of paper. Then they are to think of other, sillier names for the cities they've chosen and write them on another sheet of paper. For example, Mars, Pennsylvania, could be changed to Red Planet or Candy Bar, Pennsylvania. When the children have finished listing their "silly cities," they exchange papers. Have them refer to maps as they try to discover the actual city that each silly name applies to.

-Jane K. Priewe

## MAP IT OUT

This social studies activity can serve as an instructional bulletin board display and a learning center combined. Before you begin a unit on United States geography, make a large outline of a U.S. map on your bulletin board. As study progresses, have kids fill in the outline with construction paper models of each state. On the back of each state, have them print pertinent information such as the state's capital, largest city, biggest industry, and so on. Tack each state in the appropriate place within the outline, using one thumbtack for each.

-Marilyn Mullins

## LET'S MAKE A MAP!

Use an old wall map of the United States and assign one or two states to each student. Children are responsible for tracing and cutting their states out of rug remnants or scraps of material. These pieces can be mounted on cardboard and used as a puzzle to reinforce recognition of directionality, regions, state sizes, and shapes.      -Perry D. Stio

## CARPETMAPPERS

If you can obtain carpet samples from a local store, you can make this beautiful, colorful map of the United States. Use it to teach a variety of skills, such as matching, color recognition, directions, and so on.
Outline a large map of the U.S. on

a sheet of heavy cardboard or masonite, and draw the boundaries for each state. Then cut each state from a different carpet sample. Assign each child two or three states to place in the appropriate spots on the map. When kids have correctly matched states with their outlines, have them glue each one in place.         -Marilyn Burch

## MAP MAGIC

A certain amount of map study should be a part of every social studies curriculum. But what can you do when your school doesn't have enough maps to go around? Don't give up; make your own from a simple, roller-type window shade. Road maps of every state in the U.S. are available for low prices at most filling stations and auto club offices.
Cut a pattern from the road map and trace the outline onto the window shade. Then use a paper punch to make holes at short intervals around the outline. Hang the shade from a hook above your chalkboard and using an eraser, pat chalkdust over the holes so an outline is left on the board when the shade is raised. Since the window shade will slide along the chalkboard's overhead track, you can repeat the map several times until you run out of

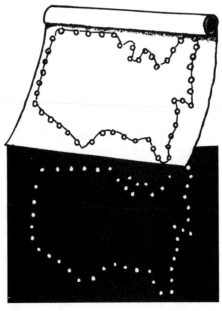

board space. Students may "connect the dots" to complete the outline, then work in small groups on various map exercises. If you would rather have some students work at their seats on desk-sized maps, but are leery about the prospect of correcting each one individually, try this idea for preparing a master copy: Mark on your own map the names of every site you want the students to locate. Now use scissors to cut out the names, leaving half-inch circles in their place. Put this key over the students' maps when grading and make red check marks in the middle of every circle that appears blank. This way, you'll have noted the students' omissions and indicated where the items should have been. This method is a real time-saver for you, and helps students pinpoint their mistakes more easily.

-Mikell Neumann

## PAINT THE PLAYGROUND!

A huge map of the United States painted on your school's playground makes a great end-of-the-year project. First divide the country into sections. Using a transparency and overhead projector, draw each section (divided into states) onto mural paper. A good size is about 20 feet by 30 feet. Next, have one crew of students take the map outside, a section at a time, and align and secure it with rocks. Another group can paint around the entire outline of the map with white paint. When it is dry, assign each student one or more states to cut out of the original pattern and outline on the large painted map. States can then be painted red, yellow, blue, and green, and reoutlined in white with names lettered on them. Children from kindergarten on up can also work on states as teams and then fill in water and land boundaries.

-Elena Dowling and Robert Heller

## SOCIAL STUDIES RED ROVER

Divide the class into two teams. The first child on Team A thinks of a country, city, or other place and gives a one-sentence clue to its identity. For example, if the place is Turkey, a child could say, "This place is also something you eat." Members of Team B try to guess the place; if they do, the child from Team A joins Team B. Now a child from Team B gives a sentence clue for Team A to guess and so on. The team with the most members at the end wins.          -Patricia Moody

## RAVES FOR REVIEW

You can make social studies review stimulating for students if you turn it into a game. Divide the class into two teams. Write relevant words from your social studies chapter or unit on the chalkboard. Give a definition of one of the words without actually identifying it, then choose a child to come to the board and erase the word you've defined. A correct response scores one point for that child's team; a wrong response, a point for the opposing team. No child may answer more than once until everyone on his or her team has had a chance. When there are just a few words left, ask for volunteers to give definitions to win two points.     -Joan Mary Macey

## SOCIAL STUDIES CHAMPIONSHIP

Turn social studies into an indoor sport! First, divide a set of index cards into three piles. Print a numeral 1 on each card in the first pile, a numeral 2 on each in the second pile, and a numeral 3 on each in the third pile. On the back of each card, print a different social studies question, assigning the simplest questions to cards in the first pile, more difficult questions to cards in the second pile, and highly challenging questions to cards in the third pile. Then divide your class into two or three teams. Have a student from each team choose a card from pile one, two, or three. If he or she answers the questions correctly, award his or her team the number of points the card represents. If incorrect, card is returned to pile and it's the next team's turn.          -Mona Kolsky

## QUESTION OF THE DAY

Here's an activity that can span the entire year and will help keep your students tuned in to current events. Start by making a news board from available bulletin-board space in your classroom. It need not be a large area—two square feet should be sufficient. Each day before the kids come in, tack up three or four pertinent articles from your local paper or any news periodical you may subscribe to. The articles may involve foreign affairs, national and local news, or human interest stories. Then choose one important fact from any of the articles you've picked and turn it into a question, such as "Who was named new secretary of state?" or "What important event took place yesterday in the Middle East?" Since headlines often capsulize information like this, you may want to omit them from the display. Print the question on a piece of plain white paper and tack it to the board under the words "Question of the Day." Students are to read the articles during free time and attempt to answer the question. They should write their answers on slips of paper along with their names and drop them in a paper sack tacked to the news board. Hold a brief news discussion at the end of the day and empty the sack to check answers.
          -Patricia Zmuda Frey

## WHEEL OF FORTUNE

A modified version of the TV show *Wheel of Fortune* can teach kids social studies and even math.

Instead of having only three contestants, everyone plays. In that way everyone pays attention, hoping to be "the one" to solve the puzzle.

For the first game, I put the following on the board, and gave them the category, "things."
☐ ☐ ☐ ☐   ☐ ☐ ☐   ☐ ☐ ☐ ☐ ☐ ☐
Then I asked each child, in turn, to supply one letter. It wasn't long before they had the correct answer—salt and pepper. Soon I began concentrating on the category, "news and current events." Everyone began to listen more closely to the news and read the newspaper for interesting facts. They were begging to emcee.

If you wish to involve math, place a numerical value on each letter. Clip pictures of appealing things to be "purchased" from magazines and catalogs with a price attached. Winners must figure out how much of their winnings is left over for a gift certificate.          -Jacqueline Armin

## FOOD FOR THOUGHT

Try this idea for motivating kids to research various topics in social studies. Soak the labels off 12 different jars (baby food jars are the best size), and number them 1 through 12. Inside each jar, place a small slip of paper, on which you've written a question pertaining to the particular social studies unit your class is studying. Instruct your students to choose questions from the jars during free time, then find the correct answers using various reference books. Have the kids record their answers on sheets of paper to be handed in when all 12 questions have been researched. Encourage students to make up questions of their own and place them inside the jars, too.
          -Jean Antony

### PLUNDER BOXES

Nothing is more fun to rummage through than "plunder"—the authentic junk found in grandma's attic. Here's how to assemble plunder boxes that will provide great history lessons.

In separate boxes collect materials that pertain to specific periods in history. Visit the library for period photos, articles, music, and art capable of being reproduced. Ask parents for personal memoirs and donations of magazines, photos, and artifacts related to your themes. And when possible, tape-record eyewitness accounts.

A 1920s' box for instance, might contain clippings, souvenirs, pictures, interviews, and ads on anything from the stock market crash and movie stars to the Hindenburg and Hitler.

After an hour with a plunder box, your students will have a much better understanding of the multitude of events that make an era—as well as many questions. Encourage them to research these questions and report their findings to the class.

*-Robert G. Brown*

### REAL PEOPLE BOOK

To help children learn about the effects of the American Revolutionary War on people, and to help them develop writing and art skills, try making a "real people" book.

On different slips of paper, write the name of a common occupation in the 1760s (innkeeper, shopkeeper, farmer, politician, soldier) or a person's relation to a British or American soldier (child of a British soldier, husband or wife of a Revolutionary soldier). Each child draws a slip from a hat and "becomes" that person. The children research what their lives were like during that period and write brief sketches of daily life during the war. For example: "I am an innkeeper. Even though I support the Revolutionary army, I must let the British soldiers stay at my inn. I don't like to, but if I refuse them, I can be put in prison." Then the children illustrate their pages.

Gather the reports and make copies of them. Bind them with staples or yarn. Finally, each child can design and draw a cover for his or her book. This "real people" book helps students understand how war affects everyone in a country, not just the soldiers.

*-Janet Spaeth*

### GRAPH A QUILT

In conjunction with a social studies unit on American colonial crafts, children can use graph paper to make patchwork patterns by coloring in and outlining boxes in a square. Older children may like to copy classical patterns from a quilting book. When all "quilting pieces" are the same size, they can be stapled together on a bulletin board and trimmed with ruffled crepe paper to make an authentic-looking quilt.

*-Mary A. Lombardo*

### REVOLUTIONARY TREASURE HUNT

My eighth graders' response to my announcement that we would begin to study the American Revolution was that they had studied it before, they knew all about it, it was spring, and let's do something else. So I devised a revolutionary war treasure hunt and started the students on a search for their own information on the war.

Each student was given a list of Revolution-era "treasures" to find, such as recipes, songs, or diaries. Students were also presented with a folder so their findings could be kept neatly in class. Two class periods and evening assignment times were set aside for initial research and preparation. Then, at the beginning of every class for seven days, students were allowed time to present their "treasures."

Many students chose to copy colonial recipes, and some cooked food—biscuits, dumplings and stew, corn bread—and brought it to class. Others proudly read their letters from Valley Forge—the pages singed and rumpled. A good number brought in copies of revolutionary war paintings, and many copied colonial flags and explained their symbolism.

*-John M. Haight*

### PRESIDENTS IN PERSPECTIVE

Use these activities on U.S. presidents to help your kids develop a sense of history.

**1.** List the birth and death dates of each president.

**2.** List the dates of each president's stay in office.

**3.** Figure out how old each was when elected.

**4.** List three important events that happened when each president was in office.

**5.** Find and trace or copy examples of hair styles and clothes that were in fashion during each president's time.

**6.** List inventions developed while each was in office.

**7.** Find grandparents' and great-grandparents' birth dates and determine who was president then.
*-Florence Rives*

## A "GRAVE" FIELD TRIP

Want an unusual way to interest students in the history of their city or town? Try a field trip to the local cemetery. Local history, early settlements and immigration patterns are just a few curriculum areas that can be studied at the cemetery. Many headstones have complete biographies engraved on them, while others contain brief epitaphs providing a sense of the language of the times. You may even discover the headstone of a famous person or reference to an historical event or local happening of an unusual nature. The artwork and symbols found on early gravestones may seem strange to us today, but they were very meaningful to members of Early American communities. Symbols like the skull and crossbones, rising sun, angels and cherubim, and winged forms were common expressions of the inevitability of death and the individual's concern for the hereafter. It would be a good idea to explain these things to your class before visiting the cemetery, and encourage the kids to do a little research on their own. You'll also need to know something about the art of gravestone rubbing, as most old stones are covered with dirt and moss. A relatively simple process, gravestone rubbing consists of transferring the design and inscription from the gravestone to paper or fabric with wax or a crayon. You will need tracing paper or cloth interfacing (special rubbing paper is also available at most art stores), and some large-sized crayons or special rubbing

wax (also available at art stores). Bring a large plastic bag to sit on, scissors and masking tape, a soft brush to clean the stone, a pad and pencil for note taking, and a litter bag.

Brush the surface lightly to remove dirt and moss from the engraving. (Be sure to check with the cemetery caretaker first.) Now tape the paper or cloth to the face of the stone with masking tape, making sure it is taut and smooth so it won't move during the rubbing. Using the flat surface of a crayon or the wax, gently rub the paper over the inscription to get an overall impression. Then repeat, using more pressure to emphasize details.

Local history, early settlements, and immigration patterns are just a few of the curriculum areas you can relate to a field trip like this, and your students will come to understand history from a personal point of view.
*-Linda M. Eccleston*

## GRAVESTONE STUDY

October is the perfect month to study a nearby, old cemetery. To stimulate interest, make a few gravestone rubbings yourself and display them along with pictures of old tombstones. You may even find stories related to strange events on gravestones of infamous or famous people. Community libraries can provide books on this subject along with details particular to your area. Discuss epitaphs and the art that appears on older tombstones. When you visit an old cemetery, bring rice paper and large crayons to make gravestone rubbings. Have children choose a rubbing and research the events that happened during the lifetime of their "person." *-William E. Heitz*

## PETROGLYPHS

Cave and rock art—
*petroglyphs*—have long intrigued historians. Here are some suggestions you can use to

design an introductory unit on this interesting and ancient concept that can be used in conjunction with a study of Southwestern American Indian tribes, cave dwellers, and primitive or aborigine peoples throughout the world.

**1.** Start by showing the kids pictures of cave and canyon wall designs. These can be found in back issues of *National Geographic* magazine and other periodicals. Check your library card catalog for additional sources.

**2.** Have students research and list some of the various subjects of rock art, such as hunters and buffalo, bows and arrows, women and children, snakes, owls, footprints, bears, eagles, dancing figures, and so on.

**3.** Have kids work in groups to discuss and list possible reasons for the creation of rock art. Some ideas may include: the desire for self-expression, the sending of messages to other tribes, superstition, or the recording of events.

**4.** Have the kids work together to create mural drawings representing events in the lives of early people—aborigines, Indians, and so on.

**5.** Let children make their own petroglyphs on pieces of sandstone, limestone, hardened clay, or slabs of plaster. They will have to use pointed objects such as nails, nail files, compass points, and so on to make their imprints; so be sure to carefully supervise this activity. Display their artwork in a special area.
*-Florence Rives*

## TIME MARCHES ON

To culminate your next social studies unit, have each child in your class select a personality in history to research and put on the cover of a mock *Time* magazine. The children should write as though they were contemporaries of their chosen subjects, focusing on specific months or years of their lives. Have them include the following items in their magazines.

1. An interview with the subject.
2. Three to five advertisements for items invented or frequently used during the time period in which their subject lived.
3. A biography of the president in office at that time.
4. A report on local happenings in your town at the time.
5. An original poem about the subject.
6. A synopsis of important national events that occurred during the chosen month or year. This activity is great for promoting research, using various sources your students may not be familiar with. Have kids laminate their finished "magazines," if possible, to give them a slick, professional appearance. -Louise Jastremski

## BRIGHT INVENTIONS

Use this social studies activity as a learning tool to reinforce your next unit on inventions. Start with a plain, manila folder. On the right side, attach two pockets large enough to hold construction paper light bulbs. Then make two sets of light bulbs—one from white paper and the other from yellow paper. On the yellow paper, print the names of famous inventors, one per light bulb. On the white ones, print the corresponding inventions. Now make an answer card and place it in a long envelope stapled to the left side of the folder. Students are to match inventors with inventions, then check their answers. -Gertrude Parker

## BIOGRAPHICAL BINGO

Biographical reports on famous people are part of most elementary curriculums, but merely having the students read their reports aloud can be tedious

and boring. Why not add a new twist to this activity by promising a game of "biography bingo" at the end of the unit? Draw an empty bingo grid on a duplicating master or reproduce the page at the right and give one copy to each student along with several cardboard markers. Make sure the squares are large enough to hold a person's name and field of endeavor. Mark the middle square FREE, to be covered automatically. The children are to move around the classroom, exchanging the name of their biographical personality and his or her talent with the other students. They are to fill in the names and endeavors on their cards in random fashion, so no two cards are exactly alike. Now fill a large container with slips of paper on which you've printed the names and endeavors of each biographical person. Draw one of the slips, read the name, and ask for a volunteer to tell you why that person is famous. All children with the name on their card must cover it with a marker. The game continues until someone has five markers in a row and calls out "bingo!" For a variation of this activity, first state the reason for the person's fame, then ask a volunteer to give the corresponding name. -Susan Horak

## TO TELL THE TRUTH

Teach your kids about famous people in history through this activity based on the old television game show, *To Tell the Truth.* Choose any historic figure you'd like your kids to know more about; then prepare a duplicating master that lists important facts, achievements, and bits of trivia about that person. Now cut small strips of paper—one for every student in your class—and number three of the slips consecutively. Draw a star on one of the three numbered slips, leave the rest blank, and put all of them together in a shoe box. Have your

students take turns drawing slips from the box while you explain that those who draw blank slips are to sit on the panel and those who draw numbered slips are the contestants. The child who picks the starred slip is to represent the actual person from history. Then give everyone a copy of the duplicating master you have prepared—except the two contestants who did not pick the starred slip. The three contestants should then go out in the hall while the rest of the kids remain in the classroom studying their duplicating masters. The contestant who drew the starred slip should also study the master. While out in the hall, he or she may share certain bits of information with the other two contestants if desired. This will enable them to stump the panel by answering a few of their questions correctly.

After they've studied the list for a few minutes, instruct panel members in the classroom to write down five questions each that will help them determine the true identity of the famous person. Now have the contestants come back inside and stand before three chairs in the front of your classroom. Ask them each to tell their names. (Of course, all three contestants will give the same name.) Then ask them to be seated. The panelists may now take turns directing their questions to the three contestants. After the designated time period is over (five minutes is usually sufficient), give the panelists index cards and instruct them to write down the number of the contestant they believe is actually representing the person from history. Each panelist must briefly explain his or her choice. Now call for the "real person" to stand up. Those who guessed correctly may help choose the next person from history to be represented. -Lynn P. Wainman

# Bingo

Reproduce this card for distribution to pupils for the idea on page 132. Use this card for other bingo-type activities.

### HISTORY AT A GLANCE
Do your students have difficulty putting historical events into perspective? If so, this idea is for you. Sometime early in the year, make two time lines and place them above your chalkboard, on the bulletin board, or on a wall in your classroom. One time line should represent the years A.D. 1 through 1775, and the other should represent the years 1776 to the present. On the first time line, one inch should equal 10 years; on the second, one inch should equal one year. Now assign a different block of time to each student in your class. Kids are to research their assigned time periods and list significant historical events or technological advances that occurred during those years. Then have the children attach their lists to the appropriate places on the time lines. Now, when your students need to place significant people, events or discoveries in historical perspective, they need only glance at the time lines! -Betty See

### MARCH OF TIME
Send your students on a path to the past. First write out a list of events that occurred in American history and have each student pick a favorite. Now give students a piece of construction paper on which to trace their footprints. When they've cut out both paper feet, they should pick one "foot" on which to write their chosen event and its date, and on the other they'll draw pictures of how this event occurred. When the drawings are finished, have students pin the series of footprints to a bulletin board in chronological order. Your student-made time line could include the question: Can you trace a path to the past?
                        -Suzanne Madero

### TIME LINE
Here's an easy-to-make, inexpensive time line that helps students put important historical events in chronological order. Tie a string across the room, high enough to be out of the way. As a date is learned or an event covered in class, write the date in large numerals on a card and clip it to the string. Tape another card to the bottom of the date card stating what makes this a date to remember.       -Pam Klawitter

### ONE COUNTY'S HISTORY
My third, fourth, and fifth grade students recently put on a program to demonstrate the growth and change of their county during the years 1800 to 1900. This program was a sound-and-light production that was engineered from start to finish by the class. The first thing the students did to get ready for the program was to research the history of the county. They obtained local history books and interviewed some senior citizens to learn about the people who had made contributions to their towns and about the history of the local landmarks that are still standing and of those that have been destroyed. They also wanted to know about famous events, legends, and life-styles of the people of the county. They hoped to include both humorous and serious stories. Once the research was completed, the students compiled the information into ten reports, each report covering the events of one decade. These eventually became the scripts for the program. Students then broke up into ten groups and began to make models portraying the county as it was during a particular decade. The models were constructed on plywood and were made of many materials including clay, boxes, and ice cream sticks. The boxes were covered and painted to look like wood-sided houses. The clay

was used to make brick homes, streets, and sidewalks. The ice cream sticks made excellent planks for the sidewalks the county had during the 1850s. The children also brought from home model trains, stagecoaches, covered wagons, and streetcars. The class even wired a one-watt bulb into a building that had the first electric light in the 1880s. The students also displayed a collection of slides and photographs. The sound portion of the program included music from the times and special sound effects such as a train whistle, church bells, galloping horses, and a streetcar clanking over its tracks. These sounds were played on cue by the narrator as he or she read the script. Three flashlights were used in the darkened room to spotlight each model as it was described. Sometimes the flashlights were turned off and a slide was displayed on a screen. By all accounts, our program was a great success!       -Jeff Deremiah

### CRUMBY CANDIDATES
To very young children, election day often means very little. The concepts involved in one vote for one candidate, privacy of choice, and majority rule are too difficult for them to understand. The following election-day activity gives my kindergartners a clearer idea of what free elections are. My voting booth is a screen borrowed from the school nurse. Inside the booth is a small table where I have placed three different boxes of cookies. The children are each given a "ballot" (a slip of paper) as they line up outside the booth. They enter, one at time, and "vote" for their favorite cookie by sliding their slip of paper under the box of their choice. When the voting is completed, the ballots are counted and the cookie with the most votes is served as a snack that day.       -Faith Solomon

## JUMP ON THE BANDWAGON

The following class activities are ways teachers can set the stage for a presidential election.

**1.** Have students collect campaign memorabilia—buttons, stickers, emery boards, posters, matches, balloons—anything candidates pass out to voters. Each item a student brings to class entitles him or her to place his or her name in a ballot box. On election day, draw a name and have a prize for that student. As students bring in the materials, plaster the classroom walls and ceiling with the materials and display other items on a table.

**2.** Each child finds pictures of the candidates in newspapers or magazines and pastes them on a poster, together with pertinent facts about each.

**3.** Create an elephant/donkey center. First draw, cut, and laminate red elephant cards and blue donkey cards. On each one paste a research question or activity. Sample activities could be: 1. On a map of the United States print the name of each president in the state of his birth. 2. Whom do you consider the greatest president? Give factual data to support your choice. 3. What would you do if you were president? Make a collage showing that.

**4.** As a class, keep track of where each major candidate travels each day during the last two weeks of the campaign.

**5.** Pin up quotes from powerful people. Discuss the power of words in politics.

**6.** Design bulletin boards that list the steps in the election of the president (primaries, convention, speeches, debates, election day, electoral college). Cut out shapes of footsteps for each one. Title the board "The Road to the White House."
            *-Virginia G. Johnson*

## AND THE WINNER IS . . .

Before the results are in, this election activity can help second through sixth graders better understand the voting process. Begin by talking with other classroom teachers about participating in a mock all-school election. Assign a state name to each class joining in. Classes with more students are assigned states with more electoral votes. Teachers can use current events and election activities to help students be informed voters. Make your own students responsible for developing a voter registration form that they ask each prospective voter to return by a certain date. Students in your class record registered voters by state and keep this

record to check off on election day. Before that day it would be good to invite a speaker in to discuss voting procedures.

As election day nears, announce voting hours and set up voting booths in your room. Have classes vote by state, and count all the votes after the polls close. To add to the excitement, announce the results by state at intervals over the intercom. Be sure to emphasize the numerical vote as well as the fact that all electoral votes for that state go to one of the candidates. Teachers of each "state" can keep a tally on their chalkboards.

After the victorious candidate is announced, it will be even more exciting to go home and watch the actual results.   *-Gloria Bernadt*

## ASSEMBLY LINE PRODUCTION

In social science work, I find first graders are not terribly interested in looking at pictures in a book and reading a few sentences about them. So, I try to create an activity that will clarify the idea. For a unit on contributing occupations, I set up a production line system. To construct a paper car, I found a simple pattern with eight parts and made patterns for each part. Next I divided the class into eight groups. Each group had one particular part to make and had to make as many parts as there were pupils. This took one class period. The next day, the eight groups were seated in the order in which each part would be pasted, starting with the chassis and ending with the bumpers. It was both fun and meaningful and kids learned to work together.

*-Freda Wittman*

## FAIRY-TALE COURT

The culminating activity of a fifth-grade study of the American legal system was a mock jury trial of Hansel and Gretel versus the witch. Students researched the law, investigated the facts, considered questions of motive and intent, and worked up the case into an 11-page script. There was a large cast: judge, bailiff, prosecutor, defense attorney, jury (formally selected the previous week), defendant (the witch), and witnesses for both sides. A character witness, for example, was the president of the Witches Association; testifying for the prosecution was an ant who had been foraging outside the witch's cottage on the day in question. Cross-examinations, objections, and outbursts were dramatic parts of the trial.

The script showed a remarkable understanding of law, accuracy in legal procedure, and insight into the logic of questioning. Any class could benefit from a similar activity, using a fairy tale or fable as part of a law unit or as an introduction to critical thinking. Oh yes—the witch was found guilty of second-degree aggravated assault and sentenced to eight years in jail.

*-Marilyn Gilbert*

## WHERE IN THE WORLD?

Second and third graders always seem to have a great deal of difficulty in mastering the concept of size and relationship when learning about the world they live in. A sturdy reinforcement to map and globe teaching is the use of nesting cups (sold where infant toys are found). Each cup should be labeled *neighborhood, city, state, country, continent,* and *planet.* Then have kids start with the smallest cup saying, "I live in the neighborhood called_____,

which is in the city of_____, which is in the state of_____, which is on the continent of_____, which is on the planet *Earth.*" As a child makes each statement, instruct him or her to place each cup in the next larger one. This audio-kinesthetic approach helps kids contrast and compare the parts which make up the total of the world in which we live.

*-Cleo Giampaolo*

## KNOW YOUR RIGHTS

If your class is studying the Constitution, this activity will make the Bill of Rights relevant. First divide students into committees. Then give a modern, day illustration of a violation of one of the basic rights. Ask one student which amendment is being transgressed. If he or she answers correctly and can state the amendment, that committee earns one point. The first committee to get 10 points wins.

*-Ronald H. Brodin*

## TEAMWORK

Get your class together to create a "Collage of Brotherhood." Not only will children think more about their relationships to the many people of different cultures with whom they share the Earth, but by working on a common project with fellow classmates, children will also create a spirit of brotherhood right in their own classroom.

To make the collage, have children find pictures of people in other countries, as well as pictures of people in the United States, and glue them all to a large sheet of brown paper. They may even wish to add photographs of themselves. Spray an art sealer on the final result for a lasting mural or backdrop for a tribute to Martin Luther King, Jr.   *-Milton Polsky*

## GOOD POSTURE WEEK

Good posture is essential for proper bone development, and children often need to be reminded of this important fact. Why not celebrate a "Good Posture Week"?

1. Show movies and filmstrips about good posture. Your audiovisual department can give you a current listing of available material categorized according to age group and date of release.
2. Ask your school nurse to demonstrate good and poor posture to the children.
3. Make sure that you and the other teachers in your school set good examples yourselves. Reward the kids for their own attempts at good posture. At the end of the week, distribute certificates saying, "I have good posture!"
4. Have the children write stories or poems about good posture. These can be typed, duplicated, and compiled into a newsletter to be sent home with every child at the end of the week. Also ask the kids to be on the lookout for events regarding good posture, physical fitness programs in your area, and so on.
5. Ask your school coach or athletic director to emphasize exercises for proper body development and to stress the importance of good posture on the field or court that week.
6. Use bulletin boards in the hallways to display posters from the health office, jackets from appropriate health and fitness books, and the children's stories and poems.
7. Ask your school librarian to set aside a special table for relevant books and magazine articles on good posture.
8. Culminate this week of special activities with a school assembly. Give special recognition to one boy or girl from every class whose posture is outstanding.

*-Barbara Conrady*

## CROSS COUNTRY JOGGING

Jogging is a terrific individualized sports activity, but sometimes you'll need to add a little spice to the regular routine. Try posting a large wall map of the United States in your school gym, with a push pin labeled to represent each jogger. Decide upon a scale, such as five laps equals one inch on the map. As jogging distances are logged, move the push pins accordingly across the map. The jogger may move in any direction he or she wants and visit as many cities and states as possible, or the class can set a destination at the start and race to see who gets there first. Try for San Francisco or the Mississippi River. Or use a world map for the contest with the heading, "Around the World in 80 Laps!" When used in cooperation with the social studies teacher, this activity can be even more enriching as the students gain information from reference material about the places they've jogged to.

*-Christina Crowley*

## VOLLEYBALL SKILLS

Younger children will find it easier to be successful volleyball players if they first use a large, lightweight beach ball. Form circles of six to eight. A person in the center tosses the ball to each in succession, going around the circle at least three times.

Then, with net up, the class forms two teams for catch volleyball. The ball is tossed to one team. A student catches it, then throws to the other team. When someone misses, the other team is given a point. As skills increase, the player who catches the ball must toss it to a team member for three catches on a side. Now, after the skills of rotation and court sense are mastered, play regular-style volleyball. The beach ball will allow the students to use the skills they have learned without having to contend with the sting and force of the heavier ball.

*-Michael Wilson*

## SELF-CONCEPTS AND PHYS ED

Every teacher knows how important it is to promote healthy self-concepts in young children. This is especially necessary during their first experiences with organized physical activity. Here are some successful strategies you can use to support a self-enhancing learning environment in physical education programs.

1. Install full-length mirrors in locker rooms. Hang signs over the mirrors reading "I look terrific today" or "I'm proud to be me."
2. Keep a camera handy to take pictures of children demonstrating correct skill form. Hang pictures on a bulletin board in the gymnasium.
3. Assign a different child to be "manager for the day" in each gym class. This student should be responsible for leading the class line, recording individual fitness scores, counting returned equipment, and so on.
4. Take individual pictures of children participating in their favorite physical activities. During art class, have the kids turn their photos into holiday greeting cards.
5. Print official physical education "happy grams" on school or department letterhead to be sent home to parents periodically during the year. These should be general in nature, stating simply that a particular child gave an outstanding performance in physical education class. This will give the kids an opportunity to explain their own achievements more specifically.

*-Robert N. Horrocks*

## HANDY EXERCISE

For a hand exercise to strengthen muscles and improve coordination, let a child attach a dozen spring-type clothespins to a coat hanger. Then, with the right hand, the child removes one pin at a time, and holds the pins in that hand until he or she has removed as many as possible without dropping one. The child must not touch the pins with any other part of his or her body. A young child may be able to remove and hold as many as five or six pins without dropping one. With practice, this number might be increased to eight or nine. Older children can hold as many as 10 or 12. When a pin is dropped, the child should begin again, using his or her other hand. Remind children to always return pins to hanger.

*-Florence Rives*

## OLD-FASHIONED RECESS
Reacquaint your students with some old favorite games.

**1. Pretzel:** A group of 10-20 people is best for this game. Have the group gather in a tight circle, with arms outstretched in front of them. In the sea of available hands, each person must grab two other hands. Without letting go, the group must then try to untangle the resulting "pretzel" and return to the original circle by ducking under or stepping over the chain.

**2. Capture the Flag:** Divide players into two different teams. Each team occupies one half of the playing area. At the back line of each team's "court" is a "flag" and a "prison." (Use two handkerchiefs for flags and simply designate two small areas behind the courts as prisons.) The object of the game is for a player from one team to capture the other team's flag and return it to his own court without being tagged. The other players protect their team's flag. Any player tagged in enemy territory must go to the enemy's prison. A prisoner can be rescued if he's tagged by another teammate, but a rescuer may not take the enemy's flag while rescuing. Only one prisoner may be rescued at a time. A team can also win by capturing all the opposing team members, though this is unlikely.

**3. Red Rover:** Divide the class into two teams and have them line up at opposite ends of a large rectangular area. Team 1 must choose a member of the other team to call on and shout, "Red Rover, Red Rover, we dare (name) to come over." Members of Team 1 must then hold hands very tightly as the person called runs across the field and tries to break through the hands of two opponents. If successful, the runner gets to pick a player from Team 1 to return with him to Team 2. Now the second team dares a player to break the chain. When recess is over, the team with the most players wins.

**4. Red Light, Green Light:** The object of this game is simply for players to move across the playing area without getting caught. One player is the leader and he or she must stand on a designated goal line. The rest of the group stands on a starting line at the other end of the playing area. The leader turns his or her back on the group and shouts "green light!" Then the group moves toward the goal line. When the leader shouts "red light!" the others must freeze. Anyone caught moving must return to the starting line . The first person to cross the goal is the new leader.

*-M. D. Thomas*

## RAINY RECESS GAMES
Here are fun games to provide a lively indoor recess period.

**Desk Ring Relay** Desks are arranged into columns with an equal number in each. A tennequoit ring is placed on each front desk. On "go", the ring is passed backward over the head until it reaches the last person in the column. This person immediately gets up, goes to the first desk in the column, and sits down in the seat as everyone else moves back one seat. The relay continues until all players are back in their original seats. To avoid collisions have all players move on the same side of the desks.

**Caterpillar** All players sit in chairs in a circle. The starting player goes to the center leaving an empty chair. He or she then calls out "slide left" or "slide right" and tries to get a seat. Players in the circle try to prevent this by moving continuously in the announced direction. The player may call a change of directions at will. When he or she gets a seat, the player who should have slid into the empty chair is in the center.

**Spin the Platter** Players sit in a circle. Each is given a number. The caller stands in the circle, spins a pie plate on its rim and calls out a number. That person must grasp the plate before it falls to the floor. If successful this person becomes the caller. Variations: Instead of assigning numbers, use colors or animals. Or throw a ball up in the air for the person called to catch before a specified number of bounces.

**Exchange Tag** One person is chosen to be "it" and stands in a predetermined place. Everyone else sits at a desk. The teacher calls out names of two players who must get up and change seats. "It" tries to tag one of these players before seats are successfully exchanged. If "it" is successful then the person tagged becomes "it." If any player touches a chair or desk that player becomes "it."

**Boiler Burst** This game begins with everyone seated. One person, the storyteller, stands and begins a story. At any time the storyteller may end the story by saying "and then the boiler burst." This is the signal for everyone to get up and exchange seats. The storyteller then attempts to get a seat. The person left standing becomes the storyteller.

*-Kathy Pattak*

## FOOD IS MORE THAN YUMMY

Introduce young children to good nutrition, important food facts, and health information with the following activity. Have children bring in labels from canned, frozen, and boxed foods and from illustrations of foods from magazines. Hold a cutting and pasting period in which the labels and pictures are neatly cut out and pasted onto cardboard pieces to fit the sizes of the pictures or labels. Leave enough space at the bottom to write the name of the food. Then do the following.

1. Hold up one picture at a time, and let the children identify the the food illustrated.

2. Have the children sit in a circle, and give each child a food picture. Tell kids to look at their picture carefully and keep in mind what it is. Now have everyone turn their picture over, and call out one food word at a time. The child holding that food picture should stand and show it to the group. Then have the children swap pictures and repeat the procedure.

3. Choose a food picture and ask a child to look carefully at the food word below the picture. Cover the picture and have the child say the word. Later, after practice, have the child say the food words, as they are flashed.

4. Introduce the basic food groups—meats, vegetables, fruits, grains, and dairy products. Let the children look at the pictures and state which group each food belongs to.

5. Have five children wear placards, each naming a different food group, and stand in front of the class. Pass out food pictures to the rest of the class. Then have each student look at his or her picture and give it to the child whose placard names the group to which the food belongs.

6. Select 13 foods (representing each of the five food groups). Collect four pictures of each food and paste them onto cardboard pieces, making 52 cards. Now play this card game with four players: Deal one card to each player and put other cards facedown in a pile. When a player gets two cards that match, he or she discards the matched pair. Players do this until all the cards are picked up or a player matches his or her entire hand. The winner is the one who "matches out" or has the least number of cards in his or her hand.

7. Use pictures to make up menus for balanced meals. Let each child select food for his own meal.
*-Florence Rives*

## FOOD PILLOWS

This art project is a perfect accompaniment to a unit on nutrition. Have each child choose a particular food, sketch it in pencil on a sheet of large, white butcher paper, place another sheet of paper underneath and cut two outlines out. Use sponges to paint both sheets with tempera paint in appropriate colors. Stuff them with wadded newspaper and staple sides together to make giant food pillows. Then hang them from the ceiling of your cafeteria for delicious companions! *-Linda Jackson, Abbey McCone, Pat Stafford*

## VITAMIN PUPPETS

Students will be full of vim and vigor as they learn about nutrition with these easy-to-make vitamin puppets.

Have each student make a set of four rectangular puppets, using two pieces of heavy paper for each. Staple or tape three sides together, leaving the bottom open (see illustration). Have students draw the letters A,B,C, or D in bold print, one on each of the four puppets. They may wish to make the letters look like

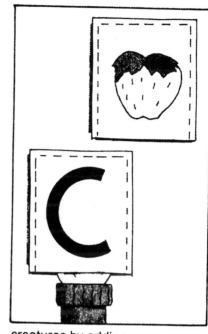

creatures by adding eyes, noses, and mouths. Next, have students cut out pictures of natural foods high in each vitamin from seed catalogs or magazines. Glue these to the back of the appropriate vitamin puppet. You may want to assign the students to research the sources of each vitamin but here is a starting list. Vitamin A: milk, eggs, liver, green and yellow vegetables; B: fish, poultry, pork chops, peanut butter, whole-grain bread and cereal; C: tomatoes, oranges, strawberries, potatoes; D: egg yolks, tunafish, fortified milk, sunlight.

Use the puppets for nutritional awareness by having small groups create poems, skits, or songs. *-Jean Stangl*

## "DO TRY IT, YOU MIGHT LIKE IT!"

Because of cultural differences and sometimes poor nutritional standards among my students, I have developed a fun learning experience dealing with food. Each Monday afternoon, we sample a tasty treat brought by a student or me. To qualify, the food has to be something we think less than fourth of the class has tasted. (Before beginning such a project, it is best to send a paper home for parents to sign inquiring about food allergies.) When tasting time arrives, I provide the students with a form to be filled out. First, we put the date. Then, we research the food in the encyclopedia or check the ingredients on the package. From this information, we list how it is grown—on a tree, bush, root, and so on; in what area of the world it is raised; or what culture makes this particular food. The next step is to smell the sample and describe its odor. Then, we get to taste! From the taste, we write at least five adjectives to describe the food. This might include words such as *green* (or any color), *sweet, sour, grainy, smooth, stringy, crunchy, bitter,* and so on. After we have devoured our samples, we circle ''like'' or '' dislike'' under the preference heading.

Some of the treats we've tried have been oysters, okra, soy nuts, seaweed (a unanimous ''yuck''), fortune cookies, hominy, fresh mushrooms, homemade pickled beans, papaya, kumquats, Clamato juice, butter (we made our own to go along with a unit on the dairy states), and made-in-class ice cream.

Since starting this adventure in eating, the students are learning they can like foods that look or sound strange. They are also picking up geographical facts and information about other cultures. I find the following tools a necessity: an electric skillet (to warm some foods), toothpicks (in place of forks), paper towels, a large spoon, paper cups, and cupcake papers. You might also use paper plates or plastic forks and spoons.              -Jane Kennedy

### EAT YOUR HAT

Here's a yummy way to culminate a unit on nutrition that stresses the avoidance of junk foods. Have every child in your class design and create an original bonnet that's good enough to eat! They can make bases for their hats from paper plates, circular poster board, or anything else suitable for millinery design—even Frisbees! Then, have them add dried fruits and vegetables, and other goodies. These can be attached with tape, ribbon, or needle and thread. Bows should provide the finishing touches, and colored ribbon can be used to hold the bonnets in place on the children's heads.

When all the hats are completed conduct a parade through the school so your kids can display their artful handiwork. Then have the class vote on the best hat, considering originality, edibility, design, and good humor. The activity should end with every child eating his or her hat, and tasting classmates' as well. This provides a truly satisfying end to the assignment, and you'll really be pleased with the kids' enthusiastic ''feedback!''

                -Bernice Cohan

### COUNTING CALORIES

This game emphasizes to students that they need to eat about 2800 calories a day and makes them aware that different foods have different numbers of calories in them. The game also strengthens addition skills through the score-keeping process.

Begin by making the game board. Take a large piece of tagboard and draw a 2-inch-wide margin around the edges of the board. Then divide this border section into about 25 equal squares. One of the corner squares will be your starting place for the game. In the other squares you must write a type of common food or drink and its calorie count per serving. (You can find calorie counts in any encyclopedia or science book.) I always intersperse these with a few squares that tell the players they miss a turn or get a free turn for landing there.

A player begins by rolling a die and moving a token the appropriate number of spaces around the board. Each time a player lands on a food square, he or she adds that number of calories to his or her score. Each player should keep a record of his or her own score and the scores of the other players. This keeps accuracy high and gives the students more addition practice. When a player scores 2800 calories, he or she is out of the game but continues to keep score with the other players. The last player in the game is the winner because he or she was able to go the farthest before reaching 2800 calories.            -Pam Pennington

### WAR ON WASTE

When we started monitoring the food waste in our school cafeteria, we found kids were throwing away 30 to 50 pounds of main dish and 60 unopened cartons of milk daily. My gifted and talented class went to work on a problem-solving campaign that cut our waste to 94 pounds a day and saved the school $8,000 during the course of the year.

My third, fourth, and fifth graders began by collecting their data—the garbage. In the back of the cafeteria they set up separate bins for vegetables, milk, fruit, main dish, and bread. By weighing the full garbage bags and charting which foods were wasted the most (pizza was wasted least), we learned the extent of the waste.

Our district dietician agreed to implement several of our suggestions on how to cut down on waste, among them that pizza be served three days a week as a second main dish.

If you try this project, you'll find students learn much about nutrition, the cost of food, graphing, and, most of all, how to go about solving a problem.

                -Joan Rademacher

## BABY DEWEY

The Dewey Decimal System is often very hard for children to remember. Here's a poem designed to help. It's divided into couplets for each division in the Dewey system.

> When you're born,
> Your thoughts are torn.
> *(000-009, General Works)*
> When you're 1,
> You think life's fun.
> *(100-199, Philosophy)*
> When you're 2,
> You believe in you.
> *(200-299, Religion)*
> When you're 3,
> You'll trust in me.
> *(300-399, Social Sciences)*
> When you're 4,
> You'll speak much more.
> *(400-499, Languages)*
> When you're 5,
> You'll come alive.
> *(500-599, Pure Sciences)*
> When you're 6,
> The things you'll fix.
> *(600-699, Technology)*
> When you're 7,
> Art will be heaven.
> *(700-799, Fine Arts)*
> When you're 8,
> Poetry is great!
> *(800-899, Literature)*
> When you're 9,
> You'll travel through time.
> *(900-999, History and Travel)*

A class discussion can help children relate the verses to the categories and remember the Dewey Decimal System!

*-Wade Olsen*

## AN AWARD-WINNING IDEA

Can your students learn to judge the quality of a book? Can they become aware that writers and illustrators make choices about how to present their ideas? They can if you interest them in the annual American Library Association Newbery and Caldecott awards. The Newbery Award is made each year for "the most distinguished contribution to American children's literature"; the Caldecott medal is awarded to an illustrator for "the most distinguished American picture book for children."

Your library should have a list of past award winners, and have at least several of them available. Explain to the class the purpose of the awards and the basis of excellence in writing and art on which the books are judged. Give children a few days to read and familiarize themselves with the books, then discuss them. What art techniques and mediums did the illustrators use? What literary devices did the authors use? Why?

Now obtain several books (not medal winners) as candidates for class awards. Announce a "Book Awards Day" and set up your panels. Start by having the panels name the awards and adopt a design for their seals of approval. Next have class members vote for best illustrated and best written, giving reasons for their choices. A nice follow-up is to write in care of the publisher to the winning author and illustrator, being sure to send a copy of the award. Children may also ask for biographies of the winners.

*-Jean Stangl*

## READING CORNER

The reading corner is a special part of any classroom. I set my reading area apart by putting a castle in the middle of it. I make the castle by painting a large cardboard appliance box and using poster board to make a turret. Over the doors of the castle I paint the words "Enter the Kingdom of Reading."

*-Ruth Neimeyer Dale*

## STREAMING TO THE LIBRARY

When I noticed that the library area in my classroom was never the "in" place to go, I decided to change the decor. I hung crepe paper streamers around the perimeter of the whole area, leaving a small opening for the "doorway." Now kids love to go in the library—it has become their own special place. I change the color scheme of the streamers each month—red and green for December, white for January, and so on—and believe it or not, the streamers stay up all month!

*-Janice Regela*

## SECRET GARDEN

Create a secret garden in a corner of your classroom. From a garden store, obtain white plastic-coated fences and deck them with multicolored tissue flowers. Bring to your garden a birdbath, watering can, sunflowers, garden tools, stuffed animals (a rabbit, squirrel, and goose are nice), real plants, and fish. Place garden and nature books, magazines, and, of course, a copy of *The Secret Garden* by Frances Hodgson Burnett on a small table. To add to the mystery, children need to show their secret garden key to enter this hideaway for solitude and quiet reading. *-Patricia Wilmott*

### BE KIND TO UGLY BOOKS!

Ugly books need loving, too! That was the theme of a schoolwide reading project enthusiastically received by students at our school. Faced with a declining book budget, we were looking for a way to interest kids in reading the many enjoyable books collecting dust on library shelves because of dull, uninviting covers. That was the start of project "Be Kind to Ugly Books."

Participants began by selecting and reading a hardback book with a worn or drab cover. (With librarian and teacher guidance, each child chose a book of appropriate reading level and interest.) The children then designed and produced colorful covers of their own, featuring the book's title and author. Call numbers were affixed to the spines; and after careful proofreading, each cover was laminated for extra durability. Finally, each of the newly covered books was placed in the permanent library collection for others to enjoy.

Not surprisingly, circulation of the formerly "ugly" books improved considerably, and the project provided an inexpensive means for making better use of the established school library collection.

If you're interested in starting a similar project in your school, here are some things you should do.

**1.** Have kids practice their printing and proposed design on scrap paper before completing covers.
**2.** Stress clear lettering.
**3.** Enlist parent volunteers to help with cutting and folding of covers.
**4.** Have kids compose short paragraphs of annotation for the inside flaps.
*-Florence Kirchner and Gary Northrop*

STRINGING UP A LINE OF GOOD BOOKS!

### FISH STORIES

Most kids like to fish and they'll like fishing for books, too. Gather together the ends of some real fishing poles (or make your own from dowel rods, sticks, or rolled-up and painted newspapers) and attach fishing strings to each one. There should be one pole for each child in your class. Turn over one or more boxes, punch holes in the box bottoms, and stick each fishing line in the hole. Write "Stringing up a line of good books" along one side of each box. After a child has read a book, tape a cutout fish to his or her line. At the end of the year, children will have a long line of fish and a good fish story to tell their friends and relatives.
*-Agnes Gregory*

### FISHING FOR BOOKS

Try this terrific reading motivator that doubles as a bulletin board display. Cover your board with dark blue paper, then use light blue to make a row of "waves" along the upper edge. In the area above the board, place large construction paper letters reading, "BOOK FISHING—NO LIMIT!" Now have each child in your class make one construction paper fish in any color, and print his or her name across the front. When everyone is finished, staple a long piece of colored yarn to each fish and tack them all in a row to the wave portion of your display. Tell your class that each time a student reads another book, he or she may make another fish and staple it to the length of yarn. At the end of a designated time period, the child with the longest "school" of fish wins—what else—a book!
*-Betty Dale*

### YUCKY-BOOK SWAP

To encourage kids to read and share, try asking them to bring in books which they DIDN'T like! With everyone sitting in a circle, have each child put his "Yucky Book" into a pile and explain why the book was awful. Then each child gets a turn to pick a book from the pile. You can be sure that they will all quickly learn the meaning of the adage "One man's meat is another man's poison."

Keep a special shelf in the classroom library for Yucky Books. Give every child a bookmark with his or her name on it to place in a book and "reserve" it until finished. This activity can be developed into a permanent trade between two kids or even into some "White Elephant" book sales.
*-Carol Gold*

### CALLING ALL MEMBERS

A lunchtime reading club is giving our kids a chance to discover the deep satisfactions that can be found in recreational reading. This is how our Book-'n'-Bag Club started. (The children call lunches they bring from home "brown bag lunches." That's how we got our name.) Visits were made to every classroom to explain the Club.

The next day 204 children were lined up outside our reading center door to sign up. We had planned for two groups of 45 each, children from the primary grades meeting on Tuesdays and children from the intermediate grades meeting on Thursdays. In order to give all children an equal chance, we put the 204 names in a bowl and had a drawing to determine our original 90 members. All the remaining names were also drawn and listed in numerical order on a waiting list. When, and if, any of the original members dropped out, new members would be added from this list.

Appealing books and magazines were placed around the room. Beanbag chairs and colorful rugs added to the inviting decor.

As the children arrived, they were checked in by a teacher-aide. Attendance records were kept since there were 110 children on the waiting list. If children decided that they would rather go outside and play or that they would just rather not be a member anymore, they came and told us. Their names were deleted from the roster and new children were invited to join. Of course if there was conflict with a school function, the children were excused for it.

Uninterrupted sustained silent reading was maintained. Children were free to walk around the room choosing and returning books and there was an occasional whisper as a child shared a picture or an interesting part of a book or magazine with a friend. During the last 10 minutes young readers were invited to

listen to a story read by the teacher.

Our Book-'n'-Bag Club is now several years old. Every Tuesday and Thursday there is a flurry of excitement as members arrive with their lunches, select books, and settle into a favorite spot. Then gradually the process of all of us quietly reading together produces an aura of tranquillity and camaraderie that permeates the room. Hopefully these pleasant connotations will become associated with reading and produce a carry-over effect that will create lifelong readers.

*-Jackee Day*

## LIBRARY CHALLENGE

Advanced readers who are ready to explore a wider range of subject areas often present a problem for teachers who may not be sure how to provide for their expanding interests. You can remedy this problem by holding weekly challenge sessions. And, if you work with other teachers with a similar problem, you can form a larger group and take better advantage of allotted library time.

Choose a different topic to present each week. Pull several interesting books on the designated topic from library shelves and display them on a long table. Then indicate the shelf area for that particular subject and have each child select two books. The students are to keep journals on the weekly topics in which they list the titles and authors of the books they've read and brief descriptions of what they've learned. At the end of each information-gathering session, offer the children a special activity pertaining to the topic of study. They don't have to complete a different activity each week, but they should be encouraged to choose at least

two a semester and present their work to the rest of the group. (Offering the kids a choice of topics to pursue will increase the likelihood of their doing a thorough job!) Here are some possible subjects and accompanying activities.

**1. Hobbies:** Learn a new game, song, or craft and share it with the group.

**2. History:** Draw a picture of some object used in the past, such as a covered wagon or a washboard.

**3. Biography:** Find a picture of a famous person who interests you. Show it to the group and tell what that person did to make him or her remembered.

**4. People and Places:** Create a travel poster illustrating a place you've read about.

**5. Science:** Find a picture of a plant or animal you've read about and tell the group where it's found, what it eats, what special characteristics it possesses, and so on.

**6. The Working World:** Describe a job or career you've learned about and tell why you consider it an important occupation.

**7. Fairy Tales:** Make a puppet to represent one of the characters in a fairy tale you've recently read. Read the tale to the group and use the puppet for his or her part in the story.

**8. Poetry and Short Stories:** Write a poem or short story of your own. It may deal with school, your family, the outdoors, leisure time, or any other topic of your choice.

**9. Fiction:** Illustrate a book jacket for a fiction book you've read and enjoyed.

At the end of the semester, ask the students in your group to fill out an evaluation sheet on which they list the three books they enjoyed most.     *-Marlene Atkielski*

## THE BOOK CONNECTION

The creative ideas below are sure to bring children and books together in some rather unusual ways!

**Book commercials** Have your kids choose books they've recently read and particularly enjoyed and write scripts for television commercials promoting them. Stipulate that each commercial must not exceed one minute in "air time." Have each child read his or her script aloud to the rest of the class, using illustrations, if desired.

**Newspaper ads** Give your students pieces of white construction paper and have them use black felt-tipped pens or crayons to design newpaper ads for their favorite books. Each ad should contain a book's title and author and a one-sentence description to capture reader interest. Bring in examples of movie advertisements for inspiration.

**Critics' corner** Bring in examples of book reviews found in newpapers and magazines. Have your kids read a few to get a sense of reviewing style, then write their own reviews of books they've recently read. Encourage the children to be as critical as possible in their writing. Display the finished reviews on your bulletin board under the heading, "Critics' Corner." The students are to read them in free time and choose at least one of the reviewed books to read themselves.

**Book Olympics** Let your kids earn bronze, silver, and gold medals by reading a predetermined number of books. Wrapping paper with a metallic look is available in most card shops and can be used to cover cardboard discs the size of Olympic medals. Decorate your bulletin board with an Olympic theme and tack the medals along its perimeter. As kids earn their medals, they may take them off the board and pin them to their clothes. You might want to bestow the medals yourself in a special ceremony. *-Albert A. Bertani*

## RELUCTANT READER CONFERENCES

Kids who can read but choose not to pose a problem for many teachers. One third-grade teacher solved this problem by using individual reading conferences. She began by collecting information for several weeks on the amount of outside reading her children were doing.

Next, she set up schedules for seven conferences a week, each lasting no more than ten minutes. All were scheduled on a regular basis so that the children had a definite goal to work toward. Because the conferences were to be held in the classroom, she designated a special corner of the room to be the "conference corner."

Record keeping was done in two ways. One method involved a student-kept record of conference dates, books discussed, and students' reactions to the sessions.

To help the project succeed, she supplemented her book collection with selections from the public library and suggested that the children borrow books, too. She also scheduled additional reading time each day, when everyone could read something on their own.

At the first conferences, the children learned the purpose of the program and were given their schedule for future meetings. The teacher helped each choose one or two suitable books and encouraged him or her to read them by the next session. Subsequent meetings centered on the kids' reactions to the books they had read since their previous conferences. Some were eager to talk; others had to be prompted with open-ended questions about the book's characters, setting, plot, and theme. For example: (1) Who is the main character in this book? (2) Does he or she remind you of anyone you know? In what way? (3) Would you like to have him or her for a friend? Why or why not? After three months, the previously unmotivated students were reading an average of two books a week, compared to fewer than one a week at the program's start. They were reading longer and more difficult books and talking about them with their classmates. *-Victoria Marone*

## WEEKLY READING MEETING

Rather than have one child read a book for a book report, let two or more children read the same book. After they have completed their book, ask them to prepare an oral presentation to share with the class.

Schedule a reading meeting where all those who've read a book act as reporters. Appoint a chairperson and a recorder. The chairperson calls the meeting to order, introduces the reporters for that session, and announces the titles of the books. After the oral presentations, the recorder reads back to the class the title and the author, and calls for questions. All of this can be recorded in the Reading Meeting Notebook. At the conclusion of the meeting, the chairperson gives each reporter a certificate or bookmark.

You can appoint new reporters for the next meeting as well as a new chairperson and recorder.

*-Kathleen Barton*

## BOOK REPORTS COME ALIVE

Make your children's book reports come alive with paper cup puppets. Ask students to select their two favorite characters from the books they have read. Have them draw and color the characters' heads and then cut them out. Next, staple each of the heads to one end of an ice cream stick. Slit the bottom of a paper cup with a pair of scissors. Then push the end of the ice cream stick through the bottom of the cup. The cup becomes the shoulders and body of the character, and it can be colored and illustrated, too. The child holds a puppet in each hand. As the class listens to the student tell about the book, the child moves the puppets to show the action of the story. You'll have the whole class listening attentively to this kind of book report.

*-Florence Rives*

## CLERI-WHATS?

Instead of a ho-hum biographical book report, let your middle and upper graders try their hands at writing clerihews. What's a clerihew? It's a novel verse form named for its originator, Edmund Clerihew Bentley. Sometimes a bit irreverent, it has a biographical theme, uses unscanned quatrain,

and always begins with the subject's name. Here is an example:

Groucho Marx
Created sparks.
His humor may have been outrageous,
Still the laughter was contagious.

A poem may be extended to more verses if desired. *-Bernice Cohan*

## SEASON UP THOSE BOOK REPORTS!

Try adding some parsley, sage, rosemary, and thyme to book report forms—it will spark interest in your students and provide you with bulletin boards, mobiles, and other ideas to spice up your classroom as well. Here are some ways kids can report on their books; you can vary these ideas or let kids make up their own. They'll enjoy reading more when they can report on their books in unusual ways!

**1.** Pretend you are the main character. Write a small diary as you think he or she would have written it.

**2.** If the book has more than eight characters, design a mobile and draw the characters as you imagine them.

**3.** Design a new book cover and write about the story and the author.

**4.** Write a poem about the book. Display it on the bulletin board.

**5.** Get a shoe box. Take a strip of tagboard and tell the story on it by drawing frames of each event.

At one end of the shoe box, cut vertical slits for the tagboard to pass through it. Put a hole at the other end so the strip can be viewed by pulling it through.

**6.** Paint a mural depicting the story or a particular scene from the book.

**7.** Get some magazines. Make a collage of the characters or items described in the book.

**8.** Advertise your book. Make a colorful poster inviting your classmates to read it.

**9.** Gather some objects that appear in the story and arrange them in an attractive display.

**10.** Write a newspaper article telling about the story as if it just happened. *-Barbara McPherson*

## BOOK FEVER

I have found a fun and easy way to keep up with students' book reports. When a child finishes reading a book, he or she fills out a 3″ x 5″ card with the book's

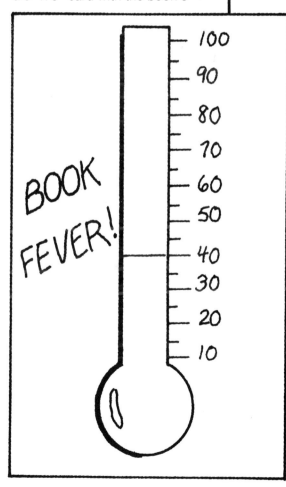

title, author, illustrator, and a paragraph summary of the book. The students file their cards in a box that has their names listed in alphabetical order. Every Friday, I count the reports and then show the students' reading progress on their individual reading "thermometers." To make these, I draw a large thermometer on white paper. Each book read moves the red "mercury" in the thermometer up one "degree."

*-Brenda McGee*

### A CLASS BOOKWORM

Your students will become avid readers as they watch their bookworm grow around the room. Make worm pieces with feet at the bottom and give one to each child. (Use the reproducible on the opposite page.) He or she then uses that pattern to trace and cut out worm pieces from construction paper, in one particular color chosen by that child. Then when a child finishes a book, he or she writes the title, author, favorite character, and best part of the book on a worm piece and attaches it to one large bookworm that's growing along the walls of the classroom. The goal is for the bookworm to go all the way around the room. This is an especially effective technique as kids are working toward a common goal rather than competing against each other.

*-Elaine Titze*

### REPORTING WITH PLEASURE

Classroom volunteers can help you get your kids excited about giving oral book reports. Choose a different volunteer for every day of the week to go out in the hall and hear students report. (You'll want to supply a desk and two chairs, if possible.) Give the volunteer index cards for each student who will be reporting. He or she should mark these cards with the books' titles, authors, and main ideas, as reported by the students. The volunteer should also summarize students' opinions of the books they've read and grade each report. Meet with your volunteer at the end of the day to discuss the reports. You might ask students who did exceptionally well to share their reports with the rest of the class. The chance to talk directly to an interested adult will keep kids excited about book reports all year!

*-Maxine L. Kaye*

### CUTTING FINE FIGURES

One picture is worth a thousand words? Not in our room! One picture, made by attaching a child's school photo (head only) to a cutout body from a department store catalog, is worth 100 pages. Each time a child reads one book or several books totaling 100 pages, he or she may move this figure along paper stepping-stones that lead to a castle.

We take great pains to match the student's head and personality to the right catalog cutout. (One child may picture herself in a Girl Scout uniform, another in a sweat suit.) When the children read the appropriate number of books (reach the castle), they get a star to paste on their outfits and they start their figures again at the first step.

Our book report stepping-stones are on the bulletin board across the top of the chalkboard, with the castle at the end. These stepping-stones and the fine figures on them are the focal point of the room.

*-Jeannetta Danford*

### BATTLE BOOK GALACTICA

Keep track of the library books your students have read by capitalizing on a Galactica theme. Starting with a plain black background on your bulletin board, use colored construction paper to make a large sun at one end followed by all the other planets in our solar system. Let each student design his or her own paper spaceship and place it on the sun. When a student reads and reports on a library book, he or she can move his or her spaceship to the next planet in line. the goal is to travel from the sun to Pluto and back again. You might want to give a small prize to the first child who makes a complete spaceflight. *-Ron Palmer*

### CERTIFIED READERS

At the Hudson Community School in Cedar Falls, Iowa, reading 25 books is worth a gold-embossed certificate, signed by the principal and librarian. For reading and reporting on 12 books, students receive silver certificates. Reading more than 25 may bring the reward of a book! The program was designed by the librarian to interest students in reading for pleasure.

*-Marilyn Lilja*

TITLE _____

AUTHOR _____

FAVORITE CHARACTER

_____

BEST PART OF THE BOOK

_____

_____

_____

# Reading Bookworm

TITLE _____

AUTHOR _____

FAVORITE CHARACTER
_____

BEST PART OF THE BOOK
_____
_____
_____

## RHYTHM BAND CUE CARDS

Small children love to play rhythm and percussion instruments, but it's not always easy to get them to complement each other when in "concert." Invariably, certain instruments ring out loud and clear while others, like maracas, for instance, may not be heard at all. The next time your students perform in a musical program involving a rhythm band, try this different method of conducting that will make them sound like polished musicians with a minimum amount of practice.

Choose a popular song with a steady beat for them to play along with. Divide the class into groups, according to the instruments they'd like to play. Now make cue cards out of 10″ × 14″ sheets of oaktag, with simple drawings of a particular instrument on each card. When you want a group of instruments to begin playing, hold up the appropriate cue card with one hand while your other hand moves with the beat of the music. For example, when you want the triangles to stop playing and the tambourines to begin, put the triangle card down on your lap and hold the tambourine card out in front of you. If you want two groups to play at the same time, hold up two cards

or one card with pictures of two instruments. You'll really be surprised at the noticeable improvement this method will bring to your music program!

-Susan Choroszewski

## INSTRUMENTAL INVENTIONS

My students made simple instruments. We began by gathering the materials needed to illustrate how sounds are produced in each family of instruments. For the strings, we collected rubber bands and empty boxes of different sizes. For winds, bottles of various sizes, tissue paper, combs and pieces of grass. For brass, rubber tubing, plumber's pipes, funnels, and nuts from a bolt. For percussion, coffee cans with plastic lids, glasses filled with water to various levels, spoons, pot lids, and boxes or cans with dried beans inside.

To illustrate how stringed instruments work, I had children stretch rubber bands over cupped hands and pluck them; then they plucked rubber bands stretched over an empty box. They heard how the box acted as a resonator and amplified the sound. They could also see how the rubber bands vibrated to produce the sound, and they noticed that longer rubber bands produced a lower pitch than shorter ones. To help kids understand how vibrating reeds can produce a sound in the woodwinds, I had them place a piece of tissue paper against a comb, put their lips to the comb, and hum. They could feel the paper vibrating. We also put pieces of grass between our thumbs (with fingernails touching) and blew on the grass; we could see the grass vibrate as well as hear the sound it made. To see how the length of the column of air determines a pitch, we filled bottles with different levels of water and blew across

the opening; empty bottles produced low tones (a longer column of air), while those filled with the most water produced the highest tones.

To illustrate how brass instruments work, I used rubber tubing and plumber's pipes for the columns of air and nuts from a bolt for mouthpieces. Students could feel their lips vibrating as they blew into the pipes. They also noticed that the longer pipes produced the lowest tones. And when we put a funnel at the end of a pipe, it made the volume of sound larger, like the bell on a brass instrument. Finally, students shook cans or boxes filled with water or objects, and hit cans or boxes with spoons to illustrate the percussive principle. When the children understood these principles, they used their imaginations to make instruments of their own. These were the only rules: no parts of real instruments could be used (except for violin or guitar strings), all instruments must produce a sound, and parents may help. I was amazed at what they came up with. One boy made a tuba from a vacuum cleaner hose with a metal mouthpiece and with a metal industrial light fixture for a bell. A plumber's daughter made a trombone from copper tubing, a metal kitchen funnel, and a washer—the slide really worked! There were cigar box violins, guitar string harps, a glockenspiel made from nails of various sizes hung on pieces of fishing wire and then hit with a big nail, flutes from pieces of chrome from a vacuum cleaner (vacuum cleaners were popular instrument suppliers!), Pan pipes from bamboo, bells from funnels, and maracas from coffee cans with beans inside. Many children were able to find parts for their instruments that fit together already; others used rubber bands, string, even parts of an innertube to hold parts together.

The finale of the unit was a classroom instrument contest, judged by the county music supervisor, the principal, parents of children in other classes, and other teachers. The judges were impressed by the interest and eagerness children brought to these projects, as much as by their ingenuity. I wouldn't be surprised if one of these students turns out to be the next Stradivari or Steinway!   -Gloria McLendon

## A VERY BIG MUSIC BOX

My "Music Box" is a compact, convenient way of organizing creative music activities for individuals and small groups. The box itself is a cardboard storage box. Reinforced handle grips and a cover hinged with scrap leather strips and yarn make the box portable, functional, and durable. The hinged cover remains upright when open, making a good place to display directions.

Directions for different activities are written on color-coded cards. They are divided into VERY EASY (on white cards), MEDIUM (on orange cards), and ADVANCED (on yellow cards). Other materials in our music box include: a small xylophone, a few rhythm instruments (sticks, hand drums, tone blocks, tambourines and sand blocks), art materials, tapes and a tape player with a headset. Some of the easy activities include making a "chance" song (pull letters out of an envelope, place them in the order chosen, and play the letters on the xylophone in that same order), making a musical setting for a poem (choose a favorite poem and make music to go with it), and making music to show different feelings.

Some of the harder activities include making a school song (turn "Are You Sleeping?" into "Are You Learning?", learning the letter names of the lines and spaces by writing notes on the staff and playing a tune on the xylophone, making music for different musical forms (AB, ABA, or Rondo), and making a rhythm score for three or four different instruments. Most of the more advanced activities require some background.

Students enjoy working in "The Big Music Box" and come up with some pretty interesting compositions! Those who want to can perform their works for the class, giving the class a chance to learn how to be a good audience and to appreciate the efforts of others.   -Martha E. Osborne

## MUSIC TO WRITE BY

If you're like most classroom teachers, your curriculum doesn't allow much time for the fine arts. There is a way you can expose your students to varied musical experiences without leaving the classroom. How? By providing them with background music during whole-class activities like handwriting practice or classroom cleanup time. Borrow a record player from your school's music department if you don't already have one, and bring in some albums from your own record collection. These should be as varied as possible, including classical, choral, and popular music, as well as musicals or movie soundtracks. You'll be surprised at what a quieting effect a little background music can have on your class — and your kids will get some valuable exposure to different types of music!   -Tom Bernagozzi

## ON THE MUSIC SCENE

As a teacher of sixth graders, I wanted to help make my students aware of the current music scene in our area. I began a weekly project based on the use of the entertainment sections of the Sunday newspapers. These papers generally contain many ads which can be studied to uncover a gold mine of information. Sample questions include the following:

**1.** Who is the principal conductor of our city's Detroit Symphony Orchestra? Who are the composers whose music will be featured in this week's concert?
**2.** What play will be opening at the Fisher Theatre next week? Who will be the leading stars in this production?
**3.** How many operas will the Metropolitan Opera Company present when it comes here on tour? Which production is already sold out?

Since our city has two major newspapers, I included separate questions for each newspaper for material other than advertisements. Besides studying the ads and columns, the students were asked to cut out pictures of musical artists who will be visiting the city.

Music listened to in music appreciation classes can be related to what is being planned for the local music scene. This makes the music students are listening to relevant.

This type of weekly project has many benefits. The students become familiar with the use of the newspaper. They become acquainted with the names of musical artists and can more readily identify these people when they appear on radio or television. They slowly come to the realization that there is a variety of music to be heard. They learn that people are interested in many different types of music. A whole new world is opened up to them. This type of exercise can be extended to the local art scene since many Sunday editions of the newspapers also have columns devoted to current area art shows. If possible, end the year with one cultural trip, voted on by the students.

-Frank W. Sosnowski

149

### CREATIVE CLASSROOM CAREER CONTEST

Here's a way to introduce pupils to a wide variety of careers. Set up a "career corner" in your classroom. You'll need an area that's relatively free from distractions, a table and chair, paper and pencils, and a good vocational reference book. (Check the career section of your local library or bookstore.) Now select an object, of your choice, such as a pumpkin, a magazine, or an article of clothing, and place it on the table. The children are to go to the career corner one at a time and list all the occupations they can think of that might be associated with the production, sale, or utilization of the chosen object. For instance, the pumpkin might involve such diverse occupations as farmhands, produce clerks, food service workers, canners, advertisers, printers, and graphic artists. The student who comes up with the longest list of occupations is the winner. Now here are some "spin-off" activities to accompany the career contest.

**1.** Pretend you are involved in one of the occupations you have listed. Write a letter to an imaginary friend describing the work you do. (This will require a little research.)

**2.** Write a poem or limerick about one of the careers listed. (This might describe a typical day on the job.)

**3.** Write a "want ad" for the career of your choice to appear in the local newspaper.      -Jill P. Gann

### THE LUNCH BUNCH

What do adults do? Our students find out every Monday at our school when adult guests come to lunch to discuss their careers and share their special interests or hobbies.

Two parent volunteers contact guests and set up a calendar. They've found that children identify best with local parents, although more renowned guests are also invited. Two or three children from each class, grades 1 through 5, attend lunch in rotation. It's voluntary, but most children are eager to go. The children carry their lunches; the guest is treated to a hot school lunch. Lunchers-to-be meet on Friday to prepare a welcome sign, name tags, appropriate questions, and a thank-you card. They are assigned tasks for Monday, such as arranging chairs in the spare classroom, greeting the guest, and cleaning up afterward.

Guests have included a doctor, an actor, an artist, a mayor, an Olympic hockey player, a taxidermist, two scuba divers, a woman deputy sheriff, an elephant trainer, a singer/guitarist, a local television newscaster, a police officer, and a mom with her newborn baby. These last two just may have been the most popular guests of all!
-Margaret Joque Williams

### WHAT'S MY LINE?

If you'd like your students to learn to ask intelligent questions, form hypotheses, and increase their awareness of many different types of careers, try this idea patterned after the old television show, "What's My Line?" Begin by selecting a "mystery guest" from among school personnel, students' parents, or community members. After making preliminary arrangements, send the person a letter confirming the agreed-upon date and explaining the procedures and goals of the program. On the day that he or she is due to arrive, put several objects on your desk that serve as clues to the person's career. The idea is to determine, by careful examination of these clues, what person would use all of these objects in his or her profession. In the final minutes before the mystery guest arrives, have the students review the evidence once again and record their hypotheses. They should also prepare three questions to ask in support of their assumptions. After the students have all had a chance to share their hypotheses, the guest may reveal his or her profession and explain to the class what it entails. On the day following the presentation, review any new vocabulary words your guest might have used and list the skills and education needed for his or her particular job. To synthesize all that they've learned, have the children write thank-you letters to the mystery guest. -Jamie Horowitz

### TOOLS OF THE TRADE

Here's an exciting contest that will foster career awareness in your classroom. Set up a display area in a corner of your room with entry blanks and a box to put them in. Also supply a pencil and reference books dealing with occupations. Each week, place a picture of a different tool in the center and let kids enter the contest by guessing what the "tool of the trade" is and which profession uses it. Some examples might be a stethoscope, mail bag, conductor's baton, or bread pan. At the end of the week, post the winning entries in the center, along with some interesting facts about the job, such as the education requirements for entering that profession, some of the duties performed, and books in which a character has that occupation. If possible, bring in tools of the trade for children to see.      -Jill P. Gann

# Early Education

Early learners need activities especially for them. This chapter includes ways to develop motor skills, recognize milestones such as birthdays and that first lost tooth, and enhance self-esteem.

Organizing a pre-school or primary classroom has its own special requirements also. Look for activities that help cut confusion when lining up on field trips. There's even a method to yawn-proof your show-and-tell.

Reading readiness, early math and science activities, art and holiday ideas, and special teaching units round out this chapter. All have a positive outlook that will keep your classroom a happy, pleasant place to be.

## MAKE-AHEAD MANIPULATIVES

Make these hands-on activities for reinforcing letter, math, classification, and perceptual skills, to use when you need them.

**Letter carriers** Discarded boxes of any size or shape can be transformed into individual letter carriers for emphasizing letters and sounds. You'll need one box for each letter. Paint the boxes bright colors and place a big letter on each lid. Inside each box, glue a colorful picture that begins with that letter. Add other small objects that begin with the letter sound or pictures of objects pasted on small cards. Kids can select a box and review a letter.

**Pick a pocket** Sew squares of scrap fabric into large pockets for holding objects that begin with each letter sound; numerals and sets of objects for children to match; colored objects and color words; pairs of like patterns; or other skill testers that can fit in the pockets. Add a loop to the pockets so that they can be stored on hooks.

**In a pickle** Make this simple classification game. Cut three brown barrels from brown construction paper. From green paper cut 11 pickles each in the shape of a whole pickle, a pickle slice, and a pickle chip. Paste one type of pickle on each barrel. Mix up the remaining 30 pickles for pupils to sort.

**By hook or . . .** ''Hook'' your kids with this skill-building activity. You'll need a sheet of pegboard or plywood with four holes drilled across the top and as many holes as possible drilled down from them. Drill holes two inches apart.

Screw hooks into the holes. Now paste pictures of objects cut from magazines or old workbooks onto small cards. Punch a hole in the top of each card. When using the board, place a card on each of the four hooks across the top. On the hooks below each card, pupils hang objects that belong in the same category because of color, beginning letter sound, and so on.

**Count the peas** Cut 10 pea-pod shapes from light green construction paper. Number the pods from 1 to 10. Use dark green

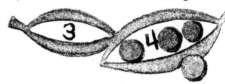

paper to cut out 55 circle-shaped peas. Store all pieces in a decorated envelope. To use, pupils will arrange the pods in order from 1 to 10, then count out the correct number of peas for each.

**Stencil fun** Make stencils of dinosaurs, snowmen, witches, popular cartoon characters (Snoopy, Garfield, Care Bears), and so on, for children to use when they want an accurate rendering. Coloring books are a good source of characters; trace onto cardboard, then cut out.

**Perceptual prism** Refine fine-motor movement and eye-hand coordination with a plastic wiffle ball and a shoelace. Make a knot in one end of the shoelace. Insert the lace through a large hole in the ball and out a smaller one so that the knot holds inside and the lace remains in place. Kids can thread the shoelace back and forth through the openings in the ball.

**Lock 'em up** Buy an assortment of inexpensive locks, many with different-sized keys. Screw or nail the locks to a sheet of scrap

plywood. Make a duplicate set of all of the keys, then attach one set to a long cord, and tie the cord to a hook at the top of the board. Pupils find the key to open each lock.

**Dressing board** On a large sheet of plywood, nail a colorful array of cloth sneakers with shoelaces and Velcro closures, buckle shoes, zippers, and snaps or hooks and eyes sewn on. Pupils practice opening and closing them.

*-Rosalee Pichler-Mosburg, Kathleen Wildstein, Ellen Javernick, Joyce Vreeland, Doris Dittmar, Barbara F. Tea, and Cheryl Potts.*

## A VINE LINE

Start a living timeline with a fast-growing vine. Ivy, philodendron, and Wandering Jew are hardy plant choices and can be pruned to a single vine. As the vine grows, train it across a wall where it will receive adequate sunlight. Ask students to predict how much the vine will have grown by such specific dates as Halloween, Washington's birthday, and the last day of school. Students should attach an index card marked with an arrow to the wall at the point where they think the vine will be by the upcoming date. When that date arrives, have students measure the distance between their arrow and the actual end of the vine. Students should record the amount of their error on their card, and then move the card to predict the growth for the next appointed date. Your students will probably discover that as they learn the vine's growth pattern, they will make better hypotheses.

*-Robert Sylvester*

## ACTION ALPHABET

When introducing pupils to the letters and sounds of the alphabet, we tend to name objects as our examples. Why not make learning the alphabet a lively experience by teaching students action words to associate with the letters? Here's a partial list of actions that could be introduced with each letter. Some letters, such as the vowels and *x*, offer a challenge in finding words pupils understand. With some explanation, you could have kids *arch* their backs or *elevate* their bodies by standing on tiptoe, or make Xs in the air.

| | | |
|---|---|---|
| b-bounce | k-kick | r-run |
| c-catch | l-lick | s-sip |
| d-dance | m-march | t-talk |
| f-fall | n-nod | v-vacuum |
| g-gallop | p-pull | w-wiggle |
| h-hop | q-quiver | y-yawn |
| j-jump | | z-zip |

*-Patricia Cunningham*

## NURSERY-RHYME OBSTACLE COURSE

Give gross-motor skills a workout while capitalizing on children's interest in nursery rhymes with this unique obstacle course. For best results, try the activity at the end of a unit on nursery rhymes so pupils will see the connections between each action and the rhyme it's based on. Here's a sample course: gallop *(Ride to Boston)*; jump over a block representing a candlestick *(Jack Be Nimble)*; climb steps of a small ladder or do a forward roll on a mat *(Jack and Jill)*; hide under a chair *(Pussy Cat, Pussy Cat)*; jump from a sitting position *(Little Miss Muffet)*; and fly to finish or back to starting position *(Lady Bug)*. *-Ellen Javernick*

## SUPER STOMPER

A jumping board is a great device for developing large muscles and improving eye-hand coordination. You will need a board that is 3 feet long, 10 inches wide, and 1 inch thick. Nail an aluminum pie plate on one end of the board. Flip the board over and measure 12 inches from the other end. At that spot, nail or screw in place a block of wood 2 inches long and 1 inch thick. When the board is turned right side up, the end opposite the pie plate should be slightly raised off the floor. To use the board, place a soft ball in the pie plate. A child jumps on the board to propel the ball into the air, then tries to catch the ball before it hits the floor.

*-Ellen Javernick*

## SNAKE EYES MEAN CRAWL

Exercise becomes an animated game when kids roll a homemade die to find out what action to perform. Cut off the top of two half-pint milk cartons. Push one inside the other to form a cube. Cover the cube with colored paper, then cut out pictures of common animals to glue to each side. Cover with clear adhesive plastic. To use, form the class into a circle. Pupils take turns rolling the cube, then imitating the animal that appears on top.

*-Ellen Javernick*

## COORDINATION CAPERS

**Walk the plank!** The balance beam can be used in a variety of ways. If your school does not have one, construct a simple version by securing a long board to two large blocks of wood. Begin by having pupils walk back and forth across the board without falling off. Then progress to more difficult exercises, such as walking backwards.

**Bend and stretch** Set aside five minutes each day to do sit-ups, toe touches, windmills, leg lifts, and so on. Work toward smooth movements and correct rhythm from each pupil.

**Bowling for accuracy** Mark off a bowling "lane" on the floor with two strips of masking tape. Set up a few blocks at the end of the lane. Have pupils take turns rolling a ball toward the blocks, working to keep the ball from touching the lines of masking tape.

**Coordination capers** Large and small balls can be used in other activities as well. Practice playing toss and catch in small groups, aiming to improve speed and accuracy in both tossing and catching. Station pupils a set distance from a box or wastebasket and have them try to toss a ball into the receptacle. As pupils' accuracy improves, increase the distance they must throw the ball. Have pupils squeeze small rubber balls to develop hand muscles.

**Hop, skip, and jump** Jumping rope is a great way to improve coordination. Try having a jump-rope marathon to see who can skip the longest without making a mistake. Award a badge (a small piece of rope glued to a paper shape) to each day's winner.

**Stay the course** Use large building blocks, chairs, ropes, and other objects in the classroom to design an obstacle course for pupils to hop, crawl, run, and walk through. Time pupils or increase the difficulty of the course as skills improve.

*-Pamela Klawitter*

## MOVEMENT WITH A PURPOSE

As pupils run and play freely, they are developing important motor skills. But directed movement is also necessary, for it gives kids a better understanding of their bodies and how they move, relate to others, and control objects. Play this Do As I Do game. Have children form a circle and imitate you as you silently touch different body parts, balance in different ways on one foot or both feet, and place arms in unusual positions. Then encourage kids to use imagination and total body control to move in response to descriptive words: *slow, fast, light, heavy, slithery, jerky,* and so on. *-Patricia J. Gilroy*

## TENNIS TASKS

Tennis balls that no longer have bounce can offer your pupils practice in improving eye-hand coordination as well as small- and large-muscle control.

1. Holding the ball in one hand and squeezing it will help build hand muscles. Use a timer to see who can squeeze the tennis ball the longest or who can squeeze the ball the greatest number of times in 60 seconds.

2. Have pupils explore ways to hold tennis balls, such as under their chins, between their knees, or under their arms.

3. Form a large circle and pass several balls from pupil to pupil simultaneously. At your signal to begin, pupils holding the balls should pass them in a specified way, such as with their right hands only or over their heads. After a few minutes, tell pupils to pass the balls in a different manner, such as between their knees.

4. Place four open boxes on their sides, about three feet away from a masking tape line. Have pupils stand at the line and try to roll a ball into one of the boxes. Move the boxes farther away to make the exercise more challenging.

5. Set four jar lids three feet from a wall and three feet from the masking tape line in the other direction. Pupils roll a ball and try to hit the lid, pushing it to the wall. Allow each child three rolls to get the lid to the wall.

6. Make a line with masking tape on the floor and have pupils bounce and catch the balls as they walk the line.

*-Eileen Van't Kerkhoff*

## ACT IT OUT

Here's an activity that combines creativity and action! As the class makes up simple rhyming poems, then acts them out, individuals will be improving coordination, plus creative writing, reading, and listening skills.

Introduce the activity in a large-group setting, using the poem below (or one of your own choice). Write the lines in large print on a sheet of chart paper:

My left foot goes tap, tap, tap
My right arm swings round and round:
My left hand just waves and waves
As my right knee bends up and down.

Read the poem aloud to the children, pointing to each line. Then have them read along with you. Now demonstrate the action for each line. Finally, have the children say the words and do the actions.

Next, as a group, compose your own four-line poem to be acted out. If your children are older, you might divide the class into small groups and ask each group to compose an action verse to teach to their peers. Or set up materials in a language arts center for individual pupils to write a poem and illustrate it, then later act it out with the class.

*-Marilyn L. Slovak*

## PAPER CRUMBLE

Pass out two sheets of paper to each child. (If possible, use paper you are planning to throw away.) Tell pupils to crumble both sheets at the same time, using only one hand to wad up each sheet. Now make a line with masking tape several feet from the wastebasket. Have pupils line up behind the tape and take turns tossing the balls into the basket.

*-Violet Johnson*

## WINTRY WALTZ

If snowflakes dance outside your window this month, have pupils join the mad swirl with this movement activity.

See the snowflakes dancing
Softly through the air.
See them spin,
Watch them glide,
They fall without a care.

All children move freely.

One by one they pirouette,
Two by two they go.
Three by three,
Then four by four,
First quickly, then so slow.

Children form a circle. On the first line, one child is chosen to move, then he or she selects a partner. Third and fourth "dancers" are chosen; all four move quickly, then slowly. Other kids wiggle fingers to simulate falling snow.

See the snowflakes dancing
Softly through the air.
See them spin,
Watch them glide,
They fall without a care.

All move. *-Carol Ann Piggins*

## BIRTHDAY BOUQUET

A bouquet of balloons is a popular birthday treat for all. Keep track of birthdays in your room by having a bouquet of balloons decorate one wall. Cut out 12 balloon shapes from construction paper and laminate each one. Write the name of a month at the top of each balloon; below it write the name of each child with a birthday then. (Use washable markers so balloons can be reused.) Attach ribbon to the bottom of each balloon and arrange the bunch on a wall at children's height.          -Oliver Sid

## THE LOST TOOTH BOARD

Here's a way to use losing a tooth as a celebration and learning experience. At the beginning of the school year, cut out nine poster board molars, approximately 9″ tall, and tack them on your bulletin board. On each one, print the name of a month, from September through June. Also cut out smaller molars, about 4″ tall, from felt and glue two of them together to make a

"tooth pocket." When a child loses a tooth, have him or her write his or her name on the poster board tooth for that month, and give him a pocket for keeping the lost tooth safe. After several months have gone by, you can use the poster board molars for math concept reinforcement. Ask such questions as: In which month were the most teeth lost? How many more teeth were lost in one month than another? How many teeth were lost in all?

          -Marna L. Bunce

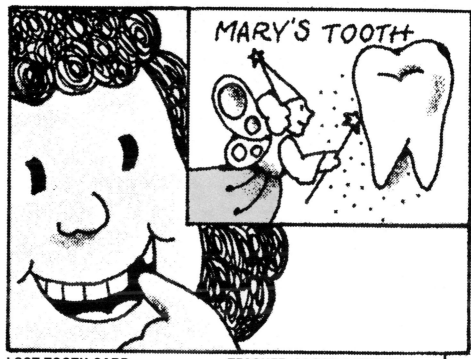

MARY'S TOOTH

## LOST TOOTH CARD

Here's a neat way to celebrate a lost tooth and insure that the tooth arrives home safely with your student. Make individual tooth cards for each child out of colored poster board. On each card, draw a picture of a large tooth with the tooth fairy waving her wand above it. Leave a space on the card for the child's name to be filled in and print the words, "A Tooth for the Tooth Fairy" across the top. You may also wish to have an appropriate poem or jingle printed on the card. When a child loses a tooth, simply tape it to the drawing and pin the card to your bulletin board until it's time for the student to take it home.          -Carol Ann Anderson

## PIN ONE ON

Let the birthday child choose a special pin to wear on the special day. Purchase round metal buttons from a craft shop, then glue a circle of colorful fabric to each. Write numerals on the pins that represent the age range of our pupils. Store in a "birthday box."          -Violet Johnson

## TEACHER, I LOST A TOOTH

Losing a tooth is an exciting event for a young child. Use these ideas in your classroom to acknowledge this important sign of growing up.

Begin by making a Lost Tooth Chart that remains in place throughout the year. Write the name of each student on the chart, and leave plenty of room beside the names for pupils to tack up paper teeth as they lose real ones. Cut out at least two teeth per child from white label paper, and place the teeth in an envelope near the chart. When a child loses a tooth, he or she takes a tooth from the envelope, peels off the back to expose the sticky surface, and places the tooth beside his or her name. Have a special chair where pupils can sit and tell the class how they lost their teeth. When each story is finished, honor the child with a song, such as this one sung to the tune of "Mary Had a Little Lamb":

> (Child) lost a tooth, lost a tooth, lost a tooth. (Child) is growing up, because he/she lost a tooth.          -Judy Meagher

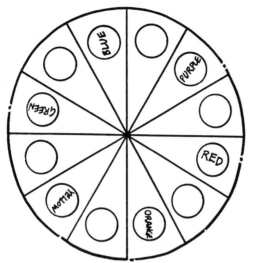

### COLOR JUGGLER

Children can review color words with this game that follows the circus theme. Cut out two tagboard circles, one 8 inches in diameter, the other 7½. Set aside the smaller circle. Divide the 8-inch circle into 12 segments; draw a ball near the top of each segment. Print the word *red* in the first ball, then color in the next ball with a red crayon. Continue with the other 10 balls, using the colors yellow, blue, green, orange, and purple. Now cut a U-shaped notch the size of the color balls in the 7½-inch circle. Sketch a juggler on the front, then attach both circles at the center with a metal brad. To use, pupils turn the wheel to the first color word, then draw a circle on scratch paper with the correct color crayon. They turn the wheel to check their answer. *-Marion Walker*

### COLOR SCOOPS

Make learning color words a treat! Cut out giant ice-cream cones from brown paper. To each cone add a scoop of ice cream cut from a different color paper. Write the appropriate color word on each scoop. Tack up the cones around the classroom.
*-Violet Johnson*

### CIRCLE SKIPPING

Review colors with this delightful game. Arrange children in a big circle. Tape large red, yellow, and blue paper circles in the center of the children's circle. Choose several pupils each time to do the action called for in each phrase below, then to skip to the circle. One-two-three and nod your head; skip to the circle, the circle that's red.
One-two-three and tap your shoe; skip to the circle, the circle that's blue.
One-two-three and shake like Jell-O; skip to the circle, the circle that's yellow. *-Carol Ann Piggins*

### COLOR THEIR WORLD

To teach my primary youngsters the skill of color mixing, I set up an activity table that six children can comfortably use at once. I fill three medium-sized bowls with water and use food coloring to make one bowl red, one blue, and one yellow. Then I give each child a white plastic-foam egg carton and a plastic medicine dropper. The children use their droppers to take color out of one bowl and drop it into a section of their egg carton. Next, they add one or two colors from the other bowls. They mix and experiment to their heart's content without polluting the primary colors in the big bowls (and without wasting any of our year's supply of tempera paint).
*-Betsy Petway*

### THE ROUND TABLE

Divide a small, round table into six pie-shaped wedges. Paint each wedge a different color, and paint six chairs to match. Collect items that are the same six colors, and place them in a round container in the middle of the table. Pupils work at the table classifying and sorting the objects, then placing them onto the correct wedge.
*-Lynn Sangerfinckenpoh*

## OUR BIRTHDAYS

Review the months of the year with this rhyme. Let kids take turns telling their birthdates.

*When's your birthday?*
*Can you say?*
*Is it close or far away?*
*What month do you*
*celebrate?*
*How long do you have*
*to wait?*
*Name the months*
*And then say*
*Which one is*
*Your special day. January*
*. . . December.*  -Carol Quinn

## HOMEMADE LACING BOARD

Learning to tie shoelaces is a great accomplishment for small children, but the learning process is often frustrating when it involves working on a tiny shoe. Try making this handy lacing board that's large enough for children whose coordination has not fully developed, and small enough to be stored inside their desks at school. Using the 8½″ x 11″ cardboard backing from a writing tablet, draw two lines, 2½″ from each side. Fold along the

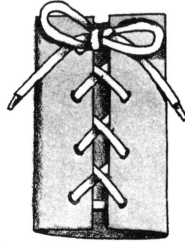

lines so that the flaps turn in toward each other. Now punch parallel rows of holes along the edges of each flap. Finally, add a heavy shoelace with strong, reinforced tips that will be manageable for small fingers.

-Lillian Koslover

## PLAYFUL PANDAS

These playful pandas offer another way to help pupils review the months and the order in which they fall.

To prepare this hands-on bulletin board, you will need 13 small pandas, one large panda, three large cardboard box tops, and string. (Coloring books are a good source of panda patterns.) Cover a bulletin board or wall space with poster paper. Tack the large panda at one end of the board. Glue a pocket on the panda's stomach and place one small panda in the pocket. It will serve as the answer key; write the names of the months in order on it.

Write a month on each of the other 12 pandas. Glue the cardboard tops in a row along the bottom of the bulletin board. Punch holes in the edges of the boxes and thread string through the holes to resemble cage bars. Place the pandas out of order in the cages.

Now explain to pupils the rules for using the bulletin board. **1.** Take all the pandas out of the cages. **2.** Read the name of the month on each panda. **3.** Arrange the pandas in the cages in order from January to December. **4.** Check your work with answer panda.  -Melinda Hammerschmidt

## IF YOU LIKE FRIDAY

Reinforce pupils' knowledge of the days of the week and give their gross motor skills a workout with this action rhyme.

*If you like Monday, shake*
*your head.*
*If you like Tuesday, wiggle.*
*If you like Wednesday,*
*stamp your feet.*
*If you like Thursday, giggle.*
*If you like Friday, jump and*
*clap your hands.*
*For Saturday, you grin.*
*For Sunday, turn yourself*
*around.*
*Then say the days again.*
*Monday, Tuesday,*
*Wednesday, Thursday,*
*Friday, Saturday,*
*Sunday!*  -Carol Quinn

## LEFT FOOT, RIGHT FOOT

Are some of your pupils still having trouble learning left from right? Make the concept an active one with this exercise.

> March with your left foot.
> March with your right.
> I'll march with you
> To Timbuktu.
> We'll get there Friday night.
>
> Hop on your left foot.
> Hop on your right.
> We'll hop and go
> To Mexico.
> And stop for just a bite.
>
> Skip with your left foot.
> Skip with your right.
> We're on our way
> To Santa Fe,
> But we'll come back tonight.
>
> Strut with your left foot.
> Strut with your right.
> We'll strut so proud
> Straight to St. Cloud.
> Our heads held upright.
>
> Sway on left foot.
> Sway on your right.
> I'll sway with you
> To Kalamazoo.
> Then we'll find a place to light.

-Marion G. Walker.

## MIX AND MATCH

Mix the use of left and right with such directions as ''touch right elbow with left hand,'' ''swing left leg and right arm,'' ''pull left ear with right hand.'' For those who need additional left and right activities, try this drawing activity. Ask pupils to draw a dog on the left side of a paper, a bone on the right side, then to draw an arrow to show the direction the dog must move to get to the bone. In which direction should the arrow go (from left to right)? Then have them draw a boy with a dish on the left side of the paper, a kitten on the right, and an arrow showing how the cat must move to reach the food in the dish. In which direction should the arrow go (from right to left)? -Theora Byrd

## DIRECTION

Mastering the concepts of left and right and top and bottom prepares pupils for reading.

**Clip 'n tell** You will need 10 computer or tagboard cards and two clip clothespins. Draw different figures on both ends of the cards. Write *left* and *right* on the clothespins, and instruct pupils to clip the corresponding clothespins over the figures on the left and right of the cards. Make the activity self-checking by drawing the same symbol for the left pictures, such as a triangle, and the same for the right, such as a dot, on the appropriate side of the back of each card. Code the back of the clothespins with these same symbols. Then the child can flip the card over to see if the triangle on the card lines up with the triangle on the clothespin, and so on. Make similar cards for top and bottom.

**Watch your step** Make 20 large footprints from oilcloth, 10 blue and 10 red. Give children a strip of blue and a strip of red paper, and tell students to tape the blue to their left shoe and the red to their right. Now tape the footprints in a path on the floor, arranging them so that when walking, pupils can place their left feet on the blue shapes, their right feet on the red shapes. -Pamela Klawitter

## LEFT, RIGHT . . . RIGHT?

Begin by explaining to the children that when their heads are facing front, their mouths and noses are in the center of their bodies. Any body part to the right of center is their right arm, leg, eye, etc. Correspondingly, any body part to the left of center is their left arm, leg, eye, etcetera. Now fasten a jingle bell to a two-inch rubber band and slip one over each child's right wrist and one over his right ankle. Emphasize that you have put the bells on their right hands and feet.

Next, direct the children to raise their right hands, put their left hands on their heads, and other activities to familiarize them with the association of the bells with the right direction.

Now your students are ready for singing. Have them stand in place beside their desks and sing the ''Hokey Pokey,'' following the directions in the song and listening for the sound of their bells when the words indicate right hand or foot movement and silence when they indicate left-side motion. This procedure results in audible and kinesthetic reinforcement that facilitates the learning of direction.

-Ruby Swickard

## LEFT, RIGHT, LEFT

Reinforce children's understanding of left and right with this very active action rhyme.

> Do the left foot tap, tap, tap.
> Do the left foot jiggle.
> Do the left foot up and down.
> Make your left foot wiggle.
>
> Do the right foot tap, tap, tap.
> Do the right foot jiggle.
> Do the right foot up and down.
> Make your right foot wiggle.
>
> Do the left hand shake, shake, shake.
> Do the left hand crawl.
> Do the left hand twist, twist, twist.
> Make your left hand small.
>
> Do the right hand shake, shake, shake.
> Do the right hand crawl.
> Do the right hand twist, twist, twist.
> Make your right hand small.
>
> Tap, tap; jiggle, jiggle; up, down; wiggle, wiggle; shake, shake; twist, twist; roll up small; that's all.

-Carol Quinn

## ACTION LEARNING

One of the best ways to help pupils understand the meanings of spatial words is to let them experience them. These activities involve spatial concepts.

**What's the hoopla?** Have kids take turns using a hula hoop to perform specified routines, such as: sit *inside* the hoop; jump *out* of the hoop, then jump back *in* the hoop; skip *around* the hoop; and so on until all the desired words are used.

**Pass the ball** Have the class form a large circle. One child begins by passing the ball, explaining in a sentence what he or she is doing. For example: "I am passing the ball *over* my head to Jim." The next child repeats that sentence, then makes up one of his own that includes a spatial word, such as: "I am passing the ball *between* my legs to Mary." Pupils who use a spatial word incorrectly are eliminated from the circle.

**Getting your goat** Read "The Three Billy Goats Gruff" to your students; then have them act out the story, concentrating on the spatial words. For example, one scene could involve a pupil, representing the troll, sitting *under* a table. Place chairs on either side of the table and have other pupils help the three "goats" climb *up* the hill (step on the chairs), go *over* the bridge, and climb *down* the hill (step off the chairs). Look for other stories with spatial concepts for pupils to role-play.

**I'm thinking of something** Use this old game to reinforce such spatial words as *high, low, near, far,* and so on. Start by saying, "I'm thinking of something in this room that is high." In turn pupils try to guess what you might be thinking of (perhaps the room clock). The winning guesser continues with "something low," "something near me," "far from me," "close to Margie," "near Peter," and so on. Pupils' guesses will tell you who has grasped the concept of the spatial words used.

*-Joseph A. Baust*

## LET'S BUILD A HOUSE

Give pupils practice in spatial relations, cutting, and counting with this exercise. Draw the outlines of two or three different-sized houses on spirit masters, and run off several copies of each. On another master, draw squares (bricks) that when cut out can be used to cover the surfaces of the houses. Give each child a house and a few sheets of bricks. Have them cut out the bricks, lay as many on their houses as needed to fill them in, then count the bricks.

*-Judy Meagher*

## LEARNING UP FROM DOWN

Directional words such as *under, over, up, down,* and so on, are often difficult for children to understand. Use these activities to teach spatial concepts. Introduce the words with bulletin board displays. For example, if *up* and *down* are being introduced, picture a seesaw with one child going up and the other going down. Label each position with an arrow and the appropriate word. Talk about children's own experiences on seesaws; ask if there is a difference in the way they feel when they go up, than when they go down.

Once pupils are familiar with the words, give each child two cards, one with *up* and the other with *down* written on it. Then show a series of illustrations, such as of a fire fighter climbing a ladder or a sky diver falling. Have pupils hold up the card with the word that describes each picture.

To reinforce pupils' understanding of the words, make task cards that ask them to

choose the word that describes the picture on the card. Or have pupils draw their own scenes to illustrate the words. Pupils could also act out a direction from you, such as, "Show me what *up* means."

*-Gaye McNutt*

## BEAN-BAG TOSS

Test pupils' understanding of spatial words with this simple game that requires just a mat and a bean bag. (An oilcloth table covering works well for the mat.) Divide the covering into 16 squares, and print a spatial word in each square, Illustrate each word as pictured above.

To play the game, lay the mat on the floor. Place a strip of masking tape one yard from the bottom edge of the mat. Have pupils take turns standing at the tape line and tossing the bean bag onto one of the squares. Each pupil then names the spatial word and demontrates its meaning

*-Joseph A. Baust*

### ALL ABOUT ME
Improve your pupils' self-awareness with these activities.
**Work and play** Label one side of an open file folder *work,* and the other side *play.* Illustrate each side accordingly. Cut out pictures showing children and adults working or playing. Child places each picture on the proper section of the folder.
**Happy or sad?** Cut two 9″ circles from cardboard. Draw a happy face on one and a sad face on the other. Cut out pictures showing pleasant and unpleasant events. Child places each picture on the appropriate circle.

**All around the house** Cut out the front of a house from a large sheet of tagboard. Cut three pieces of tagboard to glue along the bottom half of the house,

forming pockets. Draw lines on the house to separate the pockets, and label the columns *wear, play, work.* Cut out pictures of objects that can be worn, used for work, or for play for child to slip into the correct pocket.
*-Pamela Klawitter*

### WATCH THEM GROW
There's no more revealing way of measuring growth and maturation of your kindergarten students than by having them make self-portraits. At the beginning of the year, pass out drawing paper and crayons and ask children to draw pictures of themselves. Have them write (or try to write) their names on them. After they've been displayed, tuck the pictures in a folder. Around midyear, repeat the project. Finally, as the end of the year rolls around, try again. Trim and mount the three portraits in chronological order. Show the finished products to parents at conference time. The portraits make great keepsakes for parents, too.   *-Pamela Klawitter*

### MIRROR, MIRROR
Here's an open-ended activity that can be used to help kids identify facial features and focus on their own uniqueness. Give each child a small hand mirror to hold while you ask a series of

questions. For example: How many heads do you have? eyes? ears? Can you make a sound with your lips? Can you wink one eye? What makes you different from everyone else?

The list of possible questions is endless. Encourage kids to shout out some answers but to volunteer responses for more personal questions. Always end by having everyone make a big smile. *-Martha M. Lopez*

## SOMEONE NICE

Have pupils point to each body part mentioned as you read this poem. Then set out the materials included in the verse (Cheerios, jellybeans, peanuts, and so on). Give each child a sheet of white paper, crayons, and glue, and let each create a self-portrait.

What if you had
A Cheerios nose,
Jellybean eyes,
Peanut toes,
Spaghetti hair,
Macaroni grin,
Raisin teeth,
Marshmallow chin,
Popcorn arms and legs,
Hands and fingers rice?
Don't you see you'd still be
Someone very nice? *-Carol Quinn*

## ALL ABOUT ME— ALL ABOUT US

A "picture book" of your class is a great way for kids to get to know each other. Soon after school begins, take a picture of each child with an instant camera. Now have each child dictate to you three or four lines about him- or herself—pets, favorite foods, toys, games, and so on. Type the comments on plain paper, spacing them so that you have room for the child's name, address, and phone number as well as the picture. Add an introduction to the book and a little something about yourself. Let one child take the book home each night to enjoy with his or her family. *-Robert Ziegler*

**ALL SING (Key of D Major)**

Names be-gin with B.
Now it's time to see.

Names be-gin with B.
Now it's time to see.

Come on up in front if your
Now it's time to see if your

name be-gins with B.

## THE NAME GAME

Reinforce recognition of letter sounds and give everyone a moment in the limelight with this musical game. Sing the song above, asking students whose names begin with B or another letter to come to the front of the room. Then have the class say each child's name while he or she takes a bow. *-Judy Meagher*

## THE TIE GUYS

Designating special classroom jobs that students can fill is one way to help children feel important. For example, appoint "special shoe-tie helpers" the first week of school. Buy three or four shoelaces with unique designs (hearts, flowers, and so on) and tie these on the wrists of children who demonstrate the skill and willingness to tie shoes. When pupils need help with their shoes, they can go to one of the shoe-tie helpers. Change the helpers daily. *-Valerie Bang-Jensen*

## ME MOBILES

What could be more appealing to a child than a mobile about his or her favorite things? Have kids cut out outlines of four or five objects from double-thick construction paper (or cut two of each shape). Show pupils how to glue the shapes together, leaving a space at the top so that they can be lightly stuffed with tissue paper. Insert a length of yarn in each opening, then staple shut. Suspend the shapes from paper towel tubes. *-Kelly Riley*

## FIND A FRIEND

Help children learn the names of their classmates and practice following directions with this activity. Have the class sit in a circle on the floor. Choose one child to be "it." The class then chants the following, doing the motions indicated: "Clap, stand, turn around, sit down. Look who (child's name) has found." The child chooses a friend to stand behind, who now becomes "it." *-Alma Mitchell*

## THE SENSES

**Don't wake the baby!** Cut out two 9″ circles from cardboard. Glue a picture of a crying baby in the center of one circle and write *loud* under it. Glue a picture of a sleeping baby in the center of the other circle and write *soft* under it. Cut out pictures of people or

objects that are making loud and soft noises. (Make sure you have discussed loud and soft noises before putting this activity in the kit.) The student places the pictures that represent soft noises on the sleeping baby, and those that represent loud noises on the crying baby.

**Touch it** Cut out a 9″ cardboard circle and divide it into three sections. Label one section *hot,* one *cold,* and one *sharp;* then illustrate each section. Cut out pictures that could represent the feelings of hot, cold, or sharp such as a needle, an ice cube, a campfire, and so on. The student places the pictures on the appropriate section.

**Shake 'em up** Find 8-10 identical containers. Fill two containers with rice, two with dry beans, two with macaroni, and so on, but in differing quantities so that there is a distinct difference in the sound made by each pair. For self-checking, mark the bottom of each pair with a specific color. Store the containers in a small box. The student shakes each container until he or she can pair the containers according to the substance inside them.

**My five senses** Inside a folder, glue 15-20 pictures of objects that relate to senses. Then cut out pictures of hands, eyes, noses, ears, and mouths. Child looks at each of the pictures, then places the correct sense organ(s) on it. Include an answer key for self-checking on the back of the folder.          *-Pamela Klawitter*

## THOSE SENSATIONAL SENSES!

**Sight** Spread a variety of objects on a table along with several magnifying glasses. Possible objects to include are a rock, bark, an insect, grains of sand, a swatch of fabric, and a leaf. Show children how to hold the magnifying glasses to see the objects clearly. After all the pupils have had a turn at looking at the objects with the glasses, talk about what the objects looked like magnified. How were some of the objects similar? How were they different? Would pupils like to be able to see objects magnified with their own eyes, without the aid of a special glass?

**Hearing** Arrange objects that are made of different materials on a table. Include items such as a wooden block, a metal pan, a cloth pillow, a plastic plate, and a glass jar. Have pupils take turns tapping the objects with pencils or wooden dowels. Ask pupils to describe how the objects sound. Which one has the highest sound? Which has the lowest sound? The loudest? The softest? Everyone recognizes the common sounds around us—people talking, cars honking, motors running. But we usually don't hear some of the more subtle quiet sounds—fish tank filter, a faucet being turned on in another room, and so on. Ask everyone to be very quiet for one minute and to listen for sounds they usually don't hear. After the minute is up, make a class list of the sounds heard. Another day take the class outside in the hall to listen quietly for one minute. Compile another class list and compare it with the first. On other days, the class might listen outside the cafeteria, near the music room, by the gym.

**Smelling** Cut out magazine pictures of objects that have distinctive odors, such as coffee beans, perfume, an onion, a banana, and so on. Glue the pictures on individual index cards. Place small amounts of the real items—coffee beans, cotton balls soaked in perfume, minced onion, banana slices—in individual, clean yogurt cartons. Punch several holes in the lids of each carton. Now have each student smell the contents of each container, then pick out the card with the picture of the object.

**Sense of Touch** Cut two squares each of a number of textured materials, such as sandpaper, foam rubber, net, lace, velvet, corrugated cardboard, and so on. Place all the squares in a paper bag and shake the bag to distribute the squares. Now blindfold one child and have the child reach into the bag and pull out one square. Ask the child to feel the other squares inside the bag until he or she finds the square that has the same texture as the square in his or her hand.

**Tasting** Give pupils small portions of foods that look similar but have different tastes, such as sweetened and unsweetened chocolate, cornstarch and powdered sugar, and salt and granulated sugar. First have students look at the foods and describe what they see. Then have them touch and smell the foods to see whether they can identify them using those senses. Finally, suggest pupils taste the foods to identify each one. Stress the fact that you have offered safe foods for pupils to taste; caution them *never* to taste unknown substances on their own.

*-Carolyn Luetje*

## EASY I.D.

Photo name tags help the bus drivers, the librarian, and the cafeteria workers guide your pupils more easily at dismissal time. Before school begins, ask parents to send a small picture of their child n the first day. Paste each picture on a circle of colorful paper and add the child's name and his or her mode of transportation to school (walker; car pooler; bus rider, bus number). Punch a hole in the top and insert yarn to make a long necklace. —Joan Lance

## COLOR CODE YOUR KIDS

Parents who don't know most of the pupils in your class are at a disadvantage when chaperoning field trips. Cut down on the confusion by color coding kids to chaperones. For example, if Mrs. Gomez is to be responsible for five children, give her a yellow name tag and the pupils under her care yellow name tags, too. She can see at a glance which kids should be with her, and her charges can recognize her as their leader. —Ann Beyersdorf

## NIFTY NAME TAGS

You'll know who's who with these sturdy tags. Fold sheets of tagboard in half. Staple each piece two inches from the top and along the bottom. Insert a length of colorful yarn through the opening at the top so the name tag can be tied around a pupil's neck. Print child's name on both sides. The tags are ready to distribute! —Violet Johnson

## CAPTURING GOOD WORK

In order to stress the importance of learning basic concepts, our primary group set up a display using a poster of Spiderman, a genuine superhero for the kids. Each child made a pin and string web on the bulletin board with his or her name below it. A paper spider was added every time a particular skill was mastered.
—Melissa Wylie

## CLASS SECURITY BLANKETS

We all need the comfort of being close to someone or something we love, but that's not always possible, especially in the school environment. Why not have your children create their own "security blankets" to be hung in the classroom? Hang a piece of clothesline from any two corners of the room and give each student a piece of old sheeting. Tell them to think of something that makes them feel happy and draw a picture of it on the sheet with magic marker. Now hang each drawing on the line with clothespins for all to see. You'll be pleasantly surprised by the change of atmosphere in your classroom. —M.V. Myers

## OSCAR'S LITTER BAGS

Pupils can make litter bags that look like Sesame Street's Oscar the Grouch's trash can to remind them to discard their trash in the right places. To make the bags, give pupils small lunch sacks and have them use black crayons to draw vertical lines on the sacks, like the lines on a garbage pail. Now give each pupil a 6" square of green paper to cut into a circle for Oscar's head. Use crayon or paint to add his facial features, such as the bushy eyebrows and the scowl. Help pupils glue Oscar's head to the inside of their sacks so that he seems to be just peeking out of the litter bags.
—Ellen Javernick

## YES-AND-NO SPOONS

All primary teachers know that kids love to answer questions— especially the "yes or no" variety. While this is to be encouraged, it can create a problem when everyone tries to answer at the same time. Here's a simple management idea that can solve this problem once and for all!

You'll need enough white plastic spoons for the kids in your class to have two each. On half the spoons, print the word *no* with a blue felt-tipped pen. On the other half, print the word *yes* in red. Now distribute the ''yes'' and ''no'' spoons and instruct kids to raise the appropriate ones in response to your yes or no questions. This way, all your students can answer together— and your eardrums will be spared!

*-Gay Johnson*

## PETAL PLEASERS

Add a petal to a posy each day pupils demonstrate good behavior and you'll have an orderly classroom and an attractive bulletin board as well! Place a large yellow or orange circle on a bulletin board covered with a bright-colored paper. Cut out 8-10 petals (more if you want the activity to last all month), and keep those hidden in your desk. Tack up a petal each day that kids earn it.

*-Linda Martin Mercer*

## SHAPE UP YOUR LINEUP

''Don't push!'' ''Keep your hands to yourself!'' Tired of giving those commands when students are lining up? Make exits easier by giving each pupil a little space; at the same time review the basic shapes.

Using masking tape, make a series of circles, squares, and triangles near your entrance. Place the shapes far enough apart so there is distance between kids. (Plan on using a good portion of your floor space.) When lining up, review shape names and classification skills by having selected pupils stand on particular shapes. Or pass out slips of paper showing the shape each pupil is to stand on.

*-Martha Christine*

## THE DISCIPLINE TIMER

When a child gets too noisy or uncooperative during an activity, give him or her a one-minute sand timer to carry to a quiet corner of the room. While the sand runs through, the child can relax and consider correcting the problem behavior so that he or she can rejoin the group. Three-minute timers are good to have on hand when a longer time-out is needed.

*-Vi Johnson*

## PUPIL DIVIDERS

Avoid the poking and trading of places that can delay the start of any structured activity by providing pupils with their own ''personal space'' in group settings. Cut a cardboard square for each child large enough for him or her to sit on. Bring in material scraps and let each child choose the material to cover his or her square. Cut the material to fit and glue it on the square. Now write each child's name on a strip of tagboard and glue it to the cloth. Store the squares where you can pass them out easily for whole-group sessions. If a child moves away from the group, remind him or her to ''sit on your name.''

*-Catherine Wiest*

## FREEZE!

It's two minutes to lunch, an assembly, dismissal, or whatever waiting period the day may bring. Make good use of the time by playing Freeze, a game that

develops listening, observation and concentration skills.

You should be the leader the first time you play, then let pupils direct the action on other days. Tell the class to make a specific movement, such as wiggling their fingers, until you give a signal, such as shaking a tambourine or flicking the lights, and say ''Freeze!'' Eliminate those pupils who do not stop wiggling their fingers immediately. Make activity progressively harder by adding other body movements.

*-Carol Piggins*

## YAWN-PROOF SHOW-AND-TELL

The language and social values of show-and-tell make it a worthwhile activity, yet it can become a tedious affair. Ask these questions of each presenter. They'll add interest to sharing times and reinforce skills in many subjects.

*Reading readiness:*

1. What letter does your object start with?
2. Does anyone know how to spell the name of this object?
3. Are any of today's show-and-tell objects alike in some way? Could anyone classify them into a group?

*Math:*

4. How many parts does your object have? Let's count together.
5. Could you divide your object into two identical halves?
6. What shapes can you find in your object?

*Science:*

7. What is your object made of?
8. Would it sink or float? How do you know?
9. Would a magnet pick it up?
10. What senses can you use to identify your object?

*Language:*

11. Would you ask one friend to ask you a question about your object?

**12.** What will happen to this object in five years?

**13.** (Have on hand a television screen cut from a cardboard box.) Stand behind the "television" and pretend you're a news reporter. Now tell us about your object the way a television reporter would.

*Social studies:*

**14.** Where was your object made? Lets find the place on the map.

**15.** What jobs were involved in making the object?

*Social skills:*

16. How did you feel when you received this object? What "magic word" did you say?

17. How could this object be shared?

*-Susan Stewart*

## THE TEACHER'S TEA PARTY

Individual conferences with your pupils—especially if held in a tea-party setting—can help you learn how each child feels about school this year. The information you receive can also help you plan your curriculum for next year. Arrange the conferences for times when you have an aide or a parent volunteer who can take the rest of the class while you meet with individual students. Try to schedule each child's conference on a separate day so that pupils can feel that they have a special day all their own to meet with the teacher. Hold the conferences outside the classroom so you can have complete privacy, and serve a snack.

Have a prepared teacher-child report ready with specific questions; fill in the answers as you talk with each child. Possible questions could include the following. What do you think you are good at in school? What would you like to do more of in school? What haven't you been able to do that you wanted to do? Is (present grade) like you thought it would be? What do you hope to do in (next grade)?

*-Judy Meagher*

## SHOW-AND-TELL: A BETTER WAY

Show-and-tell can be a problem in a preschool or kindergarten classroom if pupils see it as a time to *show off* instead of a time to *share* new toys or interesting objects. You can make show-and-tell a more productive, enjoyable experience by turning it into a guessing game that will also build pupils' vocabulary and memory skills.

On the first day of school, announce the rules for show-and-tell. Each pupil is to bring one object for show-and-tell in a paper bag so that the item remains hidden from the class. At the designated time, a sharer gives the class two clues about what the object is, then calls on one individual at a time for questions about the mysterious item. Remind the guessers that they must ask their questions in complete sentences. The sharer must also answer in a complete sentence. Allow five guesses (and no repeated questions) before the sharer unveils the object.

This method for show-and-tell will take more time, so limit the number of children who may share on a given day. Keep a monthly chart showing who has brought something for show-and-tell and who still has a turn.

*-Ann Beyersdorf*

## THE LESS MESS SOLUTION

For those messy projects like cooking, painting, planting, and so on, spread inexpensive plastic tablecloths over tables and floors. They're more effective than newspapers, because when they get dirty, you can just wipe them with a damp cloth and mild detergent.

*-Nicki Klein*

## ME-MUSEUMS

Here's a variation on Show-and-Tell that will boost students' self-concepts and help them get to know one another quickly—and it doesn't take any preparation time at all! Ask each child to bring in one empty shoe box. Have kids decorate their shoe boxes with magazine pictures that represent their hobbies, favorite foods and television programs, special interests, and so on. Make sure they leave enough blank space on the boxes to print their names, too. When everyone is finished, put all the boxes in a row on the windowsill.

Tell the children that for the next two weeks they are to bring in one small item each day that has special significance to them. These may include snapshots of homes and families, souvenirs, greeting cards, knickknacks, stickers, small toys, and so on. Have the kids place the items in their shoe boxes each day and encourage them to view their classmates' contributions during free time. These "Me-museums" start conversations and friendships!

*-Susie Emond*

## ZIP IT UP

Do you spend a lot of time picking up stray activity cards and game pieces from the floor? Well, here's a "zippy" idea that can change all that. Store your learning games and activity cards in zip-lock bags, label each bag with the name of the game or activity inside, and hang them all on a pegboard in the back of your classroom. This way, children can tell at a glance which games are available. And if you remind them to return the bags to their proper hooks, you'll spend less time picking up after them.

*-Mary Ann Panko*

## HANG THE VOWELS TO DRY

Warm and windy weather is a good time to play this letter recognition game. On each of 26 spring-type clothespins write an uppercase letter on one side and that letter's lowercase on the other side. Cut 26 poster board ''shirts.'' Label each shirt front with an uppercase letter and the back with its lowercase. String a cord at children's eye level and let them hang up the shirts, matching pins and shirts.      -Mary Jo Fisher

## TOYS ARE FUN

Reviewing letters and sounds of the alphabet will seem less like work and more like play to children when you make toys the focus of the exercise. Gather a variety of toys, each of which begins with a different letter of the alphabet. (Try to find toys that children will readily recognize. Also, look for those that will not be known to pupils by a name other than the one you have in mind.) Now place the toys in a bag so that children will not be able to see them. Then, working with the whole class or in small groups, have pupils take turns pulling a toy out of the bag, giving the sound of the letter it begins with, and writing that letter on the chalkboard. Encourage pupils to bring other toys from home that begin with these same letter sounds.      -Marion G. Walker

## SOFT SPELLING

Large letters made from carpet-padding foam can offer a change from the usual sandpaper-letter tactile experiences. Contact carpet stores near you and request scrap pieces of foam. Padding that has a right and wrong side is best to use because pupils then have a guide for positioning letters correctly. Draw block letters on the foam freehand or trace around paper patterns.      -Ellen Javernick

## CANDY-LAND LEARNING

Their success will be sweet when youngsters use a lollipop tree to review the letters and sounds of the alphabet. Cut out a tree from construction paper and staple it to a bulletin board. Tape a lollipop for each pupil to the tree. Write a pair of uppercase and lowercase letters on each of 26 circles; staple the circles around the tree. Place in an envelope a picture of an object that begins with each letter. Have each pupil select a picture, then pin it beside the letter it starts with. When you take down the bulletin board, give a lollipop to each child.
-Loretta Welk Jung

## A YARD OF CARDS

Try a high-fashion approach to learning letters of the alphabet by having pupils make individual picture-card necklaces. First, gather together old magazines and workbooks. As you introduce each letter, have pupils search through the magazines and workbooks for small pictures of people or objects that begin with that letter. Glue the pictures onto precut 3" x 3" cards, writing the letter (or the word for more able students) below each picture. Punch a hole in the top of each card. String cards on yarn, arranging additional cards in alphabetical order.      -Carol Quinn

## HUNG UP ON THE ALPHABET

Help young children who are ''hung up'' on the letters of the alphabet with this activity. Hang a low clothesline across the front of your classroom. Now cut at least three sets of alphabet letters from stiff oaktag, mix them up, and scatter them faceup on a desk or table. Print a word such as ''house'' on the chalkboard and appoint one student to be the "cheerleader," and another to be the speller. The cheerleader calls out the letters of the word to be spelled by shouting, "Give me an 'h', give me an 'o'," and so on. The speller looks for the letters and hangs them one by one on the clothesline with a pinch-type clothespin. After the entire word has been hung on the line, the speller and the cheerleader sit down and choose two other students to play the game. Continue until every child has had a chance to participate.

*-Dave Bloom*

## LETTERS & SOUNDS

**Block play** Cut eight block shapes from tagboard. Draw lines on each block to make it appear as though three sides of the cube are showing. Glue a picture in each of those three sides that begin with the same letter and sound. (Each of the eight blocks should represent a different letter.) Trace each block on the inside of a file folder, then write one of the eight letters inside each shape. Pupils match the picture blocks to the correct letter shapes.

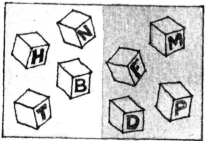

**In the doghouse** Trace and cut out identical dog-bone shapes from tagboard. Cut each bone in half, making sure you cut each at different angles or in different designs on the bone. Print an uppercase letter on one half of each bone and a corresponding lowercase letter on the other. Pupils match the uppercase and lowercase letters by finding the pieces that fit snugly together. Decorate a small box to look like a doghouse and store the bones in it.

**Letter march** Draw 26 funny characters on the inside of a file folder and have each character carry a square sign. Cut 26 small squares from tagboard and print an uppercase letter on each square. Pupils place the letters in the square signs, arranging them in sequence from *A* to *Z*.

**Bucket o' fun** Make duplicates of eight or more uppercase letters, printing the letters on tagboard. Place all the letters in a small plastic bucket. Make one card each of the same uppercase letters for yourself. Seat small groups of pupils on the floor around the bucket. On a given signal, have each pupil pull a letter out of the bucket. Then hold up one of your letter cards and ask pupils with the same letter to hold up their cards and call out the letter name.

*-Pamela Klawitter*

## WHERE AM I?

Some of your pupils may come to school able to recognize and write their own names, but for those who can't, design a worksheet that will ask them to find and circle their first names. Use a primary typewriter or print the names of all the children in your class on a spirit master. Place the names randomly on the paper, and make sure each child's name appears at least twice. Draw several lines at the bottom of the page.

When you pass out the worksheet, watch carefully for children having problems recognizing their printed names. Reassure those pupils that with your help, they'll be writing their names in no time. Then show each one how to print the first letter of his or her name, and have the child practice printing that letter on the lines at the bottom of the page. Pupils who are able to print their first name can practice printing first and last name on the lines.

*-Pamela Klawitter*

## THE CASE OF THE COINS

Use these two cheery leprechauns to review reading readiness skills. Purchase one tall and one short cardboard leprechaun figure or draw your own on cardboard. Cut two double pots from black construction paper and glue pieces together so that each pot forms a pocket. Attach one to the short leprechaun, one to the tall one.

Cut 52 "coins" from gold wrapping paper. On each print a letter to make a set of lowercase and one of uppercase letters. Pupils sort the coins, placing the uppercase letters in the tall leprechaun's pot, lowercase ones in the short one's pot.

Cut out another set of coins for practice discriminating between long and short vowel sounds. Print words or glue pictures that represent words having long- and short-vowel sounds on the coins. Pupils place long-vowel words in the tall leprechaun's pot, short-vowel ones in the other.

*-Kelly Riley*

## IDEAS TO STRENGTHEN VISUAL DISCRIMINATION

**1.** Outline the following objects on individual sheets of oaktag: a pencil, crayon, paper clip, odd-shaped button, scissors, circle, square, triangle, and a rectangle. Add other objects as desired. Store the objects together in a coffee can. Children must place

the objects on the correct oaktag sheets.

**2.** Ask your local hardware store for two identical paint-sample books. Cut apart the books. Place all of the color squares in a large box. Pupils sort through the squares to find the pairs of shades that are alike. If only one book is available, cut it apart into squares and mix up the squares in a box. Pupils sort the squares into piles of the different colors, then arrange the piles in order from darkest shade to lightest.

**3.** Glue small squares of fabric of different patterns and textures on a large sheet of tagboard. Cut a second swatch of each fabric. Children match the loose swatches of material to fixed pieces.

**4.** Play Zook! Cut out 40 tagboard rectangles the size of playing cards. Write a two- or three-letter word on each card, allowing four cards for each word. To play, divide the cards equally between two children. Sitting side by side, the two players simultaneously remove the top card from their main piles and place the cards in a second pile. If the two cards feature the same word, the first player to say "zook!" gets the opponent's second pile of cards as well as his or her own, to add to his or her mail pile. The game ends when one player is out of cards.

**5.** Cut out several squares of tagboard. Draw a line down the middle of each square. Make a pattern with marking pen on each side; on some squares make the patterns different and on some make them alike. Pupils look at each square and decide if the two patterns are alike.

**6.** Draw and cut out several small robots from construction paper. Add details with marking pen and laminate each. Cut a slit in each robot's mouth, then cut out a long strip of paper of a smaller width than the slit for each robot. On the strips, write the same words, letters, shapes, numerals, and so on, but not in the same order each time. Make a set of cards that also features those words, letters, and so on. Insert each paper strip, copy side up, through a robot's mouth. Now, working with a small group, give each child a robot. Hold up a card and ask pupils to make their robot "read out" that information by pulling the paper strip through the robot's mouth until they find the form on the card.    *-Diane Parette and Marie Jordan-Whitney*

## IDEAS TO SHARPEN VISUAL MEMORY

Visual memory is the ability to remember an object previously seen. Use these activities to sharpen this skill.

**Marble match up** Remove the top from an egg carton and divide the bottom in half vertically. Set aside one half and place a different-colored marble in each of the six cups of the other half. Show the marbles to a child, then cover them with a cloth. Give the child the other half of the egg carton and six marbles of the same colors. Have the child try to place the marbles in the six cups in the same order as yours. Then remove the cloth to see how well he or she remembered. If six cups seem too difficult at first, divide the egg carton into sets of three cups for kids to use.

**I saw . . .** Have pupils describe what they saw on their way to school, either verbally or in a drawing. Encourage them to be detailed in their descriptions. As a variation, have students close their eyes and describe, one at a time, what they have on or what the person next to them is wearing.

**Five-second flash** Arrange a number of objects, such as shapes, letters, or toy figures, on a table and cover the arrangement with a cloth. Have a duplicate of each object on hand, and show one of the objects to a child for five seconds, then remove it from view. Now uncover the arrangement and ask the child to point to the object you just held in your hand.

**Do-it-too designs** Make a design from Popsicle sticks, toothpicks, blocks or another building material. Show the design to pupils, then remove it from view. Ask pupils to duplicate the design as closely as possible using the same materials. Increase the complexity of the designs as visual memory skills improve.

**Mitten madness** From colored oaktag, cut several pairs of mittens the size of a child's hand. Or bring in several pairs of brightly colored woolen mittens. Ask three children to select a pair of mittens to hold up or put on, and have those children go to the front of the room. Ask them to show their mittens to the class, then hide them behind their backs. The class must tell what color mittens each child is wearing. Increase the difficulty of the exercise by involving more mitten-wearers.    *-Diane Parette and Marie Jordan-Whitney*

## WHICH TOY IS MISSING?

Toys are great motivators for getting young children interested in an activity. Test visual-memory skills with this game that asks pupils to name the missing toys. Cut out pictures of toys from magazines, mount each on cardboard, and back with felt for use on a flannel board. Include some toys that look alike, such as a large and a small ball. Place all the pictures on the board and identify each one with the class. Now turn the board away from pupils, remove a toy, then ask pupils which one is missing. Have

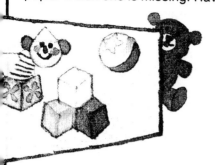

a child who answers correctly remove the next toy from the board. Make the activity more challenging by taking away two or more toys at once.   -Betty Nations

## DISCRIMINATING SOUNDS
Try these activities for improving auditory discrimination.
**Hearing test** How well do each of your pupils listen? Find out by giving each child a worksheet divided into four boxes. Then give the following directions *once*: In the top left-hand box, draw two blue balloons; in the top right-hand box, draw a brown house with a red door; in the bottom left-hand box, write your name and make each letter a different color; and in the remaining box, draw a yellow circle with a green square inside. Check all papers for accuracy.
**Odd couples or even pairs** Hone discrimination skills by giving pupils pairs of words and asking them questions about each pair. For example: Do the words rhyme? Do they begin with the same letter? Do they end with the same letter? Encourage children whose names are the same or begin with the same sound to pair up in class.
**Listening walk** If weather permits in your area, take pupils on a listening walk around the school

or community. Stop every few minutes to make a list of the sounds children hear. Back in the classroom, discuss the different sounds and how they are different.
**Opposites** Touch upon the idea of high and low sounds by plucking notes on a piano or guitar, or by playing excerpts from different records. Discuss soft and loud sounds by taping pairs of sounds on a recorder, such as the sound a hammer pounding nails makes paired with the sound of a clock ticking. Or fill pairs of plastic pantyhose eggs with opposite-sounding objects such as cotton balls and dry beans or scraps of paper and marbles. As the eggs are shaken have pupils describe the sound they hear.
**What's that sound?** Stand behind a screen and make sounds with everyday objects, such as a typewriter, rattle, drum, and so on. Ask pupils to identify each sound. Or ask them to identify tape-recorded sounds such as a doorbell ringing, a fire siren, water running, and so on.
-Pamela Klawitter

## IDEAS TO IMPROVE AUDITORY MEMORY
Auditory memory is the ability to recognize a sound being heard or to reproduce a sound from memory.
**1.** Gather together several recordings of familiar children's songs. Play each song for 30 seconds, occasionally replaying a song without warning. Ask pupils to hold up a hand when they hear a tune replayed.
**2.** Give each child a set of numerals from 1-9. Say aloud a series of three (or more) numerals, then ask pupils to hold up those numerals in the same order.
**3.** Read a short, simple story to the class. After every few sentences or every page, stop

and choose a child to summarize what he or she has heard.
**4.** Use the familiar story of *Jack and the Beanstalk* to design an activity to test pupils' abilities to recall letter sounds. Cut out a large beanstalk from oaktag. Cut out 26 leaves from construction paper and print a lowercase letter on each. Tape the letters on both sides of the beanstalk, arranging them randomly, not in alphabetical order. Now cut out a small figure representing Jack and staple an oaktag flap to his back. Cut a slit down the middle of the beanstalk and insert the flap in the slit so that Jack can slide up and down the beanstalk. Now start Jack at the bottom of the beanstalk. As pupils give the sound of the letter on each leaf, move Jack up the beanstalk. Time each pupil to see who can get Jack to the top of the beanstalk the fastest.
**5.** Cut several pieces of oaktag in rectangular shapes. Hold the cards so that the longest sides are from top to bottom. Write an uppercase and corresponding lowercase letter at the top of each card; at the bottom, glue three pictures, one beginning with the sound of the letter. In the middle of each card, attach a paper arrow with a brad. Have one pupil point the arrow to the correct picture on each card. -Diane Parette and Marie Jordan-Whitney

## AUDITORY EXERCISE
Games like these involving music and rhythm are good ways to help children develop auditory skills.
**Recognizing different sounds**
You will need three drums of different sizes (a five-gallon ice cream container, a one-gallon barrel from a fried-chicken outlet, and a plastic-foam drinking cup). Place the drums in front of the children. Focus attention first on the largest drum by tapping it several times, then on each of the

other two drums. Now have the pupils turn so that they cannot see the drums. Tap on one and have kids identify the source of the sound. Repeat, alternating drums.

**Refining auditory discrimination**
There are many similar sounds in our language. This exercise will help children learn to hear subtle differences in sound. You will need a xylophone or melody bells. Tap or ring a low note and a high note in the same family (high C, low C). Have children crouch low on the first sound and stretch high on the second. Then have pupils face away from you while you strike a variety of high and low notes. Pupils should bend or stretch depending on the sound they hear.

**Developing auditory memory** You will need a plastic-foam drinking cup for each child. Tap a short rhythm on your cup, starting with a simple one such as the first two words of ''Jingle Bells.'' Increase the difficulty of each rhythm as pupils are able to remember the preceding one, such as moving on to the first four syllables of ''Twin-kle, Twin-kle Little Star.''
-Earl R. Breiman

## ''WHAT-IS BOOKLETS''
Challenge students' imaginations and vocabulary with these tiny books made from construction paper and staples. The first type are ''shape'' booklets. I begin by cutting out triangles, squares, and circles, all big enough to carry three large words on the front. Then staple anywhere from 6 to 10 of the same shapes together. On the covers of the appropriate booklets write: ''A circle is . . .,'' ''A triangle is . . . ,'' and ''A square is . . . .'' Then let your students finish the books by writing the names of some objects that are the correct shape for each book on the blank pages.

''Size'' booklets can be titled: ''What is big?'' ''What is tiny?'' ''Tall is . . . ,'' and so on. You can make the size of the booklets themselves match the corresponding questions on the cover.

Using different-colored construction paper, you also can create ''color'' books. ''Green is . . . ,'' ''Pink is . . . ,'' and so on are possibilities for titles.
-Gertrude Parker

## A FIRST BOOK REPORT
Most preschool and kindergarten children have a favorite book that's been read to them at home or in school. Use this special story to introduce each pupil to the process of thinking critically about characters and plot in a short taped report. Have each child select a book and review it with you. Go over the title, author's name, and the general sequence of events. Then you or an aide can help each child record a report. Have the child give his or her name, the title of the book and author's name, then tell something about the book—favorite parts, most interesting characters, things about the story he or she would change. Place tapes of the reports and a copy of each book in a listening center for others to enjoy.     -Ann Beyersdorf

## TURKEY TALES
Make pictorial dictionaries and student-dictated stories part of your November language arts agenda. Prepare the dictionaries by giving each student 7 to 10 sheets of scratch paper that have been stapled together.

Brainstorm with the class a list of Thanksgiving-related words, such as Pilgrim, Native American, turkey, thanks, feast, friendship, family. Discuss what each word means. Then have pupils write one word on each page of their booklets and draw a picture to illustrate the word. For another activity, have students dictate

paragraphs on How to Cook a Turkey or If I Were a Turkey at Thanksgiving. Create an outline of a large turkey with yarn on a classroom wall and tack pupils' ''turkey tales'' around the bird.
-Violet Johnson

## READING PICTURES
Wordless picture books are great resources for helping children understand the elements of a story, and for stimulating creative thinking, language development, and an interest in reading. Follow these guidelines for enhancing the use of these books in your classroom.

Before introducing a new wordless picture book to your class, go through the book yourself several times. Get an idea of the story, and look for details you want to be sure pupils catch.

When presenting each book, arrange pupils around you so that each can see clearly. Ask pupils to describe what is happening on each page. Guide them in identifying the main characters, in describing the setting, and in summarizing the main idea of each story.

Now gather together several books and let pupils ''read'' the books to a partner. Remind pupils that because there are no words to guide them, partners may interpret illustrations differently, and that these different versions of the same story should be accepted. Sitting with different pairs at different times, take down as many of the stories as possible. Transfer the stories to chart paper. Use these pupil-produced stories, along with the illustrations from the books when needed, to teach vocabulary, spatial words, and other concepts.     -Richard Culyer

## IT'S NO JOKING MATTER

Telling jokes in preschool or kindergarten is serious business! It promotes socialization while stimulating logical thinking and use of memory and phonics skills. Here's how to capitalize on a favorite activity of young children. Set aside a Joke Time two days a week. Let pupils know that everyone may have a turn at telling a joke, but that no one must have a joke. Designate a special chair reserved for the joker. Encourage pupils to rehearse their jokes so they remember them and can tell them well. Remind children that every joke must have an answer or a punch line, never to ridicule another child's joke, and that favorite jokes may be repeated, but not on the same day.

Riddles are especially good for involving other members of the class. Limit pupil's guesses to three, and remind children that the answer to most riddles is a logical one. Knock-knock jokes also require audience participation. And because their punch lines are often based on words that sound like others, they can help reinforce and extend phonics lessons.

Occasionally, pupils may start to tell an off-color joke. A quiet word from you, such as "That's not a school joke—tell us another," should defuse the situation.

*-Mignon Morgan*

## AUTHOR, AUTHOR

Pupils ready to construct sentences can get extra practice with this independent center. You will need several cards cut from red, blue, and yellow construction paper. Write nouns pupils are familiar with on the blue cards, simple verbs on the red cards, and articles on the yellow cards. Back each card with a bit of felt so it will stick to a flannel board. Now make an envelope to hold each set of cards and place the cards along with a flannel board in a quiet corner of the room. Encourage pupils to experiment with sentence construction, using one card of each color, and try putting their sentences together to tell a story.

*-Marion G. Walker*

## THE CLASS THAT WRITES TOGETHER . . .

. . . learns about sound-symbol relationships of letters, words, sentence construction, capitalization, and punctuation, as well as how a story is created. Try introducing pupils to creative writing by composing a group story.

First, choose a subject. You might use the story as a way of highlighting the letter of the week. If it's M, for example, compose a story about a monkey. To help pupils gather ideas for the story, look at books, films or filmstrips, and other sources of pictures and information about monkeys. Talk about where monkeys live, what they look like, how they move. When you feel pupils have a good picture of monkeys in their mind, do a "word cluster" on the chalkboard. Write *monkey* in large letters in the middle and circle it, stressing the M sound as you say the word. Ask pupils to give you words or short phrases that describe a monkey, and cluster those words around the central one on the board.

The next day, review the words on the board, then ask pupils to choose one or two to make into a sentence that tells something about the monkey, such as "The monkey has a long tail." Point out that the first word begins with a capital letter and the sentence ends with a period. Now ask pupils to think about what a monkey might do with a long tail that would get it into trouble; compose several sentences that describe the event, again drawing from words in the cluster. Now is there a way the monkey can get out of trouble, using any of the remaining words on the board? Complete the session by writing down all the sentences of the story in order, from introduction to conclusion. Help pupils see that they have used words that describe what a monkey looks like and how it acts, as well as their own imaginations, to create a story.

*-Ann Beyersdorf*

## COMPREHENSION CUBES

For reading activities with hands-on appeal, I use old photo cubes. I can insert activities on the side of each cube, change the activities frequently with little fuss, and give my first graders the opportunity to work independently on sentence structure and comprehension. In the top section of each cube, I indicate which reading group these activities are for. Then on small cards, I type a sentence featuring the week's vocabulary words. I write five sentences, one for each side and for the bottom. The sentences together tell a story, but they are neither structured correctly nor in the proper order.

When pupils have free time, they can take a cube back to their desks, figure out the correct structure for each sentence, and write the proper sentences on paper. They then cut and paste the sentences (or rewrite them) on another sheet of paper in the correct order to tell a logical story. They then show me the story so I can check their work. When a number of pupils master the cubes for their reading groups, it is time to prepare more challenging ones by simply inserting new cards.

*-Carolyn M. Wilhelm*

## PUMPKIN PATCH MATH

There's no trick to learning numbers with this game, and it's a treat to play! Draw 15 pumpkins on each of two pieces of tagboard. On each pumpkin, write the number word or draw a set of objects representing a number from one to 10. Cut out 30 squares and print a numeral on each. Two players each take a board and take turns drawing a numeral card. If it matches a word or set, the child places it on that pumpkin. The first to cover all of the pumpkins wins.    -Kelly Riley

## ALL ABOARD THE ARITHMETIC EXPRESS

Children will have fun learning number concepts with this activity, an imaginary train ride. Place as many chairs in a row as you have children; the chairs represent the seats on a train. Fold sheets of construction paper in half and write a number word on one half of each sheet. Slip a number word over the back of each chair, placing "one" on the first chair and continuing in order so that the highest number is on the last chair. Now cut paper tickets and write a numeral on each ticket to correspond with each number.

Begin the activity by designating one child to be the agent who

passes out the tickets. Once each child has one, he or she finds the number word that matches the numeral on the ticket. A second child, the conductor, checks to make sure each pupil is in the proper seat. When the ticket agent and conductor take their seats, the ride begins. Ask questions or give directions to test number recognition and counting skills. For example, ask how many passengers will be left if five get off at the next stop.

-Marion Walker

## COUNT THE CARTONS

Take your kids back to the days when a milk carrier delivered products door to door with this object-numeral correspondence game.

On heavy paper draw and decorate 10 (or more) houses standing in a row. Number the doors 1-10. Cut out 55 milk carton shapes from paper. Fashion a milk truck from a clean quart carton that will hold all 55 bottles. Cut off the top of the carton. The bottom will serve as the front of the truck; leave the other end open for "loading" and "unloading" the bottles. Make wheels and a box-shaped front for the truck from the top of the carton or from paper. Add other details as desired.

To use the game, one pupil loads the cartons into the truck, then moves it down the street, delivering the number of cartons indicated by the numeral on each door.    -Kathleen Wildstein

## MAGIC MOMENTS

You may not wear a magician's hat and carry a wand, but there are probably many moments during a day when you would like to conjure up an activity to fill a restless minute or two.

**Tap on trash** Ask a pupil to tap the side of a wastebasket slowly and distinctly with a ruler. The child can tap any number of times up to a limit, such as 20, which you set at the beginning of the activity. When he or she stops tapping, classmates guess the number of taps, and the first correct guesser is the next tapper. This is a good activity for sharpening listening skills.

**Silent math** No one talks during this activity, not even you. Write a simple addition or subtraction problem on the board, or print a sequence of numbers with one number missing. Point to a student to come to the board and do the problem. If he or she answers correctly, the other pupils raise their hands. If the answer is incorrect, they cross their arms.

**The count** When you have a few minutes before lunch or dismissal, have pupils count in unison to see how high they can go before the time is up.

-Violet Johnson

## A GREAT GRAPH

Introduce bar graphing skills by capitalizing on a favorite subject with kids—their pets. First, clear a space on a wall for the graph. Then give each child a half a sheet of paper, directing each to draw his or her pet (only one), or a picture of a relative's or a neighbor's pet. When the pictures are complete, ask pupils who drew dogs to give you their papers. Tack them one above the other so that the line of pictures makes a solid bar on the graph. Do the same with pictures of cats, placing that bar beside the one for dogs, and so on until all pictures are on the graph. Then compare the number of pets, showing pupils how they can tell which pet is most popular by the height of its bar.    -Marion Walker

## A MEDLEY OF MATH GAMES

Reinforce kids' math concepts and skills with activities that ask them to identify numerals and sets, count, and compare objects for weight.

**Sets-ational** Provide practice in recognizing numbers and in forming sets. Have children march in a circle to music until you call a number. Then kids divide into sets equaling that number, hold hands, and resume marching. Ask kids who don't fit into a set to count the sets while waiting for the next number.

*-Kelly Riley*

**Number toss** Tape together four pieces of 12-inch by 18-inch tagboard to create a game board that can be folded for easy storage. Outline 21 large circles on the tagboard, and number the circles randomly from 0-20. Set out beanbags and objects to count. Here are four ways kids can use the board: 1)Throw a beanbag, then identify the numeral it lands on. 2)Throw a beanbag, identify the numeral, then count out that many objects. 3)Throw two beanbags, name the numerals, then say which is larger. 4)Two kids each throw a beanbag, then add the numbers by counting objects.

*-Ann Beyersdorf*

**How many light bulbs?** Have children count everyday objects at home, then graph the class's results. Prepare a spirit master to send to parents asking that they assist their child in counting the number of light bulbs, doorknobs, and drawers at home, as well as an object of the child's choice. On the master, the child writes in the numbers.

**Balancing act** Set up a small balance and several containers of assorted objects to weigh. Children experiment to see how many of one object are needed to balance another. Be ready to ask questions. Are larger objects always heavier than smaller ones?

*-Violet Johnson*

## COUNTING RAINDROPS

Have children hold up their fingers to indicate the number of drops, as they are mentioned, in this counting rhyme.

> I see ONE tiny drop of rain,
> Sliding down my
>   windowpane.
> Here come TWO to join the
>   one.
> They're really having lots of
>   fun.
> Now there're THREE—now
>   there're FOUR.
> My, oh, my, here come
>   some more.
> I count FIVE; I count SIX.
> They're doing funny circus
>   tricks.
> I see SEVEN, EIGHT, NINE,
>   TEN.
> I'll have to start all over
>   again.

*-Jean Brabham McKinney*

## COUNT ON CALENDARS

You can always count on calendars to help reinforce your students' number skills. Simply cut out separate number squares from your calendar pages, mount them individually on small pieces of cardboard or oaktag, and laminate for extra durability. Kids can place these number squares in numerical order, match them with other squares or corresponding numbers of objects, or use them to form equations for their classmates to solve.

*-Dorothy Zjawin*

## SEEDY SUMS

Use a popular summer fruit—watermelon—to reinforce number skills! Cut out 10 or more tagboard rectangles. Glue a watermelon slice fashioned from red, green and white paper on each rectangle. Print a numeral from 1-10 or higher below each slice. Buy one package each of dry white and black beans to represent seeds. Pupils arrange the number of seeds indicated by the numeral on each watermelon slice.

*-Joy Young*

## MR. TURKEY MATH

Test math and reading readiness skills with this holiday activity board. Decorate a bulletin board with a large colorful bird. Cut out 15 or so small turkeys, giving each three tail feathers. On the body of each turkey, write an addition or subtraction problem or draw a set of objects or an object beginning with a letter being studied. A second problem may be written on the other side. Write an answer on each tail feather, only one of which is correct. Punch a hole in each feather. A child chooses a turkey, studies the problem, then hangs the turkey on the bulletin board by placing a push pin through the correct answer.

*-Melinda Hammerschmidt*

## MITTEN MATH

**Classification** Ask each pupil to bring a pair of mittens from home. Label each child's mittens, then place them together. Count all the mittens, first singles, then pairs. Then have pupils take turns arranging the mittens in groups by color, design, texture, left hand, right hand, and so on. Discuss similarities and differences between the different groups of mittens and between the mittens in each group.

**Patterning** Cut out several pairs of mittens from construction paper and discarded wallpaper samples. Arrange a group of mittens in a particular pattern; red, blue, striped, red, blue, _____. Ask pupils to find the mitten that should go next. Repeat with more difficult patterns.

**Matching** Give each pupil one mitten and a sheet of paper. Have each draw a mitten that matches the first one but fits the opposite hand. *-Wendy Pfeffer*

## TICK TOCK TIME

This game helps students who are learning to tell time. The rules are the same as for bingo. Begin by making a game card for each student. Draw a grid with four rows across and four columns down on a duplicating sheet. Label the vertical columns with the letters T, O, C, and K. Then, in each of the 16 squares, draw a clock's face without the hands. Run off these sheets—one per student— and then fill in the clock faces on each sheet to show different times. Then cut up small scraps of paper and write a different time and one of the letters— T, O, C, or K—on each. Now you are ready to play the game. Give each student a sheet and begin to draw one scrap at a time from your pile of scrap paper. As you call out the time and a letter that are on the scrap, each student checks to see if a clock in the proper column on his or her sheet matches it. The first child to correctly fill in four clocks in a row is the winner. *-Lori Stein*

## SUPER SCOOP OF SKILLS

Set up an ice cream center in your classroom where children can review their skills.

**Number sundaes** Cut out 10 sundae dishes from brown paper, 10 scoops of ice cream from different colors of paper, and 10 mounds of whipped cream from

white paper. On each sundae dish, print a numeral from 1-10; and on each whipped cream mound write a number word from one to ten. For self-checking, write the numeral represented on the back of each item. To use, kids make sundaes by matching number word to set of objects to numeral.

**Small, medium or large?** Cut out 10 ice cream cones in graduated sizes. Number each cone on the back in order from largest to smallest. To use, have kids arrange the cones in order according to size, then check the numerals on the back to see if they are in order from 1-10.

**Split sequence** Prepare seven drawings of various stages in the creation of a banana split. For example, the first drawing might show an empty dish, the third the dish with two scoops of ice cream, the fifth with three scoops and a layer of sauce, the seventh with bananas and a cherry. Have kids arrange the pictures in the proper sequence. As a self-check, number the back of the pictures from 1 to 7.

**Shapely treats** Draw 10 ice cream treats, choosing those that are similar in appearance to a basic shape. For example, use a cone for a triangle, an ice cream sandwich for a rectangle, a sundae for a circle, and so on. Then cut out the same basic shapes from paper. To use this activity, have pupils match each treat to the paper shape it most resembles.

**Double delight** Cut out seven cone shapes and 14 scoops of ice cream. Select seven initial consonant sounds that you want to test the students on. On each cone draw or glue a picture of an object that begins with one of the sounds. On each pair of ice cream scoops draw or glue objects that begin with one of the seven featured consonants. To use, pupils look at the object on each cone, then find the two scoops of ice cream that feature objects that begin with the same sound. *-Kelly Riley*

## MATH AT WORK

Kids often come to kindergarten eager to learn to add and subtract, but they probably aren't ready for more advanced operations. However, there are activities in the areas of classification and ordering that will strengthen their ability to work with numbers in the future. And one way to generate interest in these activities is to use easily found manipulatives that appeal to kids, such as nails, wooden blocks, wallpaper, and so on. Be sure to sequence tasks to aid a gradual growth in skill, beginning at the easiest level and moving toward the more complex.

**Classification** Wallpaper can be used as a matching exercise in a number of ways. Cut out different-sized squares of wallpaper of various colors and textures. Have kids classify the squares according to size, color, texture, pattern, and so on.

Obtain two wooden blocks and drill several holes in each block. Now gather together two sets of nails (three or four of each type) that are different in at least one way, and place all the nails together in a container. Children must sort the nails into two groups, then put like nails in each of the wooden blocks.

**Ordering** Obtain another wooden block and drill two holes in it. Gather together different-sized nails, and include some very small ones and some very large ones. Mix all the nails together in a container. Ask one child to find the smallest nail and the largest nail and to place them in the holes in the wooden block. Now bring out another block with several more holes drilled in it. Have the child arrange the nails in the block in order of size.

Cut pieces of wallpaper into different-sized circles or squares and have the children take turns arranging the squares in order of size.　　　*-Joseph A. Baust*

## ARC ART

Here's a cut-and-paste activity that will give kids practice with following directions and with classifying objects by color and initial letter sounds. Have each pupil cut out a half circle from red, orange, yellow, green, blue, and purple paper in graduating sizes, red being the largest, purple the smallest. Have kids glue the circles together, placing the color that begins with R on the bottom and so on. Then have kids sort through magazines, cutting out objects of each color to glue to that arc.　　*-Phyllis Scarcell Marcus*

## PASTA PICK-UP

A game of Pasta Pick-Up teaches classification—a prelude to understanding numbers—and develops the tactile sense.

In preparation, buy boxes of pasta in as many shapes as possible. (You may be surprised at how many there are.)

To play, seat a group of children on the floor in a small circle. Have them close their eyes or put on blindfolds. In the middle of the circle, place a pile in which two kinds of pasta are mixed. Each child is to reach out and choose one item from the pile. After feeling that piece of pasta carefully, each pupil picks up as many matching pieces as he or she can. With open eyes, kids check to see that they actually did choose like shapes.

There are many possible variations:

Have each child describe the shape he or she selected. Is it smooth or bumpy?

Play the game with three or more pasta shapes in the pile.

Instead of having players match shapes, have them collect as many *different* ones as they can. Pass out a different pasta shape to each blindfolded child. Have him or her feel it carefully, then put it down. Now pass around pieces of various shapes until each child has found his or her "pet" shape. Remove blindfolds; see if each pupil really has made a match.　　*-Joseph A. Baust*

## GO-TOGETHERS

Use common household objects to assemble a classification game. Collect pairs of objects that are used together, such as a plastic cup and saucer, a washcloth and a bar of soap. Include some pairs that are obvious and others that are less so, such as a bandage and first-aid cream. Have one pair for each child. Spread all the objects on a table, and let each student have a turn at choosing two items that belong together.　　*-Carolyn Luetje*

## GRAPH IT

My kindergartners reinforce language, writing, and math skills by interviewing each other on specific topics, then presenting the results of the interviews in the form of a graph. We've made graphs showing the number of boys and girls in the class, the pupils who prefer one poem to another, whether students are more afraid of Halloween ghosts or witches, how many pupils ride the school bus, how many like to paint, and much more. I ask a pair of students to gather the information each time; then I make a master graph on the chalkboard. Children copy each graph onto a sheet of paper so they can refer to it again later. (Tracing the graphs is a great exercise for small muscles, especially when it comes to drawing straight lines to separate the columns!)

In small groups, we discuss the graphs. The concepts of "greater than" and "less than" are introduced as pupils see that one side of the graph has more marks than another. Other math concepts involving matching and counting skills also are stressed through this simple but fun activity.　　*-Rose S. Marlow*

### LET'S EXPERIMENT

What substances resist water? Pupils can find out through an experiment that lets them make predictions.

Gather several substances that are not water soluble, such as cooking oil, rubber cement, margarine, and candle wax. Give each child a sheet of paper divided into six squares, black watercolor paint (explain that it is mostly water), a brush, and crayons.

Begin by having each child paint the first square on his or her paper. Point out to pupils how easily the watercolor paint covers the paper. Now rub candle wax on each pupil's second square. Ask students what they think will happen when they paint their squares. After they paint the squares, ask pupils why they think the paint didn't stick to the wax. Repeat with the oil, rubber cement, and margarine, asking pupils to predict how each substance will react to the watercolor paint. Ask how we use wax or oil to protect objects.

Now have pupils draw a design with crayon in their last square. Have them paint over their designs, and discuss the results. Use this technique to make striking pictures. Have each child trace around a cottage cheese lid on white paper, making several overlapping circles. Draw a crayon design inside each circle. Cover the circles with a thin coat of paint.

*-Judy Meagher*

### WHAT'S LIGHT? WHAT'S HEAVY?

Help young children explore the concept of weight with these activities. Introduce the subject by reading *Let's Find Out What's Light and What's Heavy* by Martha and Charles Shapp (Franklin Watts, 1975). Then show the class as many different kinds

of scales as you can acquire—a bathroom scale, a kitchen scale, a postal scale, and so on. Weigh each pupil on the bathroom scale and make a bar graph showing the comparative weights.

Next, bring out a variety of light and heavy objects for the children to weigh on the bathroom scale. Ask pupils to find ways to classify the objects, such as placing those that weigh one pound or less in one pile and those that weigh over one pound in another. Construct a simple balance scale that pupils can use to compare the heft of common objects. To make the scale, you will need the following: two long, narrow pieces of wood, 1″ x 1″ x 12″; a 6″ square block of wood; a long nail with a large head; two margarine tubs; six 8″ pieces of string; and glue. Glue one long piece of wood upright on the square base. Drill a hole in the center of the second piece of wood, making the hole slightly larger than the diameter of the nail. Insert the nail through the hole and pound it into the upright piece of wood about one inch from the top. The horizontal piece of wood should be free to move up and down. Punch three holes,

equal distances apart, around the edge of the margarine cups. Tie one end of a piece of string in each hole, and tie the three free ends together. Hang the cups by their strings over the horizontal bar about one inch from the ends. Have pupils place handfuls of different objects, such as beans, marbles, coins, and so on, in the cups, adding more or taking away objects until the cups are balanced. Which objects are the heaviest (have the smallest number in the cup)? Which are the lightest?

Finish the project by having pupils make "weight pictures" by dipping light objects, such as feathers, string, and straws, into tempera paint and using them like brushes. Dip heavy objects, like blocks and rocks, in paint and use for printing designs on paper.

*-Carolyn Luetje*

### ELUSIVE AIR

When the wind rages, discuss that mysterious substance—air—with your young pupils. Begin by asking children to take a deep breath, then to exhale. Ask if they can see air (sometimes). Then ask if they can feel it (yes). Point the nozzle of a bicycle pump toward cotton balls or balloons to show how air can lift objects.

Now explain that wind is fast-moving air. It can move heavy objects, such as clothing on a line or sailboats in the water, because its speed makes it powerful. Tie a length of crepe paper to each pupil's arm and take the class outside. Have kids hold their arms high so they can feel the wind pull the streamers.    -Carolyn Luetje

## ANIMALS

Capitalize on kids' love of animals to develop classification skills. In addition, this kit also tests pupils' general knowledge about several different animals.

**On land, in the sea, in the air** Divide the inside of a folder into three columns. Decorate the first column to represent the sky; the second, water; and the third, land. Cut out pictures of animals that fly, swim, and walk. Have the child place the animals in the appropriate column.

**Animal families** Cut out several pictures of animal mothers and their young such as a cow and calf, deer and fawn, cat and kitten, and so on. Mount each mother and baby on opposite ends of a 3″ x 5″ tagboard card. Cut each card in half, puzzle-fashion, so that each is uniquely matched. Child must match the mother animals to their babies. If the match is correct, the pieces fit snugly.

**Farm and zoo** Cut two 6″ x 9″ pieces of tagboard. Fold each in half and cut a slot across the fold. Decorate one to look like a barn and the other a zoo cage. Cut out 5-10 farm animals and 5-10 zoo animals. Child stands the cage and the barn on a desk, then drops each animal in its proper slot.

**Home sweet home** Draw or cut out pictures of 10 different animal homes. Paste the pictures on the inside of a folder. Draw or cut out an animal that would live in each home and one type of food the animal eats. Child places the animal and its dinner on the appropriate home. Possible combinations are: hole-rabbit-lettuce; barn-cow-hay; nest-bird-worm, and so on.

## WE'RE BIG ON BIRDS!

A bird's gay tweets and chirps are some of the surest signs of spring. Welcome feathered friends into your classroom with a study of birds.

If you live near a bird sanctuary, begin your activities with a field trip to an aviary where pupils can observe many kinds of birds. Or take pupils on a walk to look for different kinds of birds.

Back in the classroom, have pupils draw pictures of the birds they observed. Discuss how the birds are alike and how they are different. Ask pupils to bring in pictures of birds for a class display. Try to categorize the birds into those that don't fly, that live near water, and so on.

If possible, keep a parakeet or a canary in the classroom for the duration of your study. Encourage pupils to observe the bird closely. How does it eat? When does it sleep? What does it do when it's angry? frightened?

Encourage children to share experiences involving birds or to bring in objects relating to birds as a way of introducing important concepts. For example, a tale of a broken egg can lead to a discussion of how the egg broke (hatching, wind, vandals—humans or warring birds). A sampling of bird food (worms, berries, seeds) can lead to a discussion of how birds get their food and why certain birds eat certain foods.

Involve bird themes in dramatic play. For example, pupils can pretend to be a baby bird hatching from an egg. They can curl up, peck, rest, peck, and finally emerge. Or have kids pretend to be birds soaring through the air.

Relate art projects to your bird study. Make flying birds by letting each pupil select a sheet of colored paper. Have each fold the paper in half, then on one side draw a bird to take up most of the paper, the belly on the fold. Help each child cut out the bird, going through both layers of paper, but not cutting the fold. Staple each bird at the front and back. Slip a length of string between the two halves and staple the string in place. Kids can hold onto the string to make their birds fly!

Bring in a variety of small twigs, string, paper scraps, and glue and let pupils make their own bird nests. Be ready to explain the process a bird follows in building a nest.

Display books on birds for kids to look at. Two to include are *A Bird's Body* by Joanna Cole (Morrow, 1982) and *A Bird Can Fly* by Douglas Florian (Greenwillow, 1980).
    -Marian Seddon

## ALL ABOUT WEATHER AND THE SEASONS

Use this kit to help pupils think about different types of weather and the time of year that we usually experience each.

**All around the seasons** Cut a 12″ circle from cardboard. Divide the circle into fourths. Label each quarter with the name of a

season, and draw a tree the way it would look at that time of the year. Cut out pictures of scenery or events easily associated with one season. Child places each picture in the appropriate section of the wheel.

**Raindrops and snowflakes** Cut 20 large tagboard cards. Illustrate the cards in matching pairs with weather symbols. For example, you might have two cards each of a lightning bolt, rainbow, hail, and so on. Children follow the rules of ''Concentration'' to match the pairs.

**What will I wear?** Divide a file folder into three vertical columns. Label the columns *hot, cold, wet;* and illustrate accordingly. Cut out pictures of seasonal clothing from catalogs. Child places each picture in the proper column.

**Weather forecast** Make 10 tagboard cards. Divide each card vertically into four boxes. In the first box, paste a small picture illustrating something typically associated with one kind of weather, such as picnickers, kids building a snowman, and so on. In the remaining three sections, draw a sun, a raindrop, and a snowflake. Child clips a clothespin on the correct weather symbol.

## TEMPERATURE TIPS

Explore concepts of hot and cold by investigating how temperature affects objects and how it can be measured.

Introduce the topic by reading *Hot As an Ice Cube* by Philip Balestrino (Thomas Y. Crowell, 1971). Now set up an experiment that will demonstrate the effect of differing temperatures on objects. Place several ice cubes in each of two small plastic containers. Set one container in a cool spot inside (or outside if it's cold in your area of the country). Put the other container near a radiator inside, (or outside in bright sunshine if it's warm in your region). Have one pupil write down the time the experiment begins. Ask the others to look at the ice every few minutes to see what is happening. Compare the length of time it takes the ice in each container to melt. Now place both containers back into a freezer, or outside if it's very cold. When the water has refrozen, show it to the kids. Discuss how heat changes a solid into a liquid, and how cold changes a liquid into a solid.

To introduce ways of measuring temperature, bring in a collection of thermometers: meat, candy, aquarium, freezer, room, weather, and so on. Explain the use for each thermometer. Point out how the temperature scales differ on the thermometers, depending on what they are used for. Demonstrate how a thermometer works by placing a candy thermometer in very hot water, then in a cup of very cold water. Explain that heat makes the liquid in the thermometer expand while cold makes it contract.

Attach the weather thermometer to a wall outdoors near the classroom and set up the room thermometer indoors. Assign students to read and record the temperatures on both thermometers at different times during the day for one week. Have a second student note the weather conditions at the time of each reading. Then make a bar graph comparing the temperatures outside and inside. How do sunshine, wind and other weather conditions affect temperature? *-Carolyn Luetje*

## SCIENCE IN A SNAP

With a few hours of planning and gathering of materials, you can set up science centers in your room that will offer ready-to-go discovery-type activities. You can use these with the whole group, or pupils can do them alone, working on their own levels.Here is a sample center based around the water table, and two activities to include in the center. If you don't have a water table, any large basin will do.

**Clay boats** Materials needed: medium-sized balls of clay; small marbles or paper clips. Begin by asking pupils: Can your clay ball float? Have them experiment by dropping the clay in the water. What happens? (It sinks.) Now ask pupils: Is there a way to change the shape of the clay so it will float? Let them experiment until they find a shape that floats. Ask: Why did the shape make a difference? (It displaced enough water to allow the clay to float.) Now have each student predict how many marbles he or she can place in the boat before it sinks. Record the predictions and see how close pupils come.

**Surface tension** Materials needed: cup, eyedropper, pitcher of water. Begin by filling a cup to the rim with water. Now ask pupils to predict how many more drops of water can be added to the cup before the water overflows. Experiment. How close did pupils come?

*-Michael Knight and Terry Lynne Graham*

## CLEVER CLOWNS

To make this entertaining art project, give each pupil a large paper plate. Provide scrap pieces of construction paper for each pupil to use in cutting out eyes, ears, a mouth, and clothing accents; glue all parts to the plate. Glue plastic grass around the features for hair. Finish each clown with a balloon nose. Blow up a balloon and knot tightly. Poke a hole in the center of a plate. Insert the knotted end through the hole and secure with tape.

*-Linda Bilyeu*

## PAINT OVER AND UNDER

Fingerpainting is a good medium for reinforcing understanding of some basic ideas. Each pupil covers a sheet of heavy butcher paper with thick fingerpaint to make a ''practice pad.'' To reinforce directional concepts, ask children to draw a line *across* the center of their papers; draw a circle *under* the line; put an X *over* the line; write their names *on* the line. Children can also practice writing letters or spelling words, and solving math problems.

*-Jean Stangl*

## DOT ART

Cotton swabs and tempera paint combine to create an imaginative art activity.

Cut enough swabs in half so you can give six tips to each pupil. Cut plastic egg cartons in half; give each child a half with a different color paint in each cup. Kids can use one tip for each color.

Have plenty of white paper on hand. The tips are great for making dots or can be used like brushes to make strokes of color.

*-Jennifer Zakheim*

## TURTLE TALES

Art projects don't have to be complicated to be creative. Draw a 9″ × 12″ oval on a sheet of green construction paper, and make an identical oval for each child. Help pupils add a turtle's head, legs, and tail to the papers. Then encourage pupils to create any designs they like on their turtles' shells. Finally, have pupils cut out the turtles and fold their legs down so they will stand up.

*-Judy Meagher*

## BROWN-BAG GOBBLER

Each child can make a turkey gobbler to serve as a Thanksgiving centerpiece. Have each pupil bring in a large brown bag. Stuff it with newspapers, then tie the end with a rubber band. Fold the gathered paper over the band to cover it. Have each child cut out a head and wattle, two wings, two feet, and several feathers from paper. Staple these parts to each bag, placing the feathers at the tied end.

*-Phyllis Marcus*

## JUST HANGIN' AROUND

Here's a spirited decoration! Gather nine white wire hangers, white string, and scrap paper.

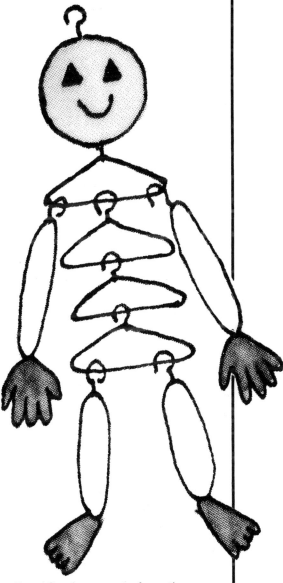

Bend five hangers to form the skeleton's head, arms, and legs. Cut out a face, hands, and feet from paper and tape in place. Attach the remaining hangers together as shown with string, then tie on the head, arms, and legs.

*-Marilyn Bennett*

## CREATE A KALEIDOSCOPE

Here's a project kids will love because each creation will be unique. Cut a circle the size of a dinner plate from tissue paper for each child. Instruct pupils to fold their circles in half, then in quarters, then again in eighths. They can continue to fold their papers if they wish, but there must remain three distinct corners on each student's paper. Set out dishes of food coloring, and show pupils how to dip each corner of their papers into a different color. Then you or an aide can unfold the circles and iron with very low heat to smooth the designs and dry the papers. Give each circle a construction paper border so the designs can be hung like mobiles.

*-Ellen Javernick*

## SPLOTCHES OF FALL COLORS

Sponge painting is fun for pupils any time of the year, but especially in the fall when splotches of red, orange, and yellow can brighten handmade leaves. Cut kitchen sponges into circles, triangles, and squares. Dip the sponges in tempera paint that has been mixed with water to create a medium consistency, then stamp out designs on green paper or cloth leaves.

*-Kathleen Allan Meyer*

## SUPER BUBBLES

Show children that bubbles can come in all shapes and sizes. Begin by making your own bubble mixture by blending ½ cup commercial bubble mix, ½ cup liquid detergent, and 2 tbs. sugar. Stir the mixture until the sugar dissolves. Then mold straws into different shapes such as squares, triangles, rectangles, diamonds, and so on. Glue each shape closed. Place bubble mixture in a large, shallow pan and dip straw figures in the mixture. Blow at or wave figure.

*-Irene Chesire*

## MAKE AN ICE MOBILE

Take advantage of cold weather to create unusual ice mobiles. Give each child an aluminum pie pan. Fill each with an inch of water, then freeze. Cut out pictures of cold-weather animals and dampen with water; stick one or two in the center of each ice block. Add another inch of water and freeze. Remove the block from the pan, poke a hole in the top with a warm nail, and insert string. Hang all mobiles outside your windows.

*-Ellen Javernick*

## FROSTY FLAKES BOARD

No two snowflakes are alike—and neither are your students! Have each child design and cut out a snowflake, then tack it to a bulletin board. Ask kids to think of words that describe their snowflakes, and print each under a flake. Label the board with a phrase such as, "Each snowflake is special . . . just like you!"

*-Janice Currier*

## THE FROSTYS COME TO TOWN

Snow persons are fun to make indoors as well as outdoors when winter rolls around. Make simple models of Mr. and Mrs. Frosty for an all-class art project. Give each pupil one large and one small white paper plate. Show the class how to position the plates so the smaller overlaps the larger as in the illustration. Help kids glue the plates together at this intersection. Provide black buttons or pieces of black felt for features and construction paper to make into hats, and then glue them onto the snow people. Add some dimension to the creatures by gluing plastic-foam packing pieces to the bodies. Finish both members of the Frosty family with scraps of cloth around their necks for scarves, and perhaps felt flowers attached to pipe-cleaner stems to adorn the missus's hats!

*-Kathleen Allan Meyer*

## CREEPY CRAFTS

Eerie art is in order for October. Here are three projects that fill the bill.

**Spider hat** Give each child one strip of 1-inch-wide black paper cut to fit his or her head, and eight 1-inch by 8-inch strips for spider legs. Have kids glue the ends of the headband together, then glue on their eight legs, folding up each end to create a foot. Add eyes by gluing a cotton ball to the center of two black semicircles.

**Ghostmobile** Pour white paint into a pie pan. Press each child's hand into the paint, then press palms, with fingers slightly spread, onto a sheet of black paper. Make four prints per child. Have kids cut out their prints, add eyes and other ghostly features on the palms, then glue to a string.

**Spaghetti webs** This is a great gooey project! Cook one package of thin spaghetti. Cool, keeping the noodles covered with a little water so that they stay soft. Have a few kids at a time work on this project. Give each a sheet of black paper. Have kids remove one noodle at a time from the pan, drain the water, then place each on their paper to form a spider's web. Allow about six strands per child. When each web is finished, have the child drop a cotton ball into a mixture of black paint and glue, then place the "spider" on its web. Dry overnight.

*-Nan Meagher and Ellen Javernick*

## PUMPKIN PLEASURE

Enjoy one of *the* symbols of fall—the pumpkin—with these ideas. Make a jack-o'-lantern for your classroom. Point out each part of the pumpkin as you cut. Let pupils help you pull out the stringy pulp and separate the seeds. Roast these for a snack or dry to feed wild birds. Pass around pictures of pumpkins growing on vines along the ground.

It's fun to make different pumpkin faces. Cut pumpkins from orange felt and glue to cardboard circles. Sew Velcro where features belong. Cut out a variety of features from black felt; back each with Velcro. Kids create faces they like.

Glow-through pumpkins make festive window ornaments. Cut orange tissue paper into small pieces. Brush a foil pan with liquid starch, then cover the bottom with tissue. Brush on more starch. Add black tissue-paper features. Dry; glue on a string for hanging.

*-Marilyn Bennett, Ellen Javernick*

## WITCH PITCH

Test eye-hand coordination with this October carnival game. Pupils can take turns trying to knock over a trio of witches using a small foam ball.

To make each witch, roll a sheet of black construction paper into a cone; glue or staple the cone in shape where the ends overlap. Cut a strip of green paper two inches wide and draw a face in the middle. Wrap the strip around the cone one inch from the top and glue or staple in place. Glue scraps of black paper around the face for hair. Cut a three-inch circle from black paper and punch a small hole in the middle. Slip the circle over the cone to form the brim of the witch's hat.

*-Ellen Javernick*

## THE SCARY STROLL

*Let kids make the sounds as you read.*

On the afternoon of Halloween/ Not one goblin could be seen./A stroll, thought the cat *(meow),* would sure be great./I'll find my

friends before it's too late./She called on the dog (bark), who grabbed his bone./"I'll walk with you so you're not alone./But let's be careful, let's beware./Soon scary witches may fly through the air."/They called on their friend, the big, brown cow (moo),/Who said, "Why, of course, I'll walk with you now./But let's not dally, let's not delay./When it gets dark the ghosts will play."/They walked without a whisper; they walked with a sound (slap alternate thighs)./The wind began to whistle (oo-oo) in the trees all around./As it grew darker, they heard something cry, "Whoo!"/ They ran (slap thighs fast) for the safety of their homes, wouldn't you?
-Carol Ann Piggins

## PILGRIM PANTOMIME AND OTHER HOLIDAY ACT-OUTS

Thanksgivingtime offers special opportunities for role-plays and other dramatics. Here are three scenes that need few props.

**Sailing on the Mayflower** Pupils can pretend to be Pilgrims crossing the Atlantic on the Mayflower. Have most of the children form the shape of a boat by holding onto a section of a long rope. Four or five others can stand in the center of the boat, holding a sign that says The Mayflower. At your signal, have the ship set sail from England (one end of the room). It should go through rough seas where it is tossed about and calm ones where it stands still until it reaches Plymouth Rock (other end of the room).

**Over the river and through the woods** Let small groups of children dramatize this familiar song while the whole class sings it or hears the record. Choose pupils to be the father, mother, children, and the horse. Yarn

reins can go around the chest of the horse and be held by one character. Give one passenger bells to jingle.

**Trembling turkey, petrified pumpkin** Poems offer lots of dramatic material. Let pupils try acting out this one of unknown origin. "Thanksgiving Day is coming,"/So Mr. Turkey said./"Now I must really be careful/Or I shall lose my head."/ The pumpkin heard the turkey./"I'm frightened, too, oh my!/They'll mix me up with sugar and spice/And I'll be pumpkin pie!"
-Vi Johnson

## SANTA'S STOCKINGS

Reinforce pupils' knowledge of vowel sounds with this holiday game. Kids fill stockings with toys that have the same vowel sound as that marked on each stocking. Cut 10 double stockings from red paper, gluing or stapling two pieces together so that each stocking forms a pocket. At the top of each, write a vowel and the long or short sound symbol. Cut out pictures of objects that feature these vowel sounds from the toy sections of old catalogs. Paste the pictures on cards. Have small groups of pupils take turns picking a card and placing it in the appropriate stocking.
Vary the game to reinforce letter recognition by making 26 stockings and labeling each with a letter.
-Kelly Riley

## HOW MANY DAYS?

Waiting for Santa is oh so hard for children, especially when they are still trying to grasp the concept of time. These Christmas chains will provide a concrete way to count down the days. Cut strips of paper in holiday colors. Have each child select 24 strips. Demonstrate how pupils can glue the strips to form links and how to connect the links to make a chain. Then give pupils a stencil of a Christmas bell or let them draw one freehand. Have them glue their chains to the bells. Distribute copies of this poem for pupils to paste in the center of the bells:

> How many days 'til
> Christmas?
> Here's a way to tell.
> Take off one link each night
> Before the sandman works
> his spell.
> And Christmas Eve will be
> here
> By the time you reach the
> bell!

Before pupils take their chains home, remind them to remove the first link on December 1 and to continue each day until the 24th. You might want to make one chain for the classroom as well.
-Marilyn Bennett

## ALONG CAME A CLOUD

Even if it doesn't snow in December in your part of the country, pupils can pretend with this poem. Have kids pantomime the actions suggested by the words.

> Along came a cloud,
> A great big cloud,
> Heavy with white snow.
> The wind did blow,
> The cloud did shake,
> And down the flakes did go.
>
> *-Carol Ann Piggins*

## GO CHRISTMAS CRAZY

Use these activities that capitalize on holiday excitement to review skills or to encourage creativity.

**What's inside?** *(creative thinking, visual discrimination).* Wrap in seasonal paper 10 or more distinctly shaped objects, such as a ball, a toy banjo, a toy drum, and so on. Place the objects on a table or under the class tree. Have pupils take turns trying to guess what is inside the packages. When kids have exhausted the guessing, have them unwrap the objects.

**Holiday cutups** *(matching)* Here's a way to use old Christmas cards. Cut off the front of 20 or so cards, then cut each picture or design into two parts. Color code matching pieces for self-checking.

**Santa's sack** *(creative drama)* Kids pretend to be toys in Santa's sack in this holiday version of musical chairs. Arrange chairs for the whole class in a U shape with the seats facing inward. Explain to the children that they are toys in Santa's sack. While the music is playing, the sack is bouncing around in Santa's sleigh. Kids are to move about in the area enclosed by the chairs, pretending to be different toys, while you remove one chair.

When the music stops, Santa has stopped at a child's house. The children should run back to their seats; the child who does not have a seat becomes the toy that will remain at that house. Pretend to be Santa and deposit the child in a ''stocking'' (the chair that was removed). Continue playing until all of the ''toys'' are out of the ''sack.''

**Paper Claus** *(creativity, following directions)* Give kids an artistic challenge: ask them to create a Santa figure using only strips of paper. Set a group of able students to work cutting strips of red, white, pink, and black paper in varying lengths and widths. Then give all pupils glue and large sheets of background paper, and let them use as many strips of paper as they need to create a jolly Santa. Encourage them to give their Santas a three-dimensional look by gluing some of the strips into links to attach to Santa's hat or to use in creating a thick white beard.

**Gingerbodies** *(creativity)* Turn your students into models for life-sized gingerbread boys and girls. Trace each student on brown butcher paper, then let him or her cut out the figure. Provide paints for pupils to use in creating a gingerbread person who looks just like them!

**Rudolph's relative** *(creative drama)* Have each pupil bring to school an old brown knee sock to use in making a reindeer puppet. Lay the sock flat with the heel facing up. Cut antlers and ears from paper. Glue the antlers behind the heel and the ears in front of the antlers. Add paper or cotton eyes and nose. Provide other scrap materials for each child to use in personalizing the puppet. Use the puppets to act out songs and stories.

*-Ellen Javernick*

## NIPPY NUMBERS

This delightful finger play about five little snowmen can help reinforce counting skills. On lines one and two of each verse, have pupils hold up the appropriate number of fingers. Ask them to raise their arms over their heads to show the sun on line three. And have them hold up fingers to show the new number indicated in line four of each stanza.

> Five little snowmen
> Sitting by the door.
> Out came the sun
> And then there were four.
>
> Four little snowmen
> Sitting by a tree.
> Out came the sun
> And then there were three.
>
> Three little snowmen
> Sitting by the zoo.
> Out came the sun
> And then there were two.
>
> Two little snowmen
> Sitting just for fun.
> Out came the sun
> And then there was one.
>
> One little snowman
> Wishing he could run.
> Out came the sun
> And then there were none.
>
> *-Carol Ann Piggins*

## HOLIDAY DISPLAY

Don't be afraid to let your students know how much you love them! This valentine bulletin board is a great way to get the message across. Any light-colored paper can serve as the background. Cut out a large red heart from red foil paper or use the top to a candy box. Give pupils a key-shaped pattern to trace around or let them draw large keys freehand. Be sure each child's name is boldly written on the key. Add an appropriate caption, such as "Who holds the key to my heart?" or the one pictured.

-Marilyn Bennett

## VALENTINE TO WEAR

Valentine minicorsages give kids who are learning to tie a bow a chance to demonstrate that skill. Give each child a long, red pipe cleaner to form into a heart. Now display cloth ribbon of various colors and patterns. Each child gets a 12-inch length of ribbon to wind around the top of the heart, then tie into a bow. Pin on with a safety pin.     -Mersha Fitzgerald

## GOIN' ON A COLOR HUNT

Red hearts and white snowflakes are among the items you can hide in your room this month for pupils to find during a color hunt.
Have students sit together on the floor. Put on brisk music and tell everyone to "look for something red." While the music plays, each pupil finds a different red object and points to it. When the music stops, yell "freeze." Ask kids to help those who have not located a red object to find one. If necessary, plant objects to make sure there is one for each child. Repeat with other colors.
Or play the game with partners. Pairs move about the room, the "leaders" spotting red objects, the "counters" counting them. Kids change roles when the music stops.     -Carol Ann Piggins

## LET'S PLAY HEART-O

Heart-o tests matching skills and visual memory, and encourages cooperative play. Cut tagboard into three cards, 4½ inches by 6 inches. Divide the cards into eight sections, and color in a heart in each section. Use a total of eight colors but not every color on every card. Now cut out 29 tagboard hearts. Leave one side of each heart plain and color in the other side, allowing three hearts of each color. Draw a zigzag line down the middle of the remaining five to create "broken hearts."
Loose hearts are spread facedown while each of three children takes a card. Players select a heart one at a time; if it matches one on their card, they keep it; if not, they return it. A player who draws a broken heart loses that turn. Play continues until all the cards are filled.

-Mary Jo Fisher

## HAVE A HEART

Celebrate Valentine's Day by incorporating hearts into all areas of the curriculum.
**Hidden hearts** To provide children with practice in noticing details, draw a picture and include 10 hidden hearts in it—a leaf on a tree, a butterfly wing, a flower petal. Show the picture to individual children or small groups. How many hearts can each child find?
**Happy hearts zoo** Stimulate creativity and reinforce tracing and cutting skills by having each child create an animal using only hearts. Provide cardboard hearts for tracing or let kids draw their own. Details can be added with markers. Ask each child to introduce his or her animal to the class and to tell a little about it. Pupils can also create people or animal puppets from paper hearts by gluing a tongue depressor to the back of each finished character.
**Counting hearts** This activity offers pupils practice in working with numbers and sets. Cut out 55 small hearts. Count out the number of hearts needed to make a set for each numeral from 1-10, and place each set in a separate envelope. On a small card, write the number word for each set. Have children match the set of hearts in each envelope with the appropriate numeral and number word.
**Chain of hearts** Cut out several dozen hearts and print a letter of the alphabet on each one. Pupils can use the hearts to demonstrate letter recognition, understanding of the order of the letters in the alphabet, or to spell words they know.
**Hearty laughs** Use valentine riddles to reinforce sequencing skills. Write each riddle on the front of an envelope; write each word of the answer on a separate

paper heart and place all the hearts in the envelope. If the pupils can read, let them figure out the answer by reading the words on the hearts and placing them in the proper sequence. If they can't, print the answer on the back of the envelope and have pupils use it as a guide for placing the hearts in the proper order.

**A little piece of my heart** Help your students to be kinder to each other with a valentine tree. Write model behaviors on separate paper hearts and hang each one on a tree branch. (Support the branch by inserting it into a dirt-filled coffee can.) Possible behaviors could include: "Help a classmate study sight words," or "Play with someone you usually don't play with today." Have each pupil pick a heart from the tree each day, then do his or her best to follow its directions.

**Heartfelt hugs** Encourage pupils to give and show affection by presenting each child with a hug coupon that reads "This coupon is good for one free hug from anyone I show it to." Let pupils use the coupon for one day in school, then take it home for more hugs.                    *-Kelly Riley*

## SPUD PEOPLE

Making paper potato people is an easy St. Patrick's Day project. Each child draws and cuts a potato shape from 9-inch by 12-inch brown or tan paper. Provide several sizes of shamrock patterns. Children trace and cut out several in sizes of their choice and paste them to the potato to form hats, collars, hair, arms, and legs. Markers make facial features; tiny lines from a fine-point black marker give the potato head a textured look.    *-Kelly Riley*

## MARCH MURALS

Decorate your room with seasonal murals this month. Here are two to make. Even if March comes in like a lamb in your area, let pupils have fun helping to create this March lion. Cover a bulletin board with light-colored paper. Cut out a lion from brown paper, without the mane, and staple to the center of the board. Add grass and other details and a title to the board. Then let pupils dip the palms of their hands in brown and yellow fingerpaint to create a handprint mane for your lion.

Make a giant wind mural by having each pupil draw and cut out something the wind might blow. Cut out a stylized Mr. Wind blowing fiercely from poster paper and tack it to one end of a bulletin board. Attach the objects, tossed and twirled every which way, at the other end.

*-Marilyn Sturdevant,*
*Carol Ann Piggins*

## MARCH MUNCHIES

Toasted oat cereal and thin pretzels add charm to March drawings. Distribute outlines of a lamb and of a lion's head. Pupils add features with markers, cut out, and glue each figure on larger paper. Thin pretzels glued around the head make the lion's mane. The oat cereal circles, glued to the lamb's body, give a woolly effect.    *-Ellen Javernick*

## PITTER-PATTER PLANS

Rain
Falls down
From clouds on high.
Rain
Falls down
From a darkened sky.
Rain grows grass and
Rain grows flowers.
Rain
Falls down in April
Showers.

Use this poem as the centerpiece for an April bulletin board. Print the poem on a giant paper raindrop and place it among silhouettes of people or objects pupils have drawn and cut out. Other rainy-day things to do. Make a list of all the things kids can see in a puddle of water. Make a list of all the objects outside that are getting wet. Classify the objects into hard and soft things, or by color or function. Count the objects in each list; count all the objects.

*-Carol Ann Piggins*

## BLOCK PLAY

**1.** Draw large outlines of a circle, square, triangle, and other common shapes on the floor in the block area, or on sheets of paper that can be stored in the area. Challenge pupils to fill as much of the shape's area as possible with various-sized blocks.

**2.** Place a figure of a person or an object, such as a car, by a set of blocks and challenge students to make something that object might need or use. For example, a doll might need a chair to sit on or a set of steps to climb onto the top bunk of its bed. A car could use a garage or it might need a bridge to get across a river or railroad tracks.

**3.** Find pictures of different kinds of buildings and tape them in the block area. Ask pupils to try to construct from blocks a building that looks something like one of those buildings. Encourage pupils to pretend that they are looking down from the top of a very tall building, such as the Sears Tower in Chicago or the World Trade Center in New York. What do the people and cars look like below?

**4.** Make construction caps for pupils to wear in the block area. Cover child-sized plastic bowls with strips of paste-dipped newspaper. When the helmets are thoroughly dried, paint them a bright color, such as orange or yellow, and add the name of your "construction company" in black on the front. (Ask the children for suggestions; then take a class vote to choose the best name.) Staple string to both sides of the helmets so they can be tied on.

*-Dorothy Zjawin*

## BOX BONANZA

Wondering what to do with all those leftover gift boxes from holiday giving and receiving? Take them to school. Large and small boxes can provide intriguing possibilities for exploring size, shape, color, and function.

Begin by reading *What's Inside the Box?* by Ethel and Leonard Kessler (Dodd, Mead, 1976). Now test pupils' group thinking skills by displaying a large appliance box. Children should decide what the box will become, how to create the object, what colors to paint it, and so on.

Bring in boxes that have a specific use, such as a tackle box, toolbox, lunch box, toy box, gift box, or bread box. Ask students to compare the materials the boxes are made of, the colors, shapes, and sizes. How is each box right for the function it serves?

Hone listening skills using four jewelry boxes. Fill each box with a different material. Have kids listen closely while you shake each one. Can they guess what's inside? Help by offering clues.

Collect six or more large boxes and an equal number of toys. Make sure each toy will fit comfortably inside one box only. First have pupils try to determine which toy will fit in which box by sight. Then have them put the toys inside the boxes, retrying if they don't all fit.

Conclude your box bonanza with marble painting. Give each child half of a fairly large box, paper to line the bottom, and several marbles. Pour tempera paint on plastic foam trays. Demonstrate how to tip and swirl the box to create designs with paint-dredged marbles.

*-Carolyn Luetje*

## DINOSAUR FUN

Dinosaurs fascinate children. Take advantage of that interest with a dinosaur learning center in your classroom. Activities in the center can reinforce basic kindergarten skills such as matching, visual discrimination, and fine-motor coordination.

You will need a large-appliance box to serve as the backdrop for a prehistoric mural that separates the center from other areas of the room. Cut off the top, bottom, and one side of the carton. Open the remaining three sides to form an angle with the floor where the carton is firmly balanced. Use markers or paint to draw a scene showing dinosaurs, swampy vegetation, water, and so on. (Use an opaque projector to enlarge illustrations from books for the mural.) Set up a low table in front of the mural to hold materials.

Here are several activities to get you and your pupils on the prehistoric path:

**Create-a-saurus** Draw a different dinosaur on each of eight sheets of 8½" x 11" tagboard. (Use an overhead projector and pictures from books for accuracy.) Cut each sheet of paper into thirds. Store the pieces together in an envelope. The child must match the correct three sections to form each dinosaur.

**Scrambled eggs** Draw and color a different dinosaur on each of six tagboard sheets, then cut out each dinosaur. Draw the same dinosaurs on each of six smaller cards and cut them out. Place each small dinosaur in a plastic hosiery egg and put the eggs in a basket. Child opens each egg and matches the dinosaur inside to the larger one.

**Prehistoric puzzler** Draw a large, brightly colored picture of a dinosaur. Mount the picture on heavy cardboard, then cut it apart into puzzle pieces. Store the pieces in a flat box. Child puts the pieces together to form the beast.

**Modelosaurus** Place several containers of modeling clay along with pictures of dinosaurs in the center. Have pupils use the clay to create likenesses of the dinosaurs.

**Matchosaurus** Cut twelve 4" x 6" tagboard cards and divide the cards into six pairs. On the first pair, draw identical dinosuars. Draw the same kind of dinosaur on the next set of cards, but make them smaller in size. Follow this procedure with the remaining sets of cards, using the same dinosaur but continually decreasing the size. Store all the cards together in an envelope. The child matches each pair of dinosuars by size.

**Me and my shadow** On eight sheets of tagboard, draw and color a different dinosaur. Cut out the dinosaurs and use them to trace onto eight other sheets of tagboard. Color those dinosaurs black, but do not cut them out. Child matches each dinosaur to its shadow. *-Pamela Klawitter*

## PRESCHOOL CORNER

Young children are often fascinated by a doctor's office, yet fearful of it, too. Help preschoolers become more comfortable with medical procedures and personnel through discussion and role playing.

First, try to arrange a visit to a hospital or to a pediatrican's office. Prior to the visit, read and discuss *Doctors and Nurses: What Do They Do?* by Carla Greene (Harper & Row); *My Doctor,* by Harlow Rockwell (Macmillan); or *The Hospital Book,* by James Howe, photographs by Mal Warshaw (Crown).

Afterward, set up a corner of the classroom to resemble the doctor's office or the area of the hospital pupils visited for free play. Make surgical masks from rectangles of white cloth and nurses' caps from rectangles of white paper. Have each pupil cut out and glue a red cross to the center of a cap before you staple the ends.

Pupils also can practice "doctoring" on a large paper figure. Give an outline of a person to each child. Let kids add facial features with crayon and clothing with fabric scraps. Then they can apply Band-Aids, gauze pads, and so on to heal imaginary wounds. *-Carolyn Luetje*

## THE MECHANICAL CENTER

Ask parents to donate old appliances and machines. Have screwdrivers and other tools handy for dismantling. Give children plenty of time for observing and for sharing their discoveries. What conclusions can pupils draw about how the various objects work? Do they have any similar parts? What might those parts do?

What can all children, but especially girls, gain from this experience? Exposure to mechanical skills and, hopefully, a curiosity about areas such as the block corner, where spatial, mathematical, and engineering concepts are learned hands-on. *-George Purvin*

## PRESCHOOL CORNER: FOCUS ON FEET

Preschool and primary pupils will enjoy the sensory, language, and dramatic-play experiences offered in this unit on feet.

Arrange a collection of different kinds of shoes on a low table. Have children try on the shoes, count them, and sort them into groups according to size, color, material, and so on. Discuss who might wear each pair of shoes, where they might be worn, and why. During free play, encourage children to pretend to be the person who would wear each pair of shoes.

Talk about the function of shoes as a way to protect our feet. Discuss the difference between walking on sand or rocks with shoes and in our bare feet. Help children realize that our feet are very sensitive, then try this activity. Obtain four or five plastic basins and partially fill each one with a material that has a different texture. Birdseed, popped popcorn, cotton balls, dry sand, wet sand, and dry beans are all good materials to use. Arrange the basins in order from the driest substance to the stickiest. Have pupils step in each basin with their bare feet. (Place a large towel beside the last basin so that children can wipe off their feet.) When everyone has had a turn and shoes and socks are back on, talk about how each material felt as pupils stepped in it, which materials were easiest to walk on, hardest, and so on.

After a light rain on another day, take a "track walk" to look for prints left by people, animals, and vehicles. At the first *small* puddle, have children walk through it *gently* to observe their own tracks. As you find others, help students determine who or what may have made them.

*-Carolyn Luetje*

## THERE'S A MOUSE IN OUR CLASSROOM!

I used to say "eek!" at the thought of a mouse until I became the mousemother to 11 furry rodents. I learned to appreciate mice when they added unexpected enrichment to my kindergarten curriculum.

My mousemothering started with a flood in my town. When I called the local department store to see if I could temporarily house any animals, they were delighted to send me 11 slightly soggy mice. While I had hoped for goldfish, the children were thrilled. They spent hours by the glass aquarium fitted with a mesh lid, where we housed our guests. The classroom was soon a scurry of mouse activities. We kept a vocabulary list of mouse-related words, adding new ones such as *rodent, gnaw,* and *nocturnal* each day. We discussed the mice's habits and wrote language-experience stories based on the pupils' observations. The children looked for books about mice at the library-media center, and familiar rhymes, such as "Hickory Dickory Dock" and "Three Blind Mice," were repeated often. We even had a build-a-better mousetrap contest, and the children designed ways to catch a mouse without hurting it. When the visiting mice were summoned back to the store, we kept two—dubbed Valentine and Suzie—so that our rodent enrichment could continue. And from fingerpainting mouse tracks to form a Mouse Club for outstanding achievers, it has!

*-Marilyn Karns*

## A HOUSING UNIT

Our "nests," be they apartments, single-family houses, or moblie homes, are important to us. This teaching unit on personal dwellings allows pupils to share with their classmates the special places where they live; it also

helps children recognize similarities and differences in dwellings within their community and beyond.

Begin the unit with a discussion of the places where pupils live. Make a chart showing the number of children who live in houses, those who live in apartments, and those who live in mobile homes. Ask pupils to describe their homes and make a list of these descriptive phrases. Then use the phrases to point out similarities and differences among the three types of dwellings. Conclude the discussion by having pupils draw pictures of their homes.

On another day, talk about the different shapes of dwellings. For example, apartment houses may be tall and rectangular. Mobile homes are also rectangular, but not tall. Many houses are square with triangular roofs. Give each pupil a geometric shape to carry on a walk in the neighborhood around your school. Ask pupils to be "detectives" and to try to find their shapes on dwellings. After the walk, set out books showing pictures of houses in other parts of the country or the world, such as the square adobe homes of the Hopi Indians in Arizona or grass huts in Southeast Asia. Have pupils look for similarities and differences in the shapes of these homes compared with the ones they saw on their walk. Focus, also, on the materials used to build dwellings. Make a list of such materials as wood, brick, aluminum, and cinder blocks; have pupils point out these materials on a second walk in the neighborhood. Back in the classroom, look at the homes from other regions again. Ask pupils to think about how climate affects the choice of materials used to make homes.

As a culminating activity, let pupils build their own homes. Set out boxes in different shapes and sizes to serve as the "frames" and lots of accessory items like wooden rods, wooden spools, toothpicks, rug and fabric scraps, yarn, and so on.          *-Ann Halpern*

## RUNNING A RESTAURANT, KINDERGARTEN-STYLE

Turn snack time into sell-and-serve time and see how quickly pupils learn some economics, and that it's important to do your job when part of a team.

Before "opening" your restaurant, talk about different jobs students have seen performed at restaurants. Narrow these to a cook, server, busperson, and cashier. Now divide the class into teams of four, and explain that each day a different team will have charge of running the classroom restaurant. Go on to make a list of those items that will be needed: hats or aprons, pad and pencil for taking orders, cash box, bucket and sponge, cups and napkins, food, cooking utensils, table and chairs, a place to prepare food, and money to pay for the snacks. Here's how a typical day might unfold at your restaurant. The team that will work meets with an aide or parent helper to organize the food (crackers and juice) in the housekeeping center. The first round of jobs is assigned. (Plan to have at least four "seatings" so that each child on a team can experience each job.) The cashier puts two pennies in each child's cubby hole to pay for the day's snack. The busperson sets the table and fills the water bucket. Then the server invites the first group of children to sit down and takes their orders. Kids may order any

two items—one cup of juice and one cracker cost a penny each. The server gives each child a bill for two cents, then takes the orders to the "kitchen," where the cook fills them. When customers finish, they pay the cashier. The busperson cleans the table, and the new busperson sets up for the next seating.
          *-Ginger Kattawar, Mary Oxley*

## WATER PLAY

**1.** Encourage creativity and experimentation by providing materials pupils can use to make their own boats. Stock the water area with foil containers from pies, cakes, frozen dinners, and so on, in various sizes and shapes. Include straws and paper or cloth for making sails, and glue or clay for affixing sails to boats. If some of the boats sink, encourage pupils to think about what parts of their boats' design may have been faulty.

**2.** Talk about reflections. Hang a mirror near the water area, and ask each student to compare his or her reflection in the mirror with that in the water. Are the reflections the same? Lead pupils to the conclusion that the movement of water distorts that reflection. Ask pupils to share their experiences with funhouse mirrors through student-dictated stories you can read to the class. Then make "reflection paintings" during art by dropping spots of paint on one side of a piece of paper and folding the other side on top to create the exact same design. Read "The Ugly Duckling," by Hans Christian Andersen, to the class. Then place plastic figures of ducks and swans in the water area so pupils can act out the story.

**3.** Introduce beach-related materials to encourage role-playing of shore activities. Fill a large bowl with water and add salt to it to simulate ocean water. Fill another container with dry sand, pebbles, and seashells; and fill a third container with damp sand. Add plastic fish, birds, dolls in bathing suits or shorts, boats, and other figures of things one might see on the beach. Question children on safety precautions on the beach, what to do if it rains, and what they like best about the beach. Ask pupils to illustrate their answers and collate the pages into a class book.

*-Dorothy Zjawin*

### A SUPERMARKET IN SCHOOL

Setting up a grocery store in the classroom can be a great way to end a unit on nutrition and the four food groups. Let pupils construct the "store" from large building blocks, or obtain a large appliance box from a hardware store. Cut off the top, bottom, and one side of the box (but save the cardboard for making signs for the store), and open the remaining three sides to balance the carton. Place a table or a large bookcase with shelves on one side of the carton to hold food. Bring in empty cereal, detergent, and other dry-food boxes. (If you bring in clean, empty cans, tape their rims to avoid cuts from small, metal shards left after opening the cans.) Encourage pupils to make price tags for the foods and to design posters to hang on the outside of the store to entice shoppers to come inside. Pupils can make their own currency or use money from board games for buying goods. *-Linda Martin Mercer*

### AUTO ACTIVITIES

Cars are both familiar and fascinating objects to children. Capitalize on that interest with a unit on automobiles.

Make the focal point of the unit an auto repair shop learning center in the classroom. To obtain the materials for the center, take a

trip to your local body shop to borrow car parts such as a steering wheel, a dashboard, hubcaps, wheels, a carburetor, and so on. Then go to a service station or to someone who tinkers with cars and obtain mechanic's tools such as a creeper, spark plugs, a screwdriver, wrenches, and so on. Have some old workshirts and hats on hand for pupils to wear in the center. Limit the number of children "working" in the repair shop to three or four at one time. Encourage them to use the creeper to slide under desks to make believe they are fixing transmissions, brakes, and so on. Keep track of vocabulary development, and present any new words used by children in the center to the whole class. Weather permitting, give pupils a close-up view of the interior, exterior, and under-the-hood parts of a real car. Compare how some of the parts look when the motor is on to when it's off. (Be sure to provide plenty of adult supervision.) Back in the classroom, put up an illustration of a large car on a bulletin board and have pupils label as many parts as possible. Then give individual pupils outlines of a car with parts omitted, and have them draw in the missing parts. Additional activities for the unit could include: creating collages of different cars, comparing pictures of old and new models, and making a chart of the ways we use cars every day.

Culminate the unit with a trip to a car dealer where pupils can see new cars as well as the garage where cars are repaired. Take photographs during the trip for a class book. *-Marcia Diefendorff*

### THE SUN'S SPECIAL FAMILY

The sun's family of planets, moons, asteroids, comets, and stars is a vast network that may seem far too complicated for young children to grasp. But through a unique combination of Bodi-Puppets (child-sized puppets worn on the front of the body) and creative dramatics, parts of the solar system can be understood.

Let the children help you design the puppets for the sun and each of the planets. By discussing the characteristics of each body while illustrating it, pupils will learn much about the sun and planets. For example, ask pupils how they think it would feel to be as hot as the sun. Ask them what colors they associate with *hot,* then pull out pieces of scrap fabric and paper in those colors. Cut out a very large circle, at least two feet in diameter, and have pupils paste the scrap materials onto the sphere. Attach two lengths of ribbon to the top of the circle so that the puppet can be tied around a child's neck.

Use a similar procedure with each planet. Make sure the size of each one is correct in proportion to the others: Jupiter being the largest, Earth fifth in size, and so on. Paste on what basic characteristics scientists have uncovered about each planet in three-dimensional or picture form, such as Saturn's rings, Jupiter's red spot, Mars' canals, and so on. When all the puppets are ready, choose 10 children to demonstrate how the planets orbit the sun. Place the sun in the middle of the room and as a group sing this chorus to the tune of "Here We Go Round the Mulberry Bush": Here we go round the red hot sun,/Red hot sun, red hot sun./ Here we go round the red hot sun,/Spinning in the universe. (Each time you sing the chorus, cue a planet to walk around the sun, following its own path.) *-Nancy Renfro*

# Computers

Whether it's basic computer literacy or learning how to create a program, this chapter covers INSTRUCTOR's best computer activities. Your kids will enjoy playing "Keyboard Twister," understanding why a computer can remember so much, and running teacher-tested programs. There are even ideas for computer bulletin boards. This is a chapter everyone can learn from.

### KEYBOARD TWISTER

Teach pupils where the letters are on a computer keyboard by recreating a keyboard on your classroom floor. Write the alphabet on cardboard, oaktag, or sturdy index cards that are about the size of a child's foot. Tape down the letters, following the order and placement of letters on a standard keyboard. Leave some space between each letter. Use a piece of tape to indicate the space bar.

Are your kids limbered up? Assign each a word four letters long. Using hands and feet, can they touch all four letters without getting twisted up? *-Michael Milone*

### COLOR THE KEYBOARD

Help primary children get acquainted with the computer keyboard through a coloring activity. Prepare a worksheet on which you draw the keyboard of your computer at the top of the paper, and write coloring instructions or general questions about the keyboard at the bottom. For example, print:

**1.** Color all of the keys that spell your name with a red crayon.
**2.** Color the RETURN key with a green crayon.
**3.** Color the space bar blue.
**4.** Color the key you would use to type your age orange.
**5.** What one letter do you use sometimes to type "yes"? (Y)
**6.** What letter do you use sometimes to type "no"? (N)
Add other directions or questions as desired. The sheet is a quick way to check which pupils need more help in mastering the keyboard. *-Kathy Marcuson*

### COMPUTER SCRABBLE

Want to put a new twist on an old game? Use a regular Scrabble game and play by the regular rules, with one exception: All the words pertaining to computers are worth triple the score they would ordinarily be worth. Your students' knowledge of computer-related terms will increase remarkably!

*-Michael Milone*

### REMEMBER SPECIAL FUNCTION KEYS

Students often find it difficult to remember the purpose of a microcomputer's many special function key combinations such as CTRL-A (control-A). A good way to remind students about these keys and their functions is to stick small colored circles on the front of the keys (not on the top of the keys where the character is usually printed). Then make a guide to the keys on a small card. Stick a dot of the same color on the card and write out the function of the keys next to the dot. Tape this card to the computer or place it on a bulletin board that is within sight of the computer user. For example, if CTRL-D means delete on your micro, yellow dots should be placed on the CTRL key and on the D key, and then on the note card. Beside the dot on the card should be written the word "delete." *-Michael Milone*

## GUESS

Need a fun way to take the confusion out of computer jargon? Write different tricky computer terms on cards and pin one on every student's back. Students then try and identify the terms on their backs by asking, "Am I hardware?" "Am I electronically charged?" Other classmates, at random, can provide yes-or-no answers to these questions until five minutes are up and everyone takes a guess at his or her hidden identity.          -Sr. Ann Claire Rhoads

## PHOTOGRAPHING COLOR GRAPHICS

One method of saving color graphics on the computer is to photograph the image from the screen. The best way to show student work on the computer to a large group is with slides. Photographing the images on a color TV or monitor is not difficult. Just follow these steps and you'll have clear slides of your color graphics.

1. Use ASA 64 color slide film. Higher speed film creates problems in color rendering.
2. Set your camera on a sturdy tripod. Make sure the camera lens is pointing straight at the monitor.
3. Be certain that you and your camera equipment are not reflected in the screen.
4. Shoot in a darkened room.
5. Take more than one frame of each graphic. Use more than one shutter speed.
6. Record the exposure procedures for each slide so when you have the slides developed, you'll be able to see which shutter speed gave you the best shots.          -Martin Nikirk

## EXPLAIN COMPUTER MEMORY

To most young children, computers seem to know everything and remember everything. Well, a computer "remembers" everything a user tells it only while it is left on. Unless the user formats a disk and saves the information on disk, all the information that has been entered will be lost when the computer is turned off. Here is a simple way to illustrate this important fact to your students. Bring in an empty ice cube tray, and point out that the tray makes ice cubes when each section is filled with water and then frozen. Now tell them that this is the way a computer operates. The computer is filled with tiny sections, like those in the ice tray. These sections in the computer are called *bytes*. When we hit a key on the computer's keyboard, each character is placed in its own section or byte inside the computer.

Just as the computer holds one character in each section, the ice cube tray holds one cube in each compartment. Taking the tray out of the freezer and dumping the cubes out of the tray is just like turning the computer off. The tray and the computer can still hold ice cubes or characters if you add more water or type in more information, but they lose everything that was inside them when emptied or turned off. I have found that this analogy makes the students in my class think twice now before turning off the computer. They check with me to see if anyone has information in the computer's memory that shouldn't be lost by turning the computer off.

-Barbara Veltri

## COLOR-CODED COMPUTERS

In our school, 350 students and teachers share seven microcomputers. The micros, which are all on carts, move from class to class all day long. To keep track of the micros and peripherals, we have devised a color-coding system that works extremely well.

First, we record the identification numbers of every piece of hardware and make two copies of the list. One copy of this chart is put away for safekeeping, and the other is posted in the teachers' room. Then we assign a color to each micro and its peripherals—disk drive, printer, language card, and so on. We put strips of colored tape on the hardware—a different color for each computer—and a strip of the same color alongside the computers' identification numbers on the chart.

This system provides an inventory checklist that we consult if any hardware needs repair. And students and teachers now find it easy to identify the different computers and their components. For instance, the "red" computer has one disk drive and a color monitor, while the "blue" computer has a language card and is the only micro that can run Logo.

-Debra Boone

## "HELP" MONITOR

A child working alone at the computer is likely to have questions while you're busy in other parts of the room. How can you keep lost moments on-line to a minimum? A "help" monitor to the rescue! This imitation video screen (made from a cardboard box with a window cut out) has a red flag on top and a class list inside. If you put the class list on a circular piece of oaktag, spacing out the names, it can be slipped around so that only one name at a time appears in the box's window.

When students run into problems, they go to your desk, raise the "help" monitor's flag, and leave their name showing on the screen. You can spot the raised flag even when you're with a reading group on the other side of the room; the child can go back to his or her seat knowing you are aware of a problem and will help as soon as you can.

-Judy A. Meagher

# Computers

## ICE CREAM DATABASE

If you've just acquired database software, but are not sure of how to begin, try having kids build a database about the subject they know the most about—themselves.

First have students brainstorm, as a class, exactly what it is they want to know about each other. Their list of attributes can include their names, sex, age, plus items such as their favorite color, food, musician—and ice cream.

At this point, help students arrange this information into "forms," the fill-in-the-blank format used by your database program. You can enter this form into the computer, and students can take turns calling it up and entering their individual data. When all students have typed in their correct age, favorite rock star, and so on, have them analyze the data. They can search for occurrences of key words such as "vanilla" under a field like "favorite ice cream." They can draw Venn diagrams that show how many students like kickball *and* tacos. They can make summary statements such as: "More girls than boys like Michael Jackson." And if you have a class party, students will be ready with data on the most popular food to serve.   -Kathy Pon

## COMPUTATHON

If you need computer equipment, but don't have the money to finance it, hold a "Computathon." Students can find sponsors who pledge a certain amount of money for every computer activity completed. For example, a sponsor might pledge 25 cents for each activity the student performs within a one-week period. Students will get a chance to contribute to their school; sponsors will see their money put to good use. And if the contest is schoolwide, the class raising the most money can be rewarded with a pizza party!   -Michelle Hicks

## AID FOR EYEBALLS

Students who have trouble reading directions will appreciate a tip on how to make the job easier.

Suppose you've given your students an exercise to complete on disk. If the directions you include are long and involved, kids can get lost reading them. But if students hit the return key after every main idea, or even after every line, the most thorny series of instructions becomes easier to understand. Not only does the extra space reduce eyestrain, but kids have to concentrate every time they decide to hit return. Students who are shown this "trick" just once are likely to use it whenever the occasion arises.   -Tom Adams

## COMPUTER CELEBRATION

When it seems time for a pick-me-up, plan a computer festival. Students have a chance to show off programs they've designed, and gain confidence, too.

At least two weeks before the event, have each child run a favorite program and make sure it's bug-free. Combine all these programs on one disk and make a backup. Before you schedule the event, estimate how long it will take children to introduce their programs and to elicit responses from the audience. Send out invitations.

At least a week in advance, make sure your equipment is all in order. If you're using a large TV (recommended so that the audience can see more easily) rather than a monitor, be sure it's compatible with your show computer, and that it will be displayed high enough to be visible to all members of the audience. Watch that electrical cords are out of traffic areas. Give your students a practice run before the big night. List the order of the presentations and the name of each student involved in the festival. And don't forget to serve refreshments.   -Miriam Furst

## NAME THAT COMPUTER

Anyone who has ever used a computer has found him- or herself talking to the machine as if it were a person (friend and enemy!). My students have one hour a week to show one of our computers all they know about math, reading, logic, and many other topics. And the more they use the computers, the more they talk to them. So I decided to run a contest to name our computers. Everyone was excited about the chance to christen a computer, and we collected hundreds of names. The students had one week to turn in their suggestions. A committee of teachers selected the top 25 entries and then made ballots with the finalists' names. Then the students voted for their favorites. Now each computer carrel in the library sports a computer-printed sign with a special name. Our students not only love to compute, they also look forward to learning with "Einstein" and "Brainiac."   -David Fiday

## DEAR DISK DIARY

Students in our computer lab don't always have enough time to run an entire disk, and sometimes, at the next session, they have trouble remembering which disk they were using last time. My solution was to make computer "diary" pages for each student. The pages look like those on a calendar, with a space for each day of the week. When a student has finished working on the computer, he or she writes the date, the disk title, and a short note of his or her progress in the space for that day on the diary page. These pages are kept in individual folders and never leave the lab; when students enter the lab, they get their folder, read their notes from the day before, and proceed to the next disk. Children enjoy writing in the diary and keeping track of their progress, and I am glad to have a record of their achievements and can know better the areas in which they need help.

-Michelle Rita Vance

## CUBBYHOLES

Now that your students have access to a printer, do they use reams of paper? Make a bulletin board with pockets for stashing all the printouts. Cover a space with printed wallpaper, then tack on double-pocket folders. Students can decorate the pockets with crayons, then use them to both display and store their work.

-Linda Eisentrout

## COMPUTER BULLETIN BOARD

Computers are everywhere, but sometimes they're hiding inside a common object. Have students collect pictures of items that you can program in some way. These could include automatic coffee makers, digital watches, office phones, copy machines, microwave ovens, and cars. Students can make a collage and title it: Where's the Computer?

-Carol S. Evans

## KID CRITIQUES

Let children evaluate the software they are using in class. They will gain experience in critical thinking and evaluation, and their input will help you select software most appropriate for their needs.

At the top of a 5 x 8 index card, write the name of a program currently being used, along with a scale showing the numbers 0 to 10. Underneath, make four columns with the heads Name, Age, Date, and Rating. After a student uses the program, ask him or her to fill in the card and give the program a rating, with 0 being the worst and 10 the best. Ask each child to give a reason

for the rating on the back of the card, and write his or her name beside the reason. Older children can fill in the cards themselves, while younger ones can dictate to you or an aide.

If you keep the cards filed by the computer and establish the rating process as an ongoing activity, in a short time you will have gathered enough data to give you a good idea of which types of programs your students use and enjoy the most. And you can build on this activity by having kids draw conclusions from the data. Which programs are the most popular? Why? Do any programs appeal more to boys than girls? What reasons could account for this? Discuss with children the criteria they used to rate the programs. Have them list the criteria in order of importance.

-Miriam Furst

## COMPUTER COLLAGE BULLETIN BOARD

Start your students on the way to computer literacy with a bulletin board that not only establishes a good definition of "computer," but also explores the realm of personal computer uses.

Have children individually write down definitions of a computer. Share the definitions, consult the dictionary, and list key words and phrases on the chalkboard. Together come up with a good, working definition. Write this on a long sheet of butcher block paper and pin it to the top of your bulletin board.

Next, ask students in the coming week to bring in computer ads from magazines and newspapers. They should also be listening to computer ads on TV and radio. After a large collection has been gathered, have students as a class make a list of all tasks a computer can do, including those they have heard about on TV and radio. You may want to suggest consulting local sales people.

This list can go on your board along with all the ads. Star the computer uses that people are also capable of doing. This is a good discussion starter on computer and technological dependency.

-Doris Dickenson

## CROSSWORD MAGIC

Using software to generate crossword puzzles is a real timesaver. It's easy to dash off a puzzle with a program like *Crossword Magic* from L&S Computerware in Sunnyvale, California, or *Crossword Puzzle* from MECC in St. Paul, Minnesota. And your students, as a result, have a fun way to practice the week's spelling words. Once the year gets going, ask students to create their own crossword puzzles.

As your kids set out to define all the words on a vocabulary list, for instance, they'll get lots of practice with the dictionary. And if you divide the class into two teams, giving each team the challenge of making a puzzle for the other, the dictionary pages will really start flying.

-Patti Littlefield

## HUNGRY MONSTER

Take advantage of the Halloween spirit. When teaching primary students how to load a program, call the computer a "hungry monster." This monster has a choice of different sandwiches (diskettes). First you open the monster's mouth (disk drive), give it a sandwich, then close its mouth—since it never chews with it open.

Turn on the mouth (disk drive and CPU), then its stomach (monitor). This is to see what it is eating. Go from there!

-Judy Nichols

## COMPUTER GRAPICS GUIDES

One of the trickiest parts of programming either text or graphics on the screen is figuring out vertical and horizontal distances. A good way to solve this problem is to put strips of clear tape across the very top and bottom of the monitor and along both sides. Then mark the horizontal and vertical strips as rulers and number each of the marks. Now you won't have to guess at distances on the screen when you create text or graphics displays.                    *-Michael Milone*

## FLOPPY SACRIFICE

Show kids how fragile a disk is. Remove the black casing from an old floppy. Kids can examine the magnetic surface inside where the data is actually stored. They'll see firsthand how flimsy it is.
*- Dolores Choat*

## MONSOON SOFTWARE

Some educational software is a lot more fun than it is academic work. Put this "edutainment" software—the kind you may have bought by mistake—in a special box. Pull it out on "indoor recess" days as a break from the weather. Or let kids play with this software as a price for good work, or use as a take-home over the summer.          *-Patti Littlefield*

## FLOPPY DISK ENCLOSED

Not too many classrooms have modems yet, but that doesn't mean students have to wait to find computer pen pals. All you need are some blank disks (even one will do), word processing software, and the help of the U.S. mail.

Simply save a text file on a blank disk, then mail it to pen pals at another school (someone with a computer system compatible with your own). After they put your disk in their computer and read your message, they can type in their response and mail the disk back. Students get used to using the computer, plus you have the option of sharing programs, graphics, and anything else you

normally store on a disk. One class can start a story; pen pals can add to it.

Remember to protect the disk with a heavy cardboard mailer, and mark it "Do not bend or fold."                  *-Dave O'Brien*

## TRAVELING TURTLE

Introduce young children to simple computer programming in Logo with an easy-to-make stuffed turtle shaped like the triangular "turtle" they see on the monitor.

At first, you should move the stuffed turtle as children make Logo commands such as forward, back, right, and left. I like to draw a grid on the chalkboard and move the turtle across the grid as children tell me how many spaces to move. Then I put a felt-tip marker through the turtle's tail. Children hold the marker with one hand and move the turtle with the other as they direct its travels over a large sheet of paper on the floor. The marker leaves a trail as the children move the turtle according to the commands given by other students.

This simulation of Logo graphics helps children program the actual Logo "turtle" when they get to use the computer.

A turtle for young children should be about 18 inches long from head to tail. Start by cutting out the pieces of material: two triangular pieces, each 1 foot long, for the body; two oval pieces, each 5 inches long, for the head; eight smaller oval pieces, each 3½ inches long, for the feet; and a strip about 7 inches long and 2 inches wide for the tail.

Begin to sew the pieces together, but leave a small space unstitched so you can stuff the turtle with pillow-stuffing material. Sew the tail in a loop and attach it to the wide bottom of the triangle so children can put a pen or marker through the tail to draw with.

Finally, embroider the letters L and R for left and right on the turtle's back to help children move the turtle according to the commands.

Increase the difficulty of the commands as children become adept at moving the turtle.
*-Jan Cardwell*

## TURTLE GARAGE

If your school owns a Turtle Tot robot or some other type of automated Logo toy, you may be worried that it will get broken. What's a good solution? When your imitation turtle isn't moving forward 40 on the floor, keep it in a garage. Kids can have fun decorating this robot-abode and will be sure to respect it. Build your garage with a cardboard barrel or box, Contact paper, and a pillow for the turtle toy to sit on inside.          *-Michelle Rita Vance*

## FROM TURTLE'S POINT OF VIEW

Here is a good "off-computer" game for reinforcing Logo programming skills—especially good when you have a roomful of kids and only a few computers. It's called *Tell Turtle*.

Select one child to be "turtle." The rest sit in their regular places, creating natural obstacles for the turtle, who is about to begin a journey from one end of the classroom to another.

Students will take turns giving commands to turtle: forward or back—plus the number of steps to be taken in the direction chosen—or right, left and the number of degrees the turn should be. The commands given must be precise for the turtle to move. "Take four steps this way" is answered with "Turtle doesn't understand that" by the rest of the class. Meanwhile, "Forward four" may be correct, but it sends turtle crashing into the nearest desk!

Once students begin to master the commands, the game gets more exciting. Now turtle must be directed toward his goal via the quickest route. Next the class has to get turtle from the closet to the door in fewer than 10 moves. This time, make counterproductive instructions count as a strike. If students get three strikes, the game is over.

Next class, try playing with two turtles. Each starts in a different part of the room, but has a common destination. Two teams alternate giving commands—a given instruction will direct both turtles. Remind students that a command that helps one team's turtle might also help the other team's turtle, too.

The carryover from *Tell Turtle* to actual computer Logo is swift. Begin by writing the students' oral directions on the board. Students at their seats can then draw an accompanying diagram of where the turtle would be walking given these directions. Eventually, students learn to turn these diagrams into correct Logo

procedures, and when they get time on the computer, they'll see how good they are at telling the turtle!　　　*-Terry Rosengart*

## TURTLE COUNTRY

Are you using line grids on the chalkboard to show kids how the Logo turtle makes geometric shapes? A better way is with a grid made out of dots. Kids can't figure distance by counting spaces; they have to concentrate on points instead.

Here are the instructions for a dot-grid board. It's a map of "turtle country" 360 steps wide and 240 steps high with a dot every 10 turtle steps:

Begin with a sheet of EXPO Marking Surface, size three feet by four feet ($15 at your local stationer's). Get a piece of 1/8-inch pegboard the same size as the marking surface, and attach the EXPO sheet by its sticky side. If you like, make *X* and *Y* axes with tape or epoxy paint.

Now you're ready to complement your students' Logo work with accurate off-computer demonstrations. Simply use a large wooden compass stuck in one of the holes of the pegboard. Use a dry-erase marker taped on to the other end to draw circles and arcs.

When your kids save a similar dot-grid on their Logo work disk, they can begin any program with a proper backdrop to geometry work. They'll simply READPICT a

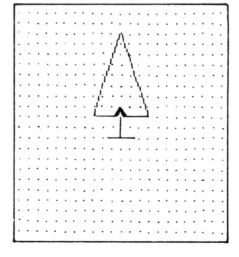

previously prepared "DOTGRID" and they're ready to connect the points.

What's a good project to start with? The TREE shown here. The first commands could be PENUP SETY 80 MAKE "TOP POS SETY-20 PENDOWN, thus fixing the height and top position. Then . . . SETX 30 SETPOS; TOP PENUP SETY-20, and . . . PENDOWN SETX-30 SETPOS STOP to complete the triangle of the tree. The BASE can be added all without a single FORWARD, BACK, RIGHT, LEFT, or SETH command.　　*-Reinhold D. Wappler*

## LEARNING NEW LOGO COMMANDS

One interesting Logo command that children learn early in their experiments with the language is REPEAT. This command simply tells the turtle to draw an already defined shape as many times as the number immediately following the command indicates. For instance, REPEAT 360 (FD 1 RT 1) will draw a circle. My students have difficulty, however, visualizing and using a command with REPEAT that turns an entire shape a certain number of degrees before it is drawn again on the screen. For example, in this command, REPEAT 24 (Diamond RT 40), the students who have already taught the computer how to draw a diamond understand REPEAT 24 and Diamond, but they have trouble visualizing what will happen with the command RT 40. To help with this, we do the following seat activity.

The children draw and cut out small diamond shapes from tagboard. Then they trace around the shape on another piece of paper. Next, they rotate the pattern to the right and trace again. They continue to do this until the tracing and turns form an interesting geometric pattern. They experiment with different shapes, number of repetitions, and degrees of turns. When the children return to the computer, they are better able to experiment with variables in the command that turns an entire shape.

-Sharon Bardus

## OBSERVE LEARNING STYLES

This on- and off-computer exercise is for teachers and students who use Logo or a program with similar "drawing" capabilities. First ask children to draw a picture of some simple object—a dog, a tree, or a house—by hand on paper. Then ask them to draw the same object on the computer, using the keyboard to put the image on the screen. Compare the pictures. In some cases they will be very different, indicating that the child has no set image of an object. Some of the children's pictures will be almost identical to their drawings.

This activity will give you a sense of the importance of visual images to different children and will help you better understand their individual learning styles.

-Louisa Birch

## BRIDGE WORK

Young writers sometimes forget to provide their readers with transitions—they jump from one point to another with nothing in between. Or sometimes they're vague; they use words like "nice" and "interesting" (instead of words that are nice and interesting).

A word processor can help with both problems. For instance, type up a short story on disk, but leave out a crucial detail:

*The spacecraft, tugged by a mysterious force, moved rapidly toward the rocky surface of the planet.*
*The crew walked toward the mountain, eager to reach its bright green peak.*

You left out the actual landing of the spacecraft! Pass the disk to a student and see if he or she can use the insert mode of your class's word processor to correct the problem. While students take care of the missing transition, they will grow more familiar with the software. Have students finish the story, or write two *new* paragraphs—leaving out an important transition. Now have students trade the disk with a friend. Can the partner bridge the gap?

To deal with the problem of vagueness, try giving students a few sentences like these on disk: The *animal* charged out of the cave.

The *person* threw a *thing* at it. Can students turn this into a story about a boar and a hunter with a spear (or a poodle, its owner, and a dog biscuit)? This time, they'll practice using the delete mode of the word processor. And once they've erased the vague words and replaced them with better choices, see if they would like to try this next exercise.

Ask students to use the word processor to create a character. Give students a disk on which you've typed: **1.** Male or female **2.** Age **3.** The character's favorite phrases **4.** The character is afraid of **5.** This character knows a lot about; (and so on). Set these categories up in a fill-in-the-blank format. You'll find that the word processor helps students keep their ideas orderly. With the insert mode on, the answer space expands as needed. (No microscopic-sized writing is necessary to squeeze in the answers.) Neat printouts help students see their ideas clearly, too. When everyone has had a chance to see printouts, divide the class into groups and encourage them to write a story

about what happens when the characters they've created meet at a party or are stuck in an elevator together. The characters can stay the same, change as the story develops, or drop out of the picture—but hopefully, not down an elevator shaft! -Tom Adams

## ALIEN SPY

Teach pupils to organize information with the help of a word processing program and an alien spy mission! Here's how. Tell kids that they will be making some conclusions about three imaginary countries: Zak, West River, and Farmington. They will read a series of "facts" about these places and then draw some conclusions about the kind of people who live there.

Give them each a disk full of facts. The facts about Zak, for instance, might include:

There are 5,600 sheep in Zak.
There are 5,600 people in Zak.
There are no cars in Zak.
The citizens of Zak walk an average of .3 miles a day.
Zak residents make an average of 25 phone calls daily.

What will kids do? Using the MOVE feature of their word processing program, they'll rearrange all the information until it begins to make sense. They'll start by putting all Zak facts together, separating them from information about West River and Farmington. They might further group together all facts about food in Zak or all tidbits about transportation.

When kids feel satisfied, have them type in their top-secret conclusions. Some may decide that in Zak, where people don't walk much and don't own cars, the main occupation is talking on the phone. But others may conclude that the Zakians produce wool. Encourage such varied conclusions, and if you want, throw in a wild card. Let kids decide which of the above facts are false! Your students will have lots of fun, and so will you.

*-Tom Adams*

## MOVABLE WORDS

A good way to give students practice using the various functions of a word processor is with a language arts lesson on disk.

Take a look at the next paragraph. It contains errors and directions on how to fix them. If you save this paragraph on disk and give it to your students, not only will they have practice with the delete and insert modes of your word processor, but they will also practice grammar.

"Out of the dense early morning fog, a large ship beggan (CORRECT SPELLING) to come into view. As the ships (MAKE SINGULAR) moved toward the beech (CORRECT SPELLING), Ned stood near the docks and tried to count the people on deck. When the ship drew closer (INSERT COMMA) he could see a large crowd. He ran to get his friends."

To increase the challenge, lay some booby traps. Insert a few mistakes without alerting students of their presence. Once students have found all the errors, have them add a paragraph that tells what happens next. (If they'd like, they can leave *you* a few errors, just as long as they include directions on how to fix them.)    *-Tom Adams*

## STAFFING SOLUTION FOR YOUR COMPUTER LAB

If staffing your computer lab is a problem, a parent-volunteer program may be the answer. Spread the word that your computer program is in need of staffing recruits by contacting your parent-teacher association. Parents who are already volunteering at the school may be

willing to spend an extra day or a few hours in the computer lab. Once you have several volunteers, arrange a meeting to show parents how to operate the computers (if such instruction is needed), where the software is kept, and what kinds of software you have. Demonstrate some of the programs, particularly the more complicated ones. Encourage questions; the more parents understand now, the easier it will be when they begin working with students on their own.

Draw up a master list showing the time periods each day when the computer room is open and when specific classrooms are scheduled to use the computers. If pupils from any classroom are welcome to use the lab during their free periods, make note of this on the schedule, too. Post the daily or weekly schedules in the lab. Prepare a class list for each classroom, and file these in a box. When students come to the computer lab, the volunteers can quickly check to make sure the right students are in the room. For your own convenience, draw up a weekly list showing when the various volunteers are scheduled to be in the computer lab. Post this list also, and ask volunteers to let you know of conflicts that may prevent them from being in the lab during their scheduled hours.

If you have only a few computers in your lab, say five, have each teacher send no more than 10 students to the lab at one time. It will be easier for the volunteers to maintain discipline and to work with children who need help. The teacher should specify which program each child is to work on. For those times when a program is not specified, show the volunteers several popular programs for various grade levels that they can offer the children.

Volunteers should keep track of how each child did at the computer, and record comments about general attitude on special sheets for the classroom teacher. Encourage parents to use the computers when pupils are not present, so that they can learn more about the machines. Hold periodic meetings and ask volunteers to suggest ways to improve the computer program. At the end of the year, have a tea or thank the volunteers in some way for their support.

*-Diane G. Murray*

## ELECTRONIC BULLETIN BOARD

Children can turn a classroom computer into an electronic bulletin board after they have learned the PRINT command in BASIC. A class electronic bulletin board is a good lesson in simple programming and a new way for children to share jokes, opinions, and news.

In a class with only one computer, this activity works best if the class is divided into groups so each group has one day of the week to compose and enter messages on the bulletin board. Once group members have decided on their messages, they enter the information on the computer as simple programs built of PRINT statements and a clear screen command. The group saves the programs under a code name that its members must agree on. The following day, other students can go to the computer and call up the message programs.

Here is an example of a simple message program.

```
10 HOME
20 PRINT: "JOHN CAREY IS
   GIVING AWAY FREE PUPPIES!"
30 PRINT
40 PRINT: "MY DOG HAS THREE
   PUPPIES THAT I WILL GIVE TO
   ANYONE WHO PROMISES TO
   PLAY WITH THEM A LOT."
50 PRINT
60 PRINT: "TALK TO ME AT
   RECESS OR CALL ME AT
```

# Computers

HOME. MY NUMBER IS 756-7766.''

As children become more proficient programmers, their messages will become more elaborate and might include graphics. Whatever the programming experience of your students, they will enjoy sharing news on the class electronic bulletin board.   *-Miriam Furst*

## THE FIRST BYTE

Here's a number game that you and your students can program your computer to play. It involves only a few simple commands in BASIC, the language that every microcomputer is ready to use when you buy it. Just type in these line commands (each line in a BASIC program is preceded by a number), type RUN, and you've got the program.

```
100 TR = 0
110 PRINT "WHAT IS THE
    RANGE OF NUMBERS
120 PRINT "YOU WISH TO
    GUESS FROM?"
130 PRINT "MINIMUM NUMBER
140 INPUT MI
150 PRINT "MAXIMUM
160 INPUT MA
170 RA = MA − MI
180 X = INT (RND (1) * RA) + MI
190 PRINT "I HAVE A NUMBER
    — WHAT'S YOUR GUESS?
200 INPUT GU
210 TR = TR + 1
220 IF GU = X GOTO 295
230 IF GU <X THEN PRINT
    "SORRY, TOO LOW, TRY
    AGAIN
240 IF GU >X THEN PRINT
    "SORRY, TOO HIGH, TRY
    AGAIN
250 GOTO 200
295 PRINT
300 PRINT "YOU GUESSED IT
    IN"; TR;" TRIES
305 PRINT
310 PRINT "IF YOU WANT TO
    PLAY AGAIN TYPE IN RUN
320 END
```
   *-Luiza Amodeo and Paul Rowland*

## HOW BIG IS A MILLION?

The computer can count to any number. How long would it take for it to count to a million? Load the following BASIC program into an Apple computer. When the computer asks, ''To what number would you like me to count?'', give it a seven-digit reply. Hit return and wait—a long time. Students can make predictions on exactly how long.

```
10 GOTO 80
20 FOR I = 1 TO A
30 PRINT I
40 NEXT I
50 PRINT "PRESS SPACE BAR
   TO COUNT AGAIN."
60 GET B$: IF B$ = ""THEN 80
70 GOTO 100
80 INPUT "TO WHAT NUMBER
   WOULD YOU LIKE ME TO
   COUNT?";A
90 GOTO 20
100 END
```
   *-Marion Beaver*

## A READABLE SCREEN

Dirt and glare make a computer monitor's screen difficult to read. To keep your screen readable, keep a soft cloth beside your computer at all times, and use it frequently to wipe the screen. Also check frequently to see how much glare is on the screen. Remember not to sit at your usual level, but to view the screen from the position your students will see it. The easiest way to eliminate glare is to change the vertical angle of the monitor by slipping pieces of cardboard under the front or the back of the monitor. Even a slight change in the angle of the monitor can eliminate most glare.   *-Michael Milone*

## RAIN

A good book for a day when umbrellas are in use is *Rain* by Robert Kalan (Greenwillow, 1978). It's a simple picture book in which the word *rain* pours down out of the sky, making everything wet.

Your students can recreate the inclement weather found in *Rain* with the help of a computer printout you've turned into a transparency. Begin by programming the computer to print ''rain'' many times over. Simply type in a small BASIC program such as:

```
10 FOR X = 1 TO 100
20 PRINT "RAIN RAIN RAIN
   RAIN RAIN RAIN"
30 NEXT X
```

Once you have a computer printout of a linguistic downpour, run it through a thermofax machine to make a transparency. Give each child drawing paper on which to create a scene—anything from a boat in a marina to an old man with a bump on his head. Next, each child will tape a piece of the ''rain'' transparency onto his or her drawing. The final effect is of a rain-flap that students can lift or pull down—depending on the weather, of course.   *-Catherine Toohey*

## MACK MICHAELS AND OTHER POEMS

Use Logo to help kids write humorous poetry. This program comes complete with an example (see below about Mack and his mincemeat) while it gives kids as much time as they need to fill in the blanks and make their own short poems. (This procedure uses the Terrapin/Krell versions of Logo.)

```
TO POEM
CLEARTEXT
PRINT [HI THERE! LET'S MAKE
  A POEM.]
PRINT[]
PRINT [CHOOSE A LETTER OF
  THE ALPHABET.]
PRINT [I WILL ASK YOU FOR
  SOME WORDS.]
PRINT [EACH OF YOUR WORDS
  SHOULD START WITH THE
  LETTER YOU CHOSE.]
PRINT [PLEASE TYPE THEM IN,
  THEN PRESS RETURN.]
PRINT []
PRINT [HERE IS AN EXAMPLE.]
PRINT []
PRINT [MY NAME IS MACK
  MICHAELS]
PRINT [I LIVE IN MISSOURI]
PRINT [I LIKE TO EAT
  MINCEMEAT]
PRINT [MY WORK IS MINING]
PRINT []
PRINT [A PERSON'S NAME:]
MAKE "NAME RQ
PRINT [A PLACE NAME:]
MAKE "PLACE RQ
PRINT [A JOB ENDING IN ING:]
MAKE "JOB RQ
PRINT [A KIND OF FOOD:]
MAKE "FOOD RQ
PRINT (SE [MY NAME IS] :NAME)
PRINT (SE [I LIVE IN] :PLACE)
PRINT (SE [I LIKE TO EAT]
  :FOOD)
PRINT (SE [MY WORK IS]: JOB)
END                    -Linda Stone
```

## PERSONAL PROGRAM

*Here is an exercise for you to put on disk and give to students. With the help of a word processing program, they can insert the answers. As you'll see below, the exercise is self-explanatory, so kids simply call it up and go to work. Just type in the text below.*

This assignment is not about math or English—it's about you. Why? If you are 10 years old, you've already lived for more than 3,500 days. A lot has happened to you. (Think of all the things you do in one day. Multiply that by 3,500.)
How much do you know? Every day you use little bits of information here and there as you need it: your phone number, the name of your friend's sister, how old you were when you first slept over at someone's house.
Think for a moment about some person you've known for at least a year. It might be a friend or a member of your family. How many facts do you know about that person?
All of these facts, memories, and happenings are things that you know. Here's a way for you to put some of that information in one place:
**People:** In your whole life, how many people have you met? Pick out one place where you spend time with people (at school, at home, shopping). List below the names of five people from that place. You can list them by first name, by last name, or by a description (such as "the man who ran the pet shop").
Next, think of people you've seen in the last week. They can be people at home, at a friend's house, or somewhere else. List 10 below. Don't include any of the people who were in list No. 1. This next group is different: People who live very far away. OK. This is the big list. Put into it anyone who isn't in one of the previous lists. There are no restrictions—the people in this list can be from anywhere, as long as you know them. Try to put at least 20 people into this list. Now take a break. Put only three people into this next list. Just make sure they are people who are older than you. Don't include any from a previous list.
Now it is time to make a really massive list. Think of other kids who have been in your classes in school. Think of your neighbors, and people you've talked to on the phone, and people you've met on a trip. The basic idea is just to list as many people as possible. Search your memory. Fill up the computer with names! Here goes . . .

*Editor's note: A student in the author's class came up with 365 names. Kids are sure to be proud of a printout of any length, however.*          -Tom Adams

## A PROGRAM TO BLAST OFF WITH

Celebrate past and future flights of the space shuttle with this simple program written in BASIC. The program simulates a countdown to lift-off and teaches students how to program the computer to count backwards.

```
NEW
10 PRINT "SPACE SHUTTLE
COUNTDOWN"
20 FOR X = 10 to 1 STEP — 1
30 PRINT X
40 NEXT X
50 PRINT "BLAST OFF!!!!!!!"
60 END
```

When this program is run, the computer prints the number 10 and then starts to count backward because of the command STEP — 1. After it prints the number 1, the computer will print the words *blast off.*
                        -Nancy Ray

# Computers

## A COMPUTER CAROL

The computer can add to December festivities. Just input the program below into any Apple computer for a rousing chorus of ''Jingle Bells'' (and a great way to demonstrate the computer's sound capabilities.)

```
10 REM
20 REM JINGLE BELLS
30 REM
40 DATA 173,48,192,136
50 DATA 208,4,198,1
60 DATA 240,8,202,208
70 DATA 246,166,0,76
80 DATA 0,3,96
90 FOR I = 0 TO 18
100 READ A
110 POKE 768 + I,A
120 NEXT
130 REM
140 DATA 103,100,103,100
150 DATA 103,140,0,5
160 DATA 103,100,103,100
170 DATA 103,140,0,5
180 DATA 103,100,127,100
190 DATA 63,100,84,100
200 DATA 103,140,0,10
210 DATA 111,100,111,100
220 DATA 111,140,0,5
230 DATA 111,50,111,50
240 DATA 0,5,103,100
250 DATA 103,100,103,50
260 DATA 103,50,127,100
270 DATA 127,100,111,100
280 DATA 84,100,63,200
290 FOR I = 1 TO 30
300 READ P: POKE 0,255 − P
310 READ L: POKE 1,L
320 IF P = O THEN 360
330 CALL 768
340 NEXT
350 END          -Michael Milone
```

## FLICKERING FLAMED CANDELABRA

Introduce students to computerized animation with the following holiday graphics program. Just input the program on any Apple computer (with or without color monitor), and a candelabra complete with eight flickering candles will appear.

```
10 REM
20 REM HOLIDAY LIGHTS
30 REM
40 HOME
50 HGR
60 REM
70 START = 100: HCOLOR = 3
80 FOR I = 1 TO 8
90 HPLOT START,50 TO
   START,100
100 START = START + 10
110 NEXT
120 REM
130 HCOLOR = 5
140 HPLOT 100,100 TO 170,100
150 BASE = 133
160 FOR I = 1 TO 4
170 HPLOT BASE, 101 TO
   BASE,110
180 BASE = BASE + 1
190 NEXT I
200 HPLOT 128,111 TO 140,111
210 REM
220 FLAME = 100:HC =
   1:HCOLOR = HC
230 HPLOT FLAME,50:HPLOT
   FLAME + 1,50
240 FLAME = FLAME + 10:HC
   = HC + 1
250 IF HC>3 THEN HC = 1
260 IF FLAME>170 THEN
FLAME = 100
270 HCOLOR = HC
280 GOTO 230          -Michael Milone
```

## OH CHRISTMAS TREE

Kids can watch the computer draw a lovely patterned tree by inputting and running the program below. The program is designed for any Apple computer, either with or without a color monitor.

```
10 REM
20 REM XMAS TREE
30 REM
40 HOME: HGR :SHADE = 0
50 HSTART = 140:VSTART = 10
   HFINISH = 70:VFINISH = 120
60 FOR I = 1 TO 140
70 SHADE = SHADE + 1: IF
   SHADE>7 THEN SHADE = 1
80 HCOLOR = SHADE
90 HPLOT HSTART,VSTART TO
   HFINISH,VFINISH
100 HFINISH = HFINISH + 1
110 NEXT I
120 FOR I = 1 TO 10
130 HSTART = 134 + I:VSTART
   = 120:HFINISH =
   HSTART:VFINISH = 140
140 HCOLOR = 5: HPLOT
   HSTART, VSTART TO
   HFINISH,VFINISH
150 NEXT I
160 END          -Michael Milone
```

## WORD PROCESSING ELVES

Dear Jane,
  Mrs. Claus and I have been very busy keeping our fire burning brightly. I see that you have been busy, too! Good work. I will try to see that you receive a puppy.
                    Your friend,
                    Santa

Dear Leonard,
  Congratulations on all your hard work! You should be very proud of yourself. I enjoyed reading your letter and will try my best to see that you find red sneakers under the tree.
                    Your friend,
                    Santa

These are just a sampling of the 500 letters seventh grade ''Santas'' wrote to primary students. Their teachers were looking for a way to get students interested in word processing. Appointing them '' Santa Claus'' did the trick. The seventh graders took their responsibility very seriously, learning how to erase mistakes carefully, move words and sentences around, and change the name on each letter to greet different children. Some teachers had their pupils write letters to Santa, telling him what gift they wanted most. The seventh graders tried to answer all these letters, altering their replies to address questions asked by the primary children. Try this word processing project in your school and see if you don't conjure up a great sack full of holiday spirit.     -James Aumack

## S. CLAUS ON COMPUTERS

Let Santa Claus introduce the computer's wide variety of capabilities to your class! Create simple programs to show how Santa could inventory his toyshop, answer children's letters, or print out Christmas lists. Program your computer to give a personal message from Santa when a child types his or her own name.

*-Lorraine B. Caramanna*

## CHILL THRILL

Children are often impressed with very cold temperatures. And they love to find out it's even colder than they thought—if you account for the windchill factor.

Some blustery day, have students type in and save the BASIC program you see below. (It runs on the Apple IIe or II+.) Once the program is up and running, kids will need to enter the temperature and wind speed they are currently enduring. Have them round these numbers to the nearest five. The program, which includes government statistics, gives the windchill in Fahrenheit degrees.

```
10 HOME : DIM C(10,8)
20 FOR W = 1 TO 10
30 FOR T = 1 TO 8
40 READ C(W,T)
50 IF C(W,T) = -56 THEN 60
60 NEXT T: NEXT W: VTAB 12
70 PRINT "TYPE THE NUMBER
   WHICH INDICATES"
80 PRINT "THE WIND SPEED"
   :PRINT : PRINT : PRINT
90 PRINT "(1)5 (2)10 (3)15 (4)20
   (5)25
100 PRINT : PRINT
110 PRINT "(6) 30 (7) 35 (8) 40 (9)
    45 (10)50
120 PRINT : PRINT : PRINT
130 INPUT W: HOME : VTAB 12
140 PRINT "TYPE THE NUMBER
    WHICH INDICATES THE"
150 PRINT "TEMPERATURE IN
    FAHRENHEIT": PRINT : PRINT
160 PRINT "(1) 35 (2) 30 (3) 25 (4)
    20"
170 PRINT
180 PRINT "(5) 15 (6) 10 (7) 5 (8)
    0"
190 INPUT T: HOME: VTAB 12:
    HTAB 1
200 PRINT "THE WIND CHILL
    FACTOR IS EQUIVALENT TO"
210 PRINT : PRINT : HTAB 14
220 PRINT C(W,T)" DEGREES F"
230 DATA 32,27,22,16,11,6,0,-5
240 DATA 22,16,10,3,-3,-9,-15,-22
250 DATA 16,9,2,-5,-11,-18,-25,-31
260 DATA 12,4,-3,-10,-17,-24,
    -31,-39
270 DATA 8,1,-7,-15,-22,
    -29,-36,-44
280 DATA 6,-2,-10,-18,-25,
    -33,-41,-49
290 DATA 4,-4,-12,-20,-27,
    -35,-43,-52
300 DATA 3,-5,-13,-21,-29,
    -37,-45,-53
310 DATA 2,-6,-14,-22,-30,
    -38,-46,-54
320 DATA 0,-7,-17,-24,-31,
    -38,-47,-56
330 END
```
*-Edward D. Watson*

## HEARTBREAKERS

This Valentine's Day your students can learn to estimate angles and line lengths while they create heart puzzles for each other to solve.

One student, in secret, will begin to draw a broken heart using the Logo turtle. This student will complete only *one half* of a heart, either the left or right half. The student's partner then comes to the computer, and like a true matchmaker, draws the broken heart's other half! (See the example.)

To aid your students, type in and save the Logo procedures that follow. Students will load these before they begin, and have them at their disposal in creating their designs. Here are a few more pointers:

The first student should move the turtle forward 70 steps before starting. This will keep the picture from "wrapping" or running off the screen. The second student should take over by moving the turtle about 40 horizontal steps away from the first student's creation. Kids may want to try easy-to-copy 90 and 45 degree angles at first, as well as line lengths that are multiples of five. Finally, when students are finished, have them print out hearts for a "HALVE-A-HEART" bulletin board!

Note: These procedures are for the PC*jr*, but are easy to adapt.

```
TO RHALF
HT ARCR 40 180
RT 30 FD 160 RT 150 ST
END
TO LHALF
HT ARCL 40 180
LT 30 FD 160 LT 150 ST
END
TO ARCR :R :D
ARC 2* :R*3. 14/360:D
END
TO ARC1 :S :D
REPEAT :D [FD :S LT 1]
END
TO ARC :S :D
REPEAT :D [FD :S RT 1]
END
```
*-Sylvia J. Foust*

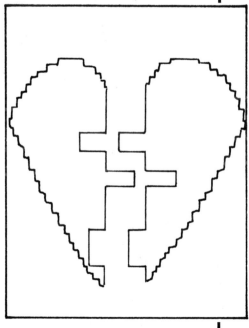

## SQUARE UPON SQUARE

Teach pupils about geometric patterns with the help of the Cartesian coordinates and the SETPOS command in Logo. First, you'll need some geoboards and rubber bands. Have students form squares and discuss how the length of the side multiplied by four equals the perimeter. Students can also figure the area of their squares by counting the number of square units on one side of the square and multiplying this number by the square units on another side. Kids will get a better grasp of equations. (For perimeter, $P = 4 \times$ Side; for area, $A = $ Side A $\times$ Side B.) Explain to kids that you'd like the geoboard to represent the positive of the four quadrants used in Cartesian geometry. For instance, if a student were to make a square with a perimeter of 120, he or she might do it by stretching a rubber band from the bottom left nail on the geoboard—which represents the meeting of the x and y axis or (0,0)—up to the geoboard's third nail or 30 on the y axis, around the bend to (30,30) and back down to (30,0) to make a square with sides of 30, an area of 90, and a perimeter of 120.

Now use Logo with its commands for Cartesian coordinates to make the same figure. These Apple Logo commands result in a square resting on the x and y axis with a perimeter of 120: SETPOS (0,30) SETPOS (30,30) SETPOS (30,0) SETPOS (0,0).

Remind students that the x coordinates are always named first, and give them a chance to draw more squares. Recommend, to start, squares with the sides of 40, 50, and 60.

Here's the most important part. Kids will start to see patterns if you have them keep track of some critical data about the squares they're creating. In a table like the one here, they'll want to record the length of the sides of each square they're drawing, the SETPOS coordinates for each, the perimeter of each, and the area for each. Finally, they should be certain to record the increase in perimeter from one square to the next, and also the increase in area from one square to the next. With the help of data laid out clearly in the form of a table, students will begin to make predictions about data to come. For instance, what will be the increase in perimeter from a square with side-length 50 to one with side-length 60? (Forty units) And the increase from 60 to 70? (Forty units)

Later, when the class is comfortable with writing the SETPOS commands as separate procedures in the Logo Editor (naming each procedure as Square 1, Square 2, and so on), teach them to use these programs as subprocedures in a program called MANYSQUARE. This deluxe program, which will draw square upon square, each bigger than the last, can lead to all kids of geometrical creations.

-Kathy Pon

## ROBOTS ON THE LOOSE!

Toy robots are valuable teaching tools. They are aids in helping kids make the jump from concrete experiences to abstract math concepts, and they are great motivators, too. Here are some lessons you can try with a classroom robot.

One inexpensive robot, called a Dingbot, is a nonprogrammable robot: Its path is random, and it changes directions randomly, every 12 inches. However, your children will soon discover that if they block this toy enroute, they can exercise some control over its movements. Kids can experiment with various obstacles (their hands, books, anything they can find) and they can build mazes for the Dingbot. One favorite activity is to tape a marking pen to Dingbot's rear as it moves along on a piece of butcher paper. "Dingbot art" is a popular center.

Some robots are programmable. These are excellent aids for teaching children about the computer language Logo. Students can program these toys to follow a procedure similar to that used in Logo (Forward 10,

| Name of Figure | Sq. 1 | Sq. 2 | Sq. 3 | Sq. 4 | Sw. 5 |
|---|---|---|---|---|---|
| Length of side | 30 | 40 | 50 | 60 | 70 |
| SETPOS Coordinates to Draw | 0,30 30,30 30,0 0,0 | 0,40 40,40 40,0 0,0 | 0,50 50,50 50,0 0,0 | ? | ? |
| Perimeter | 120 | 160 | 200 | ? | ? |
| Increase in Perimeter | — | +40 | +40 | ? | ? |
| Area | 90 | 160 | 250 | ? | ? |
| Increase in Area | — | +170 | +90 | ? | ? |

Right 90, and so on). It helps to see a procedure worked out on the floor before trying it on the computer screen. You can put colored stickers on the floor, then kids can program a robot to go dot-to-dot. Next, give kids the same dot pattern on paper, and have them connect the dots using a pencil. When kids are ready, place identical dots on the computer screen, and kids can direct the Logo turtle through the dots.

Two robots that are programmable and make good pre-Logo aids are called Omnibot and Compurobot. Another, Verbot, is voice-activated. It requires that students determine exactly which verbal commands they will give it, and what the result will be. Then they enter these commands into memory. Even bells, snaps, or other sounds will activate the robot. The catch is that later on these sounds must be duplicated exactly. A sound that isn't exact won't do the job. Because of this, a Verbot provides kids with a fun way to practice correct pronunciation. Children who speak English as a second language can give this toy commands, and if the robot responds as planned, then they've pronounced a word properly.

In general, robots are great at starting classroom discussions—about expectations and the fact that appearances can be deceiving. For instance, one toy called the Flipbot looks ''humanoid.'' Kids think it should be a robot because of what it looks like. But it can't be programmed. It does have an independent power source, though, so it's more of a robot, you'll want to point out, than the popular kids' toys GoBots and Transformers. (Kids, on their own, don't distinguish between robots and things that just look like them.)

If you do introduce your students to a classroom robot, they are sure to gain many lessons. For instance, Compurobot, mentioned above, has a keypad located on its top that includes numerals through 9. When kids want to make this robot move 10 steps, they have to resort to multiplication ($2 \times 5$). Kids will have fun experimenting. There's lots for them to discover if you let a robot loose in your classroom!

-Susan Brooks

*Editor's note: For more information on robots and robot toys, send for catalogs and fliers from Tomy Corporation, 901 East 233rd St., Dept. IM, Carson, CA 90745. Also write to Maxtron, 1825 A Durfee Ave., Dept. IM, South El Monte, CA 91733. The robots mentioned here start at about $10.*

## WACKY WORDS

Invent a game with your students that reviews the parts of speech and uses BASIC programming skills. Called *Wacky Words,* this game is modeled after *Mad Libs.* Students insert words into a plain, ordinary paragraph, and then, wackiness!

Show students how to make up their own Wacky Word games with the example that follows. It's an imaginary advertisement that reads like this:

HELP WANTED: A strong worker who can remove a tree. The tree is on top of a hill. This worker must be able to lift and carry 250 pounds. The tree will be moved to a different hill. We will have trucks to help the worker.

The first step in turning this ad into a wacky ad is to have students choose the words they would like to make wackier. Have them underline the words they want replaced. They should then label each as a part of speech. For example, above the word *worker,* they should write the word *noun.*

Now translate into BASIC. As a class, you'll assign a variable name to each different word you plan to replace. It's easy to assign variable names. A word you've labeled as a noun can be represented by the symbol N$. A verb can be represented by V$. You could assign a second noun the symbol N2$; and a second verb V2$. To keep track of what your variables are, have kids make up a chart. They'll list each word to be replaced, its variable, and the part of speech it is:

| Worker | N$ | Noun |
| Tree | N2$ | Noun |
| Lift | V$ | Verb |
| Carry | V2$ | Verb |
| 250 | NU$ | Number |
| Trucks | NP$ | Plural Noun |

This variables chart makes an easy reference guide during your next step—programming. Take a look at the program that follows. Students can use it as a model.

```
10 REM by Room 4
20 INPUT "PICK A NOUN";N$
30 INPUT "PICK A NOUN"; N2$
40 INPUT "PICK A VERB"; V$
50 INPUT "PICK A VERB";V2$
60 INPUT "PICK A NUMBER";
NU$
70 INPUT "PICK A PLURAL
NOUN"; NP$
80 REM USE ADDITIONAL LINES
85 REM FOR MORE INPUTS
90 REM AS YOU NEED THEM
100 INPUT "WHAT IS YOUR
NAME?"; NM$
110?:
120?" WACKY WANT AD"
130?" BY
140? NM$
150?
160?" HELP WANTED: A
STRONG ";N$" WHO CAN
REMOVE A ";N2$"
170?" THE";N2$" IS ON TOP OF
A HILL.
180?: THIS ";N$: MUST BE ABLE
TO ";V$"
AND";V2$" ";NU$" POUNDS.
190?" THE ";NU$" WILL BE
MOVED TO A DIFFERENT HILL.
200?" WE WILL HAVE ";NP$" TO
HELP THE ";N$".
```

This program starts with a line (line 5) that credits your class as authors of this particular Wacky Word game. Whoever plays the game will be asked by the program to pick a noun (line 20), another noun (line 30), and so on. These nouns will be substituted into the original want ad because lines 20-90 match the player's choices with the variables you've already selected (N$ and so on). Lines 100-140 name the Wacky Words Want Ad player as the author of this particular Wacky Words Want Ad. Finally, the last lines of the program (160-200) set the story up, ready for substitutions, and print it out on the screen.

When the programming is complete, your students can invite someone from another class to try their new game. The result? HELP WANTED: A strong worm who can remove a flower . . . We will have pizzas to help the worm.

This is how rumors get started!

*-Terry Rosengart*

## SPREADSHEET ACTIVITY

*The step-by-step directions below are meant for use with the AppleWorks spreadsheet package. They let kids compare the average heights of the boys in their class with those of the girls.*

**1.** Load your *AppleWorks* software.

**2.** From the main menu, select "Add files to the Desktop."

**3.** From the "Add files" menu, select the "Spreadsheet" option.

**4.** Select the option "From scratch" because you are creating a new file, then give this file a name: CLASS HEIGHTS.

**5.** You should now see the spreadsheet grid, with columns A-H and rows 1-18. (Note: There are many more rows and columns in the spreadsheet, but these are all you can see at one time.)

**6.** You are going to move the cursor by using the four directional arrows; with cursor in cell A1, type BOYS.

**7.** Move to D1 and type GIRLS.

**8.** Type the labels NAME and HEIGHT in the appropriate cells. (See diagram.)

**9.** If you'd like, use dashes to underline the various labels so they are set apart from the data kids will eventually enter. Put a quotation mark (") before your dashes (—) so that the computer doesn't confuse them with minus signs.

**10.** You are now going to put the averaging formulas into the spreadsheet. Move the cursor to cell B11 to put in the formula for the boys' height. Type @ AVG (B4 . . . B10). Do the same for the girls. In cell E11 type @ AVG (E4 . . . E10).

**Some explanation** The @ signals the computer that a formula follows. The symbol AVG means average to Appleworks. The B4 . . . B10 directs the computer to average the list of cells from B4 to B10. The E4 . . . E10 averages the cells in the E column.

Don't worry when you see an error message when you first type in the averaging formulas.

There are no heights entered yet, so the computer is trying to divide by zero (not possible).

**Some more tips** Students enter their names and heights by moving the cursor to the appropriate cell, typing in the data, then moving the cursor again or pressing the "enter" key. If at any point you or your students place data in the wrong cell, you can move your cursor to that cell and type your information over again. You can also erase by holding down the Apple key and typing B (for blank). You'll probably use this second technique when you want to clear all data to start fresh with a new class.

Finally, decimal points may be confusing to primary kids. If you like, have the computer round an average off to the nearest whole number. Move the cursor to cells B11 and E11. In each of these cells, press Open Apple-L and select the Fix option. See the manual for more information.

*-David Vernot*

## COMPUTER COTTONTAIL

This springtime Commodore Logo game gives students practice in estimating distance—the size of a bunny's hop. When the bunny hops all the way to its carrot, the computer plays "Here Comes Peter Cottontail."

First, you'll need to set the program up as described in these six steps. Then students come up to the computer, type in CARROT, and move the bunny along. They type HOP and two numbers to indicate the distance the bunny should travel. For instance, HOP 10 10 means 10 Logo steps up and 10 steps over. Have kids aim for the top of the carrot. They'll be able to play again and again because the carrot and rabbit appear randomly on the screen.

=====A=====B=====C=====D=====E====

| | A | B | C | D | E |
|---|---|---|---|---|---|
| 1 | BOYS | | | GIRLS | |
| 2 | NAME | HEIGHT | | NAME | HEIGHT |
| 3 | ------- | ---------- | | -------- | |
| 4 | | | | | |
| 5 | | | | | |
| 6 | | | | | |
| 7 | | | | | |
| 8 | | | | | |
| 9 | | | | | |
| 10 | | | | | |
| 11 | AVERAGE | @AVG(B4 . . . B10) | | AVERAGE | @AVG(E4 . . . E10) |

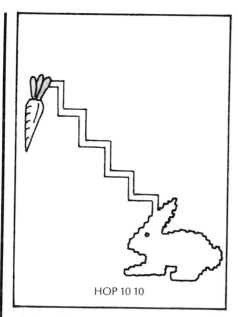

HOP 10 10

1. Load Logo, then replace the language disk with the utility disk.
2. Type: READ "SPRITES [return]. Then: READ "MUSIC [return]. Finally: READ "SPRED [return].
3. Type in the following procedures. Be sure to press CTRL and C after each one.

```
TO CARROT
    READSHAPES "BUNNY
    SET
END

TO SET
    DRAW EACH [0 1 2 3 4 5 6 7]
    [HT] SETCARROT
    SETRABBIT
END

TO SETRABBIT
    TELL 2 PC 1 BIGX BIGY PU
    SETXY 120 (−30) ST PD
    SETH 0
END

TO SETCARROT
    MAKE "X(−1) *RANDOM 100
    MAKE "Y RANDOM 50 + 50
    TELL 4 PC 8 PU SETXY :X:Y
    ST
    TELL 5 PC 5 PU SETXY :X +
    15 :Y + 10 ST
END
```

```
TO HOP:UP:OVER
    PC 1
    FD:UP LT 90
    FD:OVER RT 90
    CHECK:UP:OVER
END

TO ABS:Q
    IF:Q < 0 THEN OUTPUT −:Q
    OUTPUT:Q
END

TO CHECK:UP:OVER
    IF ABS (XCOR −:X) <10
    THEN CHECKY:UP:OVER
    STOP
    IF XCOR <:X THEN RESET
    ELSE
    HOP:UP:OVER
END

TO CHECKY:UP:OVER
    IF ABS (YCOR −:Y) < 10
    THEN YES STOP
    IF YCOR < :Y THEN HOP:UP
    :OVER STOP
    RESET
END

TO RESET
    PRINT [TRY AGAIN]
    SETRABBIT
END

TO YES
    TEMPO 6 SING [12 12 12 12 9
    5] PLAY [5] [30]
    SING [17 17 17 17 14 10] PLAY
    [10] [30]
    SET
END
```

4. You'll now need to custom-design three sprites—a rabbit, carrot, and carrot top—using the Logo sprite editor. Start with the rabbit and type: TELL 2 EDSH. A grid, filled randomly with large and small dots, will appear on the screen. Use the cursor keys to move around the grid, changing small dots to large dots and large to small as needed to create a rabbit shape like the one in the diagram below. Use the plus sign (+) or the asterisk(*) to make a large dot; the minus sign (−) or space bar to make a small dot. Press CTRL and C when you have completed the sprite.

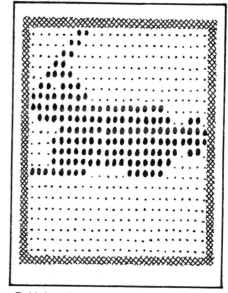

5. Using the same procedure, type TELL 4 EDSH and create a carrot shape. Then type TELL 5 EDSH and create a carrot top (see diagrams).

6. When you have completed all three sprites type: SAVESHAPES "BUNNY, then: SAVE "CARROT. Now type in CARROT and play!

*-Caroline and Elizabeth Earhart*

# For A Better Classroom

Room helpers and management, doing more with less, and review motivators are only three of the sections in this chapter that will help your classroom work. Also included are ideas on parent relations — a parent handbook, weekly activity folder, and a parents' night to remember. Your room routine will take on a new outlook with our terrific list of "57 Ways to Get Kids in a Row," proving there is a method to the madness — and helping you make your classroom a more effective learning environment.

## ROLL-CALL READING

Roll call, though necessary, always seems to take up so much valuable class time. Why not put that time to good use teaching initial sounds and vocabulary? Have each child respond to roll call by standing and giving a word that has the same initial sound as his or her name. For example, Sally could call "sand" and Bob could call "boat." Ask students to think of a different word to use each morning. *-Barbara Jacober*

## CLOTHESPIN CHORES

I use spring-type clothespins to make displays that help my students and me keep track of assignments and classroom chores. The worker wheel reminds students of the classroom housekeeping tasks they have been assigned. To make the wheel, cut out a large circle from poster board. Using markers, divide the circle into wedges, one per job, and write a classroom chore in each wedge. Print each student's name on a spring-type clothespin and clip these along the rim of a coffee can that has been covered with Contact paper or wallpaper. When assigned a chore for the week, the student removes his or her clothespin from the can and clips it to the edge of the wheel in the section that names his or her job.

I also use a board and clothespins to keep track of students' nightly homework. I write each students' name along one long edge of a rectangle cut from poster board. Across from the students' names are clothespins clipped to the edge of the board. As children hand in their homework, they move clothespins to line up with their names on the other edge of the poster board. I can then tell at a glance who has handed in their homework for the day.

*-Mary Ann Pecci*

## THE NAME GAME

How can you be fair when choosing a student to assist you in class? Try printing the names of your children on small slips of paper and place them in a box on your desk. Now when you need a helper, just draw a name from the box. Kids will enjoy the suspense! *-Jane Williams*

## GIVE OUT TITLES

Elementary students will take classroom jobs more seriously when their titles sound official. Try "internal expediters" for those who pass out papers, "horticulturist" for the plant caretaker, "courier" for the messenger, "census agent" for the child in charge of attendance. Children wil enjoy pronouncing these titles as well as explaining them to newcomers, visitors, and parents.

To display the jobs neatly, mount the "Help Wanted" section of your local newspaper on tagboard. Cover this with clear Contact paper. On separate pieces of white paper, boldly print each job title in black. Frame each job in black construction paper and attach to the large "Help Wanted" poster. Write students' names on strips of red paper, and attach these strips to the jobs they select. *-Kathy Armstrong*

## SEASONAL HELPERS

A bare tree on your bulletin board or other display area can provide a handy way to choose classroom helpers. Cut out a large bare tree from brown or black construction paper and tack it to the board. Have students design and cut out leaves from white paper, color them fall colors, and write their names on the back. Stick leaves around the tree with straight pins. Then turn one leaf over each day—that person will be the class helper for the day. When all leaves have been turned over, have kids set a new scene for the tree to fit the season by adding snowflakes and later flowers and birds. *-Jenelle Berry*

## RULES RING

The Rules Ring is a helpful aid for substitutes, new teachers, or volunteers who are called upon to take a recess duty. On small cards, print the duty times and equipment rules on one side and other items they may need to know on the other. Laminate cards, punch holes in them, and attach them to a bracelet-sized chart ring. Examples of cards could be "Recess times— 10-10:15 A.M., 2-2:15 P.M." on one side and "Drinks—none" on the other; "Slide—sitting down only" and "Bathroom—emergency only"; "Tire swings—three only" and "Lining up—by room number." Hang the ring, clearly marked, beside the whistle needed for duty. *-Judy Meagher*

### THE BAD HOUSEKEEPING AWARD

I was thrilled when, after two weeks at a new school, my fourth grader informed me she had won an award in class. Thinking in terms of gold stars and smiling faces, I read the award paper which she held out to me.
This is what it said: "Dear Parents—For some reason I save my papers instead of taking them home when I should. Because of this, I have won the 'PACK-RAT' award for this week. In the future I promise to bring my papers home."
I couldn't help but smile as I signed my name in the space provided below her's. I felt a little better when she informed me seven other members of her class also got pack-rat awards. What really made me smile was the fact that rather than scold the children, Mr. Berry, our fourth-grade teacher, had gone to all of this trouble to get a lesson across to his students and their parents.

*-Luilla Thompson*

### CASE OF THE NAMELESS PAPER

Instead of nagging over and over about students not remembering to use their names on their papers, I tape up a picture of some popular TV detective (for example, Columbo). I add a caption such as, "It Would Take Columbo to Find the Owner of This Paper!" Students are pleasantly reminded that they don't want their papers to end up in my display.  *-Carolyn Wilhelm*

### CORRECTING PAPERS WITH FLAIR

If you're faced with a mountain of papers to correct at the end of a long day, try adding some creativity to the task to relax you and inspire your students to do well. For excellent papers, use a large light-colored and a small

dark-colored magic marker to draw smiling, approving creatures. With the large marker, make a sweep of the fat tip of the pen to draw a rectangle, circle, star, triangle, or square. With the small marker, add a face, bow tie, bow, hair, buttons, belt, or whatever you wish. Your students will be excited to see these creations on jobs well done, and proud to show them to their parents.  *-Carolyn M. Wilhelm*

### GHOSTWRITERS

Here's a tip that just might get your students to remember to put their names on every paper they hand in to you. Place papers that are handed in without names on the wall under the title "Ghostwriters." Draw and cut out an unhappy-looking ghost to place next to the papers. When students don't get a paper back from you, they will know where to look for it.  *-Sandy Swartz*

### CORRECTION CLUE

How do you make certain your students read over corrected papers you return to them? When my fourth graders receive corrected papers, they know that

somewhere on the page they will find a smiling face. It will be tiny and partially hidden in a letter or number. If the face has a curl on its head, the student must show it to me within a certain length of time and also give me a corrected answer to at least one mistake in that paper.  *-Margaret Grande*

### PERMANENT SEATING CHART

This year, cut down on the time you spend keeping your seating chart up-to-date with this simple tip. Draw your original seating chart on a piece of plain, white paper. Number each row and seat appropriately. Now staple a sheet of clear plastic transparency paper to the top of this original chart. Use a wax pencil or overhead projection pen to print the names of your students in the appropriate boxes on the chart. As you change your kids' seats during the year, simply wipe off the old names and fill in the new ones!  *-Jeanne Kirchoff*

### MANILA MAKEOVERS

The tedious chore of organizing student work and assignments can be simplified by recycling those used 9″ × 12″ manila envelopes that come through the mail. Begin with a simple art project in which the children use magazine pictures to create interesting collages that will cover any undesirable print such as addresses or postmarks. Encourage them to individualize their envelopes by selecting pictures that represent their particular interests. Once created, these envelopes are great for storing daily assignments and tasks. Papers, puzzles, games, homework, and other important materials usually fit quite nicely. You also might like to make a checklist on the back of each envelope to record completion of tasks. Stars or seasonal seals instead of check marks are better motivators and look more attractive, too. After the week's assignments are completed, the task envelopes can be sent home to parents for review.

*-Leonard J. Basile*

## CREATING MORE SPACE

Give your classroom more bulletin board space by hanging 8 to 10 jumbo paper clips from the ceiling with thread. Hang them in a circle about four feet in diameter. Large pieces of lightweight cardboard can then be hung from these paper clips. Use them to display spelling words, safety signs, science pictures, or student artwork. This makes a display that is eye-catching and easy to change.  *-Debbie Feucht*

## DIVIDE AND CONQUER

Room dividers have solved many discipline problems, as well as provided for a comfortable, well-managed atmosphere in my room.

I have hung large colorful pieces of muslin or heavier material from wooden dowels to section off a particular area of the room. Next, I added traffic signs made with dowel sticks, blocks, and colored tagboard. One sign read, Quiet Zone! Serious Studies Only! Others were: Yield—Researchers Only; Stop—Game Area; Reserved for Readers; Caution—Testing Zone.  *-Julie A. McDonnell*

## MAKE A MINIFILE

Make a minifile for your desk and you can cut down on the number of trips you make to the filing cabinet. Staple several plain manila folders together, one on top of the other, so all of the tabs show. Label them with pencil so they can be reused for other topics. With this arrangement you can quickly file at your desk and put items in a permanent file at the end of the week.  *-Carolyn Schoepp*

## LOST YOUR MITTENS?

Assign each child a box, labeled with his or her name, for storing loose winter gear that can't be hung up easily. Large, oblong gift boxes are perfect for this purpose. Have children decorate their boxes in art class with pictures of winter scenes, and cut out small squares on two sides for handles. Boxes may be stored in a variety of ways, as long as they're accessible to the children at all times, and the storage spot for each box is also labeled with the student's name. Your children will quickly learn to keep their winter wear in these boxes when they see how much faster they make it to the playground!

*-Anita Klein*

## FROM SUNDAES TO STUDENT MAILBOXES

You can reduce the amount of clutter in your classroom and eliminate your students' daily search for important papers, notes, and books with this neat organizing idea. Obtain large, cardboard ice cream containers from a multiflavor outlet near you. Have the children paint their containers first, then decorate the outsides with magazine-picture collages. Now stack the cartons on top of each other, pyramid style, and hold them together by punching holes in each one and tying them with twine or pipe cleaners. They can be placed on the floor, a table, or a low platform, and each carton should be labeled with a child's name. Now your students have their own personal mailboxes to be checked and emptied every day before leaving school.  *-Anita Klein*

## MAGAZINE MEMOS

Do you often find a great idea in a magazine—but then forget the issue or page where you saw it? Here's a simple solution. Before going through a magazine to find ideas, attach a sheet of paper inside the front cover. Each time you come across an idea, jot down the page along with a note or two to remind you of the subject area or use for the idea. Not only will good ideas be at your fingertips, but you'll also make better use of your magazines and your time!

*-Leslie Snyder*

## POST OFFICE ORGANIZATION

Tired of trying to keep track of all your students' workbook pages and activity sheets? Here's an organizational unit that's easy to assemble but can do wonders to help you put everything in its place. You'll need a two-liter milk carton for every student in your class. Cut off the top of each carton so that one end is open, then wash the cartons and dry them thoroughly. You might want to brighten the cartons by covering them with colored, self-adhesive paper or ordinary construction paper decorated with designs you paint yourself. Finish by attaching a sturdy name tag to the top part of each open carton. When all the cartons are ready, place them in rows inside a large cardboard box or fruit crate. Finally, cover an empty cereal box with self-adhesive paper or decorated construction paper, and use rubber cement to attach it, open end up, to the front of the box or crate. Make a name tag for yourself and glue it to the cereal box. Now, when your students complete worksheets, they are to drop them into your "mailbox." After you've corrected the sheets, place them in the appropriate students' mailboxes to be picked up later in the day. You'll find that worksheets are misplaced less frequently this way, your classroom looks more organized and your kids enjoy the chance to play "post office," too!

*-Diane Paton*

## WHEN TIME FLIES

Are you a teacher who "fights the clock," finding it difficult to switch from one subject to the next because of deep involvement? Add a kitchen timer to your classroom. Just set the timer for the alotted time and free your mind to concentrate on the project at hand. The timer will remind both you and your children that it is time to pass to your next activity. *-Talis Byers*

## WHAT DAY IS IT?

To make your day smoother, organize. Here's one way. Section off the cover of a folder with squares. In one long row, list each child's name. Each day when the child completes an assignment, he or she puts the paper in the folder and marks the date in the square after his or her name. Use different-colored folders for different assignments. Children become aware of the day's date, and you become aware of which children need extra help to finish on time. Some may need extra time; others require time management. For best results, check the chart and papers each day.

*-Marion G. Walker*

## DETERGENT-BOX FILES

Don't throw out all those empty laundry detergent boxes you accumulate—use them instead to keep your classroom neat and uncluttered this year. Make sure the boxes are free of detergent particles before you begin by wiping out the insides with a slightly damp cloth; then use a ruler to draw a diagonal cutting line from the closed corner to approximately the middle of the opened side. (See illustration.) Use grocery bags, newsprint, or self-adhesive paper in bright colors and designs to cover each box. The finished products can be placed on your windowsill, desk top, bookcases, or any place where organization is required. They're perfect for storing a variety of classroom materials, such as magazines, activity cards, and worksheets.

*-Ruby H. Deloach*

## CARD LADDERS

To keep vocabulary words or math facts within sight of your students without using up needed bulletin board or wall space, suspend card ladders from the ceiling or light fixtures. Punch corresponding pairs of holes in the sides of 3″ × 5″ or larger cards. String them on yarn. More cards can be added as they are needed. Instead of review facts, you might put questions or math problems on the fronts of the cards and answers on the backs.

*-Connie Zane*

## JUST FOR THE RECORD

Have you wanted to keep anecdotal records on your students but found it impossible to do because you are rarely able to remember all the things that happened by the end of the day? Set up a 3″ × 5″ file box with index tabs for each student. Each morning put stacks of 3″ × 5″ cards and a felt-tipped marker in different locations around the room. These can be placed in the reading area, at learning centers, on your desk, and in your purse or pocket. Throughout the day if a student does something that should be noted for showing social growth or displays a work habit that needs improvement, quickly jot down that student's name and a quick note. At the end of the day, date each card (a date stamper makes this go extra fast) and file them in your box. These records help tremendously at report card time and during parent conferences.

*-Rosemary Diehl*

## TOUCH AND SEE DISPLAY

When putting out fragile leaves, pressed flowers, tiny seeds, or other science items that might fall apart or get lost if handled too frequently, lay them directly in the center of your nature table. Then cover them with a transparent plastic tablecloth. Place pretty rocks, vases of fresh flowers, or containers of various feathers near the edges of the table on top of the cloth. These will give students items they can touch and also will help to hold the tablecloth in place.

*-Margaret Shauers*

## HANG IT ALL

Save rigid plastic handles from soft plastic shopping bags and use them to hang charts, posters, pictures, and other visual aids. Attach the chart or poster with a clothespin to the plastic handle and slip the handle over a nail or hook previously put in your wall at a convenient spot. Wide visual aides may need two handles and pins. This method is one that causes no wear and tear on your cherished visuals and does not distract from their appearance.

*-Nancy Dickinson*

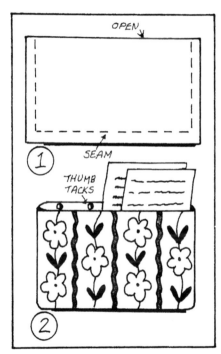

## PICK OF THE POCKETS

Make these attractive pockets to hold pamphlets or activity sheets at learning centers or on bulletin boards. Get a large-size wallpaper sample book from a decorating store — canvas-backed wallpaper works the best. Use a razor blade to slit the sheets close to the binding. Place two sheets right sides together, and machine-stitch a ½-inch seam along the two short sides and along the long edge that has been cut. Turn the pocket right-side out and mount it with thumbtacks on the bulletin board.

*-Lee Hoeting*

## USING YOUR "OLD" BASALS

I finally figured out a use for a full set of basal readers, older but in great shape. All I did was make a sign: "This is what they read in the old days!" (The books were published in the 1960s, but of course the kids think they're ancient.) I suggested that anyone finding a particularly good story make a bookmark and place it in the book with a comment for other readers. Children might note things that have changed in the last two decades. Hair or clothing styles? Male or female roles? It's gratifying to see students voluntarily reading these books when they've completed assignments.    -Margaret Hoagland

## SPEEDIE READIES

Even the most dog-eared magazines have a few good pages with interesting articles left in them. Don't throw them away. Make Speedie Readies. Speedie Readies are articles removed from old children's magazines, bound in manila tagboard and decorated with the words "Speedie Readie" on the cover. Seasonal poems, favorite recipes, games, stories, and arts and crafts projects may be put into a Speedie. Many reluctant readers will read a Speedie when they will not bother to go to the shelves and select a book.

-Violet T. Fowler

## CATALOG CUTOUTS

If you're looking for materials to use for visual aids or bulletin board displays, try sewing pattern catalogs. They contain hundreds of photos of children and adults that can be used for all kinds of craft projects. Sewing centers and fabric stores will usually give the catalogs away if you ask them to hold one for you when the next season's supply comes in. Just be sure to pick up your catalog promptly so the store manager

will be willing to help when the time comes to ask for another one.    -Margaret Shavers

## THE JOY OF JUNK

What doesn't cost a lot of money; doesn't require your precious free time to create; doesn't need glue, staples, or paint to complete; and can supply you with manipulative materials for teaching and reinforcing concepts? The answer is junk! A Saturday afternoon spent exploring your local thrift shop with a few dollars from your curriculum materials' budget can result in an acquisition of unusual teaching materials for most components of your program. You and your teaching team can supplement the commercial supplies you now have, or create your own with junk. Here are some of the most versatile objects to look for, with suggestions for their use:

1. Plastic nesting bowls to be arranged in order of size.
2. Plastic food storage containers of various shapes and sizes to help students recognize basic shapes. Have the kids match lids to containers, then arrange in order of size.
3. Old clocks, with glass removed, for practice in telling time.
4. Buttons of assorted sizes, shapes, and colors, for use in counting exercises, collages, and crafts.
5. Nuts, bolts, washers, and gears of all sizes for developing eye-hand coordination and reinforcing fine motor skills. Have the students fit nuts into bolts, manipulate gears, and so on.
6. Sweaters and jackets with zippers or buttons for practice in dressing.
7. Dish drainers, utensil holders, or silverware trays for classroom organization. Use the dish racks

to hold students' completed work or large-sized paper to keep it from folding. Utensil containers can be used to store pencils and crayons, while silver trays make good storage boxes for paint brushes, erasers, marking pens, and so on.    -Kathleen L. Gibbs

## LET YOUR FINGERS DO THE WALKING

The Yellow Pages can be useful in helping children learn the alphabet, cross references, and more about the community in which they live. Place one or more old phone books in a center. On each of a set of cards write a fictional name and the name of a place or service that person needs to find. Place cards in the center and let kids use the Yellow Pages to find an appropriate name, address, and phone number. Here are some card samples.

1. I.M. Hungry—I would like to eat in a Japanese restaurant.
2. Sue Sorry—I need to send flowers to a friend whose aunt died.
3. Running A. Fever—I need a doctor.
4. Pete Moss—I need to buy some seeds.
5. Sir G. Ree—I need an operation.
6. U.R. Drowning—I would like to take a lifesaving course.

-Rebecca Graves

## EGG CARTON STAMPS

Don't throw out those empty egg cartons; bring them to school for your kids to use in an art project instead. Cut the bottom portion of each carton into 12 different sections, and give one section to each child in your class. You'll need to supply tempera paints in different colors and sheets of butcher paper or high-gloss fingerpaint paper, if possible. Instruct the children to dip their egg carton sections into the paint, then press them on the paper a la rubber stamp. These egg carton stamps are easy to handle and great fun for primary children.

*-Joan Mary Macey*

## LAMINATED LEFTOVERS

Have you ever wondered what to do with leftover scraps of acetate that have already gone through the laminating press? Here are some suggestions:

**1.** Have children use permanent markers to design flowers or cartoon characters on small scraps of laminate. Cut them out and use to decorate a sunny window.

**2.** Have students write their names with permanent markers on short strips for name tags that will last and last.

**3.** Use small scraps of acetate for wet-look effects in collage or other artwork.

**4.** Cut large pieces into 8″ × 11″ sheets to use as handmade overhead transparencies.

**5.** Let children use narrow 8″ strips and permanent markers to create durable bookmarks for gifts for friends.

**6.** Cut larger pieces to use as acetate covers for book reports or stories written by children. Bind with staples and tape.

**7.** Use transparent tape to attach construction paper letters to long strips of laminating film. These can be tacked onto bulletin board for perfectly straight and protected letters.

*-Glenda Pearl Lassiter*

## NUMBER, PLEASE

The telephone book contains a wealth of activities for your class.

**1.** With the children make a list of the information found in a phone book: addresses, phone numbers, area codes, zip codes, time codes, city maps, and so on. Use a large cutout of a telephone

and display it in your classroom.

**2.** Create a dictionary of terms and definitions. Include such terms as: *area code, operator, local call, direct-dial call, directory assistance, emergency numbers, rate period,* and *yellow pages.*

**3.** Have kids make up five or six names, and exchange lists with a classmate. Ask students to see if the names on their list are in the phone book. If so, write the address and phone number next to each name. If not, write down on what page each name would be listed if there were such a person. What names come (or would come) before and after each name?

**4.** Have students use the rate-period chart to answer questions such as: How much will it cost to talk to your cousin in Eau Claire if you call her at 6:30 P.M. and talk for one minute? Make up story problems to go along with this activity. Use holiday rates and foreign calls, too.

**5.** Pretend your class is planning an international food fair. Let kids use the yellow pages to help them locate and list businesses that sell decorations, food, and so on.

**6.** Have each child write a septon. This is a poem based on a telephone number; it doesn't have to rhyme. Students write their number down the left side of a piece of paper, one number per line. The number on the line tells how many words should be in that line of the poem. For example, if the number is 429-3648, the first line would have four words, the second two.

**7.** Have children make a local emergency phone number guide to keep by their phones at home.

*-Kelly Riley*

## BUNNY PLAYPEN

How to house the pets that are an integral part of the elementary classroom can sometimes be baffling. This was the case when an oversized rabbit came to stay in our room. After experimenting with a variety of habitats, we found the ideal to be a used baby playpen. Chicken wire was fastened around the outside and formed into an easy-to-open top. Bunny had good ventilation and lots of space, and was highly visible.　　*-Patricia A. Wilmott*

## IDEAS ON WHEELS

An oridnary red wagon can be the answer to lots of otherwise messy classroom projects. Wagons are obtainable at a reasonable price from toy stores, antique dealers, discount houses, and so on. One of your students might even have one at home and be willing to donate it for classroom use. Clean the inside of the wagon thoroughly with detergent and water, then try some of the following ideas.

**1.** Load all of your classroom plants into the wagon. This way, you can give them the light they need all day long by simply wheeling the wagon around to follow the sun. And when it's time to water them, they won't drip all over your windowsill, either!

**2.** For special holidays, use the wagon to hold your classroom centerpiece, jack-o'-lantern, or Christmas tree. The wagon can be moved around the classroom so everyone can enjoy the view.

**3.** Use the wagon to transport items such as art projects, play props, library books, and so on.

**4.** If you've got classroom pets, load them into the wagon once a week or so and take them to visit other classrooms in your school.

**5.** Place corrected tests and worksheets in the wagon and choose one student each week to distribute them.          *-Nicki Klein*

### CONSERVATION IN THE ART ROOM

These scenes are common in too many art rooms. A student starts a project and tosses it out for the slightest error. A student needing only a scrap of paper cuts up a large sheet and discards the rest. Large amounts of paint are poured when only a small amount is needed. Empty jars, packing materials, and scraps are thrown away instead of being creatively recycled.

We teachers should stress conservation of supplies and help students to see art as a problem-solving experience—where accidents can become assets. Here are ways to do more with less.

**1.** Have students collect something that is usually discarded and display it in some unusual way. I've had students make houses from french fry containers and vests from the pop tops of soda cans.

**2.** Create a still life from some found object and make the finding part of the lesson. A walk around the school, through a park, or down the street will yield materials for a weaving, collage, or sculpture.

**3.** Visit a local lumberyard for castoffs. You will find pieces of wood and shavings that can be made into sculptures and reliefs. The possibilities for using everyday and leftover materials in the art room are endless. Once students have their eyes open to the possibilities, they will amaze you with their own ideas.
          *-Arlene Milgram*

### FURRY FRIENDS

Pets are valuable additions to any classroom. However, their *aroma* may not always be so welcome! Here are a few guidelines for keeping animals sweet-smelling and their human classmates breathing easy.

Build a cage with a wire screen for the floor. Make sure the holes in the screen are small enough so that the animals' feet cannot get stuck. Cover the screen with wood shavings. Place the cage atop four bricks so that it is elevated about three inches off the ground. This arrangement gives animals a comfortable home; the screen allows air to circulate and the shavings to dry out, giving odor-causing bacteria little chance to prosper. Change wood shavings at least every two weeks.

Slide a plastic tray beneath the case to catch any stray shavings or droppings. Sprinkle the tray with baking soda to absorb any unsavory odors.

For extra reinforcement—or if all else fails—attach an air-freshener to the outside of the case.
          *-Julia Smith*

### MARVELOUS MAGNETIC CHALKBOARDS

If the chalkboards in your school are not more than ten years old, they probably have magnetic powers. If so, you're facing an "attractive" source of visual aids for the classroom. For instance, there are dozens of inexpensive commercial science, math, reading, and readiness materials available that are already magnetized for classroom use. Or, you can use part of the chalkboard as a removable message center and area for displaying very special student work. Also, small magnets can be used to hold flashcards or stretch posters and maps across the chalkboard. When the board has served its educational purpose, use small magnets as playing pieces for leisure-time game activities like chess, checkers, or tic-tac-toe. There are many more potential uses for magnetic chalkboards; so put your imagination to work and "stick" with it!          *-Anita Klein*

### PASS THE ROLLS

Collect rolls from paper towels, foil clear plastic wrap, or toilet tissue, and use them as cores for drill-strips in phonics, vocabulary, math, social studies, and so forth. Cut a strip of paper (newsprint is fine). Write learning material on it and attach it to the roll with masking tape. Roll 'er up! Fasten with a clothespin or paper clip. Group rolls together in a basket or decorated box, and you have a ready-made learning center.
          *-Denise Kelin*

## PLASTIC SLATES

My kids have made individual slates from transparent gripper report covers for practice exercises in all subjects. One cover yields two slates. Cut cover at the fold and tape each half to a piece of colorful oak tag the same size. Use ¾" tape on all four sides. A dark crayon or a China marker will mark the plastic surface and a soft cloth will erase the marks.

These slates can be used effectively in arithmetic, language, spelling and phonics, and to review questions in social studies and science.

They allow the teacher to help one or two children with difficulties each time a problem is given. This is possible because the rest of the students will be busy doing the problem individually on their own slate. All will be busy, and time can easily be given to those who need it.

*-Anne M. Corbett*

## FLIPPY FLASH CARDS

You can solve the problem of disappearing flash cards and help reinforce your students' sequencing skills with this effective idea. You'll need several easy-open key rings or removable notebook rings. (These are available at most stationery stores.) Assemble groups of teacher-made or commercial flash cards in the order in which you'd like them to be reviewed, and punch a hole in the upper right or left corner of each card. Then simply attach each group of cards to one of the rings, and presto: flippy flash cards! These cards are especially useful for practice in sequencing. Use them to help your kids learn the months of the year, seasons, days of the week, multiplication tables, and so on.

*-Nicki Klein*

## CHALK IT UP

The use of individual chalkboards proved to be a very valuable teaching device in my second grade. We used them mainly for math. Instead of having one child

put a problem on the board, every child did the work on his or her own chalkboard. Each child then held up his or her board so I could quickly check who might have trouble with a particular concept. We also used them for various kinds of math puzzles and to review work before weekly tests. Each child had a small felt cloth with which to erase his or her board between stages of the lesson. At the end of the complete lesson, small pieces of wet sponges were passed out for washing the boards.

The children really enjoyed working on their boards and were disappointed if we didn't use them. Often on a rainy day, they would get them out and play school during recess. I found math scores improved on achievement tests after having used the chalkboards for the entire year.

*-Jane D. Fry*

## MAKE A MEASURING TAPE

Students easily can make their own measuring tapes to have for math and art projects through the year. To make a measuring tape, cut two 18-inch strips of ¾-inch-wide masking tape. Then place the sticky sides together to make one piece of tape. Take care to keep the edges even when sticking the two pieces together. If a portion of a sticky edge is exposed, just trim it off. Next, use a regular measuring tape, a ruler, or a yardstick to mark off 18 one-inch spaces. You also may want to mark half-, quarter-, and eight-inch marks. Each child can store his or her own measuring tape rolled up for future use.

*-Daisy Lynch*

## HALF-PINTS

Don't throw away those empty milk cartons, especially the half-pints. There are plenty of good classroom uses for them.

**ABC Boxes** Collect 26 half-pint cartons and cut away their upper portions. Each carton will represent a letter of the alphabet. Cover each carton with a collage designed in the shape of the particular letter and with corresponding "sound pictures" (pictures whose names begin with the sound the letter makes). Then ask students to bring in small objects and place each object in the carton that stands for the letter the name of the object begins with. For instance, a stone would go in the "s" carton. (Or would you call it a rock?)

**Circus Cages** Again cut off the upper part of the carton. Cut out pictures of circus animals and paste them to the inside of the carton. Stand the carton on its side and make bars for the cage by cutting straws and placing them in the open end.

**Paint Container** Powdered tempera can be mixed in a half-pint carton. Then, at the end of the day, if some students have not finished painting, tempera can be stored nicely by simply closing the top and fastening it with a clothespin. The next day, the paint will be ready to use after only a little stirring.    -Betty Klein

## GAME-BOARD PIECES

Need a simple solution for the problem of missing game-board markers? Try using the tops of dried-out felt-tipped pens.

-Mabel Bertram

## KEEP IT CLEAN

Tired of cleaning up globs of paint, glue, and crayon shavings from your classroom floor and art table? Here's a simple solution. Cover your table and the floor area below it with plastic shower curtains. Wipe-ups are a cinch!

-Jean Beam

## ROLL-ON GLUE

Frustrated by the messy chore of refilling your kids' individual glue bottles from a gallon container? Well, here's an idea that can change all that. Start saving your empty roll-on deodorant bottles and ask your kids to bring some in from home, too. Wrap the bottles in layers of masking tape to protect them from falls; then fill them with glue from your industrial-size container. The glue will roll on easily and won't spill out if the container falls over.

-Diane Kaufman

## REVIVE AN OLD MASTER

When an old spirit master no longer gives you a clean copy, don't make a new master—just re-ink the old one. Put the old master on the drum as usual. Place a new, blank master—ink side up—on the paper tray. Run the new master through the machine and the ink will transfer to the old master. Remove the blank master and run off pages as usual.    -Elizabeth Ramsey

## CRAYON CADDY

If you've got a plastic lazy Susan in your kitchen that you're willing to part with, and a few empty orange juice cans, you can make a nifty crayon caddy in just a few minutes. Start by cutting the juice cans down to half size, then paint them or cover them with construction paper to match the colors found in an ordinary box of crayons. Now secure the cans on the lazy Susan with rubber cement. Divide your classroom supply of crayons according to color, and drop them in the appropriate cans. Presto! A revolving crayon caddy your kids will love!

-Nicki Klein

## REUSABLE DRILL SHEETS

Tired of duplicating the same old math worksheets? Here's a way for students to use the same sheets over and over again. Using a copy machine, duplicate a worksheet onto a transparency. Place a piece of plain paper underneath the transparency, and staple both sheets into a manila folder to make a booklet.

For each problem on the transparency, write the answer on the plain sheet so it shows through below the problem. Now fold the paper lengthwise to cover the answers.

The students can write directly on the transparencies with a wax crayon. When they've finished the problems, they can unfold the plain paper and the correct answers will show through next to their own so they can correct and check their answers immediately. After wiping off their marks and refolding the answer sheet, they can now pass the folder on to the next person. To vary this idea for primary children, use a drill wheel with cartoon characters.
*-Marsha L. Henry*

## BRIGHTEN UP THOSE OLD MASTERS

A multicolored duplicating master is not hard to create and can add a new look (and new interest) to worksheets. Using a combination of the various colored inked sheets that mimeographs come in, cut and tape pieces together to approximately form the standard 8½- x 11 inch sheet of paper. This "patchwork" can be random colors or can be planned according to your needs. Be careful to tape the inked pieces edge to edge without overlapping the colors. After you finish taping the paper together, use the variegated ink sheet as you would a normal mimeograph backing. This look can be used simply for design or to enhance the function of the ditto. For instance, a worksheet can be designed to help create the problem of finding all the blue circles, red triangles, and green squares. Using blue and red ink strategically, show the circulatory system with oxygenated and deoxygenated blood flow. Designing masters this way can become an easy way to give your lessons a new look.
*-Seth J. Edwards*

## DUPLICATE USE

Why throw out those used duplicating masters when they can be recycled for future use? Back the original top sheet with an old worksheet or piece of plain paper so the carbon won't smudge when you're storing it. Now you can use the transparent middle section as a piece of tracing paper for student activities. Store them all together in a paper recycling box that the class can have free access to. The carbon paper backing can also be saved for students who might want to design a puzzle or maze to be shared with the class as a run-off.
*-Wendy Graham*

## SIGN ON THE DOTTED LINE

After 30 years of teaching, I have finally discovered a fast, easy way to make the dotted line when doing a ditto master for writing paper. Simply roll a tracing wheel (used in sewing) next to the ruler.
*-Charlene Maxey*

## RECYCLED FELT-TIPPED PENS

Here's a recycling idea for the classroom that will save you money and create an unusual tool for use in art projects. When your felt-tipped liquid markers finally dry up, you can still use them as dip pens for watercolor paints. Moisten blocks of paint with enough water to make a thin ink. Dip the felt-tipped pen into the ink and paint as you would with any paint brush. Redip and remoisten as often as necessary. Try to match felt-tipped pens with the same shade of paint, but if that's not possible don't despair—the result will be some interesting color blends! So, the next time one of your students leaves the cover off a liquid marker, or they simply run out of ink through normal use, try this idea. You'll get more mileage for your money!
*-Mary Cobb*

## THE THREE FACES OF FILE CABINETS

Short of activity space? Try turning that quiet old file cabinet into a triple-threat hands-on activity center. On one side, stick up a supply of magnetic alphabet letters and you have a reading, spelling, and language drill station. On another side, spray chalkboard paint, available at most hardware stores, for all those kids who love to write on the chalkboard. On the third side, put up felt contact cloth, also available in most hardware stores, and felt letters, and you have a "stick 'em up" center for drill or story telling. There's a lot of learning mileage *on* that file cabinet!
*-Joy Glicksberg*

## CLASSROOM GALLERY

Students will learn to take pride in their work when you set up an art gallery in your classroom. Pick up inexpensive picture frames from garage sales or secondhand stores. After an art lesson, select several pictures to be framed, or have the class choose its favorite works. Stories and poems can be glued to tagboard and framed. Change works often so that each student has a chance to get in the picture!
*-Jean Antony*

## ART GALLERY

Large appliances are often packaged in cardboard boxes. It is easy to convert one of these boxes into an art gallery where your students can display their artwork.

Cover the outside of the box with black paper. Add a few tin foil circles around the bottom of the box to represent stage lights. Tack artwork to all four outer sides.

Inside, hang pictures painted with fluorescent colors. You can place a blacklight in the box to make this art more vibrant.

In the box, you may also want to cut a window that opens and closes. This can serve as an excellent puppet theater.
*-Thomas Hilke and Eileen Hilke*

### RECYCLED SLIDES

Ever get back a roll of slide film and find that a few of the slides were black because they hadn't been properly exposed? Well, stop throwing them away! Here's an idea that can help you make use of them—and the best thing about it is that the only materials you'll need are some household bleach, a soft cloth, and a little bit of elbow grease! Simply use the cloth to apply a little bleach to the dull side of each slide. Then rub gently until all the black coating comes off. You'll be left with clear slides that can be used in lots of different ways in your classroom. For instance, you can draw small pictures on them to illustrate story scenes, print math equations for review—even let the kids use them in art projects. (They make great windows for construction-paper houses!) Just be sure that you and the children use felt-tipped pens for writing or drawing. This same procedure can be used on filmstrips.

*-Nancy S. Williamson*

### MAKE A FILMSTRIP

You can make your own color filmstrip if you own a 35mm camera and a flash unit. Begin by purchasing color slide film and learning to hold your camera with the film-receiving side (usually the right side, looking from behind camera) down.

Organize your visual presentation before your first shot. Always have the title in the first frame and a shot of a card reading "The End" in the last frame. Choose rolls of film containing 36 frames to give you enough length. With 35mm film, your shooting area or frames will be slightly restricted. Frames will be narrow and longer than necessary, but this should really fire your creativeness.

Don't try putting captions in your scene unless you are shooting a label for some object. You'll find that by including students in your shot, you must make the caption very large to be readable. Most shots of students are filmed at distances of five to ten feet. Shots of posters, objects, and pages in books are filmed at distances of three to five feet.

Discount stores usually sell slide film with developing included for about $3.50. Simply use the handy mailer to send the film in for processing. IMPORTANT: Include a notation that reads— "Special Handling—Do not cut or mount. Leave in one long filmstrip."      *-William T. Spencer, Jr.*

### MAKE YOUR OWN TRANSPARENCIES

The overhead projector is a great teaching tool, but the pictures, maps, graphs, and puzzles you want to show the class are not always available as transparencies. Here is a simple method for making a transparency of any picture, map, or graph. Cut a piece of clear adhesive-backed paper the same size as the picture you want to project. Press it onto the picture and rub firmly to remove all of the air bubbles. Now soak it in lukewarm water for a few minutes. Then carefully rub off the paper. The color and the print should adhere to the paper, and your transparency's ready.

*-Nancy Williamson*

### GET THE PICTURE?

Keep a camera ready this school year and have fun with photos. If Robby brings his pet rabbit in one day, or Amy sits up straight for penmanship class, get the picture. Halloween costumes, Christmas plays, or just everyday events are all worthy subjects for your lens. The cost isn't great but the returns are. We put our pictures in an album and labeled it "Fun Photos of Room 129." Everyone loves to look at it. Students seem to have a better class feeling after looking at it,

and a better self-image, too. Almost every evening someone asks to take it home. Parents report they have enjoyed looking at the pictures and having their children tell them about the snapshots—especially children who answer "nothing" when asked what goes on at school.

*-Ruth Townsend*

### MAKE YOUR OWN MICROSCOPE SLIDES

When studying plants or nutrition, try making microscope slides with your class. I have found that students' interest in microscopes never wanes if they can observe slides of their own making. To observe the intricacies of a plant, we took a small leaf, flower, seed, or a thin slice of a fruit or vegetable for a specimen.

In the center of $1\frac{1}{2}''$ x $4\frac{1}{2}''$ cardboard strips we cut a small hole. We then placed the cardboard strips on clear, laminated paper and stuck the specimens to the paper through the holes in the cardboard. Next, we labeled each strip and wrapped the laminating paper completely around it.

After observing the specimens through the microscope, the students drew and labeled a likeness of the slide. Some of our slides, which we store in shallow cardboard boxes, have been used as long as two years and still look great under magnification.

*-Evelyn M. Marshall*

### OUTLINE MAP

Give each child an outline map of the world. Bring in a transistor radio and together listen to a five-minute broadcast of the news. List all the places on the board that are mentioned in the broadcast. When the program is over, help pupils mark and label the places on their maps. Use this as an ongoing activity. Over a period of weeks, pupils will learn more about geography and current events.

*-Isobel L. Livingstone*

## A WELCOME FOOTNOTE

Start your Open House or Parents Day off on the right "foot" with this fun activity. Have each child trace around his or her right or left foot on a piece of drawing paper, then cut out the pattern.

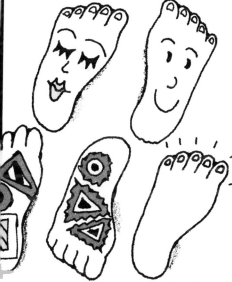

Next, let the kids draw faces on their "feet" or decorate them in any other way they choose. They might want to cover them in a collage of geometric shapes or paint their toenails in different colors. After they've been decorated, gather all of the "feet" together and tack them on your bulletin board so they spell out the word "WELCOME!"

-Sharon Rankin

## PLAN AHEAD FOR PARENTS' NIGHT

Open communication lines with a parents' night just before or soon after school begins. Make the uniqueness of each child the theme of the evening. Send invitations designed to look like mirrors to parents and children. To provide a taste of the year to come, put together a slide show of activities from previous years. Explain how coming events will give each child many ways to excel. On the special night, pass out mirror-shaped name tags to make mingling easier. After the slide show, invite parents and kids to work together on a variety of learning games.   -Marilyn Larson

## MYSTERY GHOSTS

If Parents' Night in your school happens to fall in October, you can reap double benefits from this Halloween bulletin board. Give each child in your class a white construction-paper ghost. Now have students write brief, descriptive paragraphs about themselves, leaving out their names, and paste them to the ghosts. Display these ghosts against a black background on your bulletin board under the heading "Mystery Ghosts in Room." When the display is complete, hold a contest to see who can identify the most ghosts. Parents will enjoy picking out their kids' mystery ghosts, too!

-Lisa Littlewood

## LET A LETTER HELP

Good relations between parents, students, and teachers are a must for a successful school year. If home visits are impractical in your school district, try this different "get-acquainted" technique. During the summer, write each child in your prospective class a letter. Tell kids about yourself and your family, and send along a small photo as well. At the end of the letter, ask them to do the same for you. This involves some time, but the returns are worth the effort, for the first day of school will be a meeting of friends, teacher included!

-Marjorie Shiffbauer

## BROWN-BAG IT!

"A wonderful idea; I would love to come!" "I believe that the parenting discussion group is an excellent idea." These are responses from parents sent invitations to meet at school for lunch the last Wednesday of each month. Parents bring a brown-bag lunch, and the teacher provides coffee, tea, dessert, and a place to talk informally. This is a shared teacher/parent hour to discuss classroom activities, future plans, educational issues, and school policies. Display books of interest and handouts on various subjects such as television watching, discipline, parenting skills, and peer pressure. School specialists can be invited one at a time to talk about their particular fields. Such a luncheon is a rewarding experience and a successful link between school and home. Breakfast meetings are a great idea for parents who can't make lunch.          -Amy Marotta

## SOMEPLACE SPECIAL

Get parents fired up with school spirit by holding a contest just for them! Ask parents to complete the sentence "_____ Elementary School is someplace special because . . ." in 100 words or less. Specify a deadline for entries. Only one entry per family! Your memo might also include a space for parents to write what they consider to be problems with the school, and any constructive suggestions they may have. State that all entries will be evaluated by a panel of teachers; the top 10 will receive such nifty awards as a school book bag or an all-expenses-paid lunch in the school cafeteria. Winning essays can also be displayed during a school open house.          -Robert J. Ziegler

## LISTENING LEADS TO READING

I believe that when a child is read to, all kinds of positive results occur! His or her vocabulary grows. He or she sees that reading is valued by the important people in his or her life. The child notes how the pages are turned and can be shown that pages are read from top to bottom, from left to right. In addition to creating interest and the desire to learn to read, habits of attention and listening are encouraged. Motivation, vocabulary understanding, concept formation, sequencing, and recognition of the mechanics of reading are all valuable outcomes of a pleasant sharing situation.

To encourage parents to read to their children, I send home a school library book which their child has selected and the accompanying duplicated letter.

> Dear Parent,
>     Your child chose this book at the Lincoln School Library. Since he is not able to read it yet, will you, or someone at your house, read it to him? Please send the book back by . . . . . . . .
>     Thank you for sharing this book with your child.
>         Sincerely,
>         Ms. Swickard

Beneath the letter is a return coupon like the one below:

> . . . . . . . . . . . . . . . read this book to . . . . . . . . . . . . . . .
> Name of Book . . . . . . . . . . .
> . . . . . . . . . . . . . . . . . . . .
>         Signed _____

This plan has been well received by both parents and children. The children's attitudes and reading progress have reflected their additional exposure to the pleasure of reading.
*-Ruby Swickard*

## PARENT HANDBOOK

Parents want to help their children be successful learners, but they are often hesitant to help because they're afraid of confusing children by teaching the wrong thing or in the wrong

way. It was for this reason I developed a handbook for my students' parents. The book consisted of tips ranging from "Ways to Encourage" and "Ideas for Casual Learning" to "How to Help with Spelling Words" and "The Importance of Reading to Your Child." In other sections, I diagrammed the correct formation of letters according to our penmanship program, and I prepared a glossary of math terms to help decipher directions to our math worksheets.

The most popular section was on learning through games. I gave critiques of a few of the excellent games available at toy stores, gave directions for making games at home, and described other games that could be played without props while shopping, cooking, or traveling.

The handbook, with its simple suggestions and words of encouragement, helped to open the doors of communication between the home and the school—a worthwhile project!
*-Sue Olenoski*

## WEEKLY ACTIVITY FOLDER

I launch this year-long activity at our Open House in September, when I can explain to parents how my folder project works. Every Friday morning each child arranges in the folder all the work by subject he or she has completed during the week. Papers that haven't been completed are kept separate. Sometime during the day I sit with each child and discuss the work, giving praise and encouragement, and attaching a dittoed note that says "Please complete and return to school" to the unfinished work. Then as a class we compose a letter to parents on the board. Children contribute items of interest that happened that week, and we tell of upcoming activities. Each child copies the letter; then it is put into the folder along with the schoolwork. The letter keeps

parents informed of all phases of school life, and asks them to look over the child's work sometime over the weekend with him or her. The parents have come to expect the weekly letter, and sometimes, knowing what we are studying, they have come in to share slides or talk to us. Folders and letters take a large block of time on Fridays, but the benefits gained by keeping communication open between school and home far outweigh the disadvantages.
*-Jeraldine Beakeslee*

## THIS IS A RECORDING

I used to have students write a monthly newsletter to parents, which I edited, typed, and dittoed for each family. This proved to be very time-consuming, so I tried a new technique which has been very successful—oral reporting. Using a tape cassette from a phone answering machine, students recorded special or upcoming events taking place in the school, reported something unusual that happened in the classroom, or told about a new skill or concept introduced during the week. From 4 P.M. TO 7 A.M. each day, the tape was placed in the answering machine, and parents could call a school number and listen to the recorded messages. Some parents even recorded a message in response, which was then played in the classroom for all to hear.
*-Suzanne Svejcar*

## PARENTS' NIGHT CHAIRPERSONS

Want to bring your classroom to life on Parent's Night? Try this simple art idea all your kids can have a hand in—or a face! Give your children one large plastic garbage bag each and instruct them to decorate the bags to resemble their faces. Kids can use construction paper for eyes, mouths, and noses, and colored yarn for hair. When all the bags are decorated, have each child cut his or her bag half-way up the

PARENTS' NIGHT CHAIRPERSONS

sides from the open end. Finally, help the children slide their bags over the backs of their chairs. Presto! A room full of smiling faces ready to greet parents! When Parent's Night is over, have kids stuff their face-bags with newspaper, attach a long cardboard tube, and they'll have a clone puppet to bring home!

-Carolyn Wilhelm

## AND NOW, A WORD FROM YOUR KIDS

Every year during "Back-to-School Night," we are required to give a speech explaining our grade's curriculum. After several years of a similar speech, I decided to try something different. What better way than to have the children, themselves, explain what we do in second grade! To begin with, my second graders each wrote a story accompanied by an illustration entitled, "What We Do in Second Grade." We displayed the results in the hallway.

On "Back-to-School Night" I gave a brief speech and introduction. Then I played a tape on which each child had briefly described what he liked best in second grade. The parents enjoyed hearing their children's views in their own words and voices

almost as much as the children enjoyed taping them.

It was an interesting presentation for the parents, a fun experience for the children, and a real eye-opener for me, as I learned what my class enjoyed most in school.

-Ann Moslowitz

## WHAT HAPPENED IN SCHOOL TODAY?

Parents often complain that their children are reluctant to talk about school activities and that questions like "What did you do in school today?" are usually answered with shrugs or replies of "Nothing." Here's an idea that can cut down on parents' frustration and get them more involved in their children's school lives. Each day, have your students write brief paragraphs summarizing the day's events. Then, in a class discussion at the end of the week, let them decide which events were most important. Write down their choices on a duplicating master in letter form and give them two copies each—one for themselves and one for their parents. Analyzing events this way on a weekly basis will improve students' reviewing skills and ability to discriminate between

what is and isn't important. Parents will love the way the letters help spark family discussions concerning school activities.

-Eileen Hilke

## A PARENTS' NIGHT TO REMEMBER

How can you add pizzazz to that upcoming parents' night and still get your message across? Let the kids tell the story, that's how. For the past two years, I have presented a slide show for parents at open house, depicting my students during a typical day at school. Slides cover the most important curricular areas along with a few additional subjects of interest. The entire show is narrated by the children.

Here's the way I do it. About three weeks before the big night, the class decides which subjects it wants to include in order to give an overall picture of our class program. Then I photograph them, mixing shots of materials we use with pictures of the kids using them. I try for a combination of candid and posed photos. After the slides have been processed, we choose the best ones, organize them, and write information for each. After some practice, we tape the information into a flowing narrative, with each child reading a segment which accompanies the appropriate slide. The last step is showing the slides together with the recorded narrative. Excitement builds as the kids see the finished product their parents will view.

The slide show format provides the children with a valuable learning experience in areas of language arts, organizational skills, and cooperation. It explains lengthy procedures in an uncomplicated and interesting manner and serves as an exciting culminating activity for the open house. There is nothing like watching the face of a parent as he or she sees his or her child on the screen.

-Ronna Jacobson

# Review Motivators/For a Better Classroom

## TEN-PIN PRACTICE

Good sports will enjoy reviewing facts with this bowling game. Make several sets of bowling pins of heavy paper or oak tag, and laminate or cover with clear contact plastic. With a nonpermanent marker, write a question or problem on each set of 10 pins and turn them facedown. Make a set for each team. Players on Team 1 turn over pins one at a time and give the answers, continuing until they miss. When someone misses or all 10 pins are "knocked down" (answered correctly), Team 2 takes over with its pins. Keep track of points on scrap paper. To reuse the pins, simply wipe them off and rewrite.          *-Dee Leone*

## BONUS

Write questions pertaining to a study unit on slips of paper and divide them into four groups, according to levels of difficulty. Put each group in a different coffee can and assign each can a point value of 2, 4, 7, or 10, corresponding to the difficulty of the questions inside. Also include in each can a few slips of paper labeled "BONUS." Divide the class into two teams and have the members take turns selecting and answering questions from the container of their choice. If a player draws a BONUS slip, his or her team gets the appropriate point value automatically. After all the questions have been answered, the team with the highest score wins.          *-Joan Juul-Nielsen*

## FUNNY FACE

Here's a creative activity to help your students review math problems, vocabulary words, or facts from any subject area you choose. Start by cutting parts of "funny faces" (ears, hats, collars, bows, and so on) from pieces of colored construction paper. Put each unassembled face in a separate envelope and give one to every student in your class.

Now make three or four identical sets of problem cards on which you've written questions, vocabulary words, or math equations to be solved. Divide the class into three or four groups and place a set of cards facedown on the floor in the center of each playing area. Group members are to take turns drawing problem cards from the deck. Each time a child gives a correct answer, he or she may remove a funny face piece from his or her envelope, place it on the floor in front of him or her, and return the answered problem card to the bottom of the deck. The first child to assemble an entire funny face is the winner.          *-Barby Borchardt*

## BODY LANGUAGE REVIEW

For a variation in review procedures, try this activity. Use it anytime you are going over information that can be covered with a limited number of answers, such as names of various countries, explorers, or math sums.

List each possible answer on the chalkboard. Beside each, write a body part such as eye, knee, mouth, or elbow. After you have given a question, count to three to allow all a chance to decide upon an answer and to prevent anyone's jumping the gun and giving the answer away. Students should then place one of their hands over the correct body part. Since all students are actively involved in this review, it is a quick way to check the confidence and accuracy of the students with the material and allow you to decide if further teaching or review is necessary. Occasionally you may want to ask a question and call on only one or a few students to answer using this special "body code."          *-Sandra Frey*

## ANSWER RELAY

Relays are good ways to review any subject. Give the first student in each row a sheet of paper numbered from one to ten. Ask a question; each student should quickly write down his or her response and then pass the paper on to the next student in the row, who in turn answers the next question asked by the teacher. When all 10 questions have been asked, have the first student in each row check the paper as you read off the correct answers. The row with the most correct answers is the winning row.

Give prizes occasionally or allow the row a privilege, like being dismissed first.          *-Sister Roberta Ann Leskey*

## JACKPOT!

Get your class excited about review exercises with this energizing activity that reinforces listening skills and ability to recall and recognize facts. Begin by making a list of review questions from the unit being studied. Now cut strips of tagboard and write the answers to each question on two separate strips. Mix them up and distribute them to the class facedown so that two students have the same answer in front of them. Now instruct the students to turn the strips over, look at the answer, and listen carefully to the questions asked. Be sure they understand that two people will have the same answers written on their tagboard strips. Explain that after the question is read, the student who thinks he or she has the answer in front of him or her is to jump up and yell "jackpot!" The object is to be the first one to recognize the answer and shout the "magic word." The student answering correctly receives a small tagboard button with the words "I know it!" written across the front. This activity will encourage your students to listen carefully, think faster, and recall information more readily.

*-Brenda Dalton*

## REVIEWING FUN

This year, when you're looking for a way to spice up review sessions, try this idea—it's perfect for reviewing story characters, inventory, presidents, or just about anything else! On a large sheet of white poster board

print or spray paint the name of the person you'll be reviewing. Then have your kids look through magazines, newspapers, or catalogs for words, phrases, or pictures describing that person. The students are to take turns pasting their selections on the poster board as they explain to the rest of the class why it belongs there. Post the finished product in a visible place in the room so the review and reinforcement can continue. You might also want to make a larger bulletin board display from several of these individual review posters.   *-Sister Marilyn Brokamp*

## CHOICE TUNES

This self-checking method of review will be music to students' ears! Write a series of multiple-choice questions and label the answers with letters that represent notes on the musical scale (A, B, C, D, E, F, and G). The correct answers to the set of questions will correspond to the notes of a simple musical tune.

Children jot down the answers, then try to play the tune on a piano or xylophone. If the tune sounds familiar, the student knows his or her answers are right. If there are "sour" notes, the student changes answers, then tries to play the tune again.

*-Dee Leone*

## BALLOON REVIEW SESSION

Here's an idea to help you put a little "pop" into those unexciting review sessions. Before blowing up several colored balloons, write review questions on small slips of paper and place one inside each balloon. Tie strings on the end of each one and pin them in rows across your bulletin board. The children are to go to the board, one at a time, choose a balloon to pop, and try to answer the questions inside. This game may be played individually or in teams for added excitement. You'll find that everyone looks forward to review sessions when you use this technique, and the unit you're closing will really go out with a bang!   *-Nancy Williamson*

## DINOSAUR DRILL

Every teacher knows that young children are fascinated with dinosaurs. So if you're having trouble getting your kids interested in basic curriculum areas, try the following ideas based on those large and lovable prehistoric creatures. Before you begin, you'll want to expose your students to some basic facts about dinosaurs—but don't be surprised if they already know more than you do!

**Language Arts:** Dinosaurs can be the starting points for many language arts activities. Provide reference books listing the names of major prehistoric animals and pertinent information about each one. Then let your class try these activities:

1. List the names of 10 different dinosaurs. Circle every vowel you see and count the number of syllables in each name.
2. Write a letter to a museum in your area, requesting information on dinosaurs.
3. Write a short story using one of the following titles:
   Me and My Dinosaur
   Debbie Dinosaur Goes to
     School
   The Day It Rained Dinosaurs
4. Choose five dinosaurs and make up riddles about each one for your classmates to solve.

**Mathematics:** Count on dinosaurs to liven up math drill!
1. Using reference books, compare the sizes of five different dinosaurs. What is the difference between the largest and the smallest?
2. Make several construction-paper dinosaurs and print one math equation on each one. Distribute them for classmates to solve.
3. Find the sizes of 10 different prehistoric animals. Add these numbers and compute the average.

*-Jackie Grover*

## THE BEST OF TESTS

Convinced that nothing on earth will make your students enjoy oral tests? Well, don't be too sure. If you turn the testing process into one of the creative games described below, you'll soon have your entire class "eating out of your hand." The next time you buy a bucket of fried chicken, save the container and carefully wash out the inside. Now cut lots of "chicken legs" from brown construction paper. Print a question pertaining to the material to be tested on each drumstick and put them all in the bucket. Let the kids take turns drawing drumsticks from the bucket and attempting to answer the questions that appear on each. If a student answers his question correctly, he may keep the drumstick. If not, he must

place it back in the bucket. The child with the most chicken legs in his hand at the end of the game is declared the winner.

You can use many other tasty products for this testing game. Construction paper ice-cream bars placed in an actual wrapper or oversized construction paper chocolates in leftover candy boxes make great question holders. If you'd rather not encourage these types of foods, cut vegetables from appropriately colored paper and let the kids draw them from a supermarket basket.

You might let the subject of the quiz dictate what types of cutouts you use. Questions may be printed on small, colorful construction-paper books for a reading test. An astronomy test may have questions printed on paper stars, moons, comets, and so on. Question cards may be cut in the shape of different countries or states for a social studies test. When the subject is science, print questions on cutouts of leaves, animals, raindrops, clouds, and so on. The possibilities are endless, and if you put your imagination to work, you can take the pain out of oral quizzes and turn them into the "best of tests."

*-Jane K. Priewe*

## SPELLING GOOSE

Here's a lively alternative to tiresome spelling exercises that's based on the game, "Duck, Duck, Goose." Players sit in a large circle. The leader announces the word to be spelled, then chooses one speller to start the game off. The speller moves around the outside of the circle, tapping players on the head as he says each letter of the designated word. When the last letter is said and the corresponding player is tapped, he runs around the circle chasing the speller, who tries to return to the player's spot before being tagged. If the speller is

tagged, he must sit in the middle of the circle before someone replaces him. Then the player who tagged him becomes the next speller. If the speller misspells a word, he must sit in the middle until another speller is tagged or another word is misspelled. This game keeps the whole class thinking because the players must spell the word to themselves in order to know if their position in the circle corresponds to the last letter of the word. Spelling Goose is a great activity for review and kids love the quick action involved.

*-Cheryl Callighan*

## STEPPING STONES

Use this game to reinforce skills or evoke thought for grades K-5.

**To make stepping stones:** Start with one yard of a solid-color oil cloth and one yard of heavy, clear plastic. Place matching pieces together with plastic on top of colored piece and sew across one edge. Problems to be answered are written on paper and placed between.

**To play the game:** Pretend a swift flowing stream is on your floor. Place stepping stones so they make a path across stream. The students walk across stream by successfully reading and answering each "stone" problem. If a player is not accurate, he must begin again.

**Problem variations for levels:**
**Kindergarten**—Use with shapes, colors, color words, likenesses, differences, matching, rhyming, and so on.

**First grade**—Letter recognition, phonetic sounds, words, phrases, isolated words that make sentences, math, science, social studies facts, and handwriting.

**Second through fifth grades**—Vary the above with level of difficulty. This activity provides an excellent way to study the multiplication tables and learn geography facts, too!

*-Richard Wiederholt and Mary Moen*

## TALK IS CHEAP

Do you sometimes have trouble getting your kids to settle down after recess or gym? Tired of wasting valuable time by asking for silence again and again? The next time you sense that your kids are too wound up to concentrate on learning activities, shout, "Talk time!" Then tell students that for the next five minutes, they may talk about anything that's on their minds—provided they raise their hands first and wait to be called on. Also stipulate that kids must keep their statement brief, so others will have a chance to talk. Listen carefully to your students and don't overlook the possibility that their statements may lead to other lessons. For instance, if a child tells you that he or she was injured playing darts, you might have your kids write letters to the dart manufacturer, calling for higher safety standards. This way, kids will learn the mechanics of good business letters in a way that has meaning for them. This idea will keep your class a little calmer while helping you stay in touch with your students' interests.                 -Annette Lumsden

## MINUTERS

"Minuters today" is what to say when you want everyone to sit down quietly and write for a minute. Choose one specific word as the topic, and after 30 seconds for thinking, set the timer for 60 seconds of writing.

Read five or six of the writings aloud. Then move on to the next topic. Three "minuter" topics at one sitting is usually a constructive amount. Try: island, tree, pencil, telephone, necklace, bird. Students like to suggest subjects, too.            -Joy Lindner

## NOISE POLLUTION

Is there too much noise in your classroom or hallway? Tape-record the sounds and play the tape for the class. Ask questions to start children thinking. Which sounds were not necessary? How can too much noise be harmful or dangerous? How can we improve the noise situation in our school? Have kids make a list of ways that noise pollution can be reduced.
                -Genevieve Bylinowski

## PLEASE TAKE A CARD

When I am working with one child alone or with a reading group, I ask the other children not to interrupt me. This means that students spend a lot of unproductive time standing in line waiting for me to finish with others so I can then attend to their questions.

To help solve this problem, I put index cards numbered 1 to 20 on a table near my desk. Now, when a child needs help and I am busy, he or she takes a card with a number on it and returns to work. When I am free, I call the numbers that are missing and work with each child in order. I have noticed that often children will pick up a numbered card, go back to their seats to work on whatever problem they have, and many times end up solving it themselves.

These numbered cards certainly help keep my classroom organized. They also seem to encourage students to give a problem "one more try."
                -Margaret Chianis

## THE JOB JAR

For behavior management in your classroom, use this idea that not only controls rambunctious students, but strengthens reference-using skills as well. Start with a large plastic jar and label it the "Job Jar." Fill it with small slips of paper on which you've written different assignments involving the use of reference materials. All of the assignments should pertain to some unit the class has been studying, and should indicate the

particular reference source to be used. When a student misbehaves or breaks a minor rule, he must pull an assignment from the jar and complete it within an agreed-upon time limit. This activity can be adapted to suit any grade level or subject area and will solve a variety of minor discipline problems.  -Ellen Mooney

## LINE TAMER

This handy little technique occurred to me one day as I was trying to keep a line of children in order while they were waiting for the bus. I said, "There is someone who is going to win a trip to the FRONT of the line. I can't remember the name of that person, but I think I can identify him by the way he looks." Then I began to walk up and down the line looking carefully at all the kids. I said such things as: "This person has on black shoes and is carrying a green lunch box and is wearing a red scarf and has some freckles" and so on. I kept giving clues until the child I was describing finally recognized himself or herself as the person in question. Each child listened eagerly. All the chattering stopped while the kids waited to hear if they might get to go to the front of the line. Listening skills were at an all-time peak!
                -Connie Zane

## 57 Ways To Get Kids In A Row

### LINE UP IF YOU CAN TELL ME . . .

1. what you would wish if you had one wish.
2. something people don't like: being late, sour milk, flies, noise . . . .
3. something people do like: rainbows, picnics, hugs, good movies . . . .
4. a safety rule for home or school: don't play with matches . . . .
5. a health rule for home or school: cover coughs and sneezes . . . .
6. the name of a television character or show title . . . .
7. the name of a state: Missouri, Kansas, Colorado, New Mexico . . . .
8. where your father works, mother's occupation.
9. the name of a city: New York, Boston, Detroit, Chicago . . . .
10. the name of a country: Scotland, Canada, India, Italy . . . .
11. what you would like to be when you grow up: an engineer, a news reporter, a pilot, a movie producer . . . .
12. your favorite subject in school.
13. your favorite place to visit: the woods, the ocean, the park, the gym . . . .
14. a book title, author, character, illustrator . . . .
15. a kind of fruit: banana, plum, grapes . . . .
16. a kind of vegetable: lettuce, beans, corn, cabbage, carrots . . . .
17. a type of tree: oak, maple, weeping willow, elm, lilac . . . .
18. a type of flower: rose, tulip, daisy, iris, marigold . . . .
19. the name of a movie star, singer, rock group . . . .
20. your favorite cereal: Cocoa Puffs, Rice Krispies, Raisin Bran, Sugar Smacks . . . .
21. a hobby or collection: gardening, stickers, stamps, dolls, biking, shells . . . .
22. an animal in the zoo: an ostrich, panda, monkey, rattlesnake, polar bear . . . .
23. an animal on a farm: rooster, goat, pig, cow, hen, duck . . . .
24. where your family went on vacation.
25. the name of a school worker: Mr. Manors, the cook; Ms. May, the principal . . . .
26. your address, phone number, birthday.
27. what you would do with a million dollars.
28. one thing you learned in school this week.

### LINE UP IF YOU HAVE:

1. a tooth missing, two teeth, three, four . . . .
2. aqua as your favorite color, violet, maroon, peach . . . .
3. a T-shirt on, short sleeves, long sleeves.
4. a ribbon in your hair, a watch on your left hand, a ring, a necklace . . . .
5. a "z" in your name, a "b," an "f," a "q".
6. a short vowel in your name, a long vowel.
7. a birthday in January, February, March . . . .
8. been to the circus, a rodeo, the zoo . . . .
9. sneakers on, boots, loafers . . . .
10. two persons in your family, three, four . . . .
11. a pet dog, cat, bird, fish, turtle, horse . . . .
12. seen the movies *Indiana Jones, Splash, E.T.* . . . .
13. striped socks on, pink socks, brown socks . . . .
14. taken dance lessons, Judo, swimming, voice, piano, guitar, flute lessons . . . .
15. visited other states: California, Florida, Texas, Utah, Arizona . . . .
16. participated in a wedding as a bridesmaid, flower girl, ring bearer . . . .
17. flown in an airplane, a helicopter, an air balloon, sailed, motorcycled . . . .
18. gone snow skiing, water skiing, snorkeling . . . .
19. cooked: hotdogs, hamburgers, grilled cheese sandwiches, cookies, cakes . . . .
20. helped parents mow grass, wash the car, clean the kitchen . . . .
21. performed in a recital, play, sports activity for an audience . . . .
22. moved to a new neighborhood, town, city, state, country . . . .
23. brought back your library books today, yesterday, tomorrow.
24. walked to school, ridden the bus, the subway, driven with a parent or friend.
25. been polite to a friend, teacher, parent today.
26. blue eyes, brown eyes, hazel, black . . . .
27. been to a hospital for tonsils, broken bones, to visit a friend.
28. written a poem, story, song, play . . . .
29. stood on your head, played tag, skipped rope, hung on the monkey bar, raced . . . .

*-Glenda Stroup Smithers*

# Relationships

This chapter is what it's all about — how you perceive your students and how they perceive you, each other, and themselves. The activities in this chapter are designed to help kids feel good about themselves so they can feel good about learning.

Perks for Kids has everything from offbeat awards to awards that teach. All About Me asks kids to get to know themselves and each other. Included, too, are activities that enhance teacher-pupil relationships and relationships between you and your colleagues. It's one we hope you will benefit from and enjoy.

### VERY IMPORTANT CHILDREN

To help each student know how important he or she is, my class has an Important Student Day. That day the special child receives an official proclamation, a coin is "minted" in his or her image, and an official cheer is cheered to celebrate. To choose the first special child's name, pick a name out of a hat. Thereafter let the special child pick the next one's name.

A proclamation, written on a scroll-shaped cutout pasted on construction paper, might read: "Let it be known that Sharon Jones is liked very much by her teacher and classmates. To show Sharon Jones how special she is, we have declared Sept. 20th as her day. There is only one Sharon Jones, and we are happy to have her with us. When you see Sharon Jones today, give her a great big hug or smile."

We read the proclamation at the beginning of the day and tie it with ribbon, ready to take home after school.

To use with the official cheer, we make cards which together spell out the child's full name. As we cheer for the child, we hold up the letters of his or her name.

On Important Student Day, I also take instant snapshots for the bulletin board. Before going home the class sings a special song (adaptation of "For He's a Jolly Good Fellow" or another simple song).          *-Margaret Henggeler*

### AWARDS THAT TEACH

Reinforce positive attitudes with unusual awards that honor individual students while extending the learning process. These awards can be related to a specific event, chosen with individual interest in mind, and presented for a variety of reasons. For example, you might give a small bike reflector to the student who showed the greatest concern for the safety of other riders, or you might give a brightly colored helium balloon to the one who consistently keeps class spirits high. Awards for such things as safety, conservation, and voluntary assistance provide immediate reinforcement and can launch a variety of classroom discussions concerning the nature of the objects themselves and why they are suitable awards.
          *-Karen E. Reynolds*

### "WRITER OF THE WEEK" AWARD

Motivate students to put their best efforts into writing assignments with this idea for "Writer of the Week" awards in which kids participate in choosing a winner each week! Every Friday (or any other designated day), divide your class into four or five groups. Give each group a batch of stories, poems, or essays that classmates completed during the week. Instruct each group to read these pieces carefully, discuss the merits of each, and choose one outstanding paper from the batch. Then have the groups take turns presenting their choices to the class, identifying the authors and explaining why they preferred the chosen pieces over others. Then let the entire class vote on who should be named the Writer of the Week. Present the award during a short ceremony at the end of the day. You might want to make up award certificates, bearing your school's stamp, principal's signature, and your own congratulatory message. Display award-winning papers on a bulletin board labeled "Writers of the Week." A display to make parents proud!          *-Linda Bendorf*

### OFFBEAT REWARDS

When your happy faces need a face-lift and your stars lose their glitter, try throwing away your stickers. Reward good papers by writing a poem on them!

Make sure verses promise a fun reward, like free time or a chance to go to lunch first. (You may need to stock up on some new props first, though.) Try the following:

> Boomerang!
> What a bang!
> For five minutes, play with
>     the Dracula fangs!

> Dynamite!
> This math is out of sight!
> At recess play with the
>     special class kite!

If stumped for rewards, try letting kids play with Silly Putty, go without shoes, make popcorn, play with a yo-yo, wear a cowboy hat, read a magazine, tell the class a joke, get their picture taken, sit in the beanbag chair. Whichever poetic "gems" you choose, you'll be sure to see a marked difference in student motivation.          *-Donna Raschke*

### RECESS POINTS

Recess points can be used effectively in a behavior modification program to encourage good habits in your students. Give the entire class

one plus point every time they walk quietly through the halls or are especially well-behaved during the day. When they have earned 15 plus points they are entitled to a free 10 minute recess, which should be given to them as soon as the schedule permits. Conversely, you should give the class a minus point whenever they misbehave in any way, and explain that they will lose their regular recess time if they accumulate more than 15 minus points.
                    -Nancy Lorenz

## PERSON-OF-THE-DAY DAISIES
Besides brightening up your classroom, these daisies will help children see their own strengths and recognize other persons' admirable qualities. Each day, choose one child to be the Person of the Day. Cut out large daisy petals from different colors of construction paper and give a petal to each person, including the Person of the Day. Keep one for yourself. Have each child write something he or she likes about the honored student on the petal and sign his or her name at the bottom. Glue the petals together to make daisies, eight petals to one daisy, including the one you've written. Glue a large construction paper circle onto each daisy's center with the Person-of-the-Day's name printed on it. Tack daisies to the bulletin board. Let the special person take them home at the end of the day, after everyone has had a chance to read the petals.
                    -Karen McGillivray

## STAR STUDENTS
One way to help a new student feel at home is to designate him or her as a "Star Student" for a certain period of time. The child fills out a personal data sheet telling about his or her family, likes and dislikes, ambitions, and so on. Another student interviews the "star," and he or she is given a place on the bulletin board for photos and a story about him or

her. Other Star Students can be children with birthdays or those who have accomplished something special. (Try not to omit anyone.) Such recognition does wonders for the self-concept.
                    -Linda Smith

## ALL HANDS ON BOARD
Use this friendly bulletin board to give your students a deserved pat on the back. First trace a giant hand on the board, using an opaque projector, and cut out a crepe-paper sleeve for the arm.

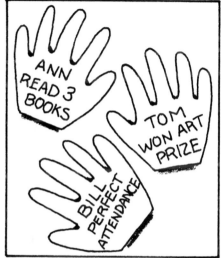

Tack the words "I've got to hand it to you" at the top of the board. Then have students trace their own hands on construction paper, cut the hands out, and sign their names at the bottom of each one. Keep the hands at your desk; when a student does something special write that achievement on his or her hand and tack it to the board for recognition.          -Sue Kreibich

## SUPER WORK
Here's an effective technique to encourage your kids to do their best written work. Positive adjectives like "super," "special," and "terrific" can be found on the advertising pages of newspapers and magazines. Start cutting out these words a few weeks before the start of school and save them in a large envelope. Then, as you review your students' work, glue

one or two of these descriptive words to any papers that merit such praise. As lettering sizes and styles differ from ad to ad, you should be able to add an individual touch to every paper. And if you're lucky enough to find some unusual or not-often-used words for praise, you can help increase your kids' vocabularies as well as their self-esteem. You'll find that papers adorned this way are more likely to be taken home, too!
                    -Joan Mary Macey

## THE BIG PEEL
Purchase a plastic banana or make one from yellow felt. Each day before school begins, place the banana on a different child's desk. That child is then "top banana," enjoying special privileges that day. Make sure pupils understand that good behavior helps determine who will be the next top banana.
                    -Violet Johnson

## GIVE YOUR KIDS A FREEBIE
On the first of every month, I give my students special tickets good for one night free from homework. They can use the tickets once during the month, whenever they choose. This helps to develop personal responsibility. First, if they lose a ticket, it is not replaced; second, each must decide for himself when to take advantage of his/her ticket. It also emphasizes the importance of homework.
                    -Sister Joanne Maskulak

## SPOTLIGHT ON TALENT
This "superstar" center is a great way for children to gain pride in their special talents. Dedicate the center to a different child each week. Children interested in sharing their talents should write a brief summary of their special interests and round up pictures and samples. Choose a class reporter to write a story about the star of the week to highlight the center, and class artists to prepare the center for a display of

the designated star's work. If the talent is a musical one, have kids help in the preparation of a cassette tape. If you have athletes or dancers, use photos of them in action. You may find you have a budding seamstress, poet, or photographer among your students! Whatever their talents, the stars from this center will make your classroom a brighter place! *-Pamela Klawitter*

## STAR OF THE WEEK

Looking for a new way to make each child in your classroom feel like a very special person? Try this "Star of the Week" program, and you'll soon have students feeling better about themselves. Every Friday throughout the year, choose a different child to be the following week's "star." Ask that child to fill out an information sheet containing questions on date and place of birth, eye and hair color, shoe size, number of household pets, and so on. This sheet may also ask for information on favorite foods, colors, school subjects, songs, and television programs. Also ask the child to bring in photographs of him- or herself to be displayed on a "Star of the Week" bulletin board. Along with the photos and completed information sheet, tack bold letters spelling the child's full name and anything else the star would like to share. You might also want to draw the child's silhouette and add that to the display as well. Sometime during the week, have the other members of your class print complimentary statements about the star on index cards and tack them to the bulletin board. Then, at the end of the week, dismantle the display, mount individual pieces on colored construction paper, and staple them together, booklet-style. Let the star take this booklet home so he or she can enjoy a little limelight there, too! *-Wendy J. Vogt*

## STUDENT OF THE WEEK

Try this clever idea for building students' self-concepts this year. Each week, choose a different child to spotlight. That child is to ask two classmates to trace the outline of his or her body on a large sheet of butcher paper. Then, during free time, instruct the three children to color in the outline appropriately, adding details such as hair, facial features, clothes, and so on. When the drawing is completed, tack it to your bulletin board or hang it on any empty wall in your classroom. Make sure to hang the drawing low enough for students to reach. Throughout the week, children are to go to the drawing, and write complimentary statements. *-Sally Braun*

## "J" IS FOR JUNK

Try having a classroom junk box on hand from which students can pick rewards for good behavior, consideration, or excellent work. Cover a cardboard carton with colored self-adhesive paper, then fill it with "junk" you've collected from home, garage sales, and so on, such as old jewelry, cereal box prizes, and other odds and ends with kid appeal. Now, when kids do exceptionally good work, print a big "J" across their papers. "J," of course, stands for junk and means a child may draw a prize from the junk box. Also, print several "J"'s on index cards and place them on students' desks when they've been well-behaved or considerate of others. *-Margaret Chianis*

## BIOGRAPHICAL BOOKLETS

Teachers in the primary grades can help promote their students' self-concepts by writing biographies of them early in the year. Start by conducting individual interviews. Take notes on special things about the child, his or her family, hobbies, and ambitions for adulthood. Preferably using a primary typewriter, type out the items about each child, one to a page, and staple them together book-fashion. Return each book to the child it pertains to and have him or her design a cover and illustrate each page. These books should be available in the classroom all year long so the children can learn more about their classmates and reinforce their understanding of themselves and their own backgrounds as well. At the end of the year, they can take the books home to share with family and friends.

*-Mary Lou Murphy*

## A LOOK INTO ME

A holiday gift students will enjoy giving is a collection of paragraphs with their own illustrations. For instance, write the phrase, ''I feel important when . . .'' and let students answer this in their own way with a picture to go along if they would like. Doing one each day before Christmas vacation, students can compile a great present for parents or simply discover more about themselves. Here are some suggestions: I feel so small when . . . . I really get temperamental when . . . . I'm shy when it comes to . . . . The worst thing I ever ate was . . . . After school I would like to . . . . I wish someday to . . . . I am happiest when . . . . Some of the things I love are . . . .

*-Eleanor D. Baumner*

## AT THE END OF OUR RAINBOW

What would you most like to find at the end of a rainbow, besides the pot of gold? That's the question you should ask your students to kick off this creative classroom project. Have the kids write brief explanations of the objects they'd most like to find at the rainbow's end and why. Then let them illustrate their choices on the same piece of paper. Now make a large construction paper rainbow on your bulletin board under the words, ''At the End of Our Rainbow.'' Display the children's illustrations and explanations around the rainbow. This will give your kids practice in writing for an audience as their creations will be viewed by the entire class. It is also a good way to reinforce higher-level thinking skills. You'll be surprised at how popular the display will be on parents' night, too!

*-Carolyn Wilhelm*

## WHAT A DAY FOR A DAYDREAM

Daydreams can tell a lot about a person. Encourage your children to share their daydreams with the rest of the class with this simple idea. Pass out paper bags and ask students to draw self-portraits on them. Open the side of each bag at the top. Then hang up the bags around the room and ask each student to write about a daydream he or she would like to share with the class. Students then place their stories inside their bags to be pulled out and read at an appropriate time. Kindergartners can put pictures of things they daydream about into their bags, after cutting them out of old magazines. This activity will give you a good idea of the wishes and aspirations of your students. You may even be able to plan classroom activities or field trips around them.

*-Carolyn Wilhelm*

## A VERY SPECIAL WAY TO CELEBRATE

Personal birthday books that are added to throughout the elementary years are a wonderful way to make every child feel special. In kindergarten, students prepare a book called ''All About Me.'' In each child's book place a photograph, birthdate, and other information about favorite foods, books, and pastimes. Also include samples of the child's best work and even a short response to ''The best thing about being 5 is . . .'' and ''I look forward to. . . .'' When the books are finished, put them in a special section of the library, filed by the birthday month and by the ''author's'' last name.

The next year during the month prior to the birthday a child checks out his or her book and adds that year's pages. This is repeated every year at birthday time. Books of children having a birthday in a particular month are put on display in the library for all the students to read. As a child moves or ''graduates'' from elementary school, his or her book can be taken along or donated to the library.

*-Jennifer Byron*

## AT REPORT CARD TIME

At report card time children are told which areas they need to improve in, but a few days later they forget these concerns. That's why I have my students make self-improvement plans after each report card day—to help them remember to take responsibility for their own improvement *all* semester. The plans are folders with covers that read ''I am going to improve my _____,'' with a blank left for children to fill in one appropriate subject, skill, or attitude.

At the end of each day, children enter the date and write what effort they made that day to improve in their particular area. My class's entries included: ''I didn't get hollered at in science today'' and ''I tried being neat in spelling today.''

*-Lois Gasparro*

## FRIENDSHIP WHEEL

Many students know little about their peers. Make this friendship wheel to bring out the interesting facts about your students' lives and to highlight their special knowledge and expertise.

First make a wheel for each student by drawing on a duplicating master a large circle. In the middle of this large circle, draw a small circle about two inches across. Then divide the large circle into eight equal pieces by drawing eight lines from the outside of the inner circle to the edge of the large circle. Number each piece from 1 to 8.

Next write in each piece of the circle or wheel a statement that the children can finish by filling in some information about themselves. Some examples are: If I could be anyone in the world, I'd choose to be . . . . The most dangerous thing I've ever done is . . . . One goal for the future I have is . . . . I have just lately learned that . . . .

Distribute wheels to students and ask them to complete each statement and to sign their names in the small circle in the middle. Then collect the wheels and save the second part of the project for the following day.

On the next day, give the wheels back to students and ask them to find someone in the class who has completed a statement in the same or almost the same way. The person with a similar answer should sign the other student's wheel under the statement that they agree on. Many students will not find other children to sign all of their spots on the wheel, but that will help your discussion later on when you use the results of the friendship wheels to talk about uniqueness and sameness in different people.      *-Joy Lindner*

## DO NOT OPEN UNTIL 2001

Years from now, how will your students look back on the time spent with you? To help jog their memories then, have them prepare posterity booklets today to record highlights of the past school year. This project not only provides an interesting year-end review but also offers the children a chance to ponder their futures—an exercise that will help them examine their current values.

Each booklet should contain a written history of the year in class. Each child can write his or her own after you've discussed highlights of the year as a class, or you can write the history as a class, with each child making contributions.

A posterity booklet can also include mementoes, such as brochures from field trips or athletic awards, examples of the student's best work (prepared, perhaps, as review exercises), messages from friends, and photographs of the class. In addition, the children can insert lists of predictions about what they will be like in the years ahead. What will their style of living be like? Where will they live? What work will they do?

To end the booklet, have students write letters to their future selves describing themselves as they are today—appearance, favorite things, hobbies, thoughts, wishes, and hopes for the future.

Complete the project with a ceremony during which everyone binds a booklet with paper fasteners and seals it with large, colored stickers.

Of course, the covers should read: "Do Not Open Until May 30, 2001."      *-Bob Tomlinson*

## ME . . . IN 20 YEARS

Duplicate or have children make a creative thinking chart. Either way make sure there is a lot of space for children to write their ideas. Explain that at the top of each section on the chart there is a heading. They are to imagine what they will be like in 20 years in each specific area.

| ME... IN TWENTY YEARS | | |
|---|---|---|
| JOB | TRAVELS | POLITICS |
| PETS | WORRIES | FRIENDS |
| APPEARANCE | FAMILY | EDUCATION |

Here are some suggestions for topics: occupation, leisure-time activities, political affiliations, clubs and organizational memberships, pets, education, friends, family, appearance, physical condition, location, future plans, places visited, major accomplishments, disappointments, worries. Have children add to these topics and encourage a classroom discussion after they have had time to think about their answers. You might want to fill one in, too, and share your answers.

*-Dorothy A. Brunette*

## DON'T MISS IT!

Helping absent students keep track of missed assignments will be a breeze with this handy chart. On a large sheet of poster board, glue enough library card pockets for everyone in your class. Label one child's name on each card. Then, as you take attendance each morning, place a colored index card in the pocket belonging to any absentee. You should choose a different student every day to be responsible for these absentees by keeping a record of the day's assignments. Then when the day is over, that child should write the assignments on small slips of paper and place them in the absentees' pockets. This way, when the children return to school, it will be easy to determine what work they've missed. Slips should be removed from the pockets as work is completed. *-Pamela Klawitter*

## HELP HOMEBOUND PUPILS

Tapes are a good way to keep a homebound child in touch with his or her peers. Classmates can record their messages and the teacher can share encouraging thoughts or directions for homework or special projects. Songs sung in class can be taped so that the child can learn them. Special stories, "radio shows," and listening games can all be added.

Another way to keep a homebound child involved is to encourage the class to write him or her letters. Post an envelope, decorated to look like a mailbox, and make a sign that says "Letters to *(name of absent child).*" Or a few children each week can put together a classroom newspaper to send to their classmate. The paper could contain stories about school events, special activities, humorous happenings, and drawings.

During a special unit of study, students can create a scrapbook about the topic, leaving room for the homebound child to make his or her additions. The scrapbook, like the other ideas, will help the homebound children feel that they are members of the class even though they can't be in school.

*-Deborra Murphy*

## GET-WELL SCROLL

A get-well scroll is a pick-me-up for children who are absent on a long-term basis from the classroom. Have the other children find magazine pictures to illustrate their feelings about the absent child. Then have them paste their pictures on either side of a roll of paper and write in a message. Begin the scroll with a message from the teacher.

*-Alice Kazimir*

## PUZZLING ILLNESS

When a student in our class is ill and absent for more than a few days, our class makes a "get well" puzzle. They write "We Miss You" or "Get Well Soon," in the center of a square of poster board and sign their names around it. Then they cut the board into puzzle pieces, put them in a plastic bag, and someone nearby delivers the puzzle to the sick child. *-Margaret Shauers*

## STUDY-BUDDY BADGES

The help you need may be right in your classroom! When a student has to be absent from class for speech, special reading, or due to illness, a study buddy helps explain the lesson missed when he or she returns. Study buddies are students chosen for their understanding of a particular skill. What makes them prize this honor are special badges that proclaim their status.

These can be made with a badge-making kit or simply by cutting paper and laminating. Students can decide what should go on the badge. An example is "I'm a study buddy." Pin them on them

yourself to make it official. Children are very pleased when they are "badged," and often ask, "When Sarah comes back, may I be her study buddy?" An important hint: Spread out your study buddies. This is a good way to boost self-confidence and recognize children who excel in one area while needing help in another. *-Kathy Marcuson*

## STEP INTO MY SHOES

What's it like to be deaf? How does it feel to be blind? Role-playing gives children a chance to find out a little bit about how their handicapped peers really feel. Have children try to perform these everyday tasks blindfolded: **1.** Using plastic glasses and a pitcher, have children try to pour a glass of water and drink it. Can they figure out how to stop pouring before the glass overflows? **2.** Have students tie their shoes. Do they find that they don't really need their sight for this task? **3.** Fill a container with various coins. Can children identify the coins? **4** Have each child find a partner to help him or her move around the classroom. What hidden obstacles might cause problems for a blind classmate?

Simulate loss of hearing with the following activities. **1.** Teach a short lesson with your back to the class and mumble. Then ask questions pertaining to the lesson. What difficulties did children encounter? How did it make them feel? **2.** Have the class write or use only gestures for 15 minutes, then discuss what it's like to communicate without spoken language. **3.** Watch a filmstrip with no sound. What can the class pick up from the film? Follow-up discussion of these activities is a must. Talk about feelings, misconceptions, and what new things children have been made aware of.

*-Pamela Klawitter*

## DEAR TEACHER

Just like adults, children often need to discuss their problems and share their joys. Unfortunately, if you're like most teachers, you don't always have the time to listen. But there is a way for you to stay in touch with your students' personal lives that only takes a few minutes of your time each week—and it's great for reinforcing writing skills, too! Set aside a half hour or so every Friday for your kids to write short, personal letters to you. Encourage them to tell you about their families, friends, hobbies, unusual experiences, fears, joys, and so on. Read the letters when you have a few extra minutes over the weekend, then return them on Monday. Make sure you say a few personal words to each child regarding the content of his or her letter as you return it. You'll be surprised at the insight these letters will give you—and your kids will appreciate your interest, too!

*-Tom Bernagozzi*

## TEACHER'S MAILBAG

Keeping open a student-to-teacher line of communication can prove valuable to both. Although intermediate students often are afraid that talking to the teacher will seem "juvenile," somehow notes are O.K. I hang a Teacher's Mailbag near the door so notes can be dropped in without fuss. It can be any type of container, but a small book bag or tote bag is ideal. All notes must be signed — unsigned notes are trashed — and absolutely no one but the teacher can remove a message. For "disregard first note" messages, keep a clothespin handy on the mailbag handle. Confidentiality is vital. This means taking notes home for disposal and taking action in such a way that no one else can trace a complaint back to any particular

person. It also means asking permission before discussing a note with anyone else — another teacher, the guidance counselor, principal, or parents. Some messages will only call for acknowledgement, others for a sympathetic ear or a frank discussion. Still others will require usual classroom management techniques such as rearranging groups and clarifying misunderstood work. Occasionally a message will clearly call for outside action. You must abide by your rule about asking permission. It is almost always given with little hesitation. The child was asking for help and depending upon you to get it for him or her.          *-Mignon Morgan*

## DIARY OF A TEACHER

Would you like to gain a little insight into what your students are really thinking about their school life? All you need to do is have the kids write a composition on what life would be like for a week as a teacher.

> Dear Diary,
>   Today I decided it was too beautiful a day to keep my poor students inside so we all had playground activity.....

Tap this obvious dimension. You may discover some secrets, likes, dislikes, ideas, and get some surprises. Seeing your world from kid-colored glasses requires a sense of humor, but the experience is well worth trying.
*-Dave Bloom*

## "SMILES THAT MAKE US HAPPY"

Even primary children seem to have days when they are just down in the dumps! So I keep a constant supply of invisible smiles in a "Happy Face Pocket" by my door. When the children seem to need a dose of smiles to pick

them up, I reach into the pocket, grab a handful of invisible smiles, close my eyes and throw the smiles out into the class! The children are instructed to wait with their hands out to catch one and put it on! When I open my eyes I always see a roomful of happy faces looking at me. The "Happy Face Pocket" is also available for individual children to "pick" smiles when they need them or even take them home for others!          *-Joanne Shartle*

## A LETTER FROM TEACHER

Personal letters from you to your students are a good way to foster positive attitudes toward writing. Once or twice a week, compose a short letter to the entire class and post it on your bulletin board. These letters should deal with various aspects of your life, such as how you spend your leisure time, what you ate for dinner the night before, and so on. Ask the children to write back to you in short letters of their own, and after they've shared them with the class, tack them on the bulletin board surrounding your original letter. You'll find that the kids really enjoy hearing about your life outside of school, and you'll be pleased with the improvement in their writing skills as well.
*-Terry Mond*

## ADVICE TO BEGINNERS

As a beginning teacher, I was nervously awaiting the first day of school when a letter from a dedicated teacher for more than 30 years set all my fears to rest. Her advice proved to be so helpful and calming to first-year teachers that I wanted to pass it on. Among her suggestions:

1. Pick a teacher in your grade level and ask him or her everything you are doubtful about.
2. If the principal or supervisor walks into your room to observe, don't lose your cool. Go right on doing what you are doing.
3. Don't let your class go pell-mell down the hall or anywhere else. Choose a good leader and instruct him or her where to stop on the way, while you bring up the rear of the line and are ready to squelch a puncher, kicker, or pincher.
4. Start out right with your class. Be nice, but crack down the minute you need to.
5. Bring a pair of old, comfortable shoes. The halls get long and feet get tired, especially at first.

She attached a list of materials to equip my classroom with, including a workable pencil sharpener, chalk, chalk liner, manuscript letter cards, flag, different kinds of paper, magic markers, gem clips, scotch tape, staples, and a number line. For the first day, the most important tip she gave was to "be pleasant, but speak in a firm, clear voice as you give directions." She also advised me to get the children settled quickly and to ask parents to leave as soon as possible (if they insist on staying, tell them the principal has asked parents to wait in the lobby or cafeteria).

*-Agnes E. Smith*

## PEOPLE OF THE MONTH

All too often, special education students don't really get to know school administrators, nurses, librarians, custodians, and other nonteaching staff members. Here's a way for you to introduce these students to unfamiliar personnel that will guarantee the establishment of good feelings among all concerned. Special students can research, develop, write, and distribute a "People of the Month" magazine which contains brief interviews with different school personnel.

Have each child choose a person to research and interview. The student must then write a short letter to the individual of his or her choice, requesting an interview appointment and explaining that information gained from the interview will be published in a special "magazine." While waiting for a response, have the child research the job description of his or her subject and develop a series of questions that will provide a framework for the interview. (Of course you'll have to offer a lot of guidance to the children throughout this activity, but don't overdo it.) After the interviews are completed, help the children compile their notes and compose brief paragraphs about their subjects to be printed or typed on masters. Have the students work in groups to design a cover for their booklet, print a title page, and create riddles, puzzles, illustrations, and any other types of "fillers" for the magazine.

Each month, when the magazine is ready to be distributed, plan a little "publishing party." Each student involved must design and deliver two invitations—one to his or her subject and one to another member of the faculty or administrative staff. At the reception, have the children play host to their guests by serving them refreshments and presenting each with an autographed copy of the magazine. This activity is sure to have positive results, with students, staff members, and administrators becoming aware of each other in a pleasurable way.

*-Roberta G. Locascio*

## NURTURING A NEW TEACHER

Help a first-year teacher settle smoothly into his or her new career.

1. Establish an advisory council for new teachers. If a network of at least three experienced staff personnel doesn't exist in your school for this purpose, join with your principal and set one up! Why? A new teacher will know that someone is always there willing to help. Some new teachers may prefer someone assigned specifically to them.
2. Express empathy. Let a new teacher know in a pleasant, even humorous way that he or she isn't the first to experience disruptive students, unsuccessful lesson plans, and general beginning-of-the-year chaos. Share how you handled the situation. Just realizing that these experiences are not unique can be the first step to building self-confidence.
3. Encourage attendance at professional meetings. Take a new teacher along with you when you go. Young teachers can share experiences and ideas with their peers and learn many valuable tips, along with making new friends.
4. Suggest community involvement. Sharing interesting classroom activities with the community is a way to build public support and enthusiasm for future projects. Suggest that the teacher invite parents to speak to their class or help with a project. Share other successful methods.
5. Give verbal encouragement. Genuine interest, recognition, and praise will encourage new teachers and help them keep going when the going gets rough. Urge new teachers to tell you their accomplishments.

*-Eva Kirkpatrick*

# Bulletin Boards

Any wall can be fun to look at with a colorful, well-designed bulletin board. And any bulletin board is better when kids have a chance to participate in creating it. Here are many examples of bulletin boards you'll want to make with your class at the beginning of the year, through Halloween, and on into winter and spring. We've also included INSTRUCTOR favorites for reading, language arts, and math. Hope you like them, and remember — let your bulletin boards do the working.

A TIME TO GET GROWING

RON  MEG  DAN  FRAN  KIM

## A-CORNY WELCOME

This "nutty" bulletin board display will ease first-day nerves. Cut out a large squirrel from red or orange construction paper and acorns from brown paper. Write each child's name on an acorn, and staple the squirrel and acorns to the board, under the words "This is 'a-corny' way to welcome you." Add a white poster board sign for the squirrel to hold with a friendly greeting on it. Now pass out paper to students and have them write "a corny" riddle question without including the

"A-CORNY" WELCOME TO YOU!

JIM  LIZ  TOM

PAM  MARK  HELLO! AND WELCOME!  KATE

SUE

answer. Staple each child's riddle under his or her acorn. Let children go to the board, read a question, and seek out that person to learn the answer to the riddle.  -Rebecca Friary

## SEPTEMBER GARDEN

To make this September bulletin board, cut out a flower for each child in the class. On the leaf of each flower, print a child's name. The caption should read: "September—a time to get growing."

A figure in the corner can be a gardener with a watering can. Ask each child to bring a photograph or draw a picture of his or her face to paste on one of the flowers. Put a picture of your own face on the gardener's figure.

For a variation, add to each flower a second leaf on which you can attach flower stickers for especially good work. Or, each child might want to display a special project near his or her flower.  -Vivian Lynn

## WISHING WELL

Encourage your students to make their new school year's resolutions with this beginning-of-the-year bulletin board. Make a wishing well from brown construction paper, drawing in tiles with heavy black pen, and a

bell in the center from sandpaper. Give the well a base of gray construction paper stones and title the board "Here's Wishing You Well All Year Long." Have each child write what he or she hopes to accomplish this year, write his or her name on the back, and put it in or around the "well." Save these "wishes" until the end of the school year, and see how many of your students kept their resolutions even after the bulletin board was changed.
-Rebecca Friary

HERE'S WISHING YOU WELL ALL YEAR LONG!

DO HOMEWORK  BE POLITE  BE HELPFUL  BE NEAT  BE ON TIME  BE KIND

## HOMEWORK PETS

Here's a bulletin board that will keep track of kids' homework for you! Ask each student to choose his or her favorite animal and draw a medium-sized (6″ by 8″ works well) outline of it. More than one child may select the same animal. Show the class how to divide animals into numerous sections, puzzle-style, using a dark marker or crayon. They may draw faces if desired, and each pet should have a collar with its owner's name clearly marked. When students have completed homework to the teacher's satisfaction, they may color in any one space on the pet. Students will work diligently on their homework assignments as no one wants to be left with an incomplete pet!  *-Mary Ann Pecci*

## WHERE DO YOU LIVE?

Help young students learn their own addresses and those of their classmates. Place a construction paper replica of your school in the middle of the bulletin board and give each child materials to create a model of his or her own home, labeling it with name and address. If yours is a neighborhood school, you might try to place homes on the board according to location. Include other area landmarks.
*-Carolyn Luetje*

## COLOR HELPS

This bulletin board keeps track of students' weekly jobs. Each crayon box is labeled with a responsibility: watering plants, helping in the library, and so on; and each child has a paper crayon with his or her name printed on the front. To assign jobs each week, I collect all the crayons, mark on the back of the crayon which job the student did

that week (so I don't reassign that job to him or her again soon), and then put the crayons into new boxes.

I can see at a glance which child is doing what job. This year I also made a crayon can to hold the

extra crayons. Should I see a need to create a new job in my classroom, I simply add another crayon box.   *-Mary Saranpaa*

### BUBBLING WITCH TALES

Stir up reading excitement with this October reading bulletin board. Each caldron is really a pocket for a Halloween-related book, a Halloween story starter, or a scary tale written by someone in your room. Children can use the board for reading and writing ideas as well as for sharing their tales with others.

-Karen Falk

### ADD-ON PUMPKINS

Use this Halloween display to motivate your kids to complete special assignments. Have each child make a plain orange pumpkin with his or her name attached and pin it to the bulletin board. As assignments are completed, the kids may add eyes, noses, and mouths to their pumpkins until they've all become jack-o'-lanterns. -Gail Madden

### SPOOKTACULAR

Turn your students into *Ghostbusters* with a bulletin board that encourages research skills. Draw a ghost pattern in a size appropriate for your bulletin board, and enlist student help in cutting out and drawing eyes on a large number of the ghosts. Cover an empty cereal box with black paper and decorate with the popular *Ghostbusters* symbol. Attach the box to the bulletin board to hold the "trapped" ghosts.
Write a question on the back of each ghost. Questions can relate to class subjects or to trivia about ghosts and Halloween. Keep a supply of additional ghosts to replace those "trapped" by the students. To trap a ghost, a student picks one from the board, researches the answer, writes the answer on the front, signs his or her name, and deposits the ghost in the trap.
You can check the box, or have students do it. You might want to

keep track of not only who has done the most trapping, but who has the most correct answers. Encourage children to contribute their own ghostly questions for classmates to solve. -Kelly Riley

241

## WINTER WORKSHOP

Here's a winter learning and display center to brighten your room. Divide the space into sections where children can share holiday cards, find winter indoor and outdoor projects, announce holiday plans. You can even have a winter poetry section, sports and games, and winter art. Keep this bulletin board up all season—simply change the sections when needed. Children will enjoy thinking of new sections.

*-Nancy Camarigg*

## A LOVE OF BOOKS

Encourage your students to develop a love of books with this Valentine's Day bulletin board. Cut large hearts out of red construction paper. Then tape or staple a book cover in the middle of each red heart. You can make lace to put around the hearts by gathering strips of white crepe paper and pasting them around the edge of each heart. The title I use for this bulletin board is "Put

Your Heart Into Reading." I also place a small Cupid at the top of the board for a loving touch. Cut out the Cupid from a sheet of red construction paper.

*-Nancy Camarigg*

## WHAT IS LOVE?

Let children provide definitions of love; you provide the space. Back your bulletin board with red or white paper and tack on an envelope containing pink hearts. Also attach a writing pen to the board. At the top write "Love is . . ." You and your class can provide the first answers, then invite everyone in the school to join in—custodians, librarians, the principal, secretaries, and other teachers. Your board will be layered with boundless ideas for this valentine month.

*-Tara Hoffman*

## MEMORABILIA BOARD

Here's a wistful way to end the year that will leave you with an attractive bulletin board display for the last few weeks of school. Search your closet or storage room for remaining parts of every monthly or seasonal bulletin board display you used during the year. For instance, you might find a schoolhouse from September, a jack-o'-lantern from October, a turkey from November, and so on. Arrange these remnants along the perimeter of your bulletin board. When they've been assembled on the board, pass out strips of colored construction paper and ask your kids to write brief reflections on the past year—about special projects, field trips, amusing experiences, and anything else they can remember. If you or the students have saved "souvenirs" from any of these events, add them to the display. The result will be a collage of memories that will remind your kids of the happy times they spent together.

*-Donna Inanen*

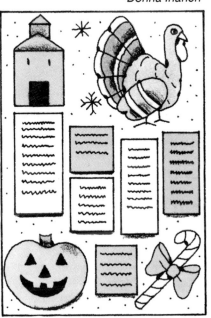

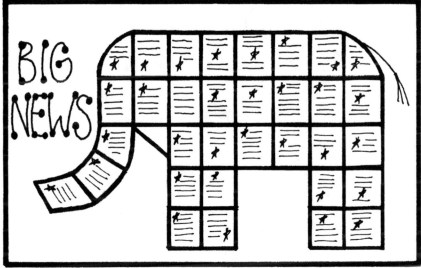

## BIG NEWS

If you would like to show off your students' work in a pleasing way but have little artistic talent, this bulletin board is for you. This elephant is constructed very simply, from 34 pieces of 8- by 11-inch gray construction paper arranged as the diagram shows. The only cutting you'll need to do to make the curves is around the head and tail and under the trunk. On each full sheet of gray paper, mount one of your students' works—stories, essays, or artwork. If you don't have enough students to cover each sheet, just leave those sheets blank. If you have more students, display their work around the elephant on gray or colored paper.    *-Jane T. Adams*

## WHAT A CATCH!

Tired of tacking up papers on bulletin boards? Try stringing fishnet in the corner of your room and let children use clothespins to hang up work that they are proud of. Materials can be easily put up or taken down. This is also a good place to hang school and classroom announcements.

*-Lori Blacksher*

## SUNNY BUNNY

What is a classroom in spring without a big white bunny and colorful construction-paper eggs? How about a rabbit painting a large egg with other multi-colored eggs nestled in a large yellow basket and in strips of green grass. The eggs are not only

cheerful and decorative but useful, too. On the back of each write a seasonal story title such as "The Special-Delivery Bunny," and "The Bunny Who Overslept." Children choose their title and write an "egg-citing" story to match        *-Nancy Camarigg*

## TAKE ME TO YOUR READER

You've probably often used a map, diagram, or picture in a bulletin board display related to a topic you're studying. Use these "content" displays to promote reading as well. For example, a bulletin board to accompany a social studies unit on regions of the world could have the title "Travel around the world in books." Along with maps and pictures, display covers of books that represent the parts of the world being studied (*Born Free, Heidi*). When you design a bulletin board to accompany a science unit on the solar system, save space for this alien and his book companions!   —*Alan M. Frager*

## GO BANANAS READING BOOKS

This is what your students will do when they are given opportunities to share their reading on this appealing bulletin board. Begin with any color background except yellow. From brown construction paper, draw and cut out a picture of a monkey holding a book; tack it to the board under the words "Go Bananas Reading Books." Then have each child cut out a large banana from yellow construction paper and draw a face at the top, with the title, author, and a short synopsis of the book he or she has read underneath. Attach bananas to board, and encourage kids to continue to keep the monkey well fed!   —*Kathleen Cullen Weisenborn*

## A CLASS OF BOOKWORMS

Celebrate the ouside-of-class reading your students have done this year with this bulletin board. The two bookworms in this picture are made from brown construction paper. Label each section of the worms with the name of one of the children in your class. After the child's name, write the number of books he or she has read this school year. If you have made outside reading a competition, you can place the sections in order, with the child who has read the most books closest to the worm's head. The children can take their personal parts of the bookworm home with them at the end of the year.   —*Ruth Neimeyer Dale*

## GREEN THUMB READING CLUB

Use this bulletin board and reading club to improve reading skills and encourage children to share and enjoy reading. Have kids trace one of their hands on colored contruction paper, cut out, and place on the green Thumb Tree. The tree can be a large tree branch or a paper tree attached to your bulletin board. The cutout hands are the leaves. Provide a suggested reading list. Every time a child finishes reading a book, he or she fills out a short form with the title, author, short resume and critique, and parent's signature. After five books have been read, the child earns a ring for his or her paper hand. When 10 books are read, the child receives a green thumb.   —*Judy Nichols*

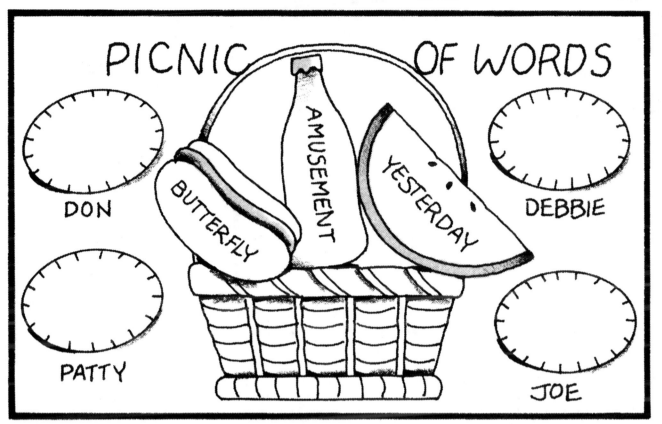

## PICNICS AND FROGS

The best bulletin board is one that children can interact with. Let them write on it, add objects to complete it, and manipulate the objects on it. Here are two with a summertime flavor.

Around a big paper picnic basket are paper plates, each identified with a child's name. In the basket are words printed on cutout shapes of hot dogs, watermelon, and pop. Each child gets a chance to fill his or her plate by drawing a word from the basket and reading the word aloud. The next child takes a turn when the first student misses a word.

For the second bulletin board, draw a big hoppy frog who will jump from lily pad to lily pad when a child reads the new vocabulary word on each pad. The caption can read: Knowing all these words makes my hoppy.

*-Dorothy Paulsen*

## BUILD A SNOWMAN

Give your kids practice in identifying antonyms with this manipulative bulletin board display. Start with a solid blue background, then arrange a piece of thick, white yarn on the board to form the outline of a snowy hill. Now make several snowmen from two construction paper circles each—a large circle for the body, and a smaller one for the head. Attach a hat to each head. Print one word on the body of each snowman, and its antonym on the corresponding head. When finished, scatter the snowmen's bodies and heads randomly on the hill and label the display, "Build a snowman." Instruct kids to build their snowmen by matching the bodies with the heads. *-Marilyn Burch*

## SYNONYMS ON RYE

Here's a bulletin board your students can really sink their teeth into! First cut out shapes that resemble sandwich parts from construction paper; use tan paper for the buns, brown for meat, green for lettuce and so on. On each of two or three bun bottoms, print a word. Place these on the board. Put all the "sandwich parts" in small envelopes along the side of the board. Then, to build a sandwich,

students choose fillings from the envelopes and print words on them that mean the same as the word on the bun. Kids then add these fillings to the sandwich, stacking it higher and higher. When children have run out of words, print a word yourself on a bun top. *-Kelly Riley*

Here's a simple game for practice in identifying angles. Students use their arms to demonstrate straight angle, right angle, acute angle, obtuse angle, and ray. The teacher selects a student to demonstrate an angle. That student then chooses a classmate who identifies the angle being demonstrated by the first student. If the second student's answer is correct, he or she then demonstrates an angle and chooses another student to identify

the angle he or she is demonstrating. If the second pupil's answer is wrong, someone else is chosen to name the angle. As a variation, try an "angle" version of Simon Says, letting children take turns being Simon. Use stick figures for a bulletin board which demonstrates these angles.          -Janet Monroe

## TRASH CAN FACTS

Oscar the Grouch invites students to practice their math facts on this "trashy" bulletin board. Trash cans are made of tagboard covered with aluminum foil and labeled with a number. Pieces of trash are also cut from tagboard and placed in the large trash can Oscar is peering out of. An addition or subtraction fact is written on each piece of trash. Students take turns picking a piece of trash, computing the answer, checking their answers with the one written on the back, then placing the piece of trash in the trash can with the correct number on it. When Oscar's trash can is empty, let children "take the garbage out" by emptying the numbered cans.     -Anne Tenerelli

## ON CLOUD NINE

This windy month, let your students fly their own airplanes and at the same time help them reinforce math skills. On a light blue background, glue tufts of cotton in nine horizontal rows. Write a math fact on 3" x 5" cards and attach one underneath each cloud. Then have each student

cut out an airplane from a different color of construction paper and print his or her name on it. Then, starting at the bottom row of clouds, students take turns "flying" their planes over the clouds as they answer each math fact correctly. If a child gives a wrong answer, his or her plane must remain above that cloud while someone else takes a turn. When a student has answered all facts correctly, he or she may place the plane in its stratospheric hangar above all the clouds.
-Dorothy Paulsen

*On Cloud Nine*

$5 \times 5 =$  $2 + 3 =$  $1 + 3 =$  $2 + 2 =$  $5 + 7 =$

$9 - 1 =$  $3 + 5 =$  $9 \times 2 =$  $7 + 1 =$  $8 - 2 =$

$4 + 3 =$  $2 \times 2 =$  $7 \times 6 =$  $8 + 1 =$  $1 + 2 =$

# Craft Ideas

Let's make something! Kids love to, and you will, too, with these craft projects made from readily available supplies. You might want to send home a letter to parents asking for contributions of plastic packing pieces, cardboard, paper tubes, wood scraps, and anything else that looks like it might inspire the imagination. And let the kids experiment and have fun. This is just a beginning to the many discoveries your class will make as students explore the 3-dimensional world of art.

# Craft Ideas

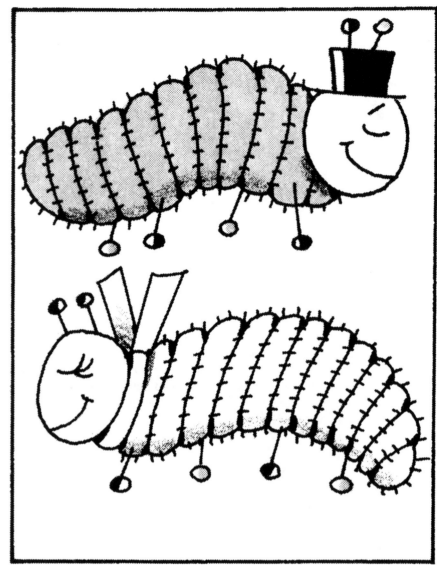

another effect, students can limit the colors to two or three crayons, then alternate those colors on the page.
*-Sally Stempinski*

## SCHOOL BANNER

A BANNER year is ahead! Help develop children's school spirit by having them design banners representative of their school. Make banners from construction paper; encourage kids to use a variety of lightweight decorations, such as magazine pictures, colorful cutouts, yarn, cotton balls. Now glue plastic straws at the top of the banner for support. Run yarn or cord through the straws and tie it, and your banner is ready to hang. *-Jacqueline Koury*

## FOLD AND DRAW SNOWFLAKES

Create beautiful snowflakes using carbon and thin white paper. Put carbon facedown on paper. Fold

together into quarters. You will use only two corners for your design. Start by drawing one snowflake point from the open corner to the middle. Use the longer folded edge to draw half a point along the fold. Inside your points, draw simple designs. Unfold, and remove carbon. Cut out your complete six-point snowflake. *-Richard Latta*

## A BRANCH FOR ALL SEASONS

A bare branch became a thing of beauty in my overcrowded classroom. The first project planned was the making of tissue butterflies. We used clothespins

## FURRY CATERPILLAR FAMILY

You can make funny, furry caterpillars from plastic-foam packing ''peanuts,'' straight pins, and colored pipe cleaners. Choose plastic-foam curls with one rounded, head-shaped end. On each curl, draw a happy face on the end with felt-tipped pens, and just behind the eyes stick in two round-headed pins. (Pins should stick up half an inch above the head and can be made more solid if you drip a little paste into the pin hole and then replace the pin.) Now anchor the end of a pipe-cleaner under the caterpillar's chin. Wind the pipe cleaner around the body, working toward the tail, and spread a little paste as you work to hold the

pipe cleaner securely. When paste is dry, give each caterpillar pin legs and feet. Hats and scarves add charm to this furry family! *-Jane K. Priewe*

## NAME ART

Intermediate students will enjoy making their names colorful with this beginning-of-the-year art project.

Instruct students to use crayon to write their names in cursive across the center of a piece of paper. Then have them select a different color crayon to trace around their names, outlining exactly the shapes of the letters. Continue this process, using different-color crayons, until the page is completely covered. For as the insect's head, abdomen, thorax and had a built-in spring for attaching our winged beauties to the limb. Presto, a butterfly bush emerged!

We have since painted and sprayed the branch with many different colors of paint, and once, wound it with strips of purple crepe paper, so we could hang clusters of green grapes on it for a little fantasyland program the children did.

In the autumn, our branch is hung with painted leaves. As Halloween approaches, we shroud it with hosts of ghosts made by placing a wad of cotton in the center of a white facial tissue, looping a rubber band around it for a head, and using a black felt pen to draw circles for the eyes and mouth. We attached modeling-clay fruits for Thanksgiving, shiny decorations for Christmas, and cutout snowflakes for January. February found a "valentine bush" in our corner. March called for shamrocks. Truly, our branch became a very necessary fixture in our classroom.

*-June Masters Bacher*

## WAYS WITH WALLPAPER

If you are fortunate enough to have acquired several out-of-date wallpaper sample books, here are five suggestions for their use in your classroom.

**1.** Have students make jackets for individual storybooks they write and illustrate themselves.

**2.** Cut the sturdiest samples into lettering for your bulletin boards.

**3.** Have children arrange cutouts of textured samples underneath thin art paper and rub with crayons or chalk for unique designs.

**4.** Cover coffee cans, orange juice containers, or small boxes with a little bit of rubber cement and the most vivid sample colors. Use to store small items.

**5.** Decorate puppets, masks, and sacks with the scraps that are left.

*-Alicia Kazimir*

## COMB IT OUT

A unique tool for your elementary art corner is the common pocket comb. Have children dip yarn or string in tempera and lay it on shiny paper like finger-paint paper. Pick up the yarn and "comb" the scroll formed with the wet yarn into a spread-out wispy abstract design. This is fun and the results are often attractive. Comb patterns into thick coatings of finger paint for an entirely different effect. Don't forget to wash comb after use.

*-Joan Mary Macey*

## BE A THUMBUDDY

Encourage students' creativity with this simple art project. Begin by making a construction paper frame for each student by cutting the center out of each piece of construction paper and gluing lighter weight paper to the back. Instruct the children to press their thumbs onto an ink pad, then make their imprints on the lightweight paper inside each frame. They can make just one or two prints or as many as they please. Then ask them to turn all the thumbprints into strange creatures, animals, people, flowers, and so on, using thin markers or colored pencils. These framed thumbprints can be shared with the entire school on a Be a Thumbuddy bulletin board. And they can be given as personalized gifts. *-Anne Pacheco*

## SPOONIES

Put those wooden ice-cream spoons from school lunches to use long after all the ice cream has disappeared.

Rinse each carefully and allow to dry thoroughly. (A damp stick will warp.) Prior to art period, have a brief discussion on birds. List the ones students may have seen in the area, the sounds they make, and talk about how they walk on the ground. You might include a creative writing activity on, "If I Were a Crow" or "Bye, Bye

Blackbird" just for fun. Next, give each child a piece of paper, one wooden spoon, and a few scraps of colored paper. Then let him or her go to work on making his or her own bird. *-Sharon Rankin*

## THE EYES HAVE IT

We recognize the need for "story starters"; why not have some "picture starters" to help launch your reluctant artists into art activity. One of my most successful "starters" is a small box of moveable plastic eyes which I purchased at a craft store. I pass two eyes to each child, and kids draw the animal or person that belongs to the eyes. Some clever youngsters have drawn two figures, side view, so that each has one eye! Eyes are easy to glue in place. *-Anthony Flores*

# Craft Ideas

### READING, RUBBING, AND SMELLING

Rub-and-smell pictures or books are easy and exciting to create. As a culminating art project for a unit on color and flavor, my students drew simple outline pictures with colored markers. We spread a heavy coat of white

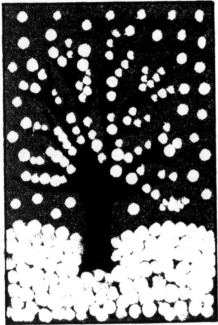

glue over each picture and smoothed it with a finger. We then sprinkled unsweetened soft drink powder over the glue and rubbed it in. It dissolved and left a fragrance, after it dried. Kids delighted in reading, rubbing, and smelling books.        -Doris Crook

### A TIP ON THE WEATHER!

Painting snow can be almost as much fun as playing in it! On a middle tone (any shade that contrasts with both black and white) background, use a brush and black paint to draw a winter scene. Let dry. Next, use a cotton swab dipped in white tempera paint to dab on "snow." Distance can be varied between dots for both solid and airy effects.
        -Vlasta Krieger

### MATCH THE SHADES

Red and yellow and...mauve and burnt sienna. Do kids know their color shades? To make a mix-and-match color game, first ask your local paint store for color sample strips in many shades. Take two strips of each color. Paste one strip of each color on the left side of squares of oaktag or poster board. Cut the other strip into individual color samples and store in a plastic bag. In free time, children match the shades, one to one. Have kids compare their names for the shades with the paint store's names.
        -Linda M. Mercer

### ART'S ALIVE

Students are often asked to imitate the style or subject matter of a certain artist, but seldom are they asked to recreate the physical context in which an artist worked. Make art history come alive—have your students put themselves in the shoes of Michelangelo!
Michelangelo painted the ceiling of the Sistine Chapel. Describe to your class the chapel and Michelangelo's daily climb up the scaffolding. Discuss the difficulties the artist must have dealt with, such as dripping paint and tired arms. Then show pictures of the chapel ceiling—students will be astounded! Now ask students to pretend that they are Michelangelo. Have them tape paper to the bottom of their desks and lie on their backs under their desks. The paper now becomes their "ceiling!" (Moving all chairs to the edge of the room is helpful.) Pass out felt-tip markers (they won't drip and possibly injure pupils' eyes) and have pupils try creating their own upside down masterpieces.
        -Laurie Parrish-Storm

### DON'T THROW AWAY BROKEN CRAYONS!

Use them instead to create beautiful abstract window decorations by ironing crayon shavings between a folded sheet of waxed paper. Have your students bring empty egg cartons from home. Gather your broken crayons, peel off any remaining paper, and use crayon or small pencil sharpeners to shave each color into an egg-carton cup. Now lay a heavy newspaper padding on top of an ironing board or other suitable surface. Cover the base of the iron with heavy foil, folding it tightly up around the sides. Set the temperature at medium and turn off steam setting.
Tear sheets of waxed paper 18" to 24" long and fold each one in half. Place a loose sheet of newspaper on top of your padding and lay a folded sheet of waxed paper on top. Then sprinkle 1/4 tsp. of several colors of shavings between the waxed paper, near the fold. Move the iron slowly over the fold; as the colors spread and blend, press outward in all directions, sealing the edges of the paper. Lift the top sheet of newspaper and use it to place the creation aside to cool. Finally, cut construction paper frames. You'll have the makings for a glittering mobile or window display, as bright as a rainbow!        -Emma Ruth Henry

### DEEP SEA MOBILES

These shimmering mobiles made from simple wire coat hangers would make a perfect accompaniment to a study of the ocean. Holding the handle of the coat hanger, pull the horizontal wire downward, changing the triangular shape into a diamond. Have kids design and color fish, animals, ships, people, or anything else found under the ocean, on white paper that will fit inside the hanger frame. Cut blue cellophane to cover the frame and tape into place. Now glue underwater scenes facedown onto the blue water. Finally, cut 8 one-inch-wide black strips of construction paper to glue onto front and back of hanger, forming a picture frame and covering up rough edges where the cellophane was fastened to hanger. Hang mobile so the light shines behind it, and it will look just like an underwater scene.

*-C. M. Armstrong*

## PUNCH HAPPY

Got a few hole punchers in your supply closet? If so, let your kids use them for an impromptu art project that will make everyone punch happy! Give each of your students two sheets of construction paper in complementary colors and instruct them to draw a simple design or shape in pencil on one of the sheets. Now have them punch holes along their pencil outlines, making sure they don't punch them too close together. Each child should then mount his or her punched outline on the second sheet of construction paper, so the complementary color shows through the holes. What to do with all those punched out circles that are left over? Collect and store them in a paper bag or shoe box. Then, when kids have free time, they can use their imaginations to arrange the circles in attractive patterns on construction paper.

*-Jacqueline Armin*

## SNEAKER PRINTS

Here's some fun spring geometry for intermediate grades. Have children just coming in from recess step onto manila paper, making sneaker prints one foot at a time. Outline each print with black markers. Color in each of the shapes in the print with different colors. Color the right and left foot in an identical way. Mount the prints on black construction paper and hang as a bulletin board. Have each child

use an index card to look at his or her own shoes. List all the geometric shapes in the prints (circles, squares, triangles). Take turns reading the geometric descriptions and see if children can identify which pair you are talking about. *-Marilyn Siegel*

## GET MORE OUT OF MOBILES

There's no question about it: kids *love* to make mobiles! And these popular displays can certainly do a lot to perk up your classroom. But any teacher knows how time-consuming it can be to take down old mobiles and replace them with new ones throughout the year. Here's a simple idea that will save you from climbing that stepladder more than once. Hang one heavy string from your ceiling for each child in your class and fasten a paper clip to the end of every string. Make sure these strings hang low enough for your children to reach. Now, when it's time to change the mobiles, simply have the kids remove the old ones and attach new ones to the paper clips. *-Connie Pribbeno*

## CATERPILLAR THRILLER

Here's a three-day art project to culminate a primary science unit on the metamorphosis of the monarch butterfly.
Gather together egg cartons, paint, and pipe cleaners to make the caterpillars. Discard the top of each cardboard egg carton and cut the bottom part in half lengthwise. Give each pupil one half of an egg carton. Have kids turn the strip of cups upside down and paint the outside of the cups to represent the caterpillar's body. The first cup should be the head. Have pupils paint eyes and attach pipe cleaners as antennas to the heads. When caterpillars

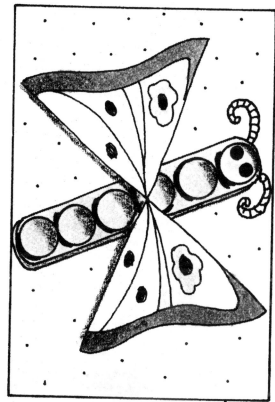

are dry, staple an oval piece of light green paper around each one to represent the chrysalis. The following day, give each child two triangular sheets of waxed paper. Instruct pupils to decorate their waxed paper to look like wings, using cotton swabs and melted crayons. After the pupils have left for the day, remove chrysalises to surprise them with beautiful butterflies the next day.

*-Gloria Bayes*

## INK BLOT DESIGNS

In no time at all, your classroom can be ablaze with color from inkblot designs your children make themselves. Start by mixing dry tempera paint with liquid starch until it resembles the consistency of finger paint. You'll want to supply several different colors for your kids to choose from. Now give each child a sheet of white construction paper, folded crosswise, then opened. Have the kids choose one central color each and drop about 1/2 teaspoon of it onto the center of their folds. Then instruct the children to drop smaller blobs of two different colors in a semi-circle around it. Students should refold their papers and use their fingertips to spread the paint outward and upward from the center of the fold, making sure that no paint squirts out of the sides. When the paint is dry, let your kids color the paper around the design.  *-Aileen M. LeBlanc*

### AND HERE'S THE RUB...
To do a rubbing of any kind is to instantly understand the meaning of texture. One of the most effective objects to use for a rubbing is, believe it or not, a plastic doily. For a unique treatment, place black paper on

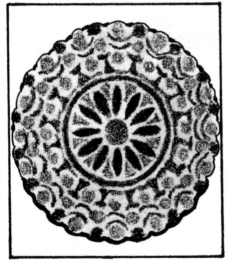

the doily and rub the surface with the side of a metallic crayon. Fill in some of the completed rubbing with a heavy colored crayon or oil pastel. This gives a rich, stained-glass look. Try cutting around the rubbing and mounting it on a contrasting background.
*-Ireene Robbins*

### FOR THE BIRDS
Here's an idea for an art project that's just right for early fall. Your kids will enjoy working with natural materials—and the birds around your school will be happy about it, too! You'll need to

purchase bags of unpopped corn, sunflower seeds, nuts, grain, oats and so on. All these things are available at grocery stores for reasonable prices. Now have each child bring in the lid to a shoebox and provide a few yourself in case anyone forgets. Make a paste of flour and water, and let the kids go to work on arranging the all-natural edibles, collage-style, on their shoebox lids. They can make abstract designs if desired, or representations of things relating to fall. For instance, unpopped corn may be used to make corn stalks, sunflower seeds to design a miniature sunflower, grains of wheat to represent a field, and so on. If your school is in a rural area, you might want to take the kids on a walk around the grounds so they can collect materials for this project themselves. Display the finished products in your classroom for a day or two, then take them outside for the birds to enjoy.
*-Ruth Ann Johnson*

### DESIGN OF THE YEAR
A new year always means new numbers to remember. How many times in January do you forget and write the wrong year on a check or letter? Here is an attractive art activity to help impress that new date on everyone's mind. Use the numerals of the new year to create a beautiful posterlike design. Draw the numerals as thick, overlapping and/or touching shapes which divide the paper into interesting areas. Fill in all the spaces and the numerals

themselves with clear, heavily crayoned color. Use only three or four colors to avoid a too-busy look. These are handsome when hung.  *-Dorothy Gordon*

### PEANUT CREATURES
Let children experiment gluing peanuts together in different and unusual animal shapes. Paint with fluorescent colors and use glass beads or paper punch dots for eyes. Paint or draw suitable backgrounds for this nutty menagerie, then display.
*-James W. Perrin*

### A DOZEN A YEAR
Pastel egg cartons make pretty calendars. Each section represents a month. Cut symbols for months from greeting cards, gift wrap, or magazines. Make sure these are small enough to glue into the compartments. Glue a bit of cotton behind each symbol to raise it before positioning. Tape paper flaps over individual sections, and letter names of months on them. Remove the flaps as months change.  *-Barbara Conrady*

### PASS THE COOKIES!
Make a pretty cookie-passing plate for summer picnics by using a dipped-and-dyed paper coffee filter. For dye, use food colorings diluted with a little water. Fold the filter into halves, quarters, or eighths, then dip the different sections in the dyes. Open carefully and let dry. Now refold and cut out designs "snowflake style." Place the completed "doily" on a paper plate, brush with liquid starch, dry, and you're ready to serve!  *-Margaret Kolak*

### CREATE YOUR OWN CROSS-STITCH!
Use graph paper as a guide for stitching on plastic foam trays. Cut your graph paper to the size

of the tray, tape it down, and "X" in your design on the paper. Using a blunt-ended needle and fine yarn, stitch right through the paper and the tray. Carefully pull away the graph paper when you are finished removing any pieces "stuck" under the stitches with the end of the needle.

*-Jane Charland*

## A FURRY FRIEND

Introduce simple sewing techniques to your students with this mouse puppet. Cut a 4-inch

circle from fake-fur fabric. Fold the circle in half, fur sides together, and sew the curved edge shut. Cut a 1-inch slit at one end of the fold and turn the mouse furry side out. Add a tail, nose, ears, and eyes of your choice. Put your index finger in the slit, and move your furry friend about! *-Mary Ann Panko*

## GRAB-BAG ART

This art activity will give your students plenty of creative challenge and will provide you with a neat way to make use of leftover art materials and any other scraps. You'll need enough brown lunch bags for every child in your class. Fill each bag with odds and ends from your art table such as scrap paper, pipe cleaners, empty thread spools, foam packing pieces, Popsicle sticks, yarn, straws, and so on. Each bag should hold a different combination of items. Staple each bag shut and place them all together in a large, plastic garbage bag labeled "Grab a bag!" Pass the garbage bag around the room and have each child close his or her eyes and choose one paper bag. The challenge is to create something using only those materials found in the bag. (Make sure kids also understand that they must use *all* the items.) You might want to make this a timed activity and allow students 15 or 20 minutes for their creations. *-Anne Pacheco*

## PERSONALIZED PUPPETS

Make puppets your students can really "relate" to. Start by taking head and shoulder photographs of each child. Next, cut puppet bodies from stiff cardboard, leaving off the head. Glue on clothes cut from old scraps of material. Then paste the photographs to the puppets' bodies. Be sure to cut around the children's heads so backgrounds don't show. Finally, glue wooden dowels to the backs of the puppets so the kids can hold on to them. Their personalized puppets are ready to perform.

*-Janet Mallery*

## A TREEFUL OF BIRDS

Show your class pictures of exotic birds, and discuss their brilliant colors and unique shapes. Have children use bright felt-tipped markers to draw their own and then cut them out. Mount on a large tree cut from wood-grained paper. Encourage children to make different-sized birds. *-James W. Perrin*

# Craft Ideas

## IMAGINATION CREATIONS

**No One Like You!** Have pupils use fingerprints to decorate their own stationery and greeting cards. Use a regular washable-ink stamp pad; or make a pad by cutting several layers of felt to fit an old jar lid, then saturating the felt with washable ink or thick tempera paint. Pupils press thumb or fingertip on the pad, then on the paper. They use colored pencils, ballpoint, or felt-tip pen to add lines that change the print into a figure or animal. Adding eyes, beaks, claws, noses, legs, and tails makes the possibilities endless! Two or three prints next to each other can make figures with heads and bodies.

**Colors Galore!** Try painting with crayons. Have pupils grow a colorful picture on a full sheet of not-too-coarse sandpaper. Put completed pictures in a warm oven (275-300° F) for one minute to melt the crayons into sandpaper.

**Creature Creation** Suggest pupils create creepy, crawly summertime bugs. Ask at a supermarket to see what days they usually discard their packing materials. Look for the kinds of plastic packing sheets used to separate layers of apples and other fruits. Trim the curved compartments and give one to each pupil for a bug body. Kids can draw spots, stripes, and other patterns with colored markers, or use scraps of material to give fuzzy or textured effects. Add pipe cleaner legs or antennae. Kids can combine the compartments to create strange new creatures.

**Add Color To Your Light** Make see-through window designs to brighten any room. Pupils draw a design on scrap paper, smooth plastic wrap over the paper, and trace the design onto the plastic with a black marker. Small pieces of colored tissue paper are glued within the outline of the design with rubber cement. Another sheet of plastic wrap is smoothed over the tissue design. Lift the plastic from the scrap paper, retrace the black lines on both sides of the plastic, and tape to a sunny window!

**Strange Effects** Want to try a project where the product looks more complicated than the procedure? Have pupils look through old magazines for a large photograph of a person's face or an interesting scene. With a ruler, each draws straight lines at any angle across the picture, marking it into strips of about the same width. Then cut these strips apart and reassemble the picture on a colored background, leaving space for the background to show between the strips. By experimenting, they can get all sorts of odd effects. They might try drawing curved lines on the picture. Part of the picture might be cut into strips that go up and down and part of it into strips that go across. Kids will be surprised at the many different effects they can achieve!

**Dye Away** Have pupils try folding, dipping, and dyeing light-colored paper with food colorings diluted with water. Then suggest they use black crayon or marker to draw a simple design on a new colorfully dyed background. It goes well with birds, dragons, flowers, and any interesting silhouettes. Suggest they experiment with the food coloring to mix new colors.

*-Katherine Bartow, Regina Cabral, Amy DeMarco, Margaret Kolak, Carolyn Martin, Ireene Robbins, Nancy Sliker, Lila Wainer, Helen Kratcha Thomas*

## PINECONE PALACES

Cover small boxes (from toothpaste, vitamins, or beauty soap) with brown paper cut from paper bags. Then glue boxes together to suggest a castle. Insert large pinecone towers in small holes cut in boxes with craft knife. Edge holes with glue to steady cones. Glue smaller cones and petals in place. Use cones from a white pine tree to get individual petals or scales that can be easily broken from the cone and trimmed with scissors. For large tower roofs, make brown paper cones. Glue petals in circles for smaller roofs. Add doors and windows with marking pen. *-Diane Crane*

## CANNED CHARACTERS

Mr. Green Beans and Ophelia Orange Blossom emerge from empty cans. (Use nonmetal cans with very young children.) Let label of can suggest a character. Glue together a paper tube that fits inside the can and is three or four inches taller. Glue head, arms, legs, and clothing cut from colored paper, pieces of advertisements, or another can label onto this tube. Add facial features and yarn hair.

*-Diane Crane*

## BROWN BAG TOTE

Insert one grocery bag in another for double strength. Fold about a 6-inch cuff to the inside. Use plastic handles cut from a thin plastic shopping bag and attach them to front and back of bag and over the handle repeatedly. Thread a strong needle with a double strand of yarn. Crayon and cut out pictures of things that might be carried in a bag. Paste to outside. If plastic handles are hard to find, reinforce top of bag with tape, punch holes, and use braided yarn. *-Diane Crane*

## SOFT SELF-PORTRAITS

Students use box cardboard for backgrounds of full-figure self-portraits in favorite back-to-school outfits. Cut circles for backing heads, and rectangles or triangles for bodies. Cover circle with batting. Then pull a larger circle cut from the top part (less likely to run) of old panty hose over batting to back and tie with thread. Make features with yarn, sewing right through cardboard, batting, and nylon. Sew tubes of panty hose fabric, and stuff for arms and legs. Cover body shapes with scraps of cloth to represent clothing. Glue all parts to background.          *-Helen Brown*

## CURLER CREATURES

Discarded plastic, foam, or mesh hair rollers can be wound with odds and ends of yarn, then glued or sewn together to make amusing animals. Use a large-eyed blunt needle for sewing, heavy craft glue for gluing. Pin mesh or foam curlers in place while gluing. Colored paper and pipe cleaners are good for adding details. Rollers may also be taped together or wired together, then covered with papier-mâché and painted.          *-Diane Crane*

## PIZZA WITH EVERYTHING

Frozen crusts and some complete pizzas are packaged on large plastic-foam circles. Cover circle with brown paper toweling soaked in wallpaper paste. Twist a ropelike piece for edge of "crust." Dry, then paint center red. Let paint dry and brush on thinned white glue. Sprinkle with sawdust. Add favorite "extras" from construction paper.

*-Nancy Wimmer*

## A PERSON FOR ALL SEASONS

Use a stuffed person as a permanent display that changes with the seasons and provides great language arts learning experiences. For the base of the person, make a cross from wood, large enough to fit the size clothing of the students you teach. Anchor the cross securely in a can or build a stand to hold it upright. As the person takes on a new look each month, use these different persons to create story-starter ideas for your students.

*September* Start by making the person a scarecrow. Have children sign up to bring in a shirt, jeans, bandana, straw hat, gloves, boots, belt, and an old pillowcase for the head. Have kids stuff the head with newspaper, and then paint it, draw in features with felt pen, and attach it to the top of the cross. Tie it securely at the neck. The shirt should be hung on the cross and then stuffed, too. Pin the other articles of clothing to the scarecrow, and let the legs hang freely.

*October* Add pumpkins around the feet. Put a mask on the person, or let kids bring masks from home and put a different mask on each day.

*November* Now the scarecrow becomes a Pilgrim. The clothing can remain the same, with white paper cuffs and a Pilgrim hat added. If someone brings in a black coat, it can go right over the scarecrow's shirt.

*December* What else — Santa Claus! Ask kids to bring in red pajamas, black gloves, and black rubber boots. Buy white fake fur or use cotton batting for the fur and beard. Red crepe paper makes a fine Santa hat. Again, fit Santa's clothing over the previous outfit.

*January* Cut out large, flat white circles and pin them over the red Santa clothing. Then make this a snowlady, with a real apron and a broom. Remove the gloves and wrap brown crepe paper around the arms to resemble sticks.

*February* Remove the white circles (save them for April), unwrap the arms, and let the red pajama suit make a valentine man or lady. Students can make and pin hearts all over the costume.

*March* Let the students decide: a kite man? A lion? A lamb? A gardener?

*April* You can make a bunny with the snowman circles. Cut the big circle into legs and pin them onto the original outfit; use the smaller circle for the body. Add ears and tie on a bright cloth bow tie. Wrap white paper over the arms, and hang a real basket over one of them.

*May* This is a good time for a favorite storybook character, like Little Red Riding Hood. Let a committee of students work on this one and bring in all the materials. Let other committees create new characters throughout the month.

*June* Use the person's original clothes to make it a "student" for the rest of the year. Let each row of kids take a turn creating a new student by using wigs and hats and bringing in items that represent summer activities. One student-person could hold a baseball and mitt, another could hold ballet slippers; and so on.

*-Judy Meagher*

# Subject Index